Luminos is the Open Access monograph publishing program from UC Press. Luminos provides a framework for preserving and reinvigorating monograph publishing for the future and increases the reach and visibility of important scholarly work. Titles published in the UC Press Luminos model are published with the same high standards for selection, peer review, production, and marketing as those in our traditional program. www.luminosoa.org

Palestinian Chicago

NEW DIRECTIONS IN PALESTINIAN STUDIES

Series Editorial Committee

Beshara Doumani, Series Editor
Samera Esmier
Rema Hammami
Rashid Khalidi
Sherene Seikaly

The New Directions in Palestinian Studies series publishes books that put Palestinians at the center of research projects and that make an innovative contribution to decolonizing and globalizing knowledge production about the Palestinian condition.

1. Loren D. Lybarger. *Palestinian Chicago: Identity in Exile.*

Palestinian Chicago

Identity in Exile

———

Loren D. Lybarger

UNIVERSITY OF CALIFORNIA PRESS

University of California Press
Oakland, California

© 2020 by Loren Lybarger

Suggested citation: Lybarger, L. D. *Palestinian Chicago: Identity in Exile.*
Oakland: University of California Press, 2020. DOI: https://doi.org/10.1525
/luminos.90

This work is licensed under a Creative Commons CC BY-NC-SA license.
To view a copy of the license, visit http://creativecommons.org/licenses.

Library of Congress Cataloging-in-Publication Data

Names: Lybarger, Loren D., 1964- author.
Title: Palestinian Chicago : identity in exile / Loren D. Lybarger.
Description: Oakland, California : University of California Press, [2020] |
    Includes bibliographical references and index.
Identifiers: LCCN 2019053432 | ISBN 9780520337619 (paperback) |
    ISBN 9780520974401 (ebook)
Subjects: LCSH: Palestinian Americans—Social conditions. |
    Palestinian Arabs—Illinois—Chicago—History—20th century. |
    Palestinian Arabs—Illinois—Chicago—History—21st century.
Classification: LCC E184.P33 L93 2020 | DDC 305.892/74077311—dc23
LC record available at https://lccn.loc.gov/2019053432

29 28 27 26 25 24 23 22 21 20
10 9 8 7 6 5 4 3 2 1

*For my daughter, Rachel,
and
for my parents, Lee and Connie Lybarger*

CONTENTS

List of Illustrations	xi
Foreword by the Series Editor	xiii
Acknowledgments	xv

Introduction	1
Protesting "Protective Edge," Chicago, July 26, 2014	1
The Project	5
Questions and Data	7
Main Assertions	7
Contextualizing the Religious Shift	9
Key Concepts: Identity, Secularism, and Religion	17
Organization of the Book	26
1. Palestinian Chicago: Spatial Location, Historical Formation	29
Early Migration from Palestine: 1890s–1940s	30
Migration, 1948–1967: Transformations of the Exilic Space	35
The New Immigrants and "Re-Palestinianization": 1967–1980s	39
The Ascendancy of Secular Nationalism: 1967–1990	43
Suburban Transition and the Religious Turn: 1980–Present	45
Browning Bridgeview: Palestinian Suburbanization and the New Islamic Milieu	48
Expanding the Islamic Milieu: Islamic Education	53

>   The Christian Milieu: Key Structures 55
>   Conclusion: *Mahjar* Spaces 56
>
> 2. Secularism in Exile 58
>   Examining Secularism: Why It Matters 60
>   Palestinian Secularism 61
>   Constituting Secularism in Chicago: The Generation of 1948–1967 62
>   The Generation of 1987–2001 70
>   A Secular Afterword 83
>
> 3. The Religious Turn: American Muslims for Palestine 85
>   The 6th Annual Conference for Palestine in the US (November 28–30, 2013) 89
>   American Muslims for Palestine's Nakba Commemoration: Palestine through an Islamic Lens 98
>   Conclusion 107
>
> 4. The Religious Turn: Generational Subjectivities 108
>   Generational Processes of the Religious Turn 109
>   Alienation and Latency in the Generation of 1948–1967 110
>   The Generation of 1987–2001: Polarization and Sectarianization 115
>   The Post-September 11 Generation 120
>   Conclusion 132
>
> 5. Dynamic Syntheses: Reversion, Conversion, and Accommodation 133
>   Syncretic Secularity 134
>   Reversion, Conversion, and Accommodation 135
>   Reversion 136
>   Conversion 142
>   Accommodation 152
>   Conclusion 157
>
> 6. Dynamic Syntheses: Rebellion, Absolute and Spiritual 159
>   Syncretic Rebellions 159
>   Absolute Rejection 161
>   Spiritualization 165
>   Conclusion 183

Conclusion 185
    Reconsidering the Religious Shift: Concluding Points 187
    Religious and Secular: What to Do? How to Live? 196

Notes 199

References 225

Index 245

LIST OF ILLUSTRATIONS

1. Palestinian flags, traditional and Islamized, alongside United States flag   2
2. Palestinian flag featuring a stencil of the Dome of the Rock; United States flag in background   3
3. Demonstrator wearing the national colors and *kufiya* scarf over hijab   4
4. Map of British Mandate for Palestine, 1922–1948   10
5. Chicago Community Areas Map   36
6. Palestinian Dabka   43

FOREWORD BY THE SERIES EDITOR

"The Palestinians" are a household word and the Palestinian condition is routinely invoked as emblematic of the dark side of the modern world: settler colonial violence, racialization and statelessness, disenfranchisement and incarceration, inequality and over-exposure to the disasters of climate change. Palestinian resistance, by the same token, is inspirational because of its persistent multigenerational struggles for justice, dignity, and the right to exist as a political community in the face of asymmetrical power relations. It is precisely because of this over-determined binary that tomes on the Palestinian-Israeli "conflict," most of which are dominated by "one land/two people" nationalist constructions of the past, still rule the shelves.

Fortunately, the past two decades have witnessed a flowering of scholarship that exceeds the colonial and nationalist frames through grounded studies of the internal complexities and lived experiences of Palestinian communities. They look at the world with Palestinian eyes. Their lines of vision intersect with the stories of many of the world's marginalized and disenfranchised populations. *New Directions in Palestinian Studies* (NDPS), the first book series of its kind in the United States, publishes books that put Palestinians at the center of research projects, to decolonize and globalize knowledge production about the Palestinian condition.

The fundamental Palestinian condition is one of ongoing process of dispossession, displacement, and statelessness, coupled with grinding generational struggles for survival across an extraordinarily diverse range of political, social, and cultural geographies. A shared trauma—the ethnic cleansing of the overwhelming majority of Palestinians from their native land in 1948—is, at one and the same time, the key reference point for the Palestinian political imagination and a centrifuge of life trajectories. The epicenter remains pre-1948 Palestine, where roughly half of the twelve million Palestinians still live; they do so under a bewilderingly complex array of differential legal, military, and economic zones and rules of mobility meant to fragment and contain their communities. A large percentage of them, moreover, live not in their ancestral homes and villages, but in refugee camps, urban neighborhoods, and unrecognized villages in Gaza, the West Bank, East Jerusalem, and Israel. The other six million or so Palestinians, most of whom live within driving distance of pre-1948 Palestine, constitute the oldest refugee population in the world, and also one of the largest.

The focus on Palestinians, regardless of geography, is why it is fitting that *Palestinian Chicago: Identities in Exile* is the first book published in the NDPS series. In an intimate portrait of the largest Palestinian community in the United States based on years of rigorous ethnographic fieldwork, Loren D. Lybarger traces the multidirectional personal journeys and forms of community activism across the secular/religious divide which inform the questions: how to live? and what to do? With sensitivity to race, gender, class, and generational forces, Lybarger shows the many counter-intuitive ways that "religion and nation remain powerful determinants of self-understanding under the conflicted, polytheistic conditions of society in the United States and in Palestine."

By laying bare the inner workings of Palestinian Chicago—especially the religious turn near the end of the twentieth century and its fraught relationship to hitherto dominant secular political imagination—Lybarger raises difficult ethical, moral, and political questions about faith, belonging, intersectionality, and the efficacy of human and international rights discourses. At the same time, his stories reveal how the messiness and contingency of the quotidian generates new identities and political possibilities.

Beshara Doumani, Series Editor

ACKNOWLEDGMENTS

In researching and writing this book, I have relied on the support of numerous individuals and organizations. My first and most important debt of gratitude is to the many individuals in "Palestinian Chicago" who participated in this project. Some are named; some appear with pseudonyms; and some receive indirect references in the pages ahead. Many others are not mentioned, but the experiences and views they shared enriched my understanding in countless ways. I wish especially to acknowledge Hatem Abudayyeh, Nicholas Dahdal, Oussama Jammal, Maha Jarad, Rami Nashashibi, and Camelia Odeh for providing insight, institutional access, and introductions to project participants.

I am also immensely grateful to my colleagues at Ohio University for their support. Neil Bernstein read multiple chapter drafts, gave constant encouragement, and advised me at every stage. Tom Carpenter and Bill Owens read grant applications and wrote letters of support. Ziad Abu-Rish provided moral backing and the suggestion to approach the editors of this series. Jonathan Dicks, Dorcas Anima Donkor, Kaltuma Sheikh, and Basileus Zeno—first-rate graduate student assistants—transcribed interviews, commented on chapters, checked translations, and tracked down references.

Several friends and colleagues gave timely guidance and read and commented expertly on individual chapters or the whole manuscript. James Damico gave unstinting encouragement and critical and repeated feedback on multiple chapters. Paul Abowd provided editorial input on the entire draft in its final stages. Jennifer Hammer and Timothy Mennel offered immensely useful revision advice at key points. Tom Abowd also gave helpful editing feedback. Maha Nassar, Paul Numrich, Atalia Omer, and Sherene Seikaly furnished detailed scholarly assessments that have immeasurably improved my analysis and saved me from several errors. Martin Riesebrodt provided theoretical perspective, offered encouragement, and wrote letters of support for grants. Martin died unexpectedly on December 6, 2014, during the period of my fieldwork. I have missed his friendship and guidance ever since. Dan Arnold and Rick Rosengarten, longtime friends at the University of Chicago, read two separate draft chapters and spoke with me about them at length. Louise Cainkar, whose pathbreaking research has provided important background information for this project, graciously offered perspective and advice at different points.

I also benefitted from several opportunities to present my findings in public. Nathan J. Brown and the Palestinian American Research Center invited me to discuss my early fieldwork at the annual Middle East Studies Association meeting in San Diego in 2010. Laurie Brand gave excellent input as the panel respondent. James Damico invited me to present at the School of Education at Indiana University-Bloomington in February 2012. That same year, in the spring, Mary Ellen Konieczny arranged for me to speak at the University of Notre Dame. Her sudden death on February 24, 2018, left a void for those of us who were fortunate to count her as our colleague and friend. Nelly van Doorn-Harder invited me to present at Wake Forest University in October 2012. She also edited a special edition of *The Muslim World* journal in which I was able to publish my paper. Joyce Dalsheim and Gregory Starrett included me in their Thematic Conversation on "Disciplining a Religious/Secular Divide" at the annual Middle East Studies Association meetings in 2011, 2012, and 2013. Those challenging sessions provided me with a multiyear opportunity to think through the broad analytic themes that became central foci of this book. Frida Furman invited me to speak at DePaul University in February 2014. Atalia Omer gave me the opportunity to address faculty and students in the Kroc Institute for International Peace Studies at the University of Notre Dame that same year. Cristina L. H. Traina and Brian Edwards invited me to present to the Middle East and North African Studies Program at Northwestern University in May 2015. Hugh Urban and Isaac Weiner invited me to speak at the Center for the Study of Religion at Ohio State University in October 2017.

I wish to thank the editors of the University of California Press's New Directions in Palestinian Studies series—Beshara Doumani, Samera Esmier, Rema Hammami, Rashid Khalidi, and Sherene Seikaly—for their enthusiasm and support for my project. I am honored that this book will be the first text to appear in this important new venue. Thank you, as well, to Executive Editor Niels Hooper and Editorial Assistant Robin Manley for expertly guiding things to completion and to Catherine R. Osborne for her professionalism and care in copyediting the manuscript. I wish to thank, too, Linda Christian for her skillful indexing work.

Multiple institutions provided financial and moral support for this project. The Ohio University Research Council granted funding for the initial exploratory fieldwork during 2010 and 2011. I owe thanks to Roxanne Malé-Brune and Carma

West for their help with the proposal. My project also received support from two National Endowment for the Humanities (NEH) awards: a summer research grant and a full-year fellowship that allowed me to deepen the fieldwork significantly. An Ohio University Faculty Fellowship Leave permitted me to extend my NEH fellowship year for an additional twelve months. This extension proved essential to completing the fieldwork. The Martin Marty Center for the Public Understanding of Religion at the Divinity School of the University of Chicago awarded me back-to-back senior fellowships during this same two-year period. The fellowships provided me with office space and an intellectual community with which to share my thoughts about my research as they were forming concurrently with my fieldwork. The Ohio University College of Arts and Sciences Humanities Research Fund and the Carnegie Foundation supported the open-access publishing of this book.

Finally, my family has been essential to sustaining me throughout this effort. My wife, Mary Abowd, whose civic engagements, friendships in the community, and journalism intertwine with the story told in this book, listened patiently and offered first-hand insights as this project unfolded. A skilled writer and editor, she read and commented perceptively on this manuscript. She also cared for our two beautiful daughters, Olivia and Rachel, during my absences. Olivia and Rachel have been wonderfully supportive, too, expressing curiosity about my work and embracing the move to Chicago. I wish to thank our extended families, as well. Their love and support have sustained me in ways I will never be able to repay.

Although I have relied on the help of so many people, I remain entirely responsible for any errors and shortcomings in this work. My book offers only one possible portrayal of Palestinian Chicago—a multi-dimensional image composed from specific moments, places, and perspectives. I intend it as a departure point for further discussion, not as a final statement. I hope it provides some insight, however incomplete, into the rich and varied lives of the individuals who so graciously shared their memories, experiences, and perspectives with me.

Introduction

PROTESTING "PROTECTIVE EDGE," CHICAGO,
JULY 26, 2014

In July 2014, as I was finishing the research in Chicago for this book, Israel bombarded the Gaza Strip in yet another attempt—the third since 2008—to destroy the military and governing capacities of the Islamic Resistance Movement, known commonly as Hamas. Labeled "Operation Protective Edge," the attack, which killed more than 2,000 civilians and injured an additional 11,000, sparked global condemnation, including a massive public response from Chicago's Palestinians (Dearden 2014; Waldroup 2014). In a well-rehearsed procedure—this was not the first time they had mobilized—the Chicago Coalition for Justice in Palestine, an ad hoc group comprising the city's major organizations active on the Palestinian cause, called for a demonstration in the Loop, Chicago's downtown area. Dramatizing their dominant role in the community, the mosques bussed hundreds of their constituents from the southwest suburbs. Event organizers claimed 15,000 demonstrators; the local NBC affiliate put the figure at 8,000 (Waldroup 2014).

Slogans at the rally and during the subsequent march down Michigan Avenue demanded "free Palestine" and declared "God is greater." The traditional flag featuring a plain triangle of red and three bars each of black, white, and green mingled with other versions of the national banner.[1] There were two Islamized variations. The first inscribed the *shahada* declaration (creedal statement) of *la ilaha illa llah/ muhammadun rasulu llah*—"There is no deity save the one God/Muhammad is God's messenger"—on the white middle field of the banner (Figure 1).[2]

The second superimposed an image of the Dome of the Rock—the site from which, according to tradition, Muhammad ascended through the heavens to the throne of God—and the words "*filastin kulluha qudsun*" (Figure 2). The words, which translate as "Palestine, All of It [is] Sanctified [or, Sacred, Holy]," played on the traditional name for Jerusalem in Arabic, "al-Quds," the Sanctified (Sacred, Holy). Both flags appeared alongside the US flag. The juxtaposition signaled a specifically Palestinian claim to American political citizenship and national affiliation.

FIGURE 1. Palestinian flags, traditional and Islamized, alongside US flag.

Religious and nationalist symbolic displays also appeared in the clothing choices of some women demonstrators. Women wearing hijab scarves in a checkered black-and-white *kufiya* (colloq: *kaffiyeh* or *hatta*) design or in the colors of the Palestinian national flag walked alongside women wearing *kufiya*-patterned scarves around their necks but nothing on their heads (Figure 3).

Signs and chants at the demonstration demanded "Israel: stop killing" and decried the attack on Gaza as "genocide." They also called for boycott, divestment,

FIGURE 2. Palestinian flag featuring a stencil of the Dome of the Rock; US flag in background.

and sanctions against Israel's "apartheid" and for ending US financial support for the Jewish state ("Not another nickel, not another dime for Israel's crime!") Other slogans revived the assertion—which the Palestine Liberation Organization (PLO) had effectively abandoned in its acceptance of the two-state principle[3]—"from the [Jordanian] River to the [Mediterranean] Sea/Palestine will be free!"

Organizers and protestors who gave interviews to NBC also presented a united front across secular, religious, and ethnic lines. Kristin Szremski, a convert to Islam and, at the time, a staff member in charge of media relations for American Muslims for Palestine (AMP), which receives detailed analysis in chapter 3, appeared on camera in hijab, declaring: "I believe Israel needs to end the occupation. Period. And that's how we're going to achieve peace" (Waldroup 2014). Executive Director of the Arab American Action Network Hatem Abudayyeh, who is profiled in the analysis of secularism in chapter 2, echoed Szremski: "The Palestinian people want peace. Absolutely. We always have. But, peace with justice" (Waldroup 2014). Deena Kishawi, a college student and protester wearing a red hijab and black-and-white *kufiya* kerchief under her scarf, also emphasized the theme of protecting civilian lives and overturning Israel's decades-long control of the Occupied Territories: "My message to Israel and to everybody out there is to stop killing Palestinians, to end the siege, to end the occupation" (Waldroup 2014). Finally, Lynn Pollack of the

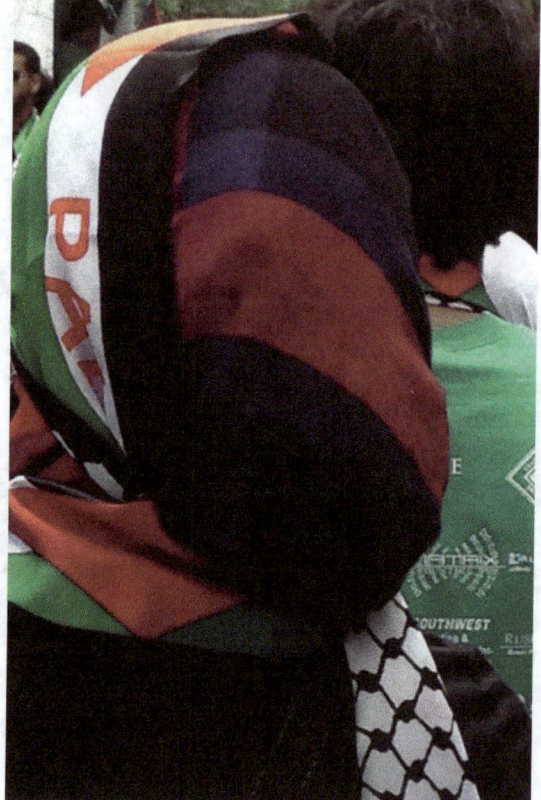

FIGURE 3. Demonstrator wearing the national colors and *kufiya* scarf over *hijab*.

anti-Zionist Jewish Voice for Peace solidarity group appealed to her fellow Jewish Americans "to stand up and take a good look at what is happening and say you don't want it done in your name either" (Waldroup 2014).

Religious and secular symbols appeared to blend seamlessly in this mass demonstration against Israel's violence. The secular, in the sense of the priority given to the crisis and question of Palestine, had seemingly assimilated Islamic signifiers as part of a nonsectarian space that included Jewish solidarity groups. But Islam, too, had embraced the nation, centering its cause as an article of faith: devotion to the One God entailed devotion to the liberation of the national patrimony, which God had made sacred. The inverse relation also seemed to hold: commitment to the nation required affirmation, at least strategically, of Islam's central importance. This religious-secular synthesis appeared an accomplished fact in 2014. Nevertheless, behind the integrated display lay a longer history of tension and shift.

THE PROJECT

This book documents and analyzes the history of this shift and its present-day impact in one of the world's most important Palestinian diaspora communities, Palestinian Chicago. At approximately 85,000 strong, this community constitutes the single largest concentration of Palestinians in North America.[4] Their sheer size has made them a target of scrutiny. Chicago's main newspaper, the *Chicago Tribune*, has periodically published exposés claiming to have uncovered connections to radical Islamic and leftist groups that the US government has listed as "foreign terrorist organizations." And, since the 1970s, the Federal Bureau of Investigation and Department of Justice have launched probes against activists suspected of supporting proscribed movements (Ahmed-Ullah, et al. 2004; Ahmed-Ullah, Roe, and Cohen 2004; Cainkar 2009, 110–52). Chicago's Palestinians have, as a consequence, become linked directly to the putative Global War on Terror; and, in response, they have fought back against interventions made against them. Since the election of President Donald J. Trump, for example, activists in the community have led protests against the "Muslim Ban," the final version of which severely limits travel to the United States from five Muslim-majority countries (Iran, Libya, Syria, Yemen, and Somalia) as well as from North Korea and Venezuela.

The analysis I present of this community in this book rests on my decades-long interaction with its members and leaders and with the situation in Palestine itself. My first encounter with Palestinian communities and the national struggle that has so powerfully defined their collective sense of identity came during a three-year stint as a volunteer English teacher in the West Bank (1986–89). The First Intifada—the mass Palestinian uprising against the Israeli occupation (1987–93)—erupted during this time. The event profoundly affected me. Several of my students were arrested in demonstrations as part of the sweeping imprisonments of leaders and youth activists, and some were severely injured. A friend was shot and killed at close range while being questioned at a military checkpoint in the town of Beit Jala. Following the military's closure of all schools in early 1988, I began work with the Palestinian Human Rights Information Center (PHRC) in East Jerusalem. I assisted PHRC's fieldworkers in collecting data on Israeli military violence in Palestinian communities across the West Bank and Gaza Strip.

In 1989, I left the West Bank to complete a master's degree in Applied Linguistics at the American University in Cairo. The first Gulf War occurred during this interval. Israel imposed a complete blockade and curfew of the Occupied Territories. After the war, in 1991, I accepted a job as an English teacher in the Gaza Strip (1991–93). The Intifada was imploding. The Gulf War had severely weakened the PLO, which had sided diplomatically with Iraq. Israel's extended closures and violent repression during the war had exhausted the population. And the relationship between Hamas and Fatah, the PLO's predominant faction, had become embittered and violent.

I left Gaza in 1993 to pursue graduate studies in religion and sociology. My dissertation project involved a full year of fieldwork in Palestine, 1999–2000. This research, occurring just before the outbreak of the Second (al-Aqsa) Intifada, became the foundation for several publications, including my first book, on the transformation of Palestinian identity in response to the deepening Islamist-secular-nationalist fracture (Lybarger 2005; 2007a; 2007b; and 2013).

While pursuing my studies in Chicago, I developed ties with the city's Palestinian immigrant community. Activist friends, some of whom I had met in the West Bank, introduced me to leaders at the Arab Community Center, known simply as "the *markaz* (center)." The *markaz* had been an anchor of the Southwest Side immigrant enclave since the early 1970s. It had a pronounced secular-left, pan-Arab, and Palestinian nationalist orientation. The center provided a range of community services, including language training, after-school cultural activities, and social work assistance. I volunteered as an English teacher for a brief period and occasionally attended organizing meetings at the *markaz* through the mid-1990s and early 2000s. I began to notice during my visits to the center that younger staff members and youth program participants were increasingly embracing outward markers of Islamic piety (beards, brimless knitted *kufi* caps, hijab scarves). This phenomenon was remarkable given the *markaz*'s secularist ethos.

The most striking manifestation of this change occurred at a fundraising dinner I attended for the Arab American Action Network (AAAN) in 1998. The AAAN was a new social service organization that replaced the Arab Community Center. The late Edward Said—the renowned Columbia University scholar and foremost Palestinian public intellectual in the United States—had come from New York to keynote the event. With dinner concluding, Said prepared to speak. Suddenly, there was a commotion. Tens of university students in the audience had risen and were forming ranks to perform the *maghrib* (dusk) prayer toward the side of the banquet space. One of the students, a young bearded man in a kufi cap, began intoning the *adhan* (call to prayer) in a resonant baritone.

As the prayer proceeded, Said waited at the podium while those who had remained in their seats shifted uncomfortably and exchanged indignant comments. The fundraiser was a secular, nonsectarian event meant to raise money for a secular, nonsectarian organization. The audience comprised Muslims as well as Christians, Jews, and many individuals who identified as secular. The unexpected intervention of the prayer—it had not been included in the program—palpably transformed the mood, producing confusion and tension.

The memory of this dramatic disruption of the AAAN fundraiser, and the interruption of Edward Said, a staunch defender of both the Palestinian cause and of secularism,[5] remained with me long after the incident. I returned to that moment frequently through the years whenever I spoke with my *markaz* friends in Chicago about the religious shift that had occurred. By the 2000s, the shift had expanded substantially as the community transitioned to the suburbs. The secular community centers had closed while the mosques, situated in the new enclave, flourished.[6] The AAAN, which had established itself in the old *markaz* premises in the Southwest Side Chicago Lawn area, was an exception to the trend. It nevertheless had accommodated the religious shift, too, in various ways (as explored in chapters 2 and 5 and elsewhere). The shift was broad and undeniable. Why this change had happened and what its impact had been became central questions for me in those early conversations. They eventually became the focus of this book.

QUESTIONS AND DATA

Four main questions orient this project. First, what historical, social, and political factors have shaped Palestinian identities in Chicago? How, specifically, did secular nationalism and religion—principally Islam in various forms but also Christianity—become primary identity frameworks at individual and community levels? Second, what explains the ascendancy of Islam, in particular, since the 1990s, and what has happened to secularism in relation to this process? Third, what forms of identity have emerged through the ensuing intersections of the religious and the secular in Palestinian Chicago? Finally, what critical perspectives does this case study provide for understanding Palestinian identity in diaspora contexts in the current moment?

I answer these questions through the description and analysis of fieldwork data. These data derive from summer research trips to Chicago occurring between 2010 and 2013 and from a two-year research residency in the city from 2013–15. The data include multiple site observations at mosques, churches, community centers, downtown protests, and community events as well as more than eighty recorded life-story interviews. Each of the interviews lasted two or more hours and in some cases included extended follow-up conversations.[7] Analysis of the data has entailed identification and interpretation of themes within and across the transcribed interviews and my field notes.

MAIN ASSERTIONS

I make several interrelated assertions about what these fieldwork data show. My first claim is that the religious turn in Chicago results from a complex interaction of homeland and diaspora-specific processes. The primary homeland factor is the development, since the late 1980s, of powerful Islamist competitors to the secular-nationalist Palestine Liberation Organization. These movements, principally the Muslim Brotherhood and its successor, Hamas, have split Palestinian society into competing secular nationalist and Islamist spheres. The division has manifested geographically: since 2007, Hamas has dominated the Gaza Strip while the secular nationalist Fatah movement, the largest of the PLO factions, remains in nominal control of parts of the West Bank. I show how the Islamic shift, in its broad sense, in Palestine and in the wider Middle East has influenced the religious turn in Chicago through family networks spanning the United States and Palestine. But the book also demonstrates the impact of other factors specific to the Palestinian experience in Chicago. These factors include the development of religious institutional structures as part of an ongoing selective assimilation process; the shuttering of secular nationalist community centers; wealth accumulation and the demographic transition to a new suburban enclave; and the anti-Muslim backlash in the long aftermath of the September 11, 2001 attacks.

My second main assertion is that the religious shift and the tensions it produces with secularism have generated a range of hybrid identities in the present. These identities defy simplistic narratives about the "Islamization" of immigrant communities or about the "decline" of secularism in the face of a global religious resurgence. This finding pushes back against prevailing scholarship on these matters. This scholarship is of two sorts. The first has tended to raise alarm about the effect of Muslim immigration on Western democracy and secular culture (Brookes and Sciolino 1995; Levitt 2006; Roy 2007; Amghar, Boubekeur, and Emerson, 2007; Sniderman and Hagendoorn 2007; Nasaw 2008; Westrop 2017). The second has focused positively on the formation of a Western *umma* (Islamic community), internally dynamic and contested, auguring a new, transcultural Western Islam (Ramadan 2004; Karim 2009; Grewal 2014; Khabeer 2016). This contradictory discussion parallels a public discourse in which racist and xenophobic portrayals of Muslim immigrants vie with counterclaims about Islam being a religion of peace compatible with a secular democratic order.

Obscured in these contending discourses is the complexity of secular-religious dynamics in the actual lives of individuals and communities. I call attention to this fact, showing how the religious turn has had multiple effects in Palestinian Chicago. As I show, secularism has not disappeared but rather transmuted, taking new forms in interaction with the religious turn. Similarly, the new religious orientations bear the imprint of secularism and in doing so develop in multiple indeterminate directions. Significantly, these transformations have analogs in the experience of Palestinian Christians, whom I also highlight in the chapters ahead. Adding to the complexities of these secular-religious interactions is the impact of a range of other mitigating factors, especially race, class, gender, generation, and space. This book analyzes these factors, showing how they shape the religious-secular dynamics in the narrative accounts of my interlocutors.

My third set of arguments pertains to the broader implications of my findings for Palestinians and non-Palestinian others in the current moment. I make two observations. First, Palestinian identity in the diaspora is likely to continue to develop in multiple directions as the religious shift deepens and as that same shift generates secular-religious hybrid responses. Second, the experiences of Palestinians in Chicago shed light on secular-religious tensions and transformations that manifest in diverse societies globally. These Palestinian accounts contribute empirical depth to arguments that Taylor (2007), Martin (2014), and Riesebrodt (2014), among others, have separately made about how the religious and the secular enter into a mutually "fragilizing" relation, each destabilizing but also conditioning the other in a dialectic that produces new syntheses. The Palestinian voices that register in this book provide crucial insight into these processes and into the possibilities they create for forging new, contrapuntal conceptions of self and other across multiple lines of difference, including the religious and the secular.

CONTEXTUALIZING THE RELIGIOUS SHIFT

Secularist and Islamist Formations in Palestine

My assertions above reflect a historical context in which secular nationalism and Islamism constitute contending responses among Palestinians to the experience of dispossession. The central defining feature of the secularist response has been its emphasis on the ethnos—the specifically Palestinian Arab nation—and its collective search for statehood. Secularism in this sense emphasizes a common identity rooted in a shared language (Arabic) and shared customs and traditions (the *'adat wa taqalid* that structured traditional village life). It also roots itself in a narrative of catastrophic loss and heroic revolution (*thawra*) flowing from successive traumas. These traumas include, principally, the wars of 1948 and 1967 but also refer to later events like the Israeli invasion of Lebanon in 1982, which resulted in the deaths of close to 20,000 Lebanese and Palestinians, 90 percent of them civilians, and in the PLO's expulsion from Beirut (Chomsky 1999 [1983], 388); the First Intifada (1987–93); and the Second Intifada (2000–05). At the heart of Palestinian secular nationalism, historically, however, is the claim to an ancestral territory according with the boundaries of the former British Mandate for Palestine (1922–48) (Figure 4).

In addition to emphasizing the ethnos and its territorially bounded space—a feature of modern nationalisms—Palestinian secularism has historically affirmed religious identities as part of the cultural mosaic and heritage of the Palestinian people. This affirmation has included the important caveat that no single religion retains a privileged position. In its Marxist forms, Palestinian secularism has at times rejected religion outright as "false consciousness" and an obstacle to national and human liberation; but the form of secularism that has predominated among Palestinians has emphasized multisectarian unity under a common identification with the nation and its cause of liberation. The core organizational structures of this form of secularism remain the various factions that constitute the PLO. Principal among these factions have been the Palestinian National Liberation Movement (Fatah/*harakat al-tahrir al-watani al-filastini*), and the Movement of

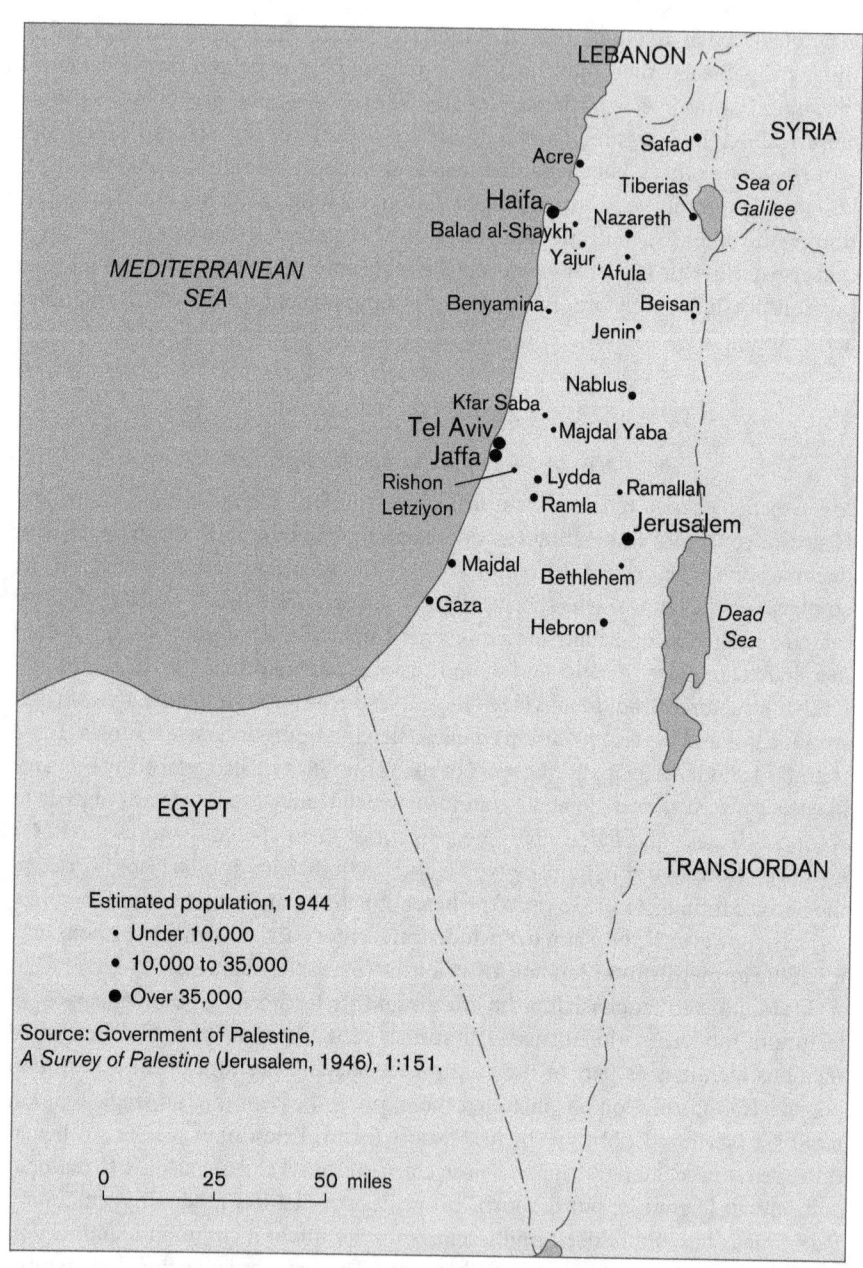

FIGURE 4. Map of British Mandate for Palestine, 1922–1948. Source: *A Survey of Palestine*, Vol. 1 (Washington, DC: Institute for Palestine Studies, 1991), 151. Used with permission of the Institute for Palestine Studies.

Arab Nationalists (MAN/*harakat al-qawmiyin al-'arab*), which, after the war of 1967, became the Marxist-Leninist-oriented Popular Front for the Liberation of Palestine.

These PLO factions first emerged during the 1950s as Palestinians contended with their traumatic mass displacement and transformation into refugees following the war of 1948. In the aftermath of the war of 1967, in which Israel occupied Arab East Jerusalem and the West Bank, Gaza Strip, Golan Heights, and Sinai Desert, the Fatah movement, in a dramatic move, took control of the PLO, transforming it into a Palestinian government in exile. With Nasser-led pan-Arabism in disarray, the phoenix-like rise of the Fatah-led PLO inspired Palestinian and Arab youth across the region to join the armed units of "the revolution" (*al-thawra*) in Jordan and, later, in Lebanon. The PLO quickly became the preeminent global tribune of the Palestinian cause: under the chairmanship of the late Yasser Arafat, it achieved the status of sole legitimate representative of the Palestinian people. Israel's invasion of Lebanon in 1982 destroyed the PLO's last independent base of operation, forcing the movement into a distant exile, first in Algeria and then in Tunisia. The First Intifada (1987–93) and subsequent Oslo Peace Process (1993–present), however, enabled Fatah, the PLO's dominant faction, to regain its position and prominence on the global stage. Ironically, the formation of the Fatah-controlled Palestinian National Authority as part of the subsequent Oslo process intensified the weakening of the PLO as a political structure for diaspora Palestinians. This weakening had already begun during the first Gulf War (1990–91), when Gulf countries cut financial support for the organization. One consequence of this process was the hollowing out of secular nationalist institutions in diaspora communities. In Chicago, the collapse of the secular nationalist community centers, which oriented politically to the various PLO factions and to the liberation programs they represented, signaled this new reality.

In contrast with Palestinian secularism, the orienting horizon of Palestinian Islamism has been the *umma* (the transcultural and transhistorical Islamic community) and its claim to sovereignty in Palestine. At the center of this claim is Jerusalem, the mythic site of the Prophet Muhammad's miraculous heavenly ascent (the *mi'raj*). Palestine has long served as a symbolic focal point of Islamic revival and anti-colonial resistance.[8] The Syrian pan-Islamist 'Izz al-Din al-Qassam, for example, whose preaching and organizing in the Galilee region helped lay ground for the Great Revolt (1936–39), thematized resistance to British domination and Zionist colonization in terms of Islamic solidarity and jihad. Hasan al-Banna, founder of the Egyptian Muslim Brotherhood in 1928, also preached extensively in towns and villages up and down the Nile River about the threat of Zionism as part of his call for a revival of Islam to counter British colonialism. The Muslim Brotherhood provided important backing for al-Hajj Amin al-Husayni, the Mufti of Jerusalem and leader of the Supreme Muslim Council in Palestine, the main organization leading the Palestinian national movement during the 1930s. The Brotherhood also sent guerrilla fighters to the Gaza Strip during the war of 1948, during which approximately 750,000 Palestinians were forcibly expelled from their towns and villages in what became Israel. Muslim support for Palestinian nationalism also extended beyond the Middle East. Leaders of the Indian Khalifat movement, for example, attended the World Islamic Congress, held at al-Aqsa Mosque under Husayni's auspices in 1931 (O. Khalidi 2009; Swedenberg 1995; Schleifer 1993; Mattar 1988; Brynjar 1988; Kupferschmidt 1987).

Since the 1980s, Hamas and Islamic Jihad have again centered Palestine within the discourse of global Islamic solidarity. They refer to "Muslim Palestine" and conceive the struggle through religious symbols and terms like *al-jihad fi sabil illah* ("armed struggle in the path or cause of God"). For these movements, the jihad for Palestine is the key to Islam's revival elsewhere. This idea mirrors Fatah and the PLO's insistence that Arab political renaissance depended on a prior commitment and solidarity among all Arabs to free Palestine through the armed struggle—in the secularist lexicon, *al-kifah al-musallah* ("the armed struggle"), not *al-jihad fi sabil illah* (Gunning 2008; Mishal and Sela 2000; Hroub 2000; Nüsse 1998; Milton-Edwards 1996). Global movements like al-Qaeda have also invoked Palestine, but in doing so have reversed the causal logic of liberation: Palestinian freedom would come only after Muslims had united as Muslims to strike against the "far enemy" (the United States) (Euben and Zaman 2009; Gerges 2009 [2005]). The Islamic State movement has similarly predicated the liberating of the territories comprising Israel, the Gaza Strip, and the West Bank on the revival of Islamic solidarity, primarily through the resurrection of the historical caliphate under its leadership. The Islamic State disdains both the PLO and Hamas as anti-Islamic because of the primary focus of these groups on Palestinian national liberation rather than on conquest of a territorial base for a revived *umma* (*Guardian* 2015).

The Islamic State's critique of Hamas is not without foundation: since its creation, Hamas has sought, through its emphasis on jihad, to wrest the mantle of armed struggle on behalf of the nation from Fatah and the PLO. In 2007, Hamas forced Fatah out of the Gaza Strip in a brief but bloody civil war that split control of the Palestinian National Authority (PNA). Since then, Hamas has dominated PNA institutions in Gaza while Fatah has retained power in the semiautonomous zones in the West Bank. In its subsequent armed engagements with Israel—such as in the 2014 "Protective Edge" invasion described at the start of this chapter—Hamas has repeatedly asserted itself as the champion of Palestinian liberation. In doing so, it has sought to cast Fatah, which has remained committed to the moribund peace process, as corrupt and compromised. One unanticipated consequence of Hamas's ascendancy has been an incipient sectarianizing reaction among some Palestinian Christians. These Christians have responded to the Islamic reframing of Palestinian nationalism by redefining belonging narrowly in relation to

Christian narratives and institutions (S. Roy 2011; Milton-Edwards and Farrell 2010; Lybarger 2007b).

Secularism and Islam in the Diaspora: The Exilic Difference

As the July 2014 demonstration in Chicago's downtown showed, and as my own observations during the 1990s also indicated, the diaspora has not been immune to the Islamic-secular competition and consequent realignments of solidarities that have arisen since Hamas's ascendancy. This phenomenon has received scant balanced attention. Journalism and scholarship on Islam, Islamic movements, Islamic revival, or Islamism in relation to Palestinians have focused primarily on Hamas or on its supposed outposts in diaspora centers like Chicago.[9] The operating assumption of the latter set of discussions is that Arab and Muslim diasporas are merely extensions of homelands situated elsewhere. Yet, as diaspora studies scholarship has demonstrated, the diaspora-homeland relationship is fluid, with influences moving in both directions (Bernal 2014; Alonso and Oiarzabal 2010; Brinkerhoff 2009; Brubaker 2005; Appadurai 1991 and 1996; Clifford 1994; S. Hall 1990). Moreover, assimilation processes in immigrant communities transform collective identities, generating new trajectories across time (Gordon 1964; Bodnar 1985; Gans 1992; Portes and Zhou 1993; Alba and Nee 1997; Deaux 2006; Serhan 2009; Kivisto 2014). Religious retrieval and revival can occur, especially in situations of racist reaction (Kivisto 2014). But, even in such instances, the retrieval always occurs within the circumstances of the exile, which are distinct from those in the homeland. Indeed, where "home" is becomes the defining question of immigrant life, especially when the legitimacy of an immigrant group's presence is continually thrown into question.

Palestinian historical experience is no exception. The conditions of life in the Palestinian diaspora differ from those in Palestine itself even if diaspora and homeland remain intertwined because of travel, electronic communication, and the perpetuation of narratives of "return" (*al-'awda*). The assumption that the secular-Islamist split in Palestine—a highly complex phenomenon not easily reducible to this binary (Lybarger 2007a, 2007b, 2013)—directly shapes an analogous fracture in the diaspora can therefore mislead. Diaspora contexts generate their own predicaments and dynamics. Palestinians in these settings confront not only the crisis of the nation "back home" but also the question of belonging within the countries to which they have immigrated. This question of belonging evolves in complicated ways across space and time. As in Palestine, identities in diaspora contexts such as in Chicago have overlapped and hyphenated in a constant negotiation of place and space.

Secularism and the Religious Turn in Palestinian Chicago

Palestinian immigration to Chicago dates to the late 1890s but began in earnest after the wars of 1948 and 1967. The period after these wars coincided with the rise of secular, multisectarian pan-Arab nationalism and specifically Palestinian liberation movements like Fatah. After the war of 1967, activists in Chicago and elsewhere in the United States created new community centers that aligned ideologically with the various factions of the reconstituted, Fatah-led PLO. The student movement also gained momentum through the activities of the Organization of Arab Students (OAS), established in 1952 at the University of Michigan; the General Union of Palestinian Students, formed in Cairo, Egypt, in 1959; and the Association of Arab American University Graduates (AAUG), founded in 1967. These structures proved instrumental to forging attachment to Palestinian national identity within and beyond immigrant enclaves during the 1970s and 1980s (Pennock 2017, 21–117).

During the 1990s, however, alongside the rise of Islamist politics in Palestine, a discernible shift toward Islam as a primary framework of solidarity occurred. Islamic organizations, such as the Muslim Brotherhood-aligned Muslim Student Association chapters (MSA), had established presences on university campuses since 1963. They openly rejected Arab and Palestinian nationalist activism, however, seeing it as "secular" and thus contrary to Islamic solidarity (Pennock 2017, 53).[10] In the 1990s, in cities like Chicago, young activists identifying explicitly with Islam as a new global framework for mobilization within and beyond the Palestinian immigrant community came to the fore. The signs of this change were evident in new forms of dress, grooming, and comportment. These forms of attire marking the new piety had even become evident in spaces once considered secularist bastions. At the Arab Community Center, the *markaz* mentioned earlier, young activists led prayers in the corners of the main room, attracting the participation of youth enrolled in the organization's programs.

Signs of a revitalized Islamic identity within the wider immigrant community were also apparent during the 1990s. Cainkar (2004, 113–14) noted the appearance of *halal* meat markets, the closing of nationalist cultural centers, and the corresponding rising attendance at mosques and private Islamic schools run by those mosques. She also reported "personally observ[ing] hundreds of individuals change from secular to religious since the mid-1990s, while conducting research and participating in the Arab and Muslim communities [in Chicago]" (114). Such developments signaled a broad shift within the ethos of the Palestinian immigrant community as a whole. At the largest Palestinian-dominated mosque, the Mosque Foundation in the southwest suburb of Bridgeview, attendance shot from an average of 75 attendees at Friday prayers in 1982, just after the mosque was built, to nearly 2,000 worshippers every week in 1994. Schmidt (2004), documenting the emergence of a generation of self-identified Muslim activists who were establishing and leading a range of new Islamic social service organizations, confirms Cainkar's observations. Similarly, Karim (2009), through a comparative ethnography of South Asian and African American Muslim interactions in Chicago and Atlanta, shows the integrative and transcending effect of an emerging transethnic Islamic solidarity rooted in what she calls "*ummah* ideals." Numrich (2012), Grewal (2014),

Numrich and Wedam (2015), and Khabeer (2016) similarly describe the development of a distinctive interethnic, intersectional, contested, and dynamic conception of *umma* among Muslim Americans. From a different angle, Naber (2012) explores the coalescence of progressive Muslim and secular-leftist groups within Arab American activist circles in the San Francisco Bay Area. Shared concerns for social justice, anti-imperialism, and resisting patriarchal authority bring these quite different trajectories into intersection.

The combined evidence from these studies seems conclusive: a shift toward Islam among Chicago's Palestinians as well as among other Arab American and Muslim-majority immigrant communities has definitely occurred and is part of a transethnic phenomenon that conceives of a transnational Islamic community or *umma* inclusive of a wide range of ethnicities (Numrich 2012; Numrich and Wedam 2015). Moreover, Chicago and the United States as a whole seem, generally, to be but one instance of a global pattern. European Muslims, for example, appear to be developing a sense of an "Islamic diaspora" within the transnational framework of the European Union. Anchoring this growing self-perception are new Muslim organizations that transcend ethnic and national boundaries. This organization-building reflects the desire of ostensibly secular European states to define an "official" Islam that legally situates Muslims as Muslims. It also responds to the needs of European Muslims to advocate and defend Islam as legitimately European (Amghar, Boubekeur, and Emerson 2007; Sniderman and Hagendoorn 2007; Roy 2004; Kastoryano 2002; Saint-Blancat 2002, 2004; Mandaville 2001).

Understanding the Religious Turn: Bringing Contingency and the Secular Back In

Yet, as obvious as it may seem that an Islamic turn has occurred and that this turn is the result of global processes, several problems arise from the privileging of religion, Islam especially, and of transnationalism above all other possible analytical lenses. Specifically, the privileging of Islam as an interpretive category and the corresponding appeal to transnational religious networks and solidarities tend to elide the social, political, and historical complexities of the communities in which Islam is but one aspect of collective life. The consequence of this elision has been an obscuring of the contingency of Islam as a shaping force within individual lives. When the focus shifts to specific communities—their constituting narratives, key historical transitions, ideological cleavages, class, gender, and generational differences, and ethnic and religious distinctions—Islam, and religion generally, cease to be an all-embracing explanation. Instead, they become a contingent and internally complex element within a broader social field (Lybarger 2014).

The data and analyses I present in this book emphasize this contingency. They do so by focusing on how the immediate social contexts within which people live out their lives—the internal social processes of diaspora communities—shape individual outlooks and responses to the world. This focus on the positive, constructive dimension of subjectivity formation departs from other interpretations of the Islamic religious shift in Chicago. These other interpretations have emphasized, not incorrectly, the effect of external forces such as majoritarian racist reaction acting against the immigrant community. Cainkar (2004) has argued, for example, that the Islamic revitalization among Palestinian Arab Muslims in Chicago has more to do with experiences that resemble those of African Americans than it does with any other factor. Like African Americans, Arabs and Muslims (including African American Muslims) have been targets of negative stereotypes, discrimination, dehumanization, political exclusion, and voicelessness: "[t]heir youth experience alienation in the schools and have to combat self-hatred imbued by textbooks, Halloween costumes, video games, talk shows and movies that portray them as barbaric" (117). Islam counters these experiences by providing dignity, identity, and strength (113).

But is racism necessarily the sole or even most important reason for the religious turn, especially among Palestinians? Racism is certainly a factor in the experiences of the individuals whose voices register in this book. The wider society has thrust the labels of "terrorist" and "Muslim" upon them as primary, pejorative identifications. Some have responded by retreating from or purposefully masking or discarding stereotypical signs of Muslimness. Many others have embraced the imposed identity, transforming it into a positive form of self-assertion. Some women, for example, explain that they wear hijab in part to proclaim their Islamic identity over and against the racist reaction. The argument emphasizing external, majoritarian pressure does have merit.

But bigotry alone does not explain why someone would necessarily embrace religious piety in response. Other nonreligious responses are possible; and even if the response is religious, that response can take a variety of forms. Why does someone choose a particular path, religious or secular? Arriving at an answer to this question requires a close look at how organizations, institutions, events, spatial processes, and generational, class, and gender dynamics positively shape a religious or secular disposition at the individual level, irrespective of majoritarian pressures.

Close empirical analysis of this sort is necessary because identities do not form purely as organic wholes in isolation. The Islamizing shift in Chicago is not an inexorable, single-track process of awakening. It is not a retrieval of some complete and unconditioned thing forgotten, for example, by a supposedly ignorant older generation too focused on assimilation.[11] It is also not necessarily a response to racism in every case. Rather, it is an indeterminate phenomenon subject to specific historical conditions and to the shaping effects of diverse, overlapping institutional settings and milieus. Religious, nonreligious, and hybrid alignments in this process unfold in new ways and in multiple directions as individuals negotiate their identities within and across different social spheres. These negotiations reshape the alignments as individuals adapt to or make compromises with competing expectations for behavior.

These points gesture back to a core question outlined at the outset of this chapter: what are the identity effects that result from crossings between social spheres and from the realignments to which they give rise? Specifically, what are the implications for secular and religious identities as they interact? The chapters ahead offer the following, multilayered answer. First, rather than disappearing as a result of the religious shift, secularism has instead persisted in revised or entirely new forms. Traditional secular nationalism continues even if its institutional frameworks have weakened. New, deinstitutionalized secularities have also appeared, often in reaction against the new piety, which, in its own right, has evolved along divergent axes in its interactions with secularism and secular spaces. A range of hybrid forms of identity that blend secularity and religiosity have emerged, as well. Secularism and religion are contingent and dynamic orientations. Their intersection and interaction generate a range of identity transformations.

KEY CONCEPTS: IDENTITY, SECULARISM, AND RELIGION

Identity

I have already repeatedly invoked the terms "identity," "secularism," and "religion" in this discussion. These terms and several others that inform the assertions and analyses in the rest of this book require specification. By "identity" I mean an emergent sense of self and other that forms and evolves narratively as "stories so far" (Massey 2005, 130) across five intersecting axes: epochal-historical; autobiographical; generational; structural; and spatial. The epochal-historical axis unfolds diachronically in relation to destabilizing, large-scale crises (for example, wars, environmental catastrophes, epidemics, mass displacements, economic depressions, revolutions and uprisings, violent state repression, vigilante violence directed at specific groups). These events create a shared experience, a shared sense of fate—memorialized in collective narratives, commemorative practices, and symbolic expressions—that become the common reference point for a generational cohort. Members of this cohort interpret subsequent events in relation to this formational crisis.

The process through which a sociohistorical generation comes into existence also entails the biological life cycle (birth, maturation, death). The life cycle facilitates a process of collective forgetting as new cohorts come to maturity under different historical conditions.[12] New cohorts do not share in the same direct way the historical memories of earlier cohorts. The historical references shift, thereby enabling a relinquishing or, more accurately, a reinterpreting of past traumas.

At the same time, however, social structures like the family, schools, religious institutions, political movements and parties, and associations of all kinds serve to instill intergenerational continuity, thus mitigating the memory-eroding effects of the life cycle. These institutional contexts constitute a range of self-referencing practices, symbols, and narratives that individuals engage and absorb through participation within these settings. Such institutions are essential to sustaining memory and social coherence across time and space. Traumatic, epochal events, however, can sever this continuity by undermining received understandings of the world and generating a search for alternative interpretive frames, narratives, institutions, practices, and symbols. New movements and associations articulating a revised interpretation of the past and present can arise in these circumstances to draw into their ranks individuals just forming or consolidating their historical and political awareness (typically between the ages of fifteen and thirty). The wars of 1948 and 1967, the Israeli invasion of Lebanon in 1982, and the First Intifada of 1987–93 were events of this sort.[13] In each case, new historical generations formed in tandem with new movements and parties as a consequence of the ensuing collective political crisis. The events marked each cohort in ways that distinguished it from other prior or succeeding cohorts.

Generational cohorts typically integrate individuals from across class, gender, religious, regional, and other salient distinctions. Palestinians who were in their late teens and twenties during the First Intifada of the late 1980s and early 1990s, for example, share a sense of a common generational location across their multiple lines of difference by virtue of having undergone this historical event together. Nevertheless, this same cohort splits internally in relation to competing interpretations of the significance of that shared experience. The most profound and enduring divide has been the one that has expressed itself in the Islamist-secular-nationalist cleavage. Such splits that result in opposing formations constitute synchronic "generational units" (Mannheim 1952, 304). These units express competing narratives about the shared epochal experience. The narratives form within contrasting, at times overlapping, sociopolitical spaces. Families, voluntary associations, religious organizations, political parties, student organizations, labor organizations, and a range of other social formations structure these spaces, institutionalizing the competing narratives of the contrasting generational units. These same institutional sites can also become divided as generational units vie to define and control them. In Palestine, secular nationalists and Islamists have fought for dominance, for example, on university campuses, within labor unions, and in associations like the Red Crescent Society (an equivalent to the International Committee of the Red Cross).

Individuals move into and out of these contentious zones. As they do so, they negotiate and integrate conflicting meanings into their own unique narratives, their own autobiographical accounts. These accounts may or may not track consistently with the social and political movements and spaces through which the contrasting generational units form. These convergences and discrepancies between the autobiographical and the generational indicate the fluidity and contingency of identity at different levels of aggregation, from the individual to the collective. The analyses in this book bring such complexities to the fore. They focus primarily on individual accounts but in doing so trace the effects of broad processes such as the generational. The individual experience as conveyed through the telling of a life story in an interview becomes a portal to collective experience, but one that reveals tensions and digressions and transgressions of dominant narratives and practices in often unexpected ways (Riessman 2008, 1–19).

The fluidity of autobiographical and generational processes in relation to diverse institutional sites is consistent with how geographers conceive of space as an emergent phenomenon. Space is "the dimension of multiple trajectories, a simultaneity of stories-so-far [. . . it is] the multiplicity of duration" (Massey 2005, 24). This idea implies not only that time-space has a narrated quality but also that it is indeterminate. Social spaces, and the identities that form within them, are, on this account, sites of open-ended narrative intersection. Space is a "coexisting heterogeneity," a "contemporaneous plurality," that is "always in the process of being made"—"it is never finished, never closed"—through these intersections (9).[14]

Space, in other words, refers to a range of co-occurring, ever forming and re-forming narrative arcs in any given moment and context. Space is not a two-dimensional reality external to the narratives we create and re-create and inhabit and abandon but rather a meaningful context constituted through our storytelling. Chicago's "South Side," for example, emerges as a place through the accounts that give it form and significance. These narratives are diverse in their trajectories and in their intersections or lack thereof. There is more than one South Side.

The emergent senses of self that constitute identity in any given site or place are the result of such narrative intersections and disconnections. This narrative process is generational, epochal, institutional, autobiographical, and spatial all at once. Moreover, the fluidity between diaspora spaces like Chicago and homeland spaces like the West Bank means that identity trajectories can imbricate: the Intifada generational cohort forms within and across both spaces, for example. This coinciding of space means that the sociomoral orientations carried within the constitutive narratives can also overlap. These orientations constitute milieus that integrate individuals structurally across class, race, religion, gender, generation, and, because of the coinciding of space, even region (Palestine and the United States, for example).[15]

At the same time, however, diaspora spaces generate their own variants of these milieus and trajectories. They undergo their own epochal events, produce their own distinct institutions, and generate their own narratives. As a result, they constitute a unique range of actual and possible trajectories. The events of September 11, 2001, have a particular salience that defines the U.S. diaspora space, for example. They have different defining effects in the homeland space of Palestine.

The key point, however, is that "diaspora" and "homeland" as meaningful, narrated contexts can and do intersect and overlap. Through migration, Palestine crosses with Chicago, giving rise intergenerationally and interspatially to the distinct place "Palestinian Chicago." Chicago, too, is interspatial within itself: multiple imbricating, intersecting spaces constitute it. This phenomenon additionally shapes the space of Palestinian Chicago in distinct ways that diverge from the interspatial dynamics in Palestine itself.

Spatial Dynamics and Identity Formation in Palestinian Chicago

Chicago, as a multisited diaspora space, has shaped the Palestinian identity dynamics that are the focus of this book in four principal ways. First, it has brought Palestinian immigrants into interaction with a wide diversity of other groups. This interaction has had a range of consequences. Black-Palestinian relationships on the city's South Side, for example, have produced conflicted economic relations. As chapter 1 shows, Palestinians have historically related to African American communities in the role of petty shopkeepers working on the edges of the segregated and impoverished black residential zones. During the 1960s and 1970s, however, new forms of relationship, new narrative intersections, developed as Palestinian political activists inspired by Third World anti-colonialism forged solidarity connections with the Black Panther Party and Black Power movements in the city and elsewhere nationally (Fischbach 2019; Feldman 2015; Pennock 2017).

Recently, these relationships have undergone renewal in the aftermath of the police killings of African Americans and the rise of the Black Lives Matter (BLM) movement (Erakat 2018). In 2014, for example, Palestinian activists from Chicago traveled to Ferguson, Missouri, site of the killing of Michael Brown, whose death at the hands of police sparked BLM's formation, to demonstrate black-Palestinian solidarity. Since then, in Chicago, young Palestinian activists, working principally through the AAAN, have collaborated with BLM chapters to address police violence and police surveillance of black and Arab communities. These past and current interactions have shaped Palestinians culturally and politically, most explicitly in the embrace among some youth of a "black" identity. This identity alignment has occurred through the encounter with black liberation politics, hip-hop, and Black Islam. Conversely, Palestine and the Boycott, Divestment, and Sanctions movement have come to serve as important symbols for a countercultural resistance identity across racial and ethnic lines. Within transnational activist networks Palestine has emerged as a rallying symbol in the effort to counter "the post-9/11 consolidation of the US-Israeli state alliance" (Collins 2011, 7–8; see also Tawil-Souri 2016, 15–28). These networks include Muslim organizational spaces and milieus, in which, as noted above, Palestine and Jerusalem, specifically, serve metaphorically to orient a cross-ethnic Islamic solidarity.

A second way in which the diaspora context of Chicago has shaped Palestinian identities in complex ways has been through socioeconomic class. Since the late 1980s, in conjunction with the Islamic shift, Palestinian immigrants in the city have transitioned in large numbers to the near southwest suburbs. This shift has occurred as part of a process of wealth accumulation among small business owners in the older urban enclave on the city's Southwest Side. The pattern of suburban shift is not unique to Palestinians. As the next chapter shows, it replicates the movements of other groups, including white ethnic communities that left the city as part of "white flight"—an exceedingly complex process, as the next chapter will illustrate—during the 1950s and 1960s. The Palestinians who speak in this book refer to their own transition to the suburbs, in fact, as a version of "white flight," thereby underlining the race and class dimensions of the phenomenon. Their reasons for invoking this term include the desire of their families, as they report, to escape gang violence and to improve their socioeconomic position and status. Scholars have often referred to this process as "becoming white" or as assimilation pivoting on a rejection of blackness (Gualtieri 2009; Roediger 2006). The desire to be categorized as white, or at least as not black, has a long history linking back to the racial categories that once determined eligibility for citizenship. Early Arab immigrants ("Syrians") fought successfully in the courts to be defined as "white," and Arab Americans to this day continue to be classified as such in the US census (Gualtieri 2009). Socially and culturally, however, the status of Arabs in the United States has remained ambiguous: US support for Israel since 1948 and the enduring perception of Muslim and Arab immigrants as a malevolent "enemy within" have repeatedly placed the Arab American, and now Muslim American, presence and claim to citizenship under suspicion (Cainkar 2009).

The Palestinian suburban transition has reconfigured the interstitial position of Palestinians in the city: it shifts their location to the near southwestern suburbs that separate white suburbia from the predominantly black and brown South Side urban space. This process points to the distinct role of the city as a mechanism of identity formation. As an intensely diverse yet also violently segregated space, the Chicago metropolitan area is a site of multiple, intersecting race, class, ethnic, and religious identity trajectories. These trajectories unfold spatially in ways that reinforce but also destabilize community cohesion. Immigrant enclaves form within the context of racial divisions that are spatially instantiated. The locations of these enclaves can shift, as the Palestinian suburban transition illustrates, but they can also become undone as individuals challenge the institutional mechanisms that instill and reinforce enclave solidarity and identity. Religion facilitates both processes. The establishment of well-endowed organizations like the Mosque Foundation in the southwest suburb of Bridgeview, for example, generates strong enclave solidarities and a new Islamic identity that parallels the Islamic revival in Palestine and elsewhere in the Middle East. Churches have played a similar boundary-marking role in Palestinian Christian communities, with Christian solidarity responding to the new Islamization in the suburbs. At the same time, however, Islam has provided an alternative context for a countercultural identity, as described above: Black Islam, especially, constitutes the space of this possibility (Khabeer 2016). The city's spatial multiplicity also opens up alternatives for individuals to break entirely with enclave solidarity and to reject or significantly reconfigure religious and national identities. Artistic milieus, youth party scenes, activist organizational spaces, and universities situated elsewhere in the city are primary mechanisms for this process.

A third complicating factor in diaspora identities is the experience of living between the *shatat* (diaspora) and the *iblad* (Palestinian Arabic colloquial for "homeland," that is, Palestine). As chapter 1 shows, since their first arrival in the city, Palestinian immigrants in Chicago have maintained familial and economic networks that tie them to "back home." Early immigrants, who were predominantly men, returned to their villages and towns to repatriate their earnings and to get married. They then travelled back to Chicago to work for years at a time, before again returning to their home communities.

After the wars of 1948 and 1967, these patterns changed as these men brought their families to the United States with them. New family reunification provisions in US immigration law allowed extended family to migrate at this point. Still, as the ethnographic analyses in the chapters to follow will show, families continued to maintain links with communities in Palestine. A common practice has been for parents and children to spend summers or even entire school years in Palestine to reinforce Arabic language abilities, attachment to Palestinian society and culture, including religion, and connections with relatives (Abu El-Haj 2015). This practice, in fact, dates to the earliest periods of family settlement in Chicago (al-Tahir 1952). It has resulted in an intergenerational bifocality that provides contrasting lenses through which to view and make sense of lived realities. This bifocality blurs differences between the experiences of recent arrivals and long-established immigrants.[16] To be a Palestinian immigrant in Chicago, regardless of generational location, often means to live across homeland and exile and thus to develop dual lenses through which to perceive space and place. This perceptual duality is facilitated as much by social media as by actual, in-person travel between the *shatat* and the *iblad*.

Gender dynamics constitute a fourth factor in diaspora identity formation. The religious shift, Islamic and Christian, has reinforced patriarchal order within the emerging Palestinian immigrant middle classes in the suburbs.[17] In doing so, it has articulated a type of gendered "respectability" that shores up enclave identity against social currents that challenge the patriarchal ethos and the gender and sexual identity norms that underlie it. Here, too, the city, as a site of multiple, overlapping spaces marked by diverging, gendered value orientations provides the opportunity for individuals to contest the patriarchalization of the enclave. Several individuals profiled in this book stake out oppositional stances from standpoints they embrace in other spheres, such as universities and domestic abuse shelters, where they develop critiques of gendered hierarchies.

At the same time, however, other individuals embrace the Islamic turn as part of a different kind of challenge to patriarchal order. Here, too, encounter with student groups like MSA chapters at universities provides the opportunity for learning and deploying an anti-patriarchal reading of religious texts against patriarchal norms in the home. Thus, even if the religious shift documented in this book has redefined what it means to see oneself as Palestinian, it has done so in tension with a range of other identity possibilities that flow not only from the traditions of secular nationalism that predate the Islamic shift but also from interactions across the class, race, *shatat/iblad*, gender, and spatial-socio-moral divides in cities like Chicago.

Secularism and Religion

The ethnographic descriptions in this book focus on identity transformations stemming from the religious shift and the deinstitutionalization, not the disappearance, of secularism. I have already discussed these two terms—religious and secular—in relation to the history of Palestinian Islamism and Palestinian secular nationalism. The terms require elaboration, however, at a general analytical level. As invoked in this book, "secular" and "religious" and "secularism" and "religion" constitute ideal-types. Drawn from empirical data, ideal-types deliberately accentuate certain features of "patterned meaningful action" that in lived reality is fluid and complex (Kalberg 2012, 99–101). The ideal-type as such does not exist, empirically. Rather, it is a provisional abstraction that enables the demarcation, comparison, and interpretation of phenomena one wishes to understand.[18] Inevitably, through application, this abstraction, the type in its pure form, will undergo revision. Instead of a single, undifferentiated image of secularism, for example, the result of application will be an empirically rich concept reflecting different developmental possibilities, including hybrid ones influenced by the interaction with religion.

Ideal-typically, then, in this book, "secularism," in its pure form, encompasses any social orientation, practice, mode of solidarity, or stance that implicitly or explicitly resists, rejects, demotes, ignores, or otherwise suspends, momentarily or permanently, the prior claim of religious authority.[19] Secularist stances manifest empirically in a range of forms. What makes an orientation or stance or mode of response in the end "secular," however, is the explicit rejection, implicit irrelevance to it, or suspension of the primacy of particular religious authority above all other considerations as a foundation for shared ethics and social and political identification. For example, secular nationalism in the Palestinian context is secular to the extent it privileges national identity and belonging above specific sectarian religious solidarities. Positively, secularism can embrace a range of value orientations, including pluralism, tolerance, individual liberty, and the like. Empirically, it can blend with religious orientations. It is possible, for example, to adhere to a religion while also adopting a secular—but not necessarily secularist—stance in social or political spheres beyond the specific religious community. Doing so entails a strategic suspending or an interpretive recasting of the priority of religious solidarity.

Similarly, secularist positions can soften to include religious solidarities through similar kinds of operations that relax the exclusion of the religious. How this occurs in Palestinian diaspora situations will be the focus of the chapters ahead.

"Religion," in contrast with "secularism," refers to institutions and practices that, in their implicit logic, presume the existence, power, and authority of superhuman forces and the capacity to interact with and gain access to these forces for the purpose of preventing or mitigating and ending crises occurring in the body, nature, and society (Riesebrodt 2010).[20] Religious solidarity is an implicit requirement for ensuring access to these powers. Religious specialists often explain human sufferings and failures in terms of an absence of religious solidarity and commitment. These explanations are theodicies—justifications for the existence of suffering (evil) despite the presence of an omnipotent and omniscient God who presumably provides protection in exchange for honor (expressed in worship) and obedience (expressed in adherence to divinely given mandates). Religious theodicies can become politically salient in periods of prolonged conflict and national crisis. The success of Hamas demonstrates how this can occur in the Palestinian context. Under such conditions, religions can reorient the social and political fields.

Hybridity and Syncretic Secularity

As I show in this book, secularism and religion constitute possible stances that individuals can adopt toward their lived conditions. A range of factors—for example, ethnicity/race, class, gender, and generation—interrelate with and shape these contrasting stances in various ways. Hybrid positions are possible. My use of "hybrid" departs from postcolonial and postmodernist conceptions of the term. In postcolonial literature, hybridity features typically in arguments about how the subaltern's subjectivity is not simply the consequence of the imposition of hegemonic colonialist discourses. Rather, the subaltern selectively appropriates and reinterprets hegemonic discourses to produce a hybrid consciousness and knowledge. Colonial discourse, too, reveals the impact of this transformative reception when analyzed critically (Bhabha 1994).

By contrast, in my broader use of the term, hybridity is less a sign and consequence of colonial power imbalances than a description of what happens to religious and secular orientations through the crossing of social circles. With Simmel and Weber, I conceive of modern societies as comprising multiple institutional spaces and sociomoral milieus. As individuals cross into and out of these various spaces, they encounter contradictions and tensions that challenge their value orientations (Simmel 1955 [1922]). One consequence of this experience is the development of reflexivity within the individual that can then lead into a process of autobiographical revision and moral reorientation. This process can entail a selective adaptation and integration—a hybridization—of orientations that serve to resolve the tensions, or "cross pressures" (Taylor 2007), which individuals can experience in negotiating moral contradictions across different social and institutional contexts. When the hybridization involves religious-secular intersection, the result is a "syncretic secularity" (Eipper 2011, and see also chapters 5 and 6 in this book).

My engagement with questions of hybridity, syncretic formations, and interaction within and across secular and religious spaces departs from much of the current debate about secularism. This debate concerns itself primarily with the modern state and with a general political logic of secularism that uniformly defines and regulates the space of the religious and the secular across different national contexts (e.g., Asad 1993, 2003; Mahmood 2005, 2006, 2010, 2016; Sullivan, Hurd, and Mahmood 2015). The problem in some of these analyses lies in the tendency to view secularism and the modern state in monolithic terms despite variations in the social and political fields from one national context to another (Joppke 2017). By contrast, I view the state as internally complex: its various bureaucratic structures interact, often at cross purposes, with diverse nonstate institutions (including religious ones), class and generation formations, social and political movements, and cultural enclaves and milieus that exist independently within a wider field of political and social tension. The field of tension can take many forms in relation to diverging national settings. Within and across these fields, secular and religious discourses, practices, and institutions can develop in multiple, indeterminate directions and in doing so give rise to a range of subjectivities, including hybrid ones.

The data I analyze, in particular, provide a detailed demonstration of the key point that "the religious and the secular exist [. . .] in a continuing dialectic that engender[s] any number of transformations" (Martin 2014, 16; see also Riesebrodt 2014). In fact, the interactions generate dynamic, synthetic forms, making it difficult to maintain the distinction between secular and religious: even if the distinction is useful for analytical purposes it nevertheless becomes a fluid line within lived realities. Palestinians have participated in this indeterminate, interactive process, just as have every other group in the West and globally. Consequently, Palestinian experience offers perspective on the diverse range of what Mahmood (2010, 295) terms "conceptions of the self, agency, and accountability that modern secularism makes possible [and] which link 'us' and 'them' indelibly (if messily) across putatively civilizational divides."[21] Mahmood has primarily political secularism—secularism as state policy—in mind, whereas my ideal-typical elaboration of the term focuses on secularism as a particular kind of individual subjectivity or agency, that is, as a "conception of self" as it is articulated and practiced by particular groups and individuals arrayed across the class, gender, generational, religious, racial, political, and spatial spectrums. These self-conceptions may or may not track with the secularizing policies and secularist political values of any given state, society, or milieu. Thus, what emerges is a multiplicity of ways to express and enact secularity. There are multiple secularisms and secularities, not a simple "modern secularism."

Much of the prevailing discussion of Palestinian and Arab and Muslim immigrants disregards this sort of fluidity that the conceptual frames I have just elaborated attempt to bring into focus. This disregard comes at a cost to understanding. When they merit attention, Palestinians and Arabs and Muslims, generally, often serve as targets of polemical caricature rather than as subjects of an informed inquiry that can elucidate questions of religion, migration, identity, and belonging. The reductive portrayal can have a parallel within Palestinian communities: the priority of representing the nation against its negation often leaves little if any latitude for individual expression. The diaspora, however, offers spaces beyond the nation and its enclaves, and some individuals seek it out to forge alternative futures.

ORGANIZATION OF THE BOOK

Chapter 1 examines the formation and historical location of Palestinian Chicago in relation to the wider history of immigration and the divisions of race and class in the city. A main concern is to show the ambivalence of the Palestinian location. Palestinians are strangers in Simmel's sense, mediating across racial lines but never fully integrating as members of the wider urban community. This status changed following the wars of 1948 and 1967 as Palestinians for the first time began to orient themselves toward permanent residency in their Chicago exile and in doing so created identifiable enclaves. The centers of these enclaves have shifted in ethos from secular-nationalist to religious—Islamic and Christian—in an arc paralleling the rise and decline of the Palestine Liberation Organization (PLO) as the diaspora's preeminent institution.

Chapter 2 shifts the focus from historical background to the ethnographic present with an analysis of the secular milieu. The chapter opens with a vivid interview with one of the founders of the Arab Community Center (the *markaz*). Steeped in pan-Arabism, this individual decries the Islamic shift in the immigrant community. The chapter continues with a generational analysis of the changes in secular subjectivities. This analysis demonstrates how the religious turn shapes secularism across historical generations.

Next, chapter 3 pivots to examine the Islamic shift through observations of two events that American Muslims for Palestine (AMP) held in 2013 and 2014, respectively. AMP is a prominent organization. It holds an annual conference on Palestine that draws thousands of participants from the Chicago metropolitan area and across the United States; and it has recently established a national advocacy office in Washington, DC. What AMP does in the Chicago community is thus representative of a wider transformation that has fused Islam with Palestinian nationalism in the diaspora.

Chapter 4 continues the focus on the religious shift, both Islamic and Christian, by examining individual subjectivity across the generational continuum. The data for this discussion derive from in-depth life history interviews with immigrants who either established or inherited the core institutions of the religious turn in its Islamic and Christian forms. Individuals for whom the wars of 1948 and 1967 were formative of their generational outlook detail key shaping experiences in Palestine and then describe the arc from that past to the realities they face in the Chicago immigrant context. This generation created the institutional foundations of the subsequent religious shift. The narratives of individuals from succeeding generations show how the earlier religious institutionalization channels their formative historical experience. This experience encompasses the First and Second Intifadas; the Oslo Peace process; the concomitant withering of the PLO as the dominant organizational structure of the diaspora; the September 11 attacks; and the subsequent intensification of the racist exclusion and law-enforcement surveillance that have persistently undermined Arab and Muslim sense of belonging in the United States. I analyze Muslim and Christian narratives, showing a mirroring of Islamic and Christian sectarian enclavization in this process of religious turning. The religious turn has the consequence of shrinking secular, nonsectarian space within which Palestinians might interact and form shared political solidarities across their confessional boundaries.

Chapters 5 and 6 continue the analysis of fieldwork data but shift the focus to the intersections of religious and secular subjectivities. The chapters elaborate the concept of "syncretic secularity" (Eipper 2011), which captures the hybridizing potential of secular and religious interactions. The analysis of case profiles in these chapters illustrates and further develops the concept by describing two main syncretic trajectories: religious secularity and secular religiosity. Religious secularity originates in the secular milieu but then arcs toward the religious; conversely, secular religiosity moves from the religious-sectarian context to the secular. Religious secularity manifests, in my data, in three subforms: reversion, conversion, and accommodation. Secular religiosity, which I describe as "rebellion" against the religious shift, can lead either to atheism or to spiritualization. Chapters 5 and 6 explain and demonstrate these sub-types in detail and examine how race, class, gender, and generation shape their development. The analyses also show that individuals can shift along the syncretic range within their own particular life trajectories. The profiles thereby illustrate not only the different types of syncretic orientation but also the fluidity that can manifest within a single autobiographical account.

The conclusion returns to the major themes of the book, principally the secular-religious interaction and its transformational effects on Palestinian identity in US exile. The current moment is a time of deep and continuing secular nationalist and Islamist political division in Palestine. Palestinians, especially through new global campaigns such as the Boycott, Divestment, and Sanctions movement, seek to re-envision politics beyond the secular-religious binary that has defined the competition between Hamas and Fatah, primarily, in the Occupied

Gaza Strip and West Bank. The binary nevertheless persists and, in diaspora communities like Chicago, produces new trajectories of identity. If there is one lesson to draw from this book it is that religion shapes Palestinian immigrant identities in infinitely complex ways. Moreover, religion is not the only conditioning force. Secularism also is an important identity framework. Even if it has appeared to be in decline, institutionally, secularism and secularity remain nevertheless relevant to the new forms of orientation that this book analyzes. Still, the individuals whose narratives are at the center of this book do not fall easily on one side or the other of the binary. The new understandings emerging in Chicago—at least among my interlocutors—of what it means to see oneself as Palestinian exceed the divisions of religious and secular, Muslim and Christian, Palestine and the United States. In doing so, they reveal the rich complexities and possibilities of Palestinian identities in and beyond the exile.

1

Palestinian Chicago

Spatial Location, Historical Formation

The hub of Palestinian immigrant life before the suburban exodus of the 1990s was a southwest corridor stretching east and west from the intersection of South Kedzie Avenue and West 63rd Street. Palestinians had settled on the North Side, too, principally between Montrose and Foster, Clark and Kimball, and Kedzie and Lawrence Avenues (Cainkar 1988, 115–16). These individuals and families lived in ethnically heterogeneous neighborhoods. The Southwest Side corridor, by contrast, was a larger, more homogenous concentration than the North Side communities. It also hosted three community centers during the 1970s and 1980s. These centers anchored group life for Palestinians across the city prior to the suburban shift at the turn of the millennium.

Members of the immigrant community citywide sold goods door-to-door, worked in factories, and owned small businesses—corner groceries, dry goods stores, gas stations, restaurants, and check-cashing operations. On the South Side, the businesses served the immigrants but also, increasingly, the larger surrounding African American and Latinx communities. After their move to the suburbs, Palestinian business owners commuted to their stores on the Southwest Side. At the end of the day, owners gated and padlocked their storefronts and drove back to the suburbs.[1] In this daily traversal, they enacted a longstanding, intermediary social relation: Palestinians in Chicago had inserted themselves between the white ethnics who had also migrated to the suburbs and the working-class and poor black and immigrant Latinx who had moved into the neighborhoods the whites had vacated. The Southwest Side Palestinians would follow the whites but live apart from them within a borderland separating the brown and black city from the expanse of white suburbia. The Palestinian exile in Chicago was, in this way, a particular kind of experience inflected by the city's racial and economic segregation.

This chapter describes this experience in detail. The discussion begins with the period of early migration in the late nineteenth century, during which Palestinians established their interstitial position between black and white residential and business zones. It then continues with developments through the wars of 1948 and 1967—a period crucial to the shift from "bimodal" migration patterns to permanent residency. The final sections of the chapter detail the organizations that have anchored the secular nationalist spaces of the Southwest Side enclave and, later, the new, Islamizing suburban community. In connection with this latter shift, the discussion also addresses the development of key Christian institutions.

EARLY MIGRATION FROM PALESTINE: 1890s–1940s

Palestinian migration to the United States dates to the 1890s. During this period, Chicago became a financial and industrial center, and its population boomed. Between 1860 and 1870 the city's residents tripled in number from 109,000 to 300,000; by 1890, the total had jumped to 1.1 million (Abu-Lughod 1999, 115–16). Foreign migration fueled this explosion. By 1900, nearly four out of five Chicagoans were either foreign-born or children of those individuals (116). The migrants came to work in the burgeoning steel and meatpacking industries. "Manufacturing establishments" went from approximately 3,500 in 1880 "to more than 10,000" in 1919 (117). Owners sited their factories along the rail lines and canals away from the Loop—and beyond municipal regulation and taxation. Worker settlements grew up around the plants. In some cases, as with the Pullman factory or U.S. Steel in Gary, Indiana, owners built company towns (Buder 1967; Mayer and Wade 1969, 188–92; Carl Smith 1995, 177–231). These settlements distanced the nascent proletariat from the wealthy downtown and became zones of white ethnic segregation.

African American migration from the southern states also intensified. Between 1900 and 1930, the city's black population skyrocketed from approximately 30,000 to nearly 234,000 (Abu-Lughod 1999, 124). Having few other options, these migrants settled within an area soon to be called "the Black Belt." This South Side zone stretched along State Street between 12th and 39th Streets (Philpott 1991, 116 and elsewhere; Drake and Cayton 1993 [1945], 174 and elsewhere; Abu-Lughod 1999, 124–26).[2] Surrounded by railroad track, a quarter mile wide, and three miles long, it became a densely populated and immiserated space (Philpott 1991, 117 and elsewhere; Drake and Cayton 1993 [1945], 198 and elsewhere; Abu-Lughod 1999, 122–25).[3] Housing covenants and white vigilante violence enforced the segregation. During a race riot in 1919, white gangs marauded through the Black Belt. The Illinois National Guard restored order only after twenty-three blacks and fifteen whites had died (Abu-Lughod 1999, 126–27; Bates 2019). The violence foreshadowed the "border wars" that flared during the 1950s and 1960s as blacks moved into formerly all-white areas (Chicago Commission on Race Relations 1922;

Philpott 1991, 120 and elsewhere; Drake and Cayton 1993 [1945], 198 and elsewhere; 1999, 124–27).

The Palestinian trajectories that intersected with these seismic and violent processes had their origins in socioeconomic shifts occurring in Greater Syria (inclusive of present-day Syria, Lebanon, and Palestine). Between 1899 and 1921, approximately 100,000 Syrians were allowed into the United States. Of this total, fewer than 6 percent were from the Jerusalem and Ramallah regions (Cainkar 1988, 68; Cainkar 1998; Serhan 2009, 12). The Chicago immigrants came mostly from these areas. Initially, most of these individuals were Christians from Ramallah; increasingly, however, Christian and Muslim peasants, who often lived together in mixed villages, began to migrate (Cainkar 1988 70–71; Serhan 2009, 15). This early migration was a direct outcome of Greater Syria's integration into a global market economy. European, especially French, naval and commercial expansion into the eastern Mediterranean during the seventeenth century initiated this process. The existing commercial classes in the Levant (present-day Syria, Palestine, Jordan, Lebanon) took advantage of newly lucrative opportunities for trade with the European states. In the process, they acquired capital that facilitated concentration of landholdings, introduction of new technology, and cultivation of cash crops such as oranges. These same elites sent their sons to study in European universities to gain new technocratic skills. Upon returning, this generation served in the commercial concerns of their families and in the new bureaucracies. They also led a host of new political movements. Some of these movements agitated for the enfranchisement of Ottoman subjects—Muslims, Christians and Jews—as citizens.[4]

The Ottoman authorities responded to these developments by instituting legal reforms that intensified the already existing divisions between the landed and commercial elites and the former peasants-turned-sharecroppers. The Land Code of 1858, for example, enabled absentee landlords and foreigners (through an amendment in 1867) to gain legal title to uncultivated expanses. It also broke up collectively owned fields—for example, the *musha'* system through which villages held land in common—into individually titled holdings. Village notables often signed legal titles on behalf of peasants, acquiring control of these lands in their own right. Absentee owners in the cities also gained control of large estates through the new legal mechanisms. And finally, the reforms opened the door to the acquisition of contiguous holdings by the nascent Zionist movement. These holdings would become the foundation for the Yishuv (Jewish settlement), which emphasized Jewish labor to the exclusion of Palestinian (Muslim and Christian) agriculturalists (Krämer 2008, 71–100). These changes in land ownership rendered sharecropping increasingly difficult. In response, young men began to abandon the villages in search of employment in new industrial hubs like Haifa and, much further afield, Chicago. Steamship company propaganda was an especially important spur to foreign migration.

The young men who migrated abroad to cities like Chicago had no intention of settling permanently in the United States. Instead, they established a bimodal pattern of residency and work: after several years, the men would return to their villages, build a house, pursue marriage, and then return again, alone, to continue work in the United States. This alternation counteracted assimilation by reinforcing family bonds "back home" and underscoring the instrumental purpose and impermanent nature of residency in the *mahjar* (literally, the place of sojourn, that is, the diaspora) (Oschinsky 1947, 23–24; Cainkar 1988, 73).

The temporary, pragmatic character of Palestinian migration manifested in the non-permanent nature of Palestinian settlement and work. The earliest immigrants did not purchase or build homes but rather rented rooms in boarding houses situated on the edge of the Black Belt. By 1912 some 150 mostly young Arab men lived in such houses in the Michigan Avenue and 18th Street area (Oschinsky 1947, 23). Within these spaces, they formed "an exclusively male community of peddlers" whose intention was to acquire wealth and return to their villages (Cainkar 1988, 74, paraphrasing al-Tahir 1952).

The First World War rendered returning hazardous, however: sea passage became dangerous and the fighting between Axis and Allied forces disrupted life in the migrants' home communities. In response, the men suspended their return visits and remained in Chicago. As their peddling capital accumulated, they began to buy small shops. One of Oschinsky's (1947) informants described peddling door-to-door with his uncle on the West Side. By 1923, he had saved enough money to start a dry goods store of his own on 18th Street (24). Between 1920 and 1935, Palestinian merchants opened numerous small stores in and along the edge of the Black Belt (23–24).

Within this "transition zone," Palestinian storeowners catered primarily to an African American clientele. In doing so, they became a "middle minority" or "stranger" group straddling the racial divide between blacks and whites (Cainkar 1988, 101–2).[5] Although most stores employed one or two African American saleswomen, the relationship with the black community could sometimes be tense and marked by stereotyped attitudes and even open conflict (Oschinsky 1947, 24–26; al-Tahir 1952, 122). One of Oschinsky's interlocutors, for example, recounted in detail how he became a target of robberies and how he violently confronted intruders in his premises after hours. He and other individuals with whom Oschinsky interacted expressed racialized views of their African American customers in describing such situations (25–26).[6] Intercommunal tensions of this sort persisted through the decades and have continued into the present (Blackistone 1981; Blackistone and Corrigan 1986; Robles 1989; Brachear 2010; Moore 2012).[7]

At the same time, however, shop owner-clientele interactions have not always been negative. Oschinsky (1947, 26) observed that the frequency of conflicts did not seem as high as his informants had indicated and that anyway Islam did not condone racism. And, although he reported bigoted attitudes among his Palestinian interlocutors, al-Tahir (1952, 193) claimed later in the same study that there was no class or racial tension between the communities.[8] He cited the example of how the Arab Club—an organization created by immigrants from Beitunia—held occasional meetings in the "Negro Muslim Temple," a Nation of Islam worship space at 824 East 43rd Street.[9] The club, al-Tahir stated, had plans to hold lectures there on Arabic language and Islamic history. This interaction seemed to indicate a desire for mutual understanding and social interaction. Al-Tahir argued that a shared commitment to Islamic ideals of equality enabled these positive relationships (al-Tahir 1952, 193).[10] Shop owner-clientele relationships could also sometimes lead to Palestinian integration into the community, for example, through intermarriage (Moore 2012). As well, various Palestinian and Muslim organizations forged alliances with African American activist groups during the height of decolonization and the Third World movement. Most recently these connections have manifested in black-Palestinian solidarity in the face of police violence in African American communities and Israel's bombardments of the Gaza Strip (Erakat 2018). During the past two decades, too, Palestinian and Muslim activists have sought to address the tensions between shop owners and their South Side clientele through campaigns to encourage stores to stock fresh produce and to cease the sale of liquor and lottery tickets (Brachear 2010; Freedman 2014).

Unlike the predominantly Muslim Palestinians in Chicago, other Arab immigrants—primarily Christians from current-day Lebanon and Syria who constituted the vast majority of the early waves of Arab immigrants—desired to remain in the United States permanently (Gualtieri 2009, 45–53 and elsewhere; al-Tahir 1952, 70–71). Beginning in 1909, these immigrants waged a sustained effort in the courts to count as "Caucasian"—a requirement for citizenship at the time. One of their key arguments was that the Middle East, the Levant region in particular, was the cradle of Christianity and for that reason was linked inextricably to Europe (Gualtieri 2009, 56–57). After a number of contradictory lower court decisions, a federal judge determined in *Dow v. United States* (1915) that Syrians, as Arab immigrants were then called, "were so related to their neighbors on the European side of the Mediterranean that they should be classed as white" according to the original intent of the 1790 statute governing immigration (74). In the wider society, especially in the South, however, they could sometimes be viewed racially as black, as the lynching of Nola Romey in Lake City, Florida, in 1929 symbolically attested (Gualtieri 2009, 114–34). Thus, even if they had won the legal right to citizenship, Arab immigrants, including Palestinians in Chicago, remained situated in a culturally ambiguous zone in which their social status could shift, at times violently.

The life of early-wave Palestinian immigrants revolved principally around the norms of work. The men kept long hours, remaining behind their counters for twelve hours a day and longer on Saturdays (Oschinsky 1947, 26). Many cooked and slept in the rear areas of their stores. After closing their shops, they played cards and backgammon late into the night at Arab-owned coffee houses and restaurants such as Mecca, Arabian Nights, and Scheherazade, which were situated along Michigan Avenue between 22nd and 45th Streets (Oschinsky 1947, 26; al-Tahir 1952, 78, 95). On Saturday nights, they went to the movies; some went to bars to drink despite the Islamic prohibition on alcohol (Oschinsky 1947, 26). Once a month, they met on Sunday to discuss the intensifying conflict between Palestinians and the Zionist movement (Oschinsky 1947, 26; al-Tahir 1952, 78 and elsewhere on Palestinian nationalist sentiment). Oschinsky noted that shopkeepers earned between $5,000 and $15,000 per year, an amount that seemed extraordinary to the men and that perhaps enabled a few of them to afford cars (26). The temptations to spend hard-earned income and ignore morality concerned some members of the community. Oschinsky described "an old pious member" of the group, who complained that his fellow merchants had lost sight of religion (29). They didn't pray, he said, and they had forgotten the *shahada* (the statement of God's unity and Muhammad's messenger status), drank alcohol, and ate pork. They also, he claimed, had affairs with their customers or with Jewish and Christian women.

Generally, however, the men Oschinsky interacted with travelled to their villages to get married and then returned to Chicago alone to continue earning money. They remained in Chicago for five to ten years or longer and then went back to their families in Palestine before again leaving for the United States. Other men traveled between Chicago and their villages every six months. A few, however, brought their wives and children with them to Chicago. A handful had "taken common law American wives of Polish, Mexican, Irish, Italian, and Jewish origin [. . .]. One was married to a Syrian Christian" (Oschinsky 1947, 27).[11] Most, though, were young and single and anticipated returning to Palestine. Relatives expected them to return with their wealth. Failure to do so was dishonorable. Repatriation, economic and personal, was a deeply felt obligation that stemmed assimilation.

This felt obligation was also, for some men, a religious one. As one individual put it, "It is very hard to be a good man in this bad land," where one could never be sure if one's eggs had been fried "in the grease of the *khanzir* (swine)" (bacon fat) and closing shop during Ramadan was potentially fatal to one's business success (Oschinsky 1947, 34). But return also brought ambivalence. One man described how after he had traveled home to get married other villagers accused him of being "stuck up," an "American," and a "city man." Another man reported that while he missed the clean air, fresh produce, and food of his village, life in Chicago provided freedom from family pressures and the chance to succeed if one worked hard (29–30). Such attractions, inevitably tinged with feelings of uncertainty, continued to draw Palestinians to the city. As the 1940s came to a close, however, political upheaval "back home" would add a further impetus for migration.

MIGRATION, 1948–1967: TRANSFORMATIONS OF THE EXILIC SPACE

The war of 1948 forced approximately 750,000 Palestinians into statelessness. The duration and extent of the violence transformed the migration calculus and bimodal migration pattern of the West Bank men who had established businesses in Chicago. The men and their families felt increasingly unsure that "home" would remain stable. Between 1936 and 1938 fewer than one hundred Palestinians arrived in Chicago (Zaghel 1976, 12); by contrast, between 1948 and 1967, the immigration rate to the United States averaged 660 individuals per year (Cainkar 1988, 74–77 and 81). Wives, children, and extended family members of already-established migrants constituted the majority of the new arrivals (Cainkar 1988, 81–86). Possessing Jordanian passports—Jordan had annexed the West Bank and East Jerusalem after the war of 1948—many of these individuals, using family networks, came to Chicago. By 1950, more than five hundred Palestinians had established residency in the city (Zaghel 1976, 12).

In an extended interview, Imm 'Umar (pseudonym), a sixty-five-year-old resident of southwest suburban Bridgeview, recounted how these changes affected her parents.[12] Versions of this story recurred frequently in interviews with those whose families had been in Chicago the longest. She described how her father had arrived in Chicago in 1939 immediately after the end of the 1936–39 Arab revolt. His uncle, who had already established himself in the city, helped him begin work as a peddler. He did not speak English and had never lived in a major metropolitan center "but he survived!" He returned to his village (Beitunia) to marry Imm 'Umar's mother in 1947. Her mother remained behind to give birth to her first child and then immigrated to Chicago through Beirut immediately following the end of the 1948 war.

Imm 'Umar's description of the experience of her parents emphasized the crucial importance of the pre-existing family networks—the "migration chain"—that had institutionalized migration as a strategy for economic advancement and wartime survival. These networks facilitated the arrival of Imm 'Umar's father and his subsequent initiation into the practices of peddling and Palestinian settlement. His decision to bring his wife and baby introduced a variation of these practices. Palestinians now began to maintain families in the city and thereby significantly alter the bimodal migration pattern. Palestinian residential locations also shifted. After 1948, immigrants began to settle further to the south and west of the city. Gradually, an enclave began to form in the Chicago Lawn, Marquette Park, and Gage Park areas. This location buffered the African American West Englewood neighborhood from the predominantly white West Lawn one (Figure 5).

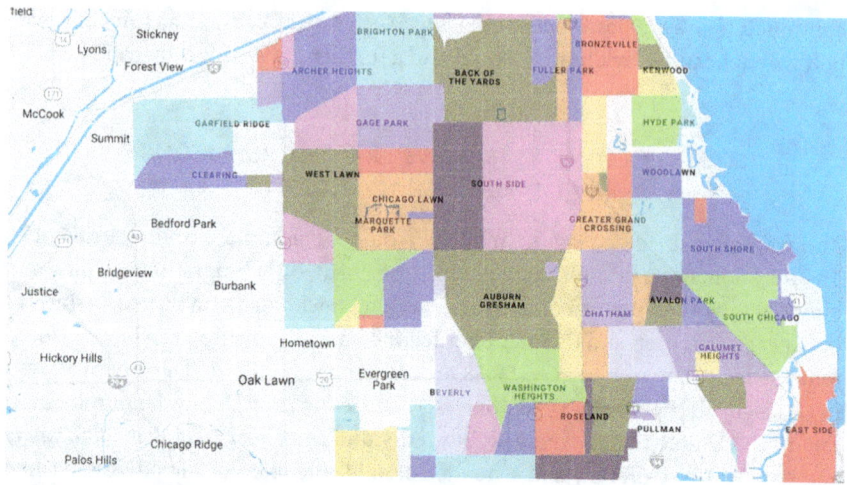

FIGURE 5. Chicago Community Areas Map. Courtesy of Peter Fitzgerald.

In situating themselves in this manner, Palestinians reprised their role as an interstitial "stranger" group. Individuals like Imm 'Umar's father still peddled, but families opened small stores on main thoroughfares such as West 63rd Street as they accumulated capital. These stores catered mostly to the growing Palestinian enclave but also to African Americans and Latinx communities that were becoming the majority of residents in the same area.[13]

Most of the Palestinian immigrants in the post-1948 period were Muslims. The preponderance came from one village—Beitunia—in the Ramallah area. A small group of Christians from the town of Ramallah, however, also migrated to Chicago. By 1946, just two years before the war of 1948, some 1,500 Ramallah Christians, roughly one-fifth of the town's Christian population, had immigrated to the United States (Zaghel 1976, 39–40). Of this total, forty individuals had migrated to Chicago (39). Within two decades this number would increase to 350 (44). Like the Beitunians, the Ramallahites peddled and then opened small grocery and linen stores. Some also worked in factories (39–52). Still, despite their shared class positions and common work practices, the Muslims and Christians lived in separate neighborhoods and congregated in separate institutional spaces (al-Tahir 1952, 67–68, 71, 93–98). In doing so, they replicated West Bank residence patterns in which they lived side-by-side, separately and symbiotically, in the same village or town (Neuhaus 1991; Tsimhoni 1993; Bowman 1993, 2001; Lybarger 2007b; Kårtveit 2014; Calder 2017).

As in the West Bank, the two segments of the community reinforced sectarian-communal separation through endogamy. Christians married Christians and Muslim married Muslims. Within these patterns, moreover, families sought to constrain marriage within kinship groupings organized along patrilocal lines and within place-specific affiliations. If one was from Ramallah, for example, one sought to marry a Ramallahite (Christian) from a particular family. Town/village-based associations or clubs strengthened the sectarian, familial, and locale-oriented solidarities that endogamy generated and relied on. The clubs not only provided spaces for leisure but also reconstituted communal ties; instilled these ties among youth, many of whom had never been to the home communities; introduced children to marriage partners; and maintained financial remittance channels to "back home."

One such club was the Children of Beitunia Club, organized in 1924. Its founding reflected an early desire to retain a placed-based affiliation and identity, resist assimilation, and facilitate the pooling of immigrant resources to support the village as a whole. The club renamed itself the "Arab Club" in the aftermath of the war of 1948. The renaming reflected a growing nationalist, pan-Arab sensibility. Club members soon formed three related organizations: the Arab Progress Club, Arab-American Aid Society, and Arab-American Women's Club, none of which now exists. The goals of these various organizations included teaching children Arabic and "Islamic values"; passing on "heritage" to youth; organizing support for the Palestinian cause; providing aid for refugees forced off their lands during the war of 1948; and funding projects in Beitunia (al-Tahir 1952, 105, 107–8). The financial assistance to the village was often substantial. During the early 1950s, the Arab Club sent $20,000 to Beitunia to build an elementary school (105).

US-based Ramallahites established their own locale-focused organization, the Ramallah Club. The Chicago chapter was organized in 1957. Like its Beitunian counterpart, the Ramallah Club promoted opportunities to socialize, meet marriage partners, and contribute financially to projects in Ramallah itself. A primary goal of the club was to resist assimilation. A club leader stated, for example, that "the objectives of the organization are: (1) to help each other here, (2) not to melt in [sic] the American society, but to preserve our heritage and (3) to help Ramallah people back home" (Zaghel 1976, 49). Toward those ends, the club held annual Christmas parties and summer picnics, at which members participated in *dabka* dancing together and introduced young people to one another (49–52). The performance of *dabka* signified the nationalist orientation of the Ramallah club. *Dabka*, along with the checkered *hatta* scarf and embroidered *thawb* (pl. *thiyab*) dress, became a marker of "heritage" (*turath*) and national patrimony. They were and have remained central to the symbolic repertoire of the Arab nationalist and Palestinian liberation movements that first emerged during the 1950s and 1960s.

The creation of the village and town clubs signaled the primacy of place, clan (*hamula*), social class (village peasants/*fallahi* versus town-dwellers/*madani*), and religious communalism (Christian or Muslim) in the identities of the early immigrants.[14] The clubs reconstructed and reinforced these axes of affiliation in the diaspora. By contrast, formal religious organizations were relatively absent in both segments of the community. According to several participants in my research, Christians relied on itinerant priests based in Michigan City, Indiana, and Spring Valley, Illinois, to perform life-passage rites such as baptisms, marriages, and funerals. Some families, Melkite Catholic and Antiochian Orthodox, attended liturgies at the combined Melkite and Maronite Church of St. John the Baptist on South Washtenaw Street. Members subsequently transplanted this church to the northwest suburb of Northlake, Illinois.

Antiochian Orthodox Christians, who constituted the majority of Palestinian Christians, began to coalesce as an identifiable group by the late 1950s. Several families met on Sundays in the Syrian-Lebanese Club in the Austin neighborhood on Chicago's West Side. Orthodox priests travelled from Buffalo, New York, to serve the community. Imm George (pseudonym), an octogenarian, recounted how eventually, as the community grew, the Orthodox bishop in Pennsylvania appointed a full-time priest to lead the group. They also leased a former Episcopalian church in the Chicago suburb of Oak Park before ultimately moving into their current permanent premises in the town of Cicero. Imm George recounted further how the church community provided a space for newly arrived immigrants like her. Soon after arriving in Chicago, her husband took her to the church, where parishioners welcomed her with flowers and food. "It was amazing!" she said.

As Imm George indicated, the early phases of Antiochian Orthodox institutionalization occurred informally and entailed interaction with a wider Arab Christian community as well as with the national Orthodox Church. Increasingly, as Palestinian Christian immigration grew during the 1960s, and especially after 1967, religious institutionalization became formalized with the purchase of a worship space in Oak Park and the hiring of a full-time priest.[15] That church and the subsequent one in Cicero—the St. George Antiochian Orthodox Church—became focal points of community life, providing, as well, important mechanisms of integration for new immigrants such as Imm George. The community was predominantly Palestinian but retained a pan-Orthodox character, attracting other Arab Christians as well as Orthodox practitioners from a variety of Southern and Eastern European backgrounds.[16]

A similar process of institutionalization also eventually occurred among Palestinian Muslims. In the earlier period, during the 1940s, however, religious practice remained individualized and ad hoc. Oschinsky (1947) observed that although some of the men with whom he interacted observed basic piety—the five prayers, abstention from pork and alcohol, fasting during Ramadan, and so on—many did not. Oschinsky noted that during Ramadan, for example, which fell during August 1946, the year he did his fieldwork, most of his interlocutors kept their shops open and ate at non-Arab restaurants, avoiding the coffee shops whose pious owners would not serve any food: "Not more than ten men kept the fast" (33–34). The necessity to sustain their businesses appeared to supersede the required ritual duties.

Less than a decade later, al-Tahir (1952) confirmed Oschinsky's observation concerning the lack of religious institutionalization and the low assiduousness of individual practice. He observed that the older generation had failed to maintain the *fard* (mandatory) rituals and had not instilled piety in their children (58, 151–52). The absence of mosques compounded the phenomenon. Nevertheless, although religious institutionalization remained weak, most Muslim immigrants still professed loyalty to Islam (173, and 207). One of the participants in my research recalled that during the 1950s Muslim Palestinians rented out banquet halls or YMCA rooms to celebrate the annual feasts marking the Muslim religious calendar. Eventually, a group began to collect money to build a small mosque (al-Tahir 1952, 207). Similar efforts would occur later, ultimately resulting, in the late 1970s and early 1980s, in the construction of the Mosque Foundation, the dominant organization within the suburban Palestinian enclave today. Prior to this occurrence, however, Islam did not constitute the primary framework of group solidarity. Rather, in the immediate wake of the war of 1967, nationalism began to galvanize identity within and across the Muslim and Christian segments of the community. Religious institutionalization did proceed, but during the first two and a half decades after the war, community life revolved around the cultural centers, locale-based clubs, and charitable foundations where a multisectarian secular nationalism took root.

THE NEW IMMIGRANTS AND "RE-PALESTINIANIZATION": 1967–1980s

The war of 1967 marked a significant shift in the size, composition, ethos, and cohesion of the Palestinian immigrant community in Chicago. The war occurred two years after the Immigration and Nationality Act of 1965 abolished the nation-of-origin quotas in effect since 1921. The new law determined immigration eligibility according to preferred skills or relationship to US citizens or residents. Arabs, along with groups that had been excluded from citizenship as non-Europeans, now had expanded access to US immigration. The liberalization of the laws, and the increasing trend of seeking permanent residence rather than pursuing the bimodal migration pattern, however, did not shift the ambivalent, interstitial nature of Palestinian life in Chicago. Anti-Arab racism and government actions targeting community activists were the main reasons for the continuing ambivalence. With each successive Middle East crisis, Arabs, and especially Palestinians, found themselves positioned as a distinct, threatening presence within US society.

Zaghel (1976) documented this phenomenon, noting the sharp backlash against Arabs in local Chicago and national media in the immediate aftermath of the wars of 1967 and 1973 (187 and elsewhere in chapters 5 and 6). Cainkar (1988), too, emphasized that law enforcement interventions and anti-Arab racism heightened Palestinian feelings of estrangement from the wider culture. She cited the case of the LA Eight (132–33). In 1987, the FBI arrested eight individuals in Los Angeles that it accused of having ties with the Popular Front for the Liberation of Palestine. The subsequent twenty-year effort to convict the men failed (Goodman 2007). The revelation, during this imbroglio, of the Immigration and Naturalization Services memorandum *Alien Terrorists and Undesirables: A Contingency Plan, 1986*, confirmed the perception of many immigrants that US society was hostile to them (Cainkar 1988, 131–32; Wofford 2016). The plan proposed placing legal resident aliens from eight Arab countries in concentration camps.[17] Additionally, in the mid-1980s Congress passed a bill to close the PLO's United Nations Observer Mission in New York. Intensified law enforcement intrusion and media stereotyping targeting Arabs and Muslims occurred, as well, in the aftermath of the bombing of the Alfred P. Murrah Federal Building in Oklahoma City in 1995 and also following the attacks of September 11, 2001. The cumulative effects of these measures and negative media coverage, beginning in 1967, produced a cross-generational feeling of alienation among Palestinian immigrants. This alienation transformed the sojourner and stranger ethos that had defined community identity from its earliest moments into a collective sense of exile (Cainkar 1988, 96; Jamal and Naber 2008).

A renewed identification with Arabness reinforced this shift. Al-Tahir (1952, 105–8) observed that attachment to pan-Arab identity had formed among the early Arab immigrants during and after the First World War. During the 1930s and 1940s, Palestinians expressed strong sympathy for the struggle against Zionism and for the plight of refugees. The war of 1967 renewed this nationalist solidarity. The arrival of new immigrants from Palestine and the formation of nationalist community organizations institutionalized it (Oschinsky 1947, 31–32, 36–43; Zaghel 1976, chapters 5 and 6; Cainkar 1988, 110).

As in 1948, the war of 1967 resulted in a mass forced exodus of Palestinians, this time approximately 250,000, from areas newly occupied by the Israeli military.[18] These areas included the West Bank, which previously had been under Jordanian control. Prior to 1967, emigration from the West Bank amounted to approximately 3 percent of the population and entailed mostly movement from the West to the East Bank of Jordan. After the war, the migration rate jumped to 20 percent of the West Bank populace: skilled labor went mostly to the Arabian Gulf states and less skilled workers headed to various South American destinations and to the United States. More than 50 percent of the emigrants were women and children (Serhan 2009, 83).

Two forces impelled the new migration: the onerous conditions of Israeli military rule and the Israeli expropriation of Palestinian land to create Jewish-only settlements (Cainkar 1988, 92 and elsewhere; Cainkar 1998).[19] Those with financial assets and transferable professional credentials were the most likely to leave. Preexisting family networks or "chains" also proved crucial. Prior to coming to the United States, "chain immigrants" had benefited from the financial remittances of their relatives. These remittances allowed their beneficiaries in Palestine to build new homes in areas that became known locally as "the American quarter." An important consequence of this phenomenon was an orientation toward the United States and the possibilities it presented for alternative life chances (Lutfiyya 1966, cited in Cainkar 1988, 111–12). Upon arriving in a city like Chicago, chain immigrants could rely on the continued support of their extended families.

Alongside chain immigrants, however, a substantial population of "new peasant immigrants" settled within interstitial zones like Marquette Park on the city's Southwest Side. In doing so, they resumed the mediating minority role, buffering predominantly African American and white ethnic neighborhoods. These new immigrants also revived the older vocational patterns. They worked, for example, as peddlers, and then opened corner stores, gas station franchises, and other similar establishments (Cainkar 1988, 105). Others worked in the factories. A smaller third group, "autonomous immigrants" comprising mostly single men, studied in universities or vocational schools or worked in companies (Cainkar 1988, 110 and elsewhere; Cainkar 1998). Some of these individuals, including a participant in my research, started financial services enterprises, such as insurance and accounting offices (chapter 2).

The new peasants, mostly concentrated on the Southwest Side, came to outnumber the chain immigrants who had preceded them. Their new demographic dominance transformed the ethos of the immigrant community as a whole. Chain immigrants had held to the patriarchal code that constituted the rural social contract. But they considerably loosened their adherence to it as they moved to the suburbs—a process that began for this established group as early as the 1970s—and generally accommodated the mores of the wider US society, for example, by allowing women freedom to leave their homes to work and attend school. Autonomous immigrants vacillated in their adherence, with some upholding patriarchal village norms and others abandoning them entirely for the middle-class individualism of their workplaces. Possessing less access to economic resources and cultural prestige, the "new peasants" mobilized tradition and nationalism as markers of authenticity in the community. Against the chain immigrants, especially, they claimed to represent "true" Palestinian identity. Having arrived involuntarily in the United States, they insisted, like immigrants of earlier periods, that ultimately they would return home to the West Bank. In the interim, as an expression of this commitment to return and the nationalism it encoded, they sought to preserve the 'adat wa taqalid ("the customs and traditions") within their families and in the community at large. In this reinvigoration of tradition, they effectively "re-Palestinianized" the immigrant community (Cainkar 1988, 110–11 and 128).

This process of re-Palestinianization was gendered, occurring in and through the home. The women—wives, mothers, and daughters—of the new peasant immigrant group performed this labor. They did so, for example, by decorating their homes with artifacts (rugs, embroidered pillows, images of Jerusalem's Old City and the Dome of the Rock, Qur'anic inscriptions); preparing traditional cuisine; deferring to elders and to men; and guarding their *sharaf*, a woman's sexual honor, the markers of which were modesty and virginity. Modesty at this time did not entail wearing hijab scarves or *jilbab* coats, practices that would accompany the Islamic shift in the 1990s. Rather, women signaled it by caring for the home and avoiding being seen in the company of men unrelated to their families. Safeguarding *sharaf* in this way signaled commitment to the patriarchal and patrilocal ethos of village life and thereby to an "authentic" Palestinian identity. Community networks reinforced these norms, primarily through gossip. Occasionally, direct coercion came to bear when husbands ordered wives back to their villages or when, in rare instances, male members of a family resorted to physical violence (Cainkar 1988, 119–29, 147–48).

Men, by contrast, had license "to escape" into the wider US society to work, seek leisure in nightclubs, and pursue extramarital relationships (Cainkar 1988, 118, 122–24). This patriarchal double standard took a more stringent form in Chicago than it did in home villages, where women typically had more latitude to move independently beyond their homes (124).[20] Cainkar (1988) attributed this phenomenon—the gendered double standard and the concomitant insistence on maintaining "tradition"—to a number of factors, including "statelessness, involuntary exile and strong attachment to the homeland, the hostility Palestinians face in the US, and above all, an ideology of exile that calls for cultural preservation" (126). Racism, especially, heightened defensiveness, rejection of the wider culture, and greater self-segregation within the home and enclave (129–33).[21]

Another likely explanation for re-traditionalization, however, one that Cainkar did not explore, was the sense of guilt that accompanied the immigrants' relationship to "back home." The relationship carried ambivalence. Those who left felt pressure to succeed and also to maintain fidelity to the culture and its values. When they returned to their communities, however, they might encounter accusations of having abandoned the ways and customs of "back home," of having "gone native," of having become "American." The desire, then, to be seen as retaining fidelity to the culture might have served as an impetus to maintain the home as a space of authenticity, that is, of tradition and patriarchal norms.

This concern to preserve authenticity registered in the observations of a participant in the research for this book, a man I had known for more than two decades, who came to Chicago in the early 1990s. He had been a political activist and member of the Palestinian Communist Party in the West Bank during the First Intifada. In our interview, he commented that the immigrant community seemed frozen in time, a relic of an era predating the 1960s. Life had moved on "back home," he said. The Chicago diaspora, however, in its concern to preserve the past, had resisted change. My friend's assessment was not entirely accurate. The diaspora had in fact transformed Palestinian identity in very specific ways. Indeed, the very attempt to retain the past—or a traditionalized reconstruction of it—constituted one such transformation. This preservation effort was necessary so long as "return" to the confiscated homeland remained the defining collective aspiration.

THE ASCENDANCY OF SECULAR NATIONALISM: 1967–1990

The retraditionalization—"re-Palestinianization," in Cainkar's terms—that the "new peasant immigrants" spurred coincided with the rising prominence of nationalism in the immigrant community as a whole. This nationalism, which became pervasive through the creation of community organizations that aligned ideologically with Arab Nationalism and the Palestine Liberation Organization, emphasized "return" (*al-'awda*) to Palestine and, symbolically, to its peasant past, from which the nation derived its territorial claim.[22] Figured primarily in terms of *turath* (heritage), the elements of this past—the checkered *hatta* scarf of Palestinian farmers, the embroidered dresses (*thiyab*) of village women, and village line dances (*dabka*) (Figure 6)—became symbols in a nationalist iconography displayed in Palestinian community spaces, gatherings, and public protests.

This symbolic array and its accompanying narrative of preservation reinforced patriarchal gender norms. In nationalist iconography, the land of Palestine frequently appeared as a woman whom the primarily male guerrilla fighters (*fida'iyun*, "fedayeen") and martyrs (*shuhada'*), situated in the exile, sought to liberate and revive by seeding her with their blood (Amireh 2003). Those communities that remained within Palestine also had a role, a feminized one, which entailed persisting physically and culturally in the land. The term *sumud* (steadfastness) entered the nationalist lexicon to describe this task for those who lived under Israel's military occupation. In tension with these terms, however, was the Marxist-inspired lexicon of revolution. "Tradition," in this perspective, was a regressive force impeding

FIGURE 6. Palestinian *dabka*. Courtesy of Sarah Canbel.

the liberation project. The "revolution," by contrast, emphasized the necessity to modernize women through education and mobilization in the struggle. The secular factions—for example, Fatah, the Popular Front for the Liberation of Palestine, the Democratic Front for the Liberation of Palestine, and the Communist Party—embraced this idea. They actively recruited women and provided avenues for their participation that served, albeit incompletely, to break the hold of traditional gender roles (Y. Sayigh 1997).

These currents—patriotic retraditionalization and revolutionary liberation—cut crosswise in the Chicago community. For example, in the Southwest Side enclave, women remained bound to the home as site of their social honor and socially prescribed role, yet, they also encountered alternative avenues of validated activity within the new, nationalist community organizations. Groups such as the Union of Palestinian Women Associations (UPWA) mobilized immigrant women on the national question and also against patriarchal norms. Based at the Arab Community Center (the *markaz*) on West 63rd Street, the UPWA accomplished these tasks through outreach to women in their homes as well as through conferences and workshops. The organization also forged public political roles for these women by bussing them to rallies and protests in the Loop (Cainkar 1988, 207–8).[23]

Post-1967 secular nationalism unified Palestinian identity across multiple sites of exile. It also linked Palestinians to the nonaligned Third World solidarity movement. Third Worldism connected US minorities to global anti-colonial independence struggles (Fischbach 2019; Pennock 2017; Feldman 2015). Locally, in Chicago, this form of activism manifested in alliances between immigrant rights and national liberation groups. The leaders of the Palestinian community organizations participated in these alliances, emphasizing the shared struggle for decolonization of the homeland and civil rights in the diaspora.

A particularly important event that cemented these links and mobilized them as a force in city politics was the 1983 campaign to elect Harold Washington, the first African American mayor of Chicago. Secular-left Palestinian leaders contributed financially to the campaign, which unified diverse minority constituencies, and staffed efforts to mobilize the vote in the immigrant community. A particularly important effect of this participation was the reorientation of the concerns of these leaders toward American domestic politics. These leaders had perceived voting as pointless, since the US government would never, in their view, change its policies toward Israel. Yet these same individuals increasingly saw the need to enter into cross-ethnic coalitions to gain support for the Palestinian cause locally and to gain access to city resources to support their community. The Washington campaign promised to divert funds away from the wealthy Loop and Near North areas to the working-class and poor neighborhoods to the west and south.

The Palestinians involved with the Washington coalition had arisen as community leaders within two main organizational contexts: Arab nationalist student groups and secular nationalist community organizations. The most prominent student formations included the Arab Students Association (ASA) and the General Union of Palestinian Students (GUPS). The ASA, which formed as an inter-Arab response to the war of 1967, held seminars, distributed fliers, and hosted a film festival. It eventually split apart into rival factions and gave way, during the 1970s, to the GUPS. GUPS linked students in the diaspora to the Palestinian national struggle. It became the center of Palestinian student activism until the PLO's abeyance following the creation of the Palestinian National Authority in the mid-1990s. Beyond the campuses, nationalist community organizations provided the principal mobilizing structures. These organizations aligned ideologically with the various PLO factions. The organizations coordinated with the university student groups. Students helped staff organization-led events. The organizations, for their part, offered post-graduation opportunities for students who wanted to continue their activism.[24]

SUBURBAN TRANSITION AND THE RELIGIOUS TURN: 1980-PRESENT

Beginning in the mid-1980s the demographic and institutional center of Chicago's Palestinian community shifted yet again to the near southwestern suburbs, especially Bridgeview but also Oak Lawn, Tinley Park, Orland Park, and Palos Hills. Wealth accumulation, professionalization, and fears associated with gun and gang violence drove the transition.[25] Some of my respondents expressed guilt about abandoning the urban enclave. They viewed Palestinian suburbanization, critically, as merely a replication of the migration of ethnic whites a generation earlier.

White suburbanization in Chicago intensified after the Second World War. Fueled partly by the GI bill, which sent thousands of returning veterans to universities, the postwar economic boom expanded the professional middle class, enabling more families to buy new homes beyond the urban core. The amplification of the racial border wars escalated this suburbanization process, which came to be known as "white flight." Of the 485 reported incidents of racial violence between 1945 and 1950, three-quarters pertained to "housing or property" (Abu-Lughod 1999, 222). More than 85 percent of the violence occurred on the edges of the Black Belt in response to attempts by African Americans to move into predominantly white urban neighborhoods (222). After 1948, when the United States Supreme Court ruled in *Shelley v. Kraemer* that restrictive covenants lacked legal enforceability, whites skittish about racial integration moved in large numbers to all-white suburbs. Seeking to profit from these conditions, real estate agents stoked panic sales and then resold the properties at inflated rates to black homebuyers. Whites lacking financial means to leave resorted to violent harassment of their new black neighbors in an effort to preserve racial exclusivity. Local and state government assisted the effort: despite the *Shelley* ruling, government agencies continued to enforce preexisting exclusionary covenants. The Federal Housing Authority, too, perpetuated "redlining" policies by insuring housing developments that had maintained racial exclusions (Hirsch 1983, 10–12; Abu-Lughod 1999, 222–23; Self 2003; Kruse 2005; Satter 2009; Rothstein 2017).

Exacerbating racial tensions, the federal Urban Redevelopment Act of 1949 mandated slum clearance and lot resale to private developers who had agreed to build homes for moderate-income people. In Chicago, most of the "slum" areas were in the Black Belt. The law required that residents who would lose their homes because of clearance be given new space in public housing. Siting these public works, however, led to new border wars, since the only available lots for such projects were toward the urban periphery near white areas. White outmigration intensified: between 1950 and 1970, the percentage of white non-Hispanics in Chicago's municipal boundaries plunged from approximately 86 percent to 65 percent (1999, 230–31, 331–32).[26] As whites left, the border wars subsided. Residents in the historic Bronzeville area (within the Black Belt) moved into the vacated neighborhoods to the south and west. The West Side, however, continued to experience tensions as poor blacks and Puerto Ricans found themselves enclosed between the expanding Loop area—large tracts had been seized for the new University of Illinois campus in what is now the West Loop—and the majority white township of Cicero. The city-suburb divide had become a simultaneous class and racial bifurcation (Abu-Lughod 1999, 221–23, 230–233; Squires, et. al., 1987, 102–17).

Chicago's intensified socioeconomic and racial segregation hardened as the decades passed. By 1990, "less than 38 percent of the city's residents reported themselves 'white non-Hispanic,' and this category included many of the most recent immigrants from the Middle East, the Indian subcontinent, and less-developed parts of Europe" (Abu-Lughod 1999, 331). In 1950, Chicago's "nonwhite" population stood at 14 percent. Ten years later, it had increased to one-quarter and within sixteen years it reached one-third of the city's population (230–31). By 1990, African Americans, specifically, who now accounted for 39 percent of the city's overall demographic concentration, outnumbered non-Hispanic whites (38 percent of the population). Hispanics—Puerto Ricans and Mexicans—contributed nearly 20 percent by that same year (334). The few suburbs housing non-white residents—including, increasingly, Arabs and Muslims[27]—were situated almost completely within Cook County, leaving the outer suburbs nearly entirely white (332). Those whites remaining in the city concentrated primarily along the lake north of the Loop and in zones abutting white suburbs at the city limits in the northwestern and southwestern sectors. African Americans tended to remain within an expanded "Black Belt" in the city's South Side; they also occupied the "second ghetto" on the West Side. Latinx (but also Palestinians) "occup[ied] 'buffer zones' [. . .] between these black and white sectors" (332).[28] By 2010, blacks and Hispanics/Latinx—32.9 percent and 28.9 percent, respectively—combined to outstrip non-Hispanic whites, now just 31.8 percent of the city's total population of 2.7 million (Mullen and Ortiz-Healy 2011).[29]

The sharp decline in heavy industry in the postwar period exacerbated the city-suburb divide. Unlike the "gunbelt"—the eastern, southern, and Southern California regions of the United States that hosted Cold War defense industries—Chicago and the Midwest, generally, never fully recovered from the Great Depression. Government demand for steel during the Second World War partly revitalized Chicago's manufacturing base, but structural adjustments—reallocation of federal investment to high-tech defense industries and relocation of steel and car production to southern states and abroad (for example, to Japan)—decimated working class livelihoods. Between 1967 and 1982, Chicago lost 250,000 (46 percent) of its manufacturing jobs (Abu-Lughod 1999, 323). The industries that remained in, or came to, the region located their plants and headquarters increasingly in the suburbs. Sharp losses also hit service-sector employment. Between 1991 and 1992, 31,000 service jobs disappeared in the city. The suburbs, meanwhile, added 19,000 service jobs during this same period (326). Still, Chicago retained its position as a node in the automated international finance network, principally through the Chicago Mercantile Exchange, known as "the Merc," which created a global marketplace for the buying and selling of commodity futures and options (derivatives). The expansion of the financial sector that the Merc fueled mostly benefited a small group of brokers downtown and in capitals abroad. Other than in the central business district, the Loop, it produced few jobs.

Taken together, these processes sharpened economic disparities. The predominantly white foreground—comprising the Loop and the Near North Side neighborhoods—gained in wealth as the non-white background to the west and south of the Loop became increasingly impoverished. Similar disparity marked the suburban-urban dichotomy. According to the 1980 census, the greater Chicago metropolitan area hosted twelve of the wealthiest communities in the nation but also ten of the sixteen poorest (Squires, et. al., 1987, 24, cited in Abu-Lughod 1999, 329). Unsurprisingly, according to a 1991 Urban League report, wealth gaps between Chicago's whites and blacks had increased far more rapidly than in other parts of the United States (Abu-Lughod 1999, 330).

The hollowing out of the urban neighborhoods that began with "white flight" continued in the near suburbs. Poverty increased accordingly in these urban areas, which had become centers of immigrant concentration, including for Palestinians, from the 1980s onward (Moser 2013). The factors driving "white flight" also propelled the Palestinian suburban shift. Imm 'Umar, mentioned earlier, explicitly identified racial factors in her account of her own family's residential shifts during the 1960s and 1970s. She and her family moved multiple times whenever "the neighborhood would change." She described the segregation between African Americans and whites and how "when blacks would move in, then everyone would move out." Her own move into the suburbs, which occurred after her marriage, followed the trajectory of white communities into these same spaces beyond the urban core.

The movement of Palestinians to the near southwest suburbs pointed toward a broader phenomenon. As Latinx, South Asians, and Arabs, primarily, abandoned older immigrant centers within the urban core, they effectively "browned" the adjacent suburbs to which they moved. The "browning" concept challenges standard assimilation theory. Logan and Zhang (2010), for example, argue that rather than assimilation, what has occurred in the suburban transition of ethnic minorities is the "globalization of the suburbs"—that is, the diversification that occurs as minority groups move into previously all-white communities. Lubin (2008), in his exploration of the movement of Latinx into Berwyn, a historically white suburb, argues similarly that Latinx are not so much assimilating as they are "Latinizing" the suburbs. They are "browning" Berwyn, effectively altering its cultural characteristics and institutional forms.

BROWNING BRIDGEVIEW: PALESTINIAN SUBURBANIZATION AND THE NEW ISLAMIC MILIEU

What the "browning" studies describe holds true as well for the nearby southwestern suburbs, such as Bridgeview, into which Palestinians have moved since the 1990s. Rather than assimilating, Palestinians have reconstituted their enclaves in these spaces, but in doing so they have also significantly reoriented the community ethos through the Islamic turn discussed in the introduction. This shift is relatively new, and its reasons for manifesting are complex.

One important factor in the reorientation has been the creation of the Mosque Foundation.[30] This organization and the nearby businesses that cater to local consumer preferences have "Arabized" and "Islamized"—indeed globalized—the near southwest suburban expanse. Significantly, the enclave that has emerged continues to perform the mediating "stranger" role, effectively buffering white communities to the west from the now predominantly African American South Side urban space. As noted earlier, in moments of conflict in which Middle Easterners have figured as "enemies," the persisting "mediator" status has given way to a perception of a malevolent "other."[31] Following the September 11 attacks, for example, white ethnics marched on the mosque in Bridgeview, unwittingly replicating previous "border war" tactics (Millar 2001; Terry and Ahmed-Ullah 2001).

The building of the Bridgeview mosque represented a significant advance in religious institutionalization. The mosques that existed prior to the construction of this new edifice were small urban storefronts that limited their services to providing a place for prayer and basic religious instruction. The shift to the suburbs marked a change in this ad-hoc institutional situation: desiring a stable meeting space, the first Palestinian migrants to the suburbs in the 1950s incorporated the Mosque Foundation and its annex organization, the American Arabian Ladies Society (AALS).

Imm 'Umar, mentioned previously, discussed the background of these developments. Her cousin was a founding member of the AALS and another distant cousin served as the mosque's first imam. The main impetus for the project, according to Imm 'Umar, was the war of 1967. Islam, she said, had not been central "to our identities" at the wider community level up until this point. In the family, her parents did instill an awareness that they were Arabs and Palestinians and Muslims. Her father recited from the Qur'an when the family gathered for occasions in the home. After the war, however, the arrival of the new immigrants catalyzed a shift in collective awareness. These individuals "were activists" who began raising consciousness about the plight of Palestinians now living under direct Israeli military rule. The older, established immigrants also began to see that "we had no country to return to" and consequently there was a need to create institutions to sustain community life intergenerationally. Imm 'Umar described efforts to start language, history, and religion classes for youth. These activities occurred alongside the formal establishment of the Mosque Foundation as a community organization in "a storefront on 79th Street, on the East Side." Along with the cultural programs, the new center hosted "welcome back [from Palestine] parties, engagements, and marriage parties." Eventually, enough money was collected to buy the plot of land that became the permanent site of the current Mosque Foundation in Bridgeview.

These developments represented a significant institutionalizing step. Prior to the creation of the Mosque Foundation, families relied on "Shaykh 'Aroubi from Dearborn [Michigan] to perform burials and marriages." After the creation of the Mosque Foundation, the organization's leaders sought to appoint their own permanent imam. Imm 'Umar's cousin, a well-respected elder, volunteered for the position and was given certification through the Jordanian embassy in Washington, DC, and by the State of Illinois. He began officiating at marriages, divorces, and funerals. He also led the community's slow effort to raise money for a new structure on the land that had been purchased in Bridgeview. He remained in the position until the early 1980s. "[My cousin] wasn't degree smart; but he was very knowledgeable and was respected in the community for his honesty," Imm 'Umar recalled.

The choice of Imm 'Umar's relative to be the first imam reflected a crucial assimilating transition among the older immigrants in response to the impact of the war of 1967. This shift entailed a transformation of traditional leadership roles. Leadership in Palestinian villages typically centered on the role of older, respected men. These male elders selected a *mukhtar*—literally, "one who is chosen"—from among their ranks to represent village interests to outsiders and mediate disputes among insiders.[32] Often the *mukhtar* was the *shaykh*, the nominal religious head of the village. The *shaykh*, like the *mukhtar*, held his position by virtue of age and reputation but was known, as well, for basic religious knowledge. This individual did not always possess formal religious training attested, for example, by an *ijaza*—an authorization to teach and preach—from an established center of learning such as al-Azhar University. He was known, rather, for being a virtuous exemplar who perhaps could recite from the Qur'an and knew the formalities of the marriage contract and other basic rituals, including burial. Imm 'Umar's cousin was accorded the status of imam because he was seen to have these qualities. He was not "book smart" but was known to be morally upstanding and to possess more religious knowledge than other immigrant elders.

In the diaspora context of the United States, formal licensing requirements transformed this family elder into a figure—the clergyman—recognizable within the American cultural milieu. By incorporating a mosque and appointing a religious leader, Imm 'Umar's relatives and their community thus began to identify collectively as Muslims and in doing so were beginning a type of social integration that had typified the experience of many other immigrant groups in the United States. The "religious turn" indexed the assimilation of the community through the formation of religious organizations that served not only ritual needs but also the functions of community representation, support, education, and leisure in a manner similar to Catholic parishes, Protestant churches, and Jewish synagogues. In this process, the community was adapting Islamic institutions to American religious organizational forms, thereby facilitating their capacity to be recognized as part of US society (Riedel 2009; Kivisto 2014, 65–66).

Assimilation processes, however, were not the only forces at work. The war of 1967 created the conditions for the renewal of political Islamic tendencies even as secular nationalism became dominant in the immediate aftermath of the conflict. This renewal culminated in the formation of powerful Islamist organizations and an accompanying religious revitalization that challenged the hegemony of secular Arab nationalism in the Middle East. These processes also affected the Palestinian immigrant community in Chicago. The impact registered most directly in a struggle to control the Mosque Foundation board in the late 1970s. The roots of this struggle lay in the composition of the new immigrants who arrived after 1967.

During the 1970s into the mid-1980s, the new immigrants came to include not only the "new peasants" whom Cainkar (1988) documented but also professionals—doctors and engineers—who possessed extensive economic and transnational institutional resources. Some of these individuals were sympathetic to reformist movements like the Muslim Brotherhood.[33] As such, they were forerunners of the generational split between secular nationalist and political Islamic movements that would occur in Palestine during and after the First Intifada (1987–93).

A group of such individuals—Palestinian and other Arab immigrants who had established themselves in professional fields and lived in Bridgeview and other adjacent southwest suburban communities—began to organize an effort to take charge of the Mosque Foundation. The initiative to build a mosque on land purchased in Bridgeview in 1973 had stalled for lack of funding. Seeing a chance to revive the campaign, the founders of the mosque project, established immigrants who had arrived from Beitunia before 1967, initially welcomed the support of the new professionals. The newcomers raised $1.2 million in total, with $369,000 coming from private sources in Kuwait, $152,000 from the government of Saudi Arabia, and $135,000 from the United Arab Emirates Ministry of Religion (Ahmed-Ullah, et al., 2004; Cainkar 2004, 112). The established Beitunians, by contrast, had required twenty years to collect $50,000 for the lot and likely would have required an equally long period to produce the funds for the mosque building itself.

Welcoming the assistance of the new professionals, however, had an unanticipated consequence: a shift of power and influence in the community. In 1978, promising to raise the necessary funds to build the mosque, the newcomers gained a majority on the Mosque Foundation board. By 1981, they had succeeded in procuring the funds and building the mosque. They then removed Imm 'Umar's cousin and installed in his place an imam who had received formal religious training and certification in the Middle East and who shared their reformist leanings.

Reformism emphasized the compatibility of Islam with the sober and rational ethos of modern middle-class professional life. This type of Islam emphasized textual orthopraxy: the Qur'an and Hadith were to be the sole authoritative determinants of faith. In this view, the traditional village piety of the established immigrants lacked foundation and consequently had allowed assimilation of non-Islamic practices. As one of the reformist leaders in Chicago put it: "We wanted to end un-Islamic practices like Easter egg hunts; [. . .] we wanted a real mosque, to raise the religious standard, and not just have a community center like the older group was thinking." The new imam installed by the reformers sought to achieve these goals through preaching, seminars, Qur'an lessons, youth education, and a range of other measures focusing especially on women's comportment. He instituted gender segregation and the requirement that women wear hijab scarves and modest clothing in the mosque, but also ideally at all times outside of the home. Through such practices, he and the board endeavored to align community identity with the reform orientation to which they were committed.[34]

The measures provoked backlash. Conflict erupted when a group of Beitunians surrounded the new board leadership in the mosque parking lot in November 1981. Bridgeview police were called to the scene to intervene.[35] That same year, the AALS, which held the deed to the mosque's land, filed suit against the new Mosque Foundation board, which was seeking to transfer ownership of the mosque to the North American Islamic Trust (NAIT) (Ahmed-Ullah, Roe, and Cohen 2004). The AALS disputed the legitimacy of the board and sought to prevent the transfer, which they feared would end local community control. According to a leader who backed the reformists, the AALS allegedly received financial support and encouragement to pursue the legal action from activists who sympathized with the dominant secular nationalist faction, Fatah. These individuals, he told me, viewed the mosque leadership transition "as a Muslim Brotherhood takeover." This was a false perception, he said. The people involved in guiding the leadership change were simply "faithful Muslims trying to improve their community."

Without the backing of the Fatah-oriented group, he alleged, the AALS would never have had the financial means to bring their suit.[36]

The AALS legal action ended in a mixed ruling. The plaintiffs retained ownership of the land on which the mosque was built but lost their challenge to the legality of the new mosque leadership and to the transfer of the mosque title. The court ruled that the transition in leadership on the board and the hiring of a new imam had occurred in a legitimate manner. The management of the Mosque Foundation would remain with the new professionals. As multiple individuals interviewed for this project indicated, this leadership transition was decisive in transforming the Mosque Foundation into the primary mechanism of the suburban reformist shift.[37]

Since its completion in 1981, the Mosque Foundation has become a well-established and expansive institution. Each Friday, it hosts two separate prayer services, one in Arabic, the other in English, which as many as 3,500 worshipers attend at a time. Having undergone a recent expansion and remodeling, the updated space features marble flooring, sage-colored "eco-friendly" carpeting, large LCD monitors in the overflow prayer areas, corporate-style conference rooms, and a bookstore with an array of classical Islamic texts, copies of the Qur'an, and children's literature addressing key practices like charity, tithing, and prayer. Mahogany-finished desks, tables, and bookcases and large-screen desktop computers furnish the offices of the mosque director (head imam) and assistant director (assistant imam). The mosque provides a range of programs: religious education; marriage and divorce counseling; conflict mediation; youth activities; a food pantry catering to a neighboring community of mostly poor whites living in prefabricated "trailer" homes; a "weekend school" for children; and the full range of ritual services.[38] On any given night, the large parking lot fills with cars as community members attend various functions in the prayer spaces and halls. During the feast to celebrate the end of the Ramadan fast, the mosque rents the neighboring Toyota Park soccer stadium to host as many as 18,000 people for the prayer. The mosque also maintains an active social media presence: its Facebook and YouTube feeds regularly post videos of conversions, prayer services, and sermons as well as announcements of upcoming programs.[39]

A second mosque, the Islamic Community Center of Illinois (ICCI), has provided an important locus for a much smaller concentration of Palestinians on the city's Northwest Side (West Belmont Avenue and North Narragansett Street area). Established in 2001, the mosque offers ritual services as well as Sunday Arabic and Qur'an instruction, an evening school for children, and youth programs. It also sponsors a private academy catering to pre-K through eighth grade students. The imams at the ICCI participate in the wider Islamic religious networks in the city and appear frequently at Mosque Foundation and American Muslims for Palestine events (chapter 3).

EXPANDING THE ISLAMIC MILIEU: ISLAMIC EDUCATION

The Islamic shift that has occurred since the 1980s has resulted not only from the reorienting of the Mosque Foundation toward a text-centered reformism but also from the establishment of two private Islamic schools on land adjacent to the mosque. Under separate administrations, the schools function alongside the mosque as the institutional anchor of the Arab-Palestinian and Muslim enclave in the southwest suburbs. The first, Aqsa School, takes its name from the al-Aqsa Mosque in Jerusalem's Old City. The school began in the Mosque Foundation basement in 1986 with seventeen students. Enrollment, limited to girls in grades six to twelve, jumped to eighty-five in the following year. In 1991, the board, under the leadership of three Palestinian professionals (two engineers and a physician), oversaw the purchase of land across from the Mosque Foundation for the school's current premises (completed in 1997). The new school offered instruction for pre-K through twelfth grade. Education was co-ed until the third grade; grades four to twelve remained entirely girls. Since the expansion, enrollment has averaged three hundred students per year. Ninety percent of these students have been Palestinian; nearly half have had Beitunian roots (Riedel 2009, 81–86).

The original rationale of Aqsa School was to create a separated space within which the "maturing daughters" of the community might be raised within an Islamic ethos and shielded from compromising moral influences in wider US society. One participant in my research illustrated how this mission manifested in the curriculum as she described her younger sister's experience at the school. The religion classes, she told me, required her sister and her classmates to read a book titled *The Ideal Muslimah* (Hashimi 1998). Her sister "hated this book" and refused to read it, and consequently religion was the only class in which she apparently did not excel. The book described the ideal Muslim woman as obedient to her husband and willing to create an environment of peace for him at home. It focused on the meaning of the Qur'anic term *qawwamun*, which appeared to establish the authority of men over women (Q4:34). It also featured a long section on the duties and responsibilities of men toward their wives.[40]

At the same time, Aqsa's general curriculum and extracurricular activities undermine the patriarchal messaging of the religion classes. Teaching in the other subjects focuses on preparing girls for college and careers. While the school's early graduates were often the first in their families to go to college, during the last three decades economic and social changes within the community have led to a growing emphasis on education. Today, most Aqsa School graduates go on to earn a bachelor's degree, and many also pursue graduate degrees or advanced professional training. Also, the religious instruction at Aqsa instills knowledge of the core texts that some girls then use to contest the patriarchal norms of their families, which they view as reflecting "culture" and not "religion."[41]

The second Islamic school, Universal School, lies across the parking lot from Aqsa School. Universal offers classes ranging from pre-K to twelve. The school is co-educational with gender segregation after the fifth grade. Universal is larger and more ethnically diverse than Aqsa. The school averages an enrollment of more than six hundred students per year and its staff comprises nearly fifty fulltime teachers. Predominantly Arab (Palestinian and Syrian, mostly) in composition, Universal's student population also includes South Asians, Africans, African Americans, and a handful of Latinx and whites.

Just as with the Aqsa School, the creation of the Universal school reflected the rising power and influence of the new professional class. The school began, for example, after the son of a Syrian immigrant physician reportedly saw pornographic images in the locker room of the public school that he was attending. Shocked by his son's account, the father organized other professionals within the Mosque Foundation community to raise money for a new school that would instill an Islamic orientation and shelter their children from corrupting influences in US society. The professionals activated the same international networks they had used to raise money for the mosque during the late 1970s and early 1980s. Within a matter of months, in 1988, they had secured enough funding to begin construction of the school on a plot of land adjacent to the mosque. The school opened two years later with 140 students and eleven teachers. A founding member of the Council of Islamic Organizations in Chicago and the Council of Islamic Schools in North America, the institution has become one of the largest Islamic schools in the United States (Riedel 2009, 82–86).[42]

A crucial difference separates the Universal and Aqsa schools. This difference reflects the ideological divide that first manifested in the struggle to control the Mosque Foundation. The Universal School embraces the Mosque Foundation's reformist Islamic program and emphasizes a broad, interethnic Islamic identity. It aims to be "universal" in the all-encompassing Islamic sense of "*umma*," or community. Aqsa School, by contrast, has drawn from mostly Palestinian families, many of whom initially resisted the reformist shift.[43] Despite centering Islam as a core identity, this group retains a focus on Palestinian national concerns. The choice to name the school after the Umayyad-era mosque situated on the Haram al-Sharif in Jerusalem is indicative of this nationalist orientation. This mosque (al-Aqsa), along with the Dome of the Rock, is the preeminent symbol of the Palestinian claim to the Holy City and to Palestine as a whole. In its choice of name, thus, the Aqsa School links Palestinian cultural and religious identities.[44]

The Aqsa and Universal schools, along with the mosque, anchor the broader immigrant enclave in which they are situated. The subdivision surrounding the mosque features single-family homes with two-car garages, late-model Toyota Camrys and Honda Civics, neatly manicured mid-sized lawns, and recently planted tree saplings that have yet to afford much shade against summer heat and humidity. The owners of these homes are predominantly Palestinians and other Muslim families who came to the neighborhood after non-Muslim families began to vacate the area. In 2009, the mosque leadership claimed that two-thirds of those who regularly participated in its ritual services and programs lived in Bridgeview and its neighboring communities, compared to only one-third in 1999 (Livezey 2000, 176; Riedel 2009, 81).

The main shopping districts and industrial zones in the Bridgeview-anchored enclave feature Arab-owned shops and enterprises. Almost every one of these business establishments combines Islamic religious and nationalist symbolic displays. The Facebook page of a popular restaurant, Al Bawadi Grill on W. 87th Street in Bridgeview, for example, not only advertises the menu but also publicizes calls to rally for protests and demonstrations in the Loop. Its Facebook site has featured photographs of the annual 'Id al-Fitr prayers at Toyota Park in Bridgeview. As well, Islamic and nationalist iconography appears in the restaurant itself, where photographs of the Dome of the Rock in Jerusalem's Old City and framed Qur'anic passages hang from the walls. These images juxtapose with the generic "Arab" sensibility of the Bedouin textiles above the booths and tables, the Arab pop music, the satellite feed from the Al Jazeera TV station, and the mix of Arabic and English conversation of the patrons. Arab Christians also come to the restaurant because of the quality of the food and because of the Levantine ambiance.

THE CHRISTIAN MILIEU: KEY STRUCTURES

Palestinian Christian families live in the southwest suburban stretches, too, congregating socially in certain informally designated spaces, such as a Starbucks coffee shop on one of the main thoroughfares. Christians own businesses—insurance, legal services, accounting—in these neighborhoods. These businesses provide one of the few points of social intersection with Palestinian Muslims. For the most part, Palestinian Christians, like Muslims, remain segregated within their own sub-milieu, interacting socially within their families, churches, and predominantly Christian organizations such as the Ramallah Club. Dispersed in an arc sweeping from the north side of the city to the northwest suburbs (for example, Northlake, IL) down to the southwest suburbs, Christians lack a single point of residential concentration. Consequently, they typically drive long distances on the expressways to attend community functions.

Three churches serve as primary community anchors. St. George, mentioned earlier, became established slowly in a manner similar to the Mosque Foundation as a response to the communal and liturgical-ritual needs of a growing Orthodox community after 1967. The purchase of a former Korean Presbyterian church building in Cicero in 1984 positioned the community for growth: Cicero is centrally located between the northwestern and southwestern suburbs in which parishioners live.

Today St. George counts approximately 1,500 mostly Palestinian families in its membership. The church has become a pilgrimage site because of its purportedly weeping icon of the Virgin Mary (Theotokos). This icon was first seen to weep in 1994. Older parishioners still recall the event with amazement. That same year, the Antiochian Orthodox Christian Archdiocese of North America declared the icon the "Miraculous Icon of Our Lady of Cicero." Cicero's town council has since declared the street in front of the church "Our Lady of Cicero Court" (Hanania 2015).

Leadership of St. George originally oscillated between priests of Arab and European ethnicity. From 1985 until the conclusion of my fieldwork, however, the church remained under the control of Fr. Nicholas Dahdal. Dahdal, a Palestinian, frequently represented St. George and, by extension, Palestinian Christians as a whole, at meetings that community activists called in periods of political crisis in the Middle East.

Like the Mosque Foundation, the church's liturgical services mix Arabic and English. But, whereas the Mosque Foundation provides separate English and Arabic prayer times, St. George combines the languages into its single Sunday morning liturgy, which can last for two hours or more. The church bulletin also appears in side-by-side Arabic and English scripts. The church provides a range of activities for children, teenagers, and young adults. One of its lay parish leaders has also created a bookstore featuring a sophisticated selection of theological, historical, and ethnographic studies on Orthodoxy and Orthodox religious communities globally. This individual, a Jordanian immigrant, also sponsors occasional lectures by authors in the church's basement community hall. In November 2014, for example, he invited Fr. Sidney H. Griffith of the Catholic University of America to speak about his recent book on the Arabic Bible (Griffith 2013).

Two other churches also draw Palestinian Christian membership. These include St. John the Baptist Melkite Catholic Church, described earlier, in the northwest suburb of Northlake, and St. Mary Antiochian Orthodox Church in the southwest suburb of Palos Hills. Established in 1969, but having origins in late nineteenth century Lebanese immigrant groups, St. John caters to Melkites and Roman Catholics and features Sunday liturgies in Spanish, Arabic, and English. Membership is predominantly Lebanese, Syrian, and Palestinian. Like St. George, the church's bulletin appears in Arabic and English. St. Mary's is a bilingual, primarily Jordanian congregation with some Palestinian members. It began in 2003 to accommodate Arab Orthodox families that had moved into the far southwest suburbs. In 2011, the church purchased a 42,000-square-foot property to house the congregation.

CONCLUSION: *MAHJAR* SPACES

The secular and religious milieus that have come to structure the social and political spaces of the Palestinian immigrant *mahjar* in Chicago have been and remain shifting zones within which diverse narrative trajectories—different "stories so far"—have intersected. These trajectories, religious and secular, have shaped individual immigrant subjectivities in multiple ways. As I show in the chapters ahead, individuals move through and across secular and religious space, engaging in a range of negotiations and reconfigurations of belonging. These journeys bear the traces of passage through and between other kinds of zones, too. Palestinian immigrant spaces emerge along the boundaries of Chicago's bifurcations: front-stage glittering city/backstage gritty city; white ethnic neighborhoods/the African-American "black belt"; white far suburbs/black and brown inner city and near suburbs. The immigrant space introduces a bifurcation of its own, transnational in character, between *amrika* and the *iblad* (back home). And within these many spatial-temporal polarities, race, class, generation, and gender intersect. These intersections add additional complexity to the negotiations of identity within and across the secular and religious space of Palestinian Chicago.

The next chapter offers an in-depth analysis of the secular milieu and the stories that intersect and shift therein. Despite a prolonged moment of attenuation, secularism has not entirely disappeared. Its traditions persist intergenerationally within its remaining organizational spaces. These spaces are no longer predominant in the immigrant community. But they constitute zones in which an alternative non-sectarian mode of communal-national belonging continues to exist. Secularism also re-emerges in new forms—ironically, as later chapters will show, in response to experiences of disenchantment within the Islamized suburban milieu.

2

Secularism in Exile

ليس فينا عيسوي أو مسلم
واحد نحن ألا فليعلموا
ديننا أوطاننا فليفهموا
إنَّا عرب تحاشينا الفتن
آه...فلتحيا فلسطين لنا
ولتحيا فلسطين الوطن

There are among us neither Christian nor Muslim.
We are one! Let them know
Our religion is our homelands! Let them understand
We are Arabs! We shun sedition!
O! Long live Palestine for us!
Long live Palestine, the homeland!

Seventy-two years old and recovering from surgery, Khairy Abudayyeh ("Abu Hatem," 1940–2019) leaned forward across his dining room table, face animated, voice deep and gravelly, to denounce "the religious fever" in Chicago and in the Middle East, especially in "what's going on in Syria." A poster of Naji al-'Ali's "Handala" figure—which depicted the Palestinian refugee—hung from the wall behind him.[1] Instead of uniting to resist Western imperialism and Israeli colonialism, he said, the "religious fanatics" had divided the Arabs, offering illusions of divine salvation. But secularists, too, were to blame. Their passivity had abetted the division and mimicked the religious mindset: "We just cannot ignore things," he said. "The solution does not come from God, it comes from us!" Abudayyeh sat up straight in his chair and gestured dramatically with his hand as he recited Iskandar al-Khouri al-Beit Jali's poetic declaration of Arab unity in the epigraph above. The performance hearkened to the Arab nationalist past and its principle that one's religion was the nation, that the nation was Arab, and that Arabs shunned sectarian division leading to "sedition."

Abudayyeh had memorized Khouri's poem as a schoolboy in the West Bank village of al-Jib some sixty years earlier. His teachers, swept up in the pan-Arabism of the 1950s, backed the Movement of Arab Nationalists (*harakat al-qawmiyin al-'arab*). Reeling from the war of 1948, they hearkened to its call to unite against Zionism and the West. Their students, including Abudayyeh, joined them in mass protests against the signing in 1955 of the Baghdad Pact, a Western-led military alliance that pan-Arabists viewed as propping up the monarchical regime in Iraq.

Six decades later, however, as Abudayyeh surveyed those early years, pan-Arabism lay in disarray. The regimes that still espoused it had either fallen or were teetering in the face of the massive Arab Spring protests (December 2010–13, approximately) and the horrendously destructive wars that followed in their wake in Libya, Yemen, and Syria. Among Palestinians, too, the unity forged historically through the leadership of the Palestine Liberation Organization (PLO) had collapsed. An ascendant Hamas ruled Gaza; a sclerotic Fatah clung to the West Bank. And, it seemed, the malaise had spread: the mosques were on the rise in Chicago and secularism had weakened in the diaspora.

Abudayyeh was right about Palestine. He had a point—his provocative, polemical flourish notwithstanding—about Chicago, too. Organizations like the Mosque Foundation, Muslim Legal Fund of America, Council on American-Islamic Relations, and American Muslims for Palestine had become dominant within the immigrant community. These groups had also helped to form citywide bodies such as the Council of Islamic Organizations of Greater Chicago and national organizations like the Washington, DC-based lobby, the US Council of Muslim Organizations. The ascendancy of these groups mirrored a rise in Islamic religiosity among Palestinians and other Muslim-majority immigrant communities, as well. More women had begun wearing headscarves; more men had grown beards; more weddings featured gender-segregated celebrating; more stores advertised *halal* grocery items of various sorts (Cainkar 2004 and personal observations). The September 11 attacks and their long aftermath had cemented the shift by intensifying a media-driven perception of Islam as the primary identity of Muslims, generating a racist, anti-Muslim backlash, and thrusting religious leaders into the role of community representatives.

Yet, despite these developments, secularism persisted. It animated leaders of the Arab American Action Network (AAAN), the sole remaining secular social service and community organization on the Southwest Side. It informed the political orientations of activists involved with Students for Justice in Palestine chapters and with the Boycott, Divestment, and Sanctions (BDS) campaign on university campuses (Lybarger 2014). Other types of deinstitutionalized secularism had also emerged as part of a disenchanted response to the new piety.

The individuals who continued to express secularist or secular sensibilities—among those who participated in this project—lived with their families and neighbors in the suburbs, where they accommodated yet also felt alienated by the religiosity pervading their communities.[2] Others resided elsewhere in the city, far from the suburban enclave. As the scope of secular nationalist institutional space receded, these individuals increasingly lacked a nucleus around which they could cohere as an identifiable presence. To embrace a secular orientation was, in the context of the religious turn, to inhabit a marginal, disconnected space, to live a disenchanted exile within the exile.[3]

EXAMINING SECULARISM: WHY IT MATTERS

If secularism in the Palestinian immigrant community has become marginal, why examine it? Three reasons present themselves. First, since the September 11 attacks and the subsequent wars in Afghanistan and Iraq, journalists and scholars have focused on Islam's compatibility with the West.[4] This concern has led to an increasing emphasis on cultural-religious location in the analysis of Muslim politics and identity (Malik 2009). The contingency of Islam in the identities of Muslims has receded from view as a result. This obscuring of contingency prevents an appreciation of complexity. Muslims in Europe and the United States do not necessarily identify primarily in religious terms, and they hold often-contradictory viewpoints on the salience and meaning of Islamic religious norms (*BBC News* 2007; Pew Research Center 2007, 2011; Nagel and Staeheli 2011). By emphasizing persisting forms of secularism, I seek to acknowledge such contingency and, in doing so, to caution against the Islamizing of Muslims in scholarly and public discourse. I do not deny the fact of Islam's ascendancy as an identity frame within immigrant Muslim communities. Indeed, this book analyzes this process in detail as it has manifested in Palestinian Chicago. My point, simply, is that in their focus on Islam's growing cultural and political prominence, scholars and journalists often lose sight of how secularism and secularity shape the identities of individuals who happen to have Muslim backgrounds.

My second justification for focusing on secularism is methodological: understanding religious revitalization requires attention to secularism and secularity because the two phenomena exist in a dynamic, mutually constituting relation (Riesebrodt 2010; Casanova 2011). We see this dynamic manifesting among Palestinians. Combating secularism and secularization in Gaza's refugee camps, for example, was the primary objective of Hamas's precursor, the Islamic Collective, during the 1980s, and a main concern of organizations like the Mosque Foundation and various churches in the Palestinian immigrant community has been to inoculate families against "corrupt" secular influences in US society and culture.[5] Any discussion of religious revival among Palestinians, then, requires, on theoretical and empirical grounds, a discussion of secularism as a competing, interacting formation.

Finally, and in connection with the previous point, the vicissitudes of Palestinian secularism demonstrate how social orientations reconstitute intergenerationally. Secular structures, even when they are weak, continue to instill secular orientations in new cohorts of activists. And the pious milieu itself can produce disenchantment and a search for secular (if not secularist) alternatives (see chapter 6). Palestinian secularism, and how it has developed over time and space, is then a highly complex phenomenon that bears directly the imprint of the religious turn.

PALESTINIAN SECULARISM

The secularism concept has had wide currency among Palestinians (Lybarger 2014). Khairy Abudayyeh offers a starting point for delineating a specifically Palestinian ideal-type. I do not claim that Abudayyeh is representative of Palestinian secularism as a whole. On the contrary, as a pan-Arabist (*qawmi*), his orientation constituted a very particular and contested trajectory of specifically political secularism. Still, the perspective he articulated conveys certain common features of secularism as Palestinians across the political spectrum have deployed it in Palestine and in the diaspora.

One of these shared features, the importance of national unity, appears in the poem Abudayyeh recited at his dining room table. The poem insists that Arab fraternity trumps religious solidarity: the nation—Arab and Palestinian—comes first. To promote Muslim or Christian solidarities at the expense of the nation is a treasonous act. One has to understand that one's religion, in the sense of a corporate loyalty, is the homeland. Such a perspective does not entail atheism per se but rather a reinterpretation of the purpose and meaning of religious practice. As Abudayyeh later explained, rituals like the pilgrimage to Mecca or fasting or prayer were salutary exercises that enabled, among other things, sharing experiences and solving problems, strengthening the body, and developing empathy for the poor. Such virtues were conducive to national unity. Palestinian secularism, as it emerges ideal-typically from Abudayyeh's self-presentation, then, annexes religions as contributing traditions that functionally nurture national cohesion: Palestinian Christians and Muslims are Arabs in the end, but what it means to see oneself as Arab includes, among other things, an ecumenical integration of subnational religious cultures (Islamic and Christian).

Palestinian secularism has proven to be historically resilient. This resiliency lies in the events, structures, and processes that reproduce it. Abudayyeh's secularism, for instance, stemmed, on his account, from the memory of his father participating alongside veterans of the Great Arab Revolt (1916–18) to fight the British during the 1936–39 Arab Revolt in Palestine. Abudayyeh described attempting later, as a child, to emulate his father's example by helping to distribute food to Palestinian fighters during the war of 1948. The pan-Arabism he later absorbed from his teachers during the 1950s provided an ideological framework for the nationalism he had learned through his family and through the experience of war. In Chicago, he would convey these values to Palestinian youth through community institutions he helped to create. Secularism thus reconstitutes itself intergenerationally through its formational experiences, organizational structures, and discourses. The success of this process has depended on the ability of its institutions and narratives to render secularism meaningful to new cohorts of activists in each successive crisis.

CONSTITUTING SECULARISM IN CHICAGO: THE GENERATION OF 1948–1967

The founders of the secular nationalist organizations that predominated within the Chicago immigrant community prior to the 1990s came of age, politically, during the period of 1948–67. I fuse these two dates into a single generational event because it was during this nineteen-year span that the secular nationalist factions took form and coalesced into a coherent Palestinian national movement. This process imbued young adults who were forming their historical and political outlooks during this time with a shared sense of fate. Variations in orientation due to differences in temporal and spatial relation to the two wars certainly existed, but the common experience of these wars and of secular nationalism as the dominant framework of political solidarity and action in this period is the key point.[6]

Social Backgrounds

Arriving in the United States during the 1950s through the 1960s and early 1970s, members of the cohort of 1948–67 who participated in this project came from varied social backgrounds. Some were from families of the professional, landowning, and commercial strata in the towns and cities of Palestine. These individuals attended elite schools prior to their arrival in the United States. Musa (pseudonym) (1930–2018), a long-time leader in the Palestinian community, provided insight into the experience of this echelon during a 2011 interview for this project. Musa grew up in an elite Muslim family in a mixed Christian, Druze, and Muslim town near Haifa and Nazareth. His family owned land and many of its members had entered professional fields (medicine, teaching, engineering). He scored well on a British Mandate placement exam and was admitted into an exclusive school to prepare for civil service employment.[7] After the war of 1948, Musa immigrated to the United States, arriving in the mid-1950s to begin medical school. He eventually became a surgeon at a large city hospital, serving there until his retirement in 1990. His wife, who was from an elite Christian family with a secular orientation, became the head administrator of a large nonprofit organization. Their children would eventually study for advanced degrees, work in professional fields, and move to the northern suburbs.

Other individuals in the generation of 1948–67 who gave interviews for this project came from less privileged backgrounds. Typically, they grew up in villages and attended public schools in nearby towns. Khairy Abudayyeh attended a government school in his village and then, in 1960, when he was twenty years old, immigrated to the United States to join his father and brother in Chicago. Originally intending to go to college, he instead began helping his brother with his business. He later took courses sporadically at Roosevelt University in the Loop while holding various jobs, often more than one simultaneously. He eventually spent the majority of his working life as a purchasing agent for the Guarantee Trust Life Insurance Company. Abudayyeh's children would go to college and enter professional fields. His son, Hatem, for example, earned a bachelor's degree at the University of California-Los Angeles and then returned to Chicago to work as an athletics coach in a local public school before becoming the executive director of the AAAN in 2002.

Ali Hussain, born in the early 1950s, followed a similar trajectory. After attending grammar school in his village, he enrolled in a government high school in nearby Ramallah, a predominantly Christian town north of Jerusalem. In 1971, at the age of eighteen, Hussain travelled to the United States for college. "I knew no one and barely had a hundred bucks on me," he recalled. He rented a room in a student dormitory for twenty-five dollars a month and began studies at the YMCA Community College. Progress was slow. He had to take various jobs, including in a downtown hotel, to pay for his rent and meals. Eventually, he launched a financial services business on West 63rd Street in the heart of the former Palestinian enclave in Chicago Lawn. He currently lives in a southwestern suburb and commutes to his West 63rd Street office.

Generational Processes in the Formation of the Cohort of 1948–1967

Musa, Abudayyeh, and Hussain differed in their socioeconomic backgrounds, yet, they shared a similar secularist outlook and commitment. The signal events that shaped their common orientation were the two wars of 1948 and 1967 through which Israel established itself and then conquered the remainder of British Mandate Palestine. Direct experience of the violence instilled a sense of national solidarity and a commitment to resistance. Musa briefly joined one of the Palestinian guerrilla groups operating in the Galilee region. Abudayyeh, as noted, also experienced the fighting in 1948. Hussain witnessed the war of 1967 and the violent imposition of Israeli military occupation. He recounted an Israeli raid on his village to search for weapons in the aftermath of the war. Soldiers detained several men, including Hussain and his uncle. At the jail, soldiers beat his uncle in front of him until he admitted to having a Mandate-era rifle in his home. This experience and others like it politicized Hussain as a teenager.

The reinvigoration of the Palestinian national movement had an equally influential impact on the cohort of 1948–67. The main event in this revival was Fatah's takeover of the PLO in 1968. Fatah, active since the 1950s, had consistently prioritized independent Palestinian decisionmaking even as it negotiated Arab regime sponsorship and access to sites from which to launch cross-border guerrilla raids against Israel. The other major Palestinian resistance movement, the Movement of Arab Nationalists (MAN), had taken a different strategic and ideological approach. It predicated Palestinian liberation on Arab nationalist revolutions that would first overthrow monarchical regimes aligned with the West and then act in concert against Israel. The MAN aligned closely with Egyptian President Jamal ʿAbd al-Nasser, who had become the preeminent tribune of secular pan-Arabism and a leader of the global Non-Aligned Movement.

The stunning defeat of Egypt, Syria, and Jordan in the war of 1967 dealt a severe blow to Nasser and the pan-Arabist cause, however, weakening the MAN as a consequence. In response, George Habash reconstituted the MAN as the Popular Front for the Liberation of Palestine (PFLP). The PFLP subsequently joined the PLO, becoming an important opposition force to Fatah within this framework. The forging of a unified national resistance prioritizing the armed struggle (*al-kifah al-musallah*) had an electrifying impact on young Palestinians. Even as the Middle East reeled in shock from the 1967 defeat, Palestinian and other Arab youth rallied to "the revolution," especially joining the guerrilla groups that had established bases in Jordan.

As in the Middle East, the war of 1967 generated a surge of nationalism within the Chicago community. Musa, Abudayyeh, and Hussain each cited this intensification of feeling as their motivation to become community organizers. Abudayyeh spoke of 1967 and its aftermath not as a defeat of Arab nationalism but rather as a moment of rejuvenation, in Chicago, of a commitment to Arab solidarity. He described a "birth of nationalism, a strong national movement" and cited the groups that formed from the Movement of Arab Nationalists as the inspiration. Musa, as well, noted that "'67 sparked people's awareness," whereas before the war "there was little political activism in the community."

Specific responses to the surge of nationalism varied in the community. Musa, for example, became a leader in organizations that leaned ideologically toward Fatah, the main PLO faction. He also helped found the Chicago chapter of the American-Arab Anti-Discrimination Committee. Through these involvements he became an important mediator across political and sectarian lines in the immigrant community. At one point, Musa assisted a predominantly Palestinian Christian group to conduct a needs assessment, collect money, and obtain a plot of land for a community center associated with their church. "Back then we didn't ask about religion [. . .]. We saw ourselves as Palestinians. As far as I am concerned Christianity is part of my heritage as a Palestinian Muslim."[8]

Hussain responded to the post-1967 nationalist sentiment by joining the Arab Student Association (ASA), which had emerged to counteract pro-Israel groups (Pennock 2017). The ASA held annual conventions that drew participants from "all Palestinian political factions and also from Iraq, Kuwait, Libya, Yemen." But, beginning in 1978, the organization fractured when Palestinian students split to form the Palestinian Students Association. Hussain commented: "That was one of the biggest mistakes the leadership made at that time [. . .]. We started excluding the activists in the community who were defending the Palestinian cause and we reduced it to only the Palestinian students." The Palestinian organization lacked funding and soon folded. Despite the fractures, the networks that grew from these groups mobilized young leaders within an emerging secular nationalist milieu in the city. Significantly, religious movements such as the Muslim Brotherhood did not present viable alternatives because they did not address the core national question that so urgently confronted the cohort of 1948–67. Hussain stated: "I'm proud to be Muslim, but the Islamists in the early '70s here in Chicago were not active toward the cause [. . .]; they would rather have somebody from Africa convert to be Muslim than unite as Arabs to liberate Palestine."[9]

The post-1967 nationalist response also gave rise to new community-level organizations. For example, Abudayyeh and Hussain, along with a third individual, Samir Odeh, who had arrived in Chicago at the same time as Hussain and had studied with him at the YMCA Community College, helped found the Arab Community Center (the ACC, the *markaz*) in 1972. The center's activities included instruction in the Arabic language, in Arab and Palestinian history and politics, and in practices like *tatriz* (traditional embroidery) and *dabka* (village line dancing) that had become symbols of Palestinian identity. These activities replicated the way the PLO factions and their associated organizations in the Occupied Territories and in the refugee camps in Jordan and Lebanon raised national awareness. They generated a sense of national cohesion within the Chicago immigrant community, thereby marking a distinctive Palestinian and Arab presence in the city's Southwest Side.

Institutionalizing Secularism

The ACC would become a main social and political anchor of the Palestinian enclave in the Chicago Lawn area during the 1970s and 1980s. Two other centers, also situated on West 63rd Street, came into existence at approximately the same time. Their leaders and base constituencies were known to align ideologically with Fatah and with one of Fatah's opposition groups in the PLO, respectively. By contrast, the Arab Community Center was understood to orient toward pan-Arabism, Third World internationalism, and the political left within the PLO.[10] All three centers sought to mobilize Chicago Palestinians in relation to the national liberation effort. They did so through cultural programing, financial support for families and communities locally and in Palestine, and protest actions. The ACC and its successor organization, the Arab American Action Network (AAAN), with which I have had the strongest connection and familiarity, reflects this organizing work in a broad sense.[11]

The ACC's initial location was on the North Side near the intersection of North Belmont and West 42nd Street. A small Palestinian community had formed in this area, and some of the organizers, including Khairy Abudayyeh and Ali Hussain, were living there at the time. The majority of Palestinians, however, had settled on the city's Southwest Side. This fact led the center's leaders to relocate the ACC to premises near South Rockwell and West 55th Street in the Gage Park area. "The rent was $650 and we were wondering where the hell we were going to come up with the money; it was a huge place," Hussain remembered. Searching for an affordable alternative, they relocated again in 1978, this time permanently, to a building in the Chicago Lawn area on West 63rd Street near South Kedzie Avenue. The ACC continued until 1995. A year later, a new organization, the AAAN, took its place in the same premises under a new generation of leaders. These leaders had grown up attending ACC events as well as participating in the Union of Palestinian Women Associations (UPWA) programs, which also had been situated at the ACC.

The ACC's social outreach focused on youth. Parents dropped off their children after school. Abudayyeh and Hussain and their fellow activists, who went directly from their jobs to the center, taught the language, history, and culture classes. Hussain brought his own children and typically "ten to fifteen of their neighborhood friends" with him in his van. "I was teaching Arabic classes there from 1972 all the way to 1995," he recalled. This focus on youth became a guiding concern of the center's programs. Samir Odeh (1951–94), one of the founders and also a director of the ACC, for example, launched the Youth Delinquency Program, the first initiative of its kind to address the needs of Palestinian and Arab teenagers on the Southwest Side (Abowd 1995). The ACC initiatives became a model for other community centers nationally. In 1979, Odeh participated in the creation of the National Network for Palestinian Community Empowerment, an organization that trained local community organizers. He traveled across the United States, visiting Arab community centers and helping their staff recruit membership and build programs (Abowd 1995).

The ACC also became a social and political hub during major crises such as the Israeli campaign against the PLO in Lebanon in 1982 and the First Intifada (1987–93). ACC organizers facilitated communication with loved ones "back home" and coordinated letter-writing campaigns, marches, blood banks, clothing drives, and an extensive sponsorship program for families in Palestine. These efforts sometimes drew the scrutiny of law enforcement. During the 1982 Lebanon war, for example, Chicago police arrested Ali Hussain on drug-smuggling charges after suspicious neighbors reported seeing discarded medical equipment—syringes—in the dumpster behind the center. The association had collected the implements but deemed them inadequate for sending to Lebanon. Hussain's colleagues immediately fanned out across the Southwest Side to collect funds for his bail. A National Lawyers Guild attorney—an individual of Irish ethnic descent who supported the Republican cause in Northern Ireland—volunteered to defend Hussain.[12]

The willingness of this lawyer to volunteer his time revealed an additional dimension of the work that Hussain and his colleagues had undertaken in their effort to organize Palestinians in the city: building ties to other immigrant and minority groups and their community centers. These ties solidified during Harold Washington's campaign to become the first African American mayor of

Chicago in 1983. The ACC's leaders contributed financially and volunteered their labor to that campaign, their first ever venture into city politics. After the election, the new mayor held his first Southwest Side "town hall" meeting at the ACC (Abowd 1995). Hussain and other ACC leaders like Odeh remained involved in efforts to build coalitions and run Arab candidates for local office. Odeh, for example, chaired the outreach committee for Illinois Voters for Middle East Peace from 1985–90. The committee focused on Arab voter registration and sought avenues for Arab participation in city government. These efforts led Washington to institute the Advisory Committee on Arab American Affairs. Odeh and the ACC also joined Reverend Jesse Jackson's Rainbow Coalition in 1988, strengthening bonds with African American civil rights leadership nationally (Abowd 1995).

Hussain, Odeh, and other ACC activists had learned that mobilizing political pressure and developing political access were crucial to defending the Palestinian community and its interests. They worked within established entities like the Democratic Party but also forged alliances with other minority and immigrant community organizations in order to build Palestinian and Arab political capacity. Referring to his arrest in 1982, Hussain reflected on the importance of those ties and on their later weakening:

> The community and our allies came together, and that support helped to place pressure on elected leaders to dismiss the charges. Leaders of other [ethnic] communities, including business people, testified that our center were good people who actually worked against drug crime in the area. Our situation today is different [. . .]. We don't come together like this anymore."

Deinstitutionalization and Attenuation

In 1991, a fire gutted the building in which the Fatah-oriented Palestinian Community Center was situated.[13] The center's leadership never rebuilt the institution. The second center associated with one of Fatah's competing factions also closed at this time. A year later, the ACC sealed its doors. The shuttering of these centers signaled the deinstitutionalization and corresponding social and political weakening of secularism—a process that paralleled the crippling of the PLO during and after the first Gulf War (1990–91) and also the powerful rise of Islamist competitors, principally Hamas, in the Occupied Territories (primarily, the Gaza Strip). Even though the AAAN would soon replace the ACC—largely due to a successful effort to transform the *markaz* into a grant-funded social service organization—the institutional shift favoring Islamic religious organizations in the southwest suburbs had become decisive. Individuals committed to Palestinian liberation would participate in these new Islamic institutions, but the religious framework would not have the same intersectarian Arab and Palestinian nationalist focus as the community centers in the former Chicago Lawn enclave. The creation of American Muslims for Palestine (AMP) in 2006 would address this lack of a political advocacy structure (see chapter 3). Significantly, however, the AMP, as its name suggests, oriented itself explicitly in religious sectarian terms.

The events leading to these changes were complex. They included the demographic transition and corresponding religious institutionalization in communities like Bridgeview beginning in the latter half of the 1980s (see chapter 1). Ali Hussain, Musa, and Khairy Abudayyeh acknowledged these processes but pointed to two other factors: the decision not to move the secular community centers to the suburbs and the inability of the Oslo Peace Process (1993–present) to produce an independent Palestinian state. Working in tandem, these two factors, they argued, undermined the capacity of secular nationalists to respond effectively to the growing influence of the Islamic organizations. Hussain observed:

> After 1995 [two years into the Oslo Peace Process], people were really in despair about politics and our community centers weren't there [for them in the suburbs]. This opened the door to the Islamist people taking over the community. It became the trend to follow the *shaykh* wherever he goes, do whatever he says; whether it's the right thing or wrong thing, people followed them. We lost our entire base, practically.

The Islamic shift also gained momentum from the perception, in Hussain's recounting, that "the [Fatah-led] nationalist movement was not doing good over there [in Palestine], there was no liberation, no state." The disenchantment with secularism, he said, led to the embrace of religion as an alternative. The change was dramatic: "You used to walk in this neighborhood [Chicago Lawn] back in the '80s and you would hardly find women with hijab [. . .]. But now, suddenly, in Bridgeview, you hardly see anyone without it."

Khairy Abudayyeh echoed Hussain's assessment. "Oslo discouraged everybody [among the secular nationalists]," he said. "It put a damper on our activities." In addition to the demoralizing psychological impact, there was the problem of legitimacy stemming from a perception that the PLO had betrayed the cause of liberation and statehood: "The religious fanatics started saying to us, 'Your cause is useless! See what nationalism did to you! See what Communism did to you! See what Arafat did to you!' We didn't have an answer."

The difficult position reflected in Abudayyeh's comments reflected how the Oslo Peace Process had transformed the terms of the conflict by bringing the PLO, which had become politically isolated and financially undermined during the first Gulf War, into alignment with Israel and the United States. Diaspora activists confronted a situation in which the objectives of solidarity and advocacy were no longer clear. The agreement appeared to fall short of what had been the PLO-led consensus goal, independent statehood within the post-1948 ceasefire lines and the return of the refugees. With Oslo, the PLO seemed to have capitulated to a limited form of autonomy within highly circumscribed territorial zones (the patchwork of areas, delimited as A, B, and C, with differing levels of Israeli security control). This dispiriting result left diaspora activists despondent and adrift. As Abudayyeh noted, Islam-oriented leaders saw an opportunity to declare the failure of secular nationalism and propagate the message that only with a return to Islam would Palestinians, and Muslims globally, recover the homeland. As late as 2014, in fact, this exact idea was the main message of a speech that a Mosque Foundation imam gave at the annual American Muslims for Palestine Nakba Day commemoration (see chapter 3).[14] Palestine would return to Palestinians one day, the imam said, but the key to this eventuality lay in the return of Arabs and Muslims to Islam.

In addition to the changed political context, Abudayyeh pointed to other factors contributing to the weakening of secularist organizations. "We also were busy with our families and jobs," he said, "six or seven of us, the founders and some other people, we had jobs and families and less time to give the community and that gave an opening to the religious fanatics, too." The reliance on volunteer labor indicated a relative lack of professionalization at organizations like the Arab Community Center. By contrast, from the 1980s through the 2000s, the Mosque Foundation significantly enlarged its complex, alongside the two new Islamic schools, providing a full range of religious and social programing as it did so. The Islamic institutions, in this way, became an all-encompassing canopy for community life and individual leisure time in the expanding suburban enclave (Lybarger 2014).

Nostalgia marked the outlook of the secularists of the 1948–67 cohort as they reflected on what had occurred since the 1990s. During his 2012 interview for this project, Khairy Abudayyeh recalled a gathering of the old guard at the home of a family whose daughter had just graduated from college that summer. The party featured Palestinian food and a musician who played nationalist songs. "The women were not wearing hijab scarves," he remembered, "it was like the old days when we would get together, women and men, Muslims and Christians, without boundaries."

Musa also commented on the difference between past and present: "The leftists," he said, "had a devout Muslim as president of their community center [the ACC] for many years!" He added:

> That was an example of how people separated the two. You could be religious in your personal life but in public you were a Palestinian [. . .]. What's going on now is Saudi-influenced [. . .]. People start meetings of supposedly secular organizations with "*al-salamu 'alaykum*" ["Peace be upon you"—a typical Islamic greeting and also a phrase that ends the mandated ritual prayers] and they pause their activities for prayer [. . .]. It didn't used to be like this; this is Saudi stuff.

The extent to which Saudi influence had propelled the religious turn in the suburbs was unclear. What was relevant in Musa's comment, however, was how it reflected his estrangement from the Islamized present. Marked by piety, even in ostensibly secular settings, this present had become foreign to what was, in his view, genuinely Palestinian. For secularists of the generation of 1948–67, to see oneself as Palestinian was to embrace an ethic of national solidarity that acknowledged religious differences but insisted that such distinctions should remain bounded within individual life. In public, one was Palestinian. To assert otherwise, whether through rhetoric or sartorial practice, was to divide the nation.

Yet, as Musa's remarks indicated, a younger cohort of secular activists—which formed in the period of 1987–2001—appeared to be at ease with an overt hybrid construction of public space as simultaneously religious and secular. These activists seamlessly incorporated Islamic invocations at the start of supposedly secular events. This shift appeared to signal a new conception of the normative boundaries of the religious and the secular in public life. Interviews with leaders in this new cohort, however, nevertheless revealed an underlying ambivalence about the change.

THE GENERATION OF 1987–2001

Since the 1990s, leadership of secularist institutions within the Palestinian immigrant community in Chicago has passed to a new cohort of activists. I demarcate this generation in relation to the period of 1987–2001. This period encompassed several key events: the First Intifada, a mass uprising against the Israeli occupation in the West Bank and Gaza Strip; the Gulf War, in which the United States led a military campaign to force the Iraqi army out of Kuwait in 1990–91; the Oslo Peace Process, which began in 1993 but then ground to a halt with the outbreak of the Second Intifada (the al-Aqsa Intifada); and, finally, the September 11, 2001 attacks in the United States. These events, carried into living rooms via cable and satellite television, mobilized a new generation of secular nationalist activists.

During this same period, the Islamic shift began to reshape Palestinian social and political identities in Palestine and in diaspora communities like Chicago. The resulting secular-Islamist split defined the generation of 1987–2001 in both places. In Chicago, the Islamic shift corresponded with an enfeeblement of secular nationalist structures. The new generation of secularist leaders had to adjust to this transformation. A flexible accommodation of the public assertion of religion and of the predominance of Islamic institutions in the suburbs distinguished their outlook from the attitudes of secularists of the 1948–1967 cohort, who, like Musa, insisted that religiosity be restricted to personal life or, like Abudayyeh, saw religious sectarianism as a threat to national unity. The three profiles that follow illustrate how the generation of 1987–2001 accommodated the new religiosity but also expressed deep misgivings about it.

Manal

Manal (pseudonym), a former volunteer at the ACC on the Southwest Side of the city, was a family physician in private practice when I interviewed her in her large home in a southwestern suburb. Born in Jerusalem in the mid-1960s, she had spent much of her childhood in Austin, Texas, where her father completed an engineering degree at the University of Texas. She returned to Palestine in the 1980s to attend high school in the Jerusalem area. This high school, which featured an English-language curriculum and American teachers, catered to wealthy, US-born Palestinian children.

Manal described becoming conscious of her American identity while at the school. Local residents referred to her and her classmates as *"amrikan."* The political factions, she told me, generally avoided recruiting students at her school because "[we] were not really seen as 100 percent Palestinian [. . .]. You were somehow tainted by America because you grew up there, and you were frowned upon by those who were less educated." Manal commented further that the perception stemmed from observed differences in social comportment: "We had no problem walking out into the street in t-shirts and jeans, going and coming freely—most girls back home [in Palestine] don't do that—and speaking with the opposite sex, with American [Palestinian-American] boys at the school; we saw that as normal." Manal's comments about the suspicion she encountered indicated how Palestinians in Palestine—or, at least, those individuals who lived near her school—could perceive the diaspora as a morally corrupting force, especially for girls.

Despite the local skepticism, Manal nevertheless became politically active. She participated in after-school demonstrations, school council, and a *dabka* dance troupe that toured the West Bank. The artistic activity was especially important to her. Her family had urged her to avoid public protests and political organizing, but the dance troupe "was acceptable, it was art—political action in artistic form that would not necessarily subject you to danger [. . .]. We were allowed to do that."

Manal did eventually become involved in organized activism, but that development only occurred after her return to the United States, to Chicago, to begin college in the late 1980s. Manal's description of this phase reflected, in particular, the importance of the organizations that activists of the generation of 1948–67 had established during the post-1967 period. It also reflected how Chicago's wider metropolitan area afforded her freedom from community social controls. Living on her own in a rented apartment near the university, Manal had the ability to engage in political activity in ways that had not existed for her in Palestine due to the close scrutiny of female public behavior.[15]

Manal's integration into the specifically secular nationalist political milieu in Chicago occurred through the General Union of Palestinian Students (GUPS) chapter at her campus. She joined GUPS after meeting some of its members at an event. She then became president of the chapter during her senior year. Through GUPS she established connections with the ACC. Leaders at the center invited her to join in their programs and activities. As a single woman living on her own, she especially appreciated the "chance to meet people [. . .]. There was a Palestinian women's organization [the Union of Palestinian Women Associations] and I was a member of that, was very active there, and a *dabka* group that would meet every Friday night to practice, and they held Thanksgiving complete with turkey and *hummus* for those who didn't have families [. . .]. All the other major holidays were celebrated there."

Through such activities, the ACC eased the transition for newly arrived immigrants and for students living on their own. It provided a home and the support of friends. Equally important, however, was the opportunity to engage in various types of activism on behalf of the Palestinian cause. In her comments, Manal described a time of heightened political advocacy in the period after her graduation from college in 1985. In December 1987, the First Intifada began. The ACC's premises quickly became a site of round-the-clock activity. Community members came frequently to the center to learn about events and take part in food and medicine drives.

The Union of Palestinian Women Associations (UPWA), which was headquartered at the ACC, played a key role in facilitating the logistics of these efforts. It integrated women into the work of the campaigns and empowered them politically in the process. Manal described, for example, how English classes attracted women initially and then how teachers would recruit their students into UPWA and ACC work. This process led to the formation of a core of activists who staged conferences and conventions. At these events, Manal and her fellow organizers would perform *dabka*, lead singing of nationalist songs, plan activities, and educate the community, women especially, about current events and the need for gender equity. The UPWA also held an annual banquet that attracted more than a thousand participants. "At that time," Manal commented, "people felt they had a national identity and wanted to have these gatherings and were willing to contribute money [. . .]. Now, no one wants to talk about contributing [to nationalist organizations], but, people back then were giving thousands and thousands of dollars to the [refugee] camps and to Palestine."

After medical school, during the 1990s and 2000s, Manal continued to engage in Palestinian activism. She described this period as a moment of secularist collapse that left the immigrant community without an organizational structure through which to advocate for Palestine. I reminded her of American Muslims for Palestine (AMP), which was founded in 2006 in the wake of Israel's "Summer Rains" bombardment of the Gaza Strip in retaliation for Hamas's abduction of Israel Defense Force Corporal Gilad Shalit. Hadn't this organization filled the gap created by the collapse of the community centers? I asked. Manal claimed not to know much about AMP but pointed out that it had an explicitly Islamic identity: by definition it ruled out the inclusion of Palestinian secularists, atheists, and Christians. She noted that locale-oriented organizations like the Ramallah club did integrate non-Muslims into the Palestinian community, but these structures were "more social than political." In moments like Israel's repeated attacks on Gaza, there was no mechanism, no *secular* mechanism, to bring all Palestinians together. "That's the flaw in the political organizing of the Palestinians in this community [. . .]," she commented. "The will and desire are there, and you can tap into it and into the resources, and you can massage the anger that builds up, but what's the mechanism through which all of this is going to flow?" The absence of such a mechanism led Manal to conclude there was no "organized community" other than at the Mosque Foundation and its associated groups, but these religious associations excluded important segments of Palestinian Chicago.

Faced with the lack of a secular organizational alternative, Manal found that she could not avoid participating in the new pietistic milieu and its structures. She described, for example, sending her children to the Islamic schools next to the Mosque Foundation to learn Arabic and Islamic heritage. "I'm not a religious person," she said, "however I wanted them to have a little bit of religion in them and I wanted them to know the language [. . .]. People have different reasons for sending [their kids]—not just because we want to indoctrinate them into religion, but for limited purposes, like language and culture." She monitored her children's experience and eventually removed them: "[I took them out] when it reached the point, where, in my view, what they were learning had nothing to do with Palestinian values, and they were being brainwashed, in my opinion." She placed her children in the public schools, instead.

In these comments, Manal revealed how the Islamic religious turn had begun to affect secularist practices and sensibilities. Her perspective toward religion was continuous with the attitudes of the generation of 1948–67, which viewed Islam as an historical inheritance or individual practice but resisted it as a frame for shared political identity. The difference in the generation of 1987–2001, of which Manal was part, lay in its pragmatic participation in religious institutions. In the aftermath of the religious shift, this generation of secularists had few other options for retaining ties to Palestinian immigrant life and identity in Chicago.

Reflecting on this predicament, Manal commented on the need and the prospect for reviving a nonsectarian, secular space in the community. The lack of such a space became particularly apparent when children began to search for marriage partners. The capacity of the secularist milieu to regenerate itself resided partly in its ability to institute and transmit its value orientations intergenerationally within families. Meeting marriage partners was critical to perpetuating these family structures. She commented:

> We all got married through the *markaz*, we all met our spouses there. Now, when your child is older and he's dating and he says, "Mom, introduce me to someone," where am I gonna send this kid? Where? Where??! There really is no community. We don't go to church or mosque. The mosque isn't an environment for this kind of social interaction.

The absence of secular spaces also had eroded intergenerational collaboration, a factor in the weakening of secular structures. "One thing our organizations are not doing," Manal said, "is reaching out to the older people for guidance [. . .]. You still need the old group that has access to wider circles, families that can organize, that have access to people and to money [. . .]. The younger people do not have this access." As Manal described: "We used to raise maybe twenty, thirty, forty thousand dollars at our annual banquet, and we thought it was a million bucks back then, but, today, the *shaykhs* at the Mosque Foundation can raise a million dollars in less than a half-hour on a Ramadan night."

Having lost their place in community life, the secular nationalist organizations faced difficulty sustaining their fiscal viability. The break in intergenerational ties had compounded this problem. The occasional moments when secular spaces did reemerge brought their relative absence into stark relief. When I described Khairy Abudayyeh's account of a party someone had given to celebrate a daughter's university graduation, Manal said she remembered the event, too:

> You know what it was? It was the *markaz* on a Friday night twenty-five years ago! Arabic music, singing, Arabic food, old and young, women and men, freely socializing. We were there as Palestinians: Christians and Muslims and secularists. No one wearing hijab, no one going off to pray. We need to revive this type of thing, because that will turn into political organizing on a much higher level. I don't have the anger Abu Hatem [Abudayyeh] has. You really can't blame anybody. It was a natural state of affairs given our leadership overseas and the current situation [the failed Oslo process].

The nostalgic tone in Manal's recollection of the graduation party emphasized the fact that the secular ethos no longer existed as it once did. The heart of organized community life lay elsewhere, in the mosque programs and Islamic schools and in social gatherings structured according to reformist, pietistic norms such as weddings featuring gender-segregated celebrating. There was no intersectarian, secular alternative for gathering and leisure other than the occasional dinner party. Like Ali Hussain, Manal blamed the dispiriting impact of the Oslo agreement and failed peace process. Still, she said, "we could revive our gatherings and organizations with some extra commitment."

Whether or not the secular milieu could actually revive itself in the manner that Manal suggested remained uncertain. Younger Palestinian activists had a range of options for continuing their involvement in the cause after they finished college. Many joined in AMP activities, for example (see chapter 3). As Hatem Abudayyeh, son of Khairy Abudayyeh and Executive Director of the AAAN, told me, "We are in a bit of a competition with AMP over these kids—we don't know which way they'll go."

The religious shift had also drawn in secularists themselves. Manal mentioned several former leftists who had become pious and "converted." She interpreted this phenomenon as a reaction to the failures of secularism and the corresponding need for meaning and direction in life:

> Many of the old guard at the *markaz* that had been very involved in organizing the community went into depression mode [after Oslo]. They asked themselves, what place do I have in this process now? Everything we've been struggling for has suddenly vanished. Where do we go from here? And many of them to this day have not

found the answer. They have disappeared off the political spectrum. Some have even gone in the Islamic direction. These people [who embraced the Islamic turn] felt abandoned. The mosque was there to say: 'See where your secularism got you! It got you nothing but failure and corruption. But, we have the answer! Join us now!' You were no longer feeling Palestinian; it no longer did anything for you. Islam now was what mattered, what seemed to give hope, the way forward. You were Muslim now. A lot of people converted. People who used to call themselves socialists were now wearing hijab and praying five times a day.

Manal, by contrast, had found a third path between withdrawal and conversion. Secularism persisted within her outlook in this intermediate trajectory. She combined guarded participation in the Islamic institutions—limited attendance at Saturday morning religion classes for her children, for example—with the nurture of informal gatherings in which the former secularist ethos could again revive, albeit momentarily. She also occasionally volunteered for the AAAN. Secularism had dissipated but not disappeared, and this was the case even in the suburbs where Manal and other secularists had moved along with their piety-minded neighbors.

Mahmoud

The next profile of an individual of the generation of 1987–2001 illustrates a different developmental track from the demoralization-to-conversion and the accommodation-and-persistence trajectories that Manal witnessed and experienced. This alternative movement extended to a space of secularity beyond the Palestinian immigrant milieu. Within this space, Palestinian identity broadened into a multisectarian, cross-national Arab American solidarity that transcended the dilemma, for secularists, of the religious shift.

My interview with Mahmoud (pseudonym), a chemical engineer in his late thirties at the time of our conversation, provides insight into this other possible trajectory. We began our discussion in his downtown office and then continued for several hours at his favorite restaurant in the Loop. Born in the Arab Gulf region in 1975, Mahmoud arrived two years later in the United States. His father, a trained accountant in the United Arab Emirates, joined his brothers in a restaurant business on the Northwest Side. Five years later, the family moved to the immigrant enclave in Chicago Lawn, where Mahmoud's father started a new restaurant. The restaurant failed, at which point the father recertified as an accountant and began work in the City of Chicago's taxation department.

Mahmoud had limited contact with Palestinian community organizations on the Southwest Side. His lack of connection stemmed partly from the fact that his family had moved into the area during his final year of high school. He had not grown up in the community. Still, he described sporadically attending the Saturday Arabic classes at one of the secular nationalist community centers (not the *markaz*). These classes, he recalled, lacked discipline and a coherent curriculum. He attended a few initial sessions but then stopped. Mahmoud also described going to community fundraisers at the center to support charitable causes in Palestine. The family was still on the North Side at the time. Attending those events required a thirty- to forty-minute car ride across the city. "I think this was around the time of the Israeli invasion of Lebanon in 1982," he told me, "but I was too young to appreciate what was going on."

After graduating from high school in 1993, Mahmoud followed his father's example by pursuing a two-year degree at a South Side city college. Attending this college had the unforeseen consequence of integrating Mahmoud into a Palestinian student milieu and into organizing structures such as GUPS. He initially participated in GUPS, but the factional infighting alienated him. He recalled one event in particular: an election for the governing board at the college:

> You had all the [PLO] factions in GUPS [. . .]. I remember making the argument that we were a small group on the South Side at this small community college so who gives a shit about this [factional loyalty] stuff. We were sitting around in the cafeteria smoking and arguing but we weren't accomplishing anything. We had the elections and we shut down the entire cafeteria. And all the other students were like, what the hell! Everyone else has a small ballot box but the Palestinians have to shut down the entire cafeteria because they are fighting over the results. I remember when I walked in to vote, some guy who was not from the college, he was from UIC (University of Illinois at Chicago)—there was this hierarchy with the UIC GUPS chapter controlling our chapter [. . .], it was like organized crime the way the territory was divided up—this guy takes my ballot before I even walk into the room and he scribbles something on it in Arabic. I said, 'What the hell is that!' He said, 'Don't worry about it.' I said, 'Fuck you! Don't worry about it?! You can't write on my ballot!' I said, 'Fine, I'm turning in a blank ballot!' My cousin, who was at UIC, said later, 'So, Mahmoud, you turned in a blank ballot!' [laughter]. I said, 'How the hell did you know?!?' I really did not like the whole faction nonsense. One faction would win, take over the office, and never do anything. Absolutely useless. At that point, I figured I could do a lot more to benefit the community as a whole, Palestinian and non-Palestinian, Arab, Muslim and Christian.

Mahmoud's recollection highlights the extent to which, in the early 1990s, secular nationalism and its ideological factions remained the dominant structure of politics and identity on the college and university campuses that drew immigrant Palestinian enrollments in the city. This period coincided with the beginnings of the Oslo Peace Process, an event that momentarily rehabilitated the international status and authority of Yasser Arafat and the Fatah movement. Oslo, however, also deepened the factional divides among secular nationalists. The leftist Popular Front and Democratic Front groups, for example, rejected Fatah's decision to enter into the Oslo process. Mahmoud encountered this deepening divide—and a corresponding demand for party loyalty—on campus.

After two years at the community college, Mahmoud transferred to the University of Illinois at Chicago (UIC), where he earned bachelors and masters degrees in chemical engineering. During this period, he joined the American-Arab Anti-Discrimination Committee (ADC), a civil rights organization that advocated for Arab Americans as a distinct, cross-national ethnic group in the United States. Mahmoud's interest in the ADC developed after seeing its spokesperson, James Zoghby, defend Arabs and Muslims on national television following the Oklahoma City bombing in April 1995.[16] Inspired by Zoghby's public advocacy, he contacted ADC to see how he might contribute. Within a year he was serving on the board of the organization's Chicago chapter. At Zoghby's invitation, he also took part in an ADC factfinding trip to Palestine. The objective was to support the Oslo process and to hear directly from the Palestinian Authority leadership about how Arab Americans, especially, could advance Palestinian interests in the United States. This trip, which introduced Mahmoud to Palestinian politics at the highest level, solidified his sense of Palestinian identity. But it also situated this identity and his activism on behalf of it within an Arab American framework.

Soon after returning from the ADC trip, Mahmoud founded an association for Arab professionals and assisted in the creation of an Arab American advocacy group within the city's Democratic Party. These activities brought Mahmoud to the attention of Mayor of Chicago, Richard M. Daley. Immediately following the September 11 attacks, Daley invited Mahmoud to join the Arab Advisory Board. This entity, established under the previous Harold Washington administration, provided a channel of communication and patronage to the city's Arab American community. Similar advisory boards existed for other ethnic blocs in the city, as well.[17] Within a year, Mahmoud accepted a three-year appointment as an advisor to the Daley Administration.

The embrace of an Arab American identity, as well as mainstream political assimilation through that identity (for example, within the Chicago Democratic Party), allowed Mahmoud to resist and transcend the pressures of political factionalism in the Palestinian immigrant community. Those pressures became irrelevant and disappeared for him within the broader Arab American space. Similarly, the Arab American context allowed him to negotiate the Islamic religious shift by providing him with an alternative reference group that reinforced an ethos of pluralism.

The religious shift directly affected Mahmoud. His mother and aunts began to wear the hijab scarf, for example, and his parents started to fast and pray regularly during the early 1990s. Mahmoud linked the changes to the process of religious institutionalization in the suburbs. "It had to do with the conservative movement in Chicago," he said. "Maybe it's the *shaykh* at the Bridgeview Mosque who started it; he and his supporters insisted that [. . .] women had to wear hijab, everybody had to pray, everybody had to come to the mosque, and a lot of people kind of went in that direction." Mahmoud had resisted this trend. "I haven't fasted or prayed for twenty years," he told me. His refusal to conform sometimes caused tension and awkwardness. He described how feelings of estrangement arose during large family gatherings:

> Sometimes I feel like an outlier. For example, over the weekend we had two *iftars* [the meal that occurs after sunset and that breaks the daylong fast during Ramadan] with one hosted by my uncle, the other by my cousin. And there were some very conservative, very religious family members in both groups. And there were also a lot of non-observant family members—some, I should say some, not a lot.

The awkwardness Mahmoud experienced at these Ramadan dinners disappeared, by contrast, when he convened with his friends in the professional organization he had established. In this space, a middle ground existed, made possible by a tacit agreement to allow and respect diverse lifestyles:

> If I'm out with a lot of the younger Arab Americans—like this group I started for Arab American professionals—a lot of them are non-observant. We have drinks when we go out. We don't pray five times a day. Some of us might fast, but like me not everyone does. A lot of us have the same opinion: respect for the religion, just not observant. Some of us have a problem with religion because of the leadership, seeing them use religion for political gain, distorting the religion for their own interests [. . .].

As he reflected on the ethos of this group of peers, Mahmoud recounted how his father had instilled a basic "live and let live" orientation within him as a child. He recalled two incidents, in particular, in which his father conveyed the importance of accepting difference and of placing moral rectitude above religious observance:

> [Once] when I was 11 [. . .], after we had someone who was religious over for dinner, my father said, 'Listen, religion is good, and it's good if you observe religion, but that's not the only thing you should strive for. You can be a good person without religion, and there are people who are religious who are bad people. So, you need to be a good person first and foremost, and then accept religion or not. It's your decision.' Religion was never forced on us, never shoved down our throats. Another time, my sister and I, when she was in seventh grade and I was in sixth, were telling our dad [about] this guy in school named Ethan and he's Jewish. My dad asked us what he was like. My sister and I, being goofy and silly, both said, 'He's ugly.' We thought it was hilarious, we said it at the same time. But then we got lectured by my father, let me tell you! He said, 'That's unacceptable, you can't do that, you don't judge somebody by their religion, there are a lot of good Jewish people. Our problem is not with Jewish people; it's with the Israeli government—the policies. Never judge anybody based on their background.'

Out of place within the Islamizing spaces of the family and wider immigrant community, Mahmoud attempted to mirror his father's values of acceptance but did so from the contrasting stance of someone who "didn't care for religion," personally. Like his father he sought to respect the choices of others. In doing so, he articulated a type of soft secularism that bridged the religious and the secular, or at least allowed them to coexist within the community that his professional peers constituted. His father, especially after his turn toward a heightened piety during the 1990s, likely would not have spoken of his values as "secular." Mahmoud, however, had clearly adapted them to a secular sensibility that above all else privileged individual autonomy in matters of belief and practice, religious and political.

As with Manal, Mahmoud accommodated the religious shift: it was a fact he accepted. But, unlike Manal, he defied its institutional gravity by joining and creating alternative Arab American spaces that transcended the nationalist and religious particularisms of the Palestinian immigrant milieu. This transcendence did not necessarily mean disengagement from Palestine advocacy. The Arab American context, as his work with the ADC demonstrated, retained a central concern for Palestine. What Mahmoud transcended was the specifically Palestinian political and communal space. He was not nostalgic, as Manal and Khairy Abudayyeh were, for the secular nationalist ethos that once prevailed. Its factionalism had alienated him from the start.

Hatem Abudayyeh

My final profile of the generation of 1987–2001 features Hatem Abudayyeh, Executive Director of the AAAN and son of Khairy Abudayyeh.[18] Abudayyeh has dedicated his entire working life to Palestinian community empowerment and Palestinian advocacy within the secular nationalist structures that his father helped to create. His path thus contrasts sharply with Mahmoud's transcendence of the Palestinian political space and with Manal's and even his father's sense of living in the aftermath of secularism's marginalization.

In our conversations, Abudayyeh vigorously denied that the Islamic religious shift had made secularism irrelevant. The religious shift did not signal a fundamental change. The conditions of Palestinian life, in his view, remained inexorably secular. The central matter of Palestinian liberation was still unresolved. Moreover, the social and political challenges that the immigrant community faced in Chicago required approaches and resources the mosques simply could not provide. Secular organizations devoted to political advocacy and community support were therefore indispensable.

Abudayyeh has been the AAAN executive director since 2002. During this time, he has overseen significant expansion of AAAN's social programs. The organization provides translation and transportation services as well as referrals for legal, housing, counseling, childcare, and domestic violence assistance. It has developed a range of youth and women's programs. It also provides English as a Second Language classes. In addition to service provision, the AAAN has engaged in public advocacy to counter anti-Arab racism and discriminatory policies. In doing so, it has forged strategic alliances with other immigrant communities and immigrant rights organizations. These alliances have proved crucial to supporting the public positions that AAAN has taken, for example, against US government actions such as the Trump Administration's "Muslim Travel Ban" in 2017.[19] Individual AAAN personnel, including Abudayyeh, have also helped lead protests against Israel's actions in the West Bank and Gaza Strip as well as against

US Department of Justice investigations targeting community leaders since the September 11 attacks. These activities have occurred through separate coalitions, not necessarily as AAAN initiatives.[20]

Abudayyeh described his individual activism and his work at the AAAN as stemming from the tradition of Arab nationalism that inspired his father's generation. He spoke with great pride of this political inheritance: "Syrian Ba'athists, Iraqi Ba'athists, the Arab National Movement, the Nasserites, all of those different trends of Arab nationalism in general, that's the political background my parents came from. And, that, by osmosis, is the political background that I learned."

The osmosis metaphor was apt. It connoted immersion and absorption within a larger political culture that preserved, reinforced, and instilled the traditions of secularism intergenerationally. Abudayyeh described this culture, which pervaded the ACC, the AAAN's organizational predecessor, as integrating Arabs of diverse backgrounds who shared a commitment "not only to Arab nationalism but to internationalism." This international focus led the *markaz* founders to "support [. . .] other national liberation struggles—it's why our organization today has great relations with the Puerto Ricans in Humboldt Park, with the Mexican nationalists and Chicano nationalists in Pilsen and Little Village, with the African American communities [. . .]. It's because of the political perspective these people brought from the Arab world." Americans, he said, did not understand this fact. They viewed Arab nationalism through the lens of the Iraq War and the corresponding media discourse that portrayed the late Saddam Hussein and Ba'athism as totalitarian and repressive. They did not know "about the different Arab nationalist parties, how some of them built the first leftist organizations and instituted very progressive policies in their countries." Abudayyeh expressed pride in this history: "I grew up in a progressive home and community. The issues of women's rights and class contradictions were at the forefront of everything I understood about my struggle and the struggle of other peoples."

Ironically, Abudayyeh's transformation into a community organizer and ultimately the AAAN director would not begin in the Palestine activist community in Chicago but at the University of California-Los Angeles (UCLA), where he completed his bachelor's degree. The first Gulf War (1990–91) erupted during this time. Anti-war protest gripped the UCLA campus. Abudayyeh became involved with the students organizing these protests. The organizers forced him to confront inconsistencies between his professed beliefs and actual behavior. "I had the tendency to talk a lot [at rallies]," he said, "because I read the stuff [radical political theory], I understood the stuff, but I wasn't really an activist or an organizer." He recalled one female student, in particular, who challenged him: "She told me: 'Confronting these rich students and their privilege is absolutely correct, but, you know, you don't do any work, you're not an organizer, not an activist, you're not involved in any activism work!' [. . .]. For her, it was all rhetoric and it didn't mean shit!" Challenged in this way to enact his principles, Abudayyeh decided to abandon his medical school plans and instead return to Chicago to "make a difference in the community."

The establishment of the AAAN in that same moment provided Abudayyeh with an opportunity to shift into community organizing. After a brief stint coaching athletics in a local high school, he applied for a position as a coordinator of the youth program at the new organization. "I called Dima [pseudonym] out of the blue," Abudayyeh recounted, "and asked if there was anything available." Dima, a close family friend, had worked with Abudayyeh's mother to lead the Union of Palestinian Women Associations. She encouraged Abudayyeh to apply for the coordinator position. The organization soon offered him the job.

In taking a staff position at the AAAN, Abudayyeh completed his transition to the vocation and identity of an activist. In doing so, he continued the commitments his parents embodied, embracing a politics of Palestinian liberation and Arab community empowerment. He did so, however, at the exact time the secularist milieu had begun to collapse despite the AAAN's debut. Like other *markaz/* AAAN activists, he pointed to Oslo's failures, as well as to the collapse of the Soviet Union and the transition to a unipolar world dominated by a single United States superpower allied with Israel, as reasons for the loss of secular influence. He also stressed the failures of secularists to offer viable and attractive alternatives in the suburbs. This failure, however, did not mean that there was no longer a place for secular community organizations. "Ninety percent of our social services clients come from the southwest suburbs," he observed, "so those issues of economic sustainability for families and the community are still there even though those folks seem to be upwardly mobile." Moreover, some Palestinians continued to live in the Southwest Side neighborhoods. "I would say if you look at the economic levels," he commented, "it's not a whole lot different. A large percentage [is] still under the poverty line in the suburbs just like in Chicago Lawn." The claim, then, that the base had become wealthy and did not need the services that the AAAN offered was only partly accurate.

Abudayyeh admitted, nevertheless, that "we have to move to the suburbs; when it comes down to it, we have to." The organization's identity as an "urban organization" committed to "progressive change" in alliance with other oppressed minority communities, especially "the black and Latino communities," however, made it difficult for its members to imagine a move. "It's the core of our identity," he said, "something we have worked hard at, these alliances, ever since my father's time, and it's been really hard for some of us to understand that moving to the suburbs, where our base is located, is the correct path."

But, if the AAAN did move, it would recover its relevance, Abudayyeh asserted. The premises would be "jam-packed, alive from 8:00 a.m. till 10:00 p.m. like the *markaz* used to be in the '70s and '80s." This would happen because few other groups offered programming focused on the community's most pressing needs:

> I think people in the southwest suburbs, families, want the type of youth programming that we provide. We offer a safe social and political space for young men and young women to come together in programming, respectful programming, respecting class differences, respecting gender differences, understanding systems of oppression, discussing and challenging systems of oppression. I don't think that every single family in Bridgeview wants to send their children to the mosque for their youth development. Many would prefer the programming we offer here. We discuss Palestine and the Arab world but also the taboo issues: violence in the home, double standards, and patriarchy, all of those things. I don't think anybody's talking about patriarchy in the Islamic institutions in the southwest suburbs. The Mosque Foundation and other Islamic centers seem like they're the main institutions because there are no attractive secular organizations nearby. If I want my kid to learn Arabic, he's going to have to go to an Islamic school. There is no Arabic language instruction in Chicago's public schools or in the suburban public schools, even those with huge Arab populations.[21] I know some parents who say, 'Listen, I want my kid to learn Arabic but not just in the context of Qur'an memorization.' That stuff might not be part of my political or even my cultural background, you know, this, faith-based political Islamic stuff; but where else am I supposed to go?

The appearance of an Islamic turn within the community was therefore deceptive, according to Abudayyeh. The community's needs were still secular in character. Those needs stemmed from, among other things, the persisting challenges of poverty, domestic abuse, and political repression of Arabs and Muslims, generally. The "Islamic turn," for Abudayyeh, reflected an absence of secular organizations capable of answering to non-"faith-based" needs rather than a substantial change in the value orientations of the community.[22] Secularism remained relevant even if secularist structures had weakened or were missing in the spaces in which Palestinians now lived.

Still, for many young AAAN program participants and staff, Islam was a manifest identity orientation. These individuals wore headscarves or beards and prayed in the corners of the AAAN's premises. During Ramadan, as I noticed on one occasion, their computers were set to the times that sounded the *adhan*—the call to prayer—for the breaking of the fast. Whatever else it might have meant, seeing oneself as Palestinian now intertwined with the embrace of an Islamic piety that typified the religiously transformed ethos of the suburban enclave.

Abudayyeh implicitly acknowledged this fact. He accommodated the piety of the younger activists in the AAAN workspace, whereas twenty-five years earlier *markaz* leaders had resisted public expressions of religiosity.[23] He also partnered with the mosques and with groups like American Muslims for Palestine to solicit support for AAAN programs and for social justice campaigns and protest actions: he simply could not ignore the Islamic religious leadership, which could mobilize thousands of constituents, as coalition partners. At the same time, Abudayyeh insisted correctly on the inescapable priority of the secular. The Islamic turn had not cancelled or overcome the fundamental struggle for Palestinian liberation and community empowerment. In Abudayyeh's view, secularism's continuing relevance and the possibility of its renewal remained latent within this ineluctable reality.

A SECULAR AFTERWORD

On May 15, 2014, the Students for Justice in Palestine (SJP) chapter at the University of Chicago commemorated the *Nakba* ("the Catastrophe"), the Palestinian Arabic term for the forced displacement of nearly three-quarters of a million Palestinians in 1948. The SJP remembrance featured photographs and brief speeches and a buffet of hummus, falafel, and shawarma. The main event was an impassioned performance by Remi Kanazi, a young Palestinian spoken word artist from Brooklyn.

Of Christian background, Kanazi, in his poetry, excoriates sectarianism. The poem "Religious Harmony," for example, which Kanazi performed, begins with an indignant oath in which the speaker declares, "If I hear one more person ask my religion, [thinking it] would shape and define my worldview," then "I'm gonna flood his people, kill his firstborn [. . .]" (Kanazi 2011, 27). The poem proceeds to scorn Zionist claims that Muslims persecuted Jews and Christians in Palestine before 1948. Zionist militias, the poem says, killed and dispossessed Palestinian Muslims and Christians alike. The next stanzas deride Republicans and "liberal secularists" alike for stoking fears about Islam while ignoring poverty and racism in the United States.[24] It ends with the narrator declaring that even though he was raised a Christian he cannot see why that should matter in a world in which one also hears, while walking in Brooklyn to the subway, the call to prayer on Fridays. The speaker in the poem proclaims to never have known "religion by name" in such a world but instead holds above all else to a "faith in my people" (Kanazi 2011, 28). Throughout Kanazi's performance, the audience, including the SJP chapter president, a young woman who grew up in Chicago's suburban Palestinian enclave, attended the Islamic schools next to the Mosque Foundation, and wore a hijab scarf, snapped their fingers in appreciation. As he concluded, they applauded enthusiastically.

Kanazi's performance at the SJP event underscores the core assertion of this chapter: that despite its weakening, secularism nonetheless persists. The weakening is certainly evident. With the notable exception of the AAAN, the institutional structures of the secular nationalist milieu in Chicago have atrophied or disappeared entirely since the 1990s. This phenomenon has occurred alongside the withering of the PLO and the imploding of the diaspora as an organized political force generally (Frisch 2012). At the same time, however, secularism has not entirely disappeared. As Manal and Hatem Abudayyeh show, the institutions and traditions that the cohort of 1948–67 established reproduced secularist orientations within the generation of 1987–2001. Manal's narrative demonstrated this fact: organizations like the General Union of Palestinian Students as well as the Arab Community Center and Union of Palestinian Women Associations integrated her into the secularist milieu, and in the process reinforced a secularist orientation within her. Abudayyeh's narrative revealed additional elements of this process: crises like the first Gulf War and the political formations that mobilized a wider US antiwar response proved critical as catalysts for the reappropriation and reproduction of the progressive and secular Arab nationalism that he had absorbed in his family. A wider US institutional context was also crucial for trajectories leading to a secular transcendence beyond the immigrant enclave and its sectarian tensions, religious and political. Mahmoud, who had assimilated through participation in the American-Arab Anti-Discrimination Committee into a wider Arab American activist and US political culture, exemplified this process.

Secularism persisted, as well, as the "background," or condition of possibility, of the religious shift itself. The next two chapters—which show how the religious milieu has constructed itself in tension with secularism—demonstrate this fact. At the same time, the religious turn has generated new hybrid forms of "syncretic secularity." These forms are reactions to Islamization, in particular (see chapters 5 and 6). In each of these respects—in the continuity of its traditions and structures, in the role it plays as the foil of the religious turn, and in the ironic production of new forms of secularity through the disenchantment that the religious shift provokes—secularism has retained its relevancy and force.

3

The Religious Turn

American Muslims for Palestine

May 17, 2014 dawned crisp and bright as I drove west on East 87th Street toward Bridgeview, a near southwestern suburb. American Muslims for Palestine (AMP) was staging its Nakba Day commemoration in the Aqsa School parking lot across from the Mosque Foundation. Every year, Palestinians honor this day to mark their dispossession in 1948. In Palestine, they fly black flags and recount the events of that formative "catastrophe" (the literal meaning of "*nakba*") through commemorative displays, gatherings, and speeches.

In the United States, activist groups use Nakba Day to raise awareness about the Palestinian situation and cause. Two days prior to the AMP event, for example, Students for Justice in Palestine chapters held remembrances on university campuses across Chicago featuring historical photographs of the eras of 1948 and 1967 and also a large replica of the wall that Israel had built in the West Bank and around Jerusalem. Members passed out flyers advocating the Boycott, Divestment, and Sanctions campaign and talked with fellow students about Israeli repressive measures in the Occupied Territories. AMP's commemoration featured a comparable photographic display as well as a similar wall replica.[1] There were also speeches by the imam of the Mosque Foundation, who invoked the Prophet Muhammad's *isra'* (journey from Mecca to Jerusalem on the back of the winged steed Buraq) and his *mi'raj* (ascent from the Haram al-Sharif platform through the heavens to the foot of God's throne). With the mosque's dome and minaret as a backdrop, the link between Islam and the Nakba in AMP's commemoration was hard to miss. To remember "the catastrophe" at this particular event was simultaneously to assert the centrality of Islam to the Palestinian territorial claim, narrative of dispossession, and demand to return.

Secularists, as seen in the previous chapter, claim that the religious turn in the suburban Palestinian enclave is superficial. The core national problems—

dispossession, occupation, and the necessity of liberation—inescapably define the Palestinian condition. Putatively religious groups like AMP, as the argument goes, respond to this condition: behind the Islamic construal is the secular predicament of a nation in exile in search of a free and independent existence within a territorially bounded state in its ancestral homeland. The seeming turn to religion signals disillusionment with the historical secular national liberation movement: Palestinians are searching for alternative solutions to their collective predicament and Islamic groups have stepped forward to offer them. In Chicago, moreover, the failure of the secular community centers to relocate to the suburbs has created a gap in Palestinian organizing that AMP and the mosques have filled. Islam has become influential, secularists say, not because of Islam's predominance in Palestinian society but rather because of secularism's institutional absence. Secularists also point to the anti-Muslim backlash that has frequently erupted in American society, for example, after the bombing of the Alfred P. Murrah Federal Building in Oklahoma City on April 19, 1995 or following the September 11 attacks. The apparent Islamic turn, in addition to indicating disillusionment and secular absence, is a collective reaction, they claim, to the vilification of Islam and not an indication of a thoroughgoing restructuring of identity per se.

Taken together, these arguments, aside from the analytical validity they might have, minimize the extent to which religious, specifically Islamic, revitalization has transformed how individuals understand themselves as Palestinian. In doing so, they implicitly reinforce secularism as a normative condition and value of collective Palestinian life and, correspondingly, construe religion as a type of false consciousness: that is, the turn to Islam is not really about religion but rather about something else. A religious shift, however, has undeniably occurred. And it has contoured Palestinian identities in important ways in both Palestine and the diaspora. This shift certainly responds to the national predicament and to secularism and its vicissitudes. But to claim that it is merely an effect of secularism's absence or failure or of the seemingly secular conditions of Palestinian life or of anti-Muslim sentiment in the wider US society is to miss its positive, constructive character. As the next two chapters will show, the religious shift constitutes a distinct and deliberate standpoint grounded deeply in narratives and practices that relate the Palestinian situation to divine imperatives and promises.

At the center of that standpoint is the salvific drama in which God confers restitution on those who hold fast in faith and suffering (the believers) and chastisement on those who refuse the divine commandments and oppress the innocent (the unbelievers). In the Palestinian context, holding fast to faith entails the selfsacrificial, divinely mandated, and just struggle to redeem the Holy Land, which God, in Islamic perspective, has granted to those who bear witness to his exclusivity and to the fact that Muhammad is his final messenger. This perspective appears within the ideological formulations of the Muslim Brotherhood and its Palestinian offshoot, Hamas (Nüsse 1998). A Christian variation of this standpoint—as articulated, for example, in the writings of Palestinian liberation theologians—draws on prophetic discourse in the Bible to cast the national struggle as enactment of the divine commandment to free the oppressed and establish "justice and only justice." Only through an end to the occupation, restitution of the dispossessed, and creation of equality for all can there be "a new heaven and a new earth"—a new peace among peoples—in the Holy Land (Ateek 1989; Ateek, Ellis, and Ruether 1992). Understanding how standpoints like these have textured Palestinian identities, especially during and after the 1990s, requires close attention to the religious discourses, practices, and institutions of Palestinian communities.

This chapter, the first of two detailing the religious shift in Palestinian Chicago, undertakes this task through an in-depth focus on AMP. Established in 2006 during "Operation Summer Rains," Israel's euphemistic code name for its bombardment of the Gaza Strip that year, AMP has become one of the most prominent groups advocating for the Palestinian cause in the United States. Significantly, it goes out of its way to emphasize its American identity. Its Statement of Principles says that AMP "is an American organization founded by Americans" for the purpose of "educat[ing] the American public and media about issues related to Palestine."[2] The statement further insists:

> We are a strictly an American [sic] organization working for Americans in America. We are donor-funded. All of our fundraising is conducted within the United States; all of our funds and work is [sic] kept within the US. We are an independent, American organization and not affiliated with any foreign entities or organizations.

The repetition of the descriptor "American" is noteworthy in two respects. First, it aims to deflect questions about ties to proscribed Islamic political movements and about reliance on foreign funding sources and foreign government control. After the September 11 attacks, US government agencies targeted Muslim organizations, freezing the assets of large charities like the Holy Land Foundation for Relief and Development, whose leaders were convicted of providing material support to designated terrorist organizations, principally Hamas.[3] Well aware of this past and its continuing relevance for any Muslim organization, AMP stresses its specifically American identity, mission, and funding streams.

The second main significance is the consequent cultural positioning of Muslims and Palestinians as Americans above all else. In this positioning, AMP fuses these three terms, "American," "Muslim," and "Palestine," within a comprehensible American identity idiom that hyphenates immigrant belonging (for example, as Muslim American, Iranian American, Arab American, Jewish American, Mexican American, German American, Irish American, African American, and so on). In doing so, it performs a type of assimilation that nevertheless preserves critical identity distinctions, for example, from "white" or "Christian."

The second term in the organization's name, "Muslims," establishes these distinctions with the majority culture. The choice of term imposes a second important difference, however: the stress is on "American Muslims" and not "Palestinians" or "Palestinian Americans" or even "Arab Americans." The phrasing, in other words, defines the unit of solidarity in sectarian-religious rather than ethnic-national terms. This shift mirrors the way American Jewish organizations that focus on Israel, among other concerns, project identity (Jewish Voice for Peace, J Street, the American Jewish Congress, the American Jewish Committee, the Jewish Federations of North America, etc.). It also reflects the transformation of "Muslim" into a religious transethnic identity inclusive of the wide range of groups comprising Muslim communities in the US (African Americans, whites, immigrants of varying national origin, Latinx, and so on). "Jewish" functions in a similar manner as a category that incorporates an equally diverse range of backgrounds (European, Iraqi, Yemeni, Moroccan, Iranian, Ethiopian, South Asian, etc.). Strategically, the choice to frame solidarity in religious-sectarian terms allows AMP to expand the Palestine advocacy community beyond the particular Palestinian and Arab context. This recontextualization is not just strategic, however: it entails a shift in subjectivity, too. By centering "Muslim," AMP changes the discursive frame from a nationalist to a religious-nationalist emphasis. This alteration simultaneously transforms Palestinian and American Muslim self-understanding by making the two identities central to one another.

AMP counts eight chapters in New Jersey, California (Bay Area and Southern California), Michigan, Missouri, Chicago, Detroit, New York, and Wisconsin. The chapters do not maintain a formal membership base. Its organizational model is that of a nonprofit advocacy group that maintains a paid staff and relies on donations and volunteer support. Headquartered nationally in the Chicago suburb of Palos Hills, it also has an office in Washington, DC, to facilitate Congressional lobbying. Its activities include the production of carefully researched and documented publications on the Palestinian issue, media outreach, advocacy training, community education, and participation in public protests.

Given its local and national prominence, AMP affords a particularly useful and important perspective on the religious turn in Palestinian Chicago. In this chapter, I provide a close look at two events: AMP's sixth annual conference in 2013 and its Nakba Day commemoration in 2014.[4] These events illustrate how AMP fuses the identities of "Muslim" and "Palestinian." They also reveal important tensions that persist within the fusion. My analysis is primarily an outsider one. Unlike the other chapters, this one does not draw extensively on interview data but relies, instead, on my direct observations as recorded in my notes. The perspective inevitably skews, therefore, toward my subjective experience and interpretation of these events. The voices that speak directly in the next chapter help, however, to balance and expand the perspective I present here. The two chapters, therefore, should be read together. The questions and insights that arise within them, moreover, carry forward into chapters 5 and 6.

THE 6ᵀᴴ ANNUAL CONFERENCE FOR PALESTINE IN THE US (NOVEMBER 28–30, 2013)

"A Blessed Land, A Noble Cause"

AMP holds a conference every year during the Thanksgiving holiday that draws thousands of participants from Chicago and across the country. AMP leaders say they choose this day to take advantage of cheap hotel rates, but the scheduling choice also implicitly resists affirming the settler colonial Christian past. AMP thereby signals that Muslims active on Palestine refuse assimilation of the US cultural mythos and rites that resonate with the form of domination they resist in Palestine. Not everyone necessarily agrees with ignoring Thanksgiving, however. At its 6ᵗʰ Annual Conference for Palestine in 2013, attendees in an open forum questioned the timing, asserting that many community members observe the holiday and therefore organizers should have chosen a different date. In this way, AMP's boundary-marking encounters counterconceptions of the diaspora and its relationship to US society and culture. Such contestation suggests a plurality within the community that has already become apparent in the previous chapter on secularism and secularists and will continue to emerge in the chapters ahead.

The theme of the 2013 conference, held at the Crowne Plaza Hotel near Chicago's O'Hare Airport, was "A Blessed Land A Noble Cause [sic]." The publicity included, in Arabic, the Qur'anic gloss "*al-ladhi barakna hawlahu.*" This phrase, which translates as "the surroundings of which We have blessed," comes from the Qur'anic passages traditionally considered as describing Muhammad's *isra' wa al-mi'raj*, his nocturnal flight from Mecca to Jerusalem and his subsequent heavenly ascension from the Haram platform (Qur'an 17:1). The surroundings that God blesses refer to an area extending around al-Aqsa Mosque. Islamic religious scholars have debated the spatial extent and the theopolitical implications of the blessing. But the fact of the Qur'anic reference and the resulting status of Jerusalem as Islam's third-holiest site, after Mecca and Medina in present-day Saudi Arabia, have become central to Islamist discourse in the Occupied Territories and abroad.

The image on the conference logo and poster, which appeared also on the conference badges, showed the Old City in the middle distance with the Qubbat al-Sakhra, the Dome of the Rock, rising above it in the center.[5] At the top of the poster was the AMP logo and a heading stating "The Conference for Palestine in the US: A Blessed Land A Noble Cause [sic]." Beneath this banner was the Qur'anic slogan referring to how God had blessed the area around al-Aqsa. These words were superimposed over a map of the Middle East. The map floated faintly in the background sky above the barbed wire and dome. Iraq and Syria, labeled in English, appeared centrally. Palestine, too, appeared, in bold capitalization. Israel registered in its utter absence of mention even though the boundaries marking the West Bank and Gaza Strip in relation to the area in which Israel proclaimed its sovereignty following the 1948 war were nevertheless visible in the map.[6]

This same imagery provided the backdrop for the stage in the main plenary hall. In the stage backdrop, the golden dome predominated, deemphasizing and excluding non-Muslim (Christian and Jewish) sacred landmarks.[7] The only reference to Jewish presence in the conference imagery occurred implicitly, for example, in the foregrounded loops of barbed wire that framed the Dome of the Rock. These unmistakably evoked Israel's domination of the city and its use of walls and fences to exclude Palestinians, specifically Muslim Palestinians. The barbed barrier marred the image of the Old City and the Dome, although olive trees still appeared within the compound. The greenery suggested that the signs of the divine blessing (the *baraka* said to pervade and surround the Holy City)—which, according to the *tafsir* literature (scholarly Muslim commentary on the Qur'an), consist of the flourishing of flora and fauna—persisted even as Islam's enemies had disfigured the land.[8]

"Give Me a Break for [sic] Your Hypocrisy, Dear Brothers and Sisters"

The gesture toward Iraq and Syria in the map background of the poster and badge image hinted at the reasons for emphasizing Jerusalem and the divinely blessed land surrounding it as the conference theme. In the bulletin's welcome note, the organizers made these reasons explicit:

> [P]alestine does not exist in a vacuum. What happens in Syria, Egypt and elsewhere in the region also has an impact on the future of the Palestinian people. With the tragedies occurring in Syria and unrest in Lebanon and Israel's continual grinding military occupation of Palestine, it is important to remind ourselves that this is the Holy Land. This is the land, [sic] which Allah swt [*subhanahu wa ta'ala*, "Glorious Is He and Most High"] has blessed.

The references to the turmoil in Syria, Egypt, and Lebanon and its effects on Palestine evoked the Arab Spring uprisings and the profound political changes they had produced. The conference program note explicitly underscored the allusion, asking, "How do we move forward? How do we relate our work for Palestine to the struggles for freedom and democracy throughout the Middle East?" After brutally suppressing massive nonviolent demonstrations demanding democratic reform in 2011, the Syrian regime had become mired in a devastating armed conflict in different regions of the country. In 2012 and 2013, the al-Qaeda-linked Jabhat al-Nusra, which had drawn in foreign fighters and was known to receive money from Qatari sources, carried out a series of devastating attacks targeting Alawite, Christian, and Shi'a communities.[9] These attacks deepened sectarian divisions in Syria and increasingly mired the Lebanese Hezbollah movement, a client of Syria and Iran, in the fighting. The violence extended into Lebanon itself. In August

2013, for example, bomb attacks targeted two Sunni mosques in Tripoli (Saad and Hubbard 2013). Thousands of Syrian refugees also had crossed into Lebanon.

Egypt, too, had experienced a mass uprising that forced President Hosni Mubarak, in power since 1981, to step down. Unprecedented elections brought the Muslim Brotherhood candidate, Mohamed Morsi, to the presidency in June 2012. Thirteen months later, the military, riding a wave of protests opposing Morsi's declaration of emergency powers, deposed the newly elected president, massacred more than eight hundred of his supporters in Rabaa Square, and installed Field Marshal 'Abd al-Fattah al-Sisi in his place (Human Rights Watch 2014).

Locally, in Chicago, these cataclysmic events generated a number of fissures. Syrians, Lebanese, and Egyptians were influential in the leadership of the Mosque Foundation, the largest predominantly Palestinian mosque in the southwest suburbs. The Mosque Foundation provided substantial support for AMP, hosting annual Ramadan fundraisers for the organization and providing space for events. Just two months before AMP's 2013 conference, the head imam of the Mosque Foundation publicly called upon the Obama administration to use military force against Syrian regime targets in response to a chemical weapons attack in the Damascus suburbs.[10] The demand reflected the sympathy of the Mosque Foundation's leadership for the victims of Syria's civil war and for Syrian opposition movements, such as the Muslim Brotherhood, which the Assad regime had brutally targeted. This endorsement of US bombing, however, did not receive universal support in the wider community. The head of another, smaller, predominantly Palestinian mosque, whose leadership sympathized with the type of revolutionary Islamic anti-imperialism that the Lebanese Shi'i Hezbollah movement, an ally of the Assad regime, had pioneered, issued an opposing statement that declared any such intervention an attack on Muslims and Islam. God prohibited Muslims from killing one another, he said. Calling for an attack against Syria was tantamount to the unpardonable sin of *fitna* (destroying Muslim unity through violence against fellow Muslims).[11] The target of these remarks—the Mosque Foundation—was unmistakable.

Tension would again break out in public a year later in October 2014. In this instance, AMP found itself at odds with Syrian Muslim leadership in the city. The instigating event in this case was the forcible entry by religious Jewish settlers onto the Haram al-Sharif compound to commemorate Sukkot (Chag HaAsif, the biblical Festival of Tabernacles). This provocative act, from the Palestinian standpoint, violated the status quo concerning the Haram. In an email communication, AMP declared "Aqsa in danger" and demanded the Obama administration censure the State of Israel for allowing the aggressive intrusion to take place. A prominent Syrian-American activist, Dr. Zaher Sahloul—past president and board chairman of the Mosque Foundation; former board member and chairman of the Council of Islamic Organizations of Greater Chicago; and president of the Syrian American Medical Society (SAMS)—stated in a Facebook post shared publicly on October

14, 2014, that al-Aqsa was indeed in danger and that Muslims must defend it. But, then, in the same statement, he asserted that over the course of three and a half years not one large Muslim demonstration had occurred in Chicago to protest, in his words, "the criminal regime's" destruction of Syrian lives and holy places. "We condemn Israel!" he wrote. "[But] give me a break for [sic] your hypocrisy dear brothers and sisters."[12]

Two years later, in 2016, Syrian-Palestinian tension again burst into public, this time along lines extending beyond the Islamic context. Sahloul, now an immediate past president and senior advisor of SAMS, again took to social media—Twitter, this time—to accuse prominent Palestinian and Jewish Palestine solidarity activists of serving traitorously as a "fifth column who have been [sic] promoting war criminals, supporting the genocidal politics of Assad and Putin, promoting idiotic conspiracy arguments, disregarding the sacrifices of the Syrian people and probably getting paid by Russian and Assad PR firms. They are the equivalent of the propaganda machine of Hitler." In the same tweetstorm, Sahloul asked bitterly, "How can they claim that they care about Palestinian children in besieged Gaza while they ignore the suffering of Syrian children in besieged Aleppo?" The targets of this attack were Ali Abunimah, co-founder of *The Electronic Intifada,* and Max Blumenthal, a well-known Jewish American writer.[13] Both individuals were relentless critics of Israeli policies in the Occupied Territories. They also had taken uncompromising stands against purported Palestinian National Authority corruption, misrule, and connivance with Israel's occupation. Abunimah advocated a single democratic state of Israelis and Palestinians (Abunimah 2006). Blumenthal embraced a similar position, earning sharp rebuke from Jewish commentators who saw in his views a dangerous Jewish self-loathing abetting anti-Semitism.[14] Both activists also had expressed concern for the violence in Syria—Blumenthal explicitly denounced the Syrian regime—but had come to oppose US intervention.[15]

By 2016, the question of intervention in the Syrian civil war was dividing the Islamic, secular left, and Jewish anti-Zionist activist circles that had previously shared a common opposition to Israel's repression of the Palestinians.[16] On one side were individuals and groups categorically opposed to US military intervention. Drawing lessons from the United States's invasion and occupation of Iraq, they argued that US action could only result in even greater misery in Syria and in expansion and consolidation of US and Israeli hegemony in the region. Supporting intervention was backing Zionism and imperialism and consigning Syria to complete ruin. On the other side, those advocating intervention pointed to the Assad regime's indiscriminate violence against its own people, including deliberate bombing of civilians, rampant use of torture in its prisons, and use of chemical weapons. They called for international solidarity in support of the grassroots forces seeking to overthrow the regime and establish a new democratic order in the country. To oppose intervention was, in effect, to back Assad, sell out the opposition, and abet wholesale destruction of Syria and Syrian lives.

Sahloul's tweets reflected the increasing bitterness of the divide, as did Blumenthal's writings, to which Sahloul was responding. Blumenthal, in particular, had authored a damning Alternet exposé in 2016 that linked Sahloul, SAMS, and other anti-regime Syrian activist groups like the White Helmets to US government agencies; Turkish and Qatari intelligence services; Jewish organizations that supported Israel's hard line on the Palestinians and on Iran; and Syrian Islamist movements like the Muslim Brotherhood and al-Qaeda-linked groups (Dot-Pouillard 2012; Giovani 2018; Jay 2012; Blumenthal 2012, 2016, 2018). Blumenthal also asserted that SAMS was a key participant in the effort to pressure the Obama and Trump administrations into launching military reprisals against the Syrian regime. This campaign, he alleged, used sensationalist accounts of Syrian government atrocities and the supposed use of chemical weapons by the Syrian regime to create this pressure (Blumenthal 2016, 2018). To Sahloul, these accusations smacked of slander and of abject support for the murderous and criminal Syrian regime.

Abunimah's response to Sahloul's flurry of tweets was blistering. He stated that Sahloul's assertions were baseless and, tag teaming with Blumenthal, accused SAMS of collaborating with the "anti-Palestinian group [Jewish United Fund of Chicago]." Abunimah took aim, as well, at Sahloul's supporters, especially Ahmed Rehab, the Egyptian American Executive Director of the Chicago office of the Council on American-Islamic Relations (CAIR), an organization that benefited from the support of groups that Sahloul had headed at different points, including the Mosque Foundation. Abunimah was especially critical of Rehab for describing Blumenthal, a friend and collaborator of Abunimah, as a Nazi, which Rehab denied doing.[17]

This embittered breach cut especially close in Chicago. Abunimah, Sahloul, and Rehab lived and worked there. In response, a number of AMP representatives attempted to intervene in the dispute, calling on the belligerents to recognize the damage they were inflicting on Muslim and Arab unity.

Expanding "The Holy," Transcending the Schisms

The AMP conference in November 2013 endeavored early on to transcend these incipient tensions and return the focus to Palestine. It attempted both of these maneuvers through its call to remember, in the midst of the horrendous violence, that Palestine, Syria, Lebanon, and Jordan, as well as Iraq and Egypt—as indicated in the map image in AMP's conference publicity—constituted the very lands that God, in the Qur'an, had blessed and made holy to Muslims. The inclusion of these other countries beyond Palestine, an interpretive move that expanded the limits of the Holy Land well in excess of its traditional, historical, and religious boundaries, served the unifying purpose of the conference. By recalling the centrality of the Holy Land, and by seeing their respective countries included in this central focus, Arab Muslims, in particular, were to step back from the divisions that had sundered their solidarity in the United States and in the Middle East. The semiotics of the conference publicity achieved this refocusing by redirecting attention to Israel as the foremost threat. The barbed wire that cut off the Dome of the Rock and al-Aqsa—a reference to Israel's domination of these sacred Islamic sites—symbolized the repression of all believing Muslims in the region. The implication was hard to miss: to free Jerusalem, to return it to Muslim suzerainty, was to free Muslims throughout the Middle East. In this way, the symbolic logic of the conference publicity forcefully returned Palestine to the center of Muslim American concern even as it acknowledged the suffering in the surrounding countries in the region.

The compelling force of this symbolic move derived from a long history in which Jerusalem and the Holy Land had served as symbolic proxies for Arab and Muslim anti-colonial struggles.[18] During the 1920s and 1930s, for example, Grand Mufti of Jerusalem al-Hajj Amin al-Husayni (c. 1895–1974) made Jerusalem central to an appeal for global Islamic support for the Palestinian cause as part of the shared resistance to European imperialism. The crowning moment in this effort was the World Islamic Conference, which he convened at al-Aqsa Mosque in 1931. Islamic solidarity focusing on Palestine also inspired 'Izz al-Din al-Qassam (c. 1881–1935), a Syrian pan-Islamic preacher whose clandestine organizing of armed cells provided a precedent and network for the 1936–39 Arab Revolt against Zionist settlement and the British Mandate. Hasan al-Banna (1906–49), founder of the Muslim Brotherhood in 1928, also made Palestine a core theme in his public preaching. Hamas and the Islamic Jihad, which have long argued that the key to reestablishing a unified and free Muslim umma lies in the struggle to liberate Jerusalem and indeed the entirety of Palestine, appeal directly to the memory of al-Qassam and al-Banna (Kupferschmidt 1988; el-Awaisi 1998; Swedenburg 2003; Schleifer 1993; O. Khalidi 2009; Milton-Edwards and Farrell 2010; Euben and Zaman 2009).

The claim here, to be absolutely clear, is not that any sort of direct organizational or material link exists between AMP and Hamas or Islamic Jihad—I have no evidence of any such link and was not searching for it—but rather that AMP draws on a set of tropes that are common to Palestinian Islamism generally. In doing so, AMP does not simply reproduce these discursive figures but instead adapts them to the diaspora. In contrast to the Islamist movements in Palestine, for example, AMP does not directly invoke jihad discourse and does not explicitly refute the legitimacy of Israel through open references to Palestine as an Islamic patrimony or *waqf*.[19] Rather, it hews to the international consensus that has deemed Israel's occupation of the West Bank and Gaza Strip to be illegal. It adopts the language of international covenants and rights, a discourse that suppresses particularistic national and religious claims. It also refrains from advocating any specific end-of-conflict scenario, whether one state or two, and remains silent on whether or not the objective should be the creation of a *shari'a*-based state, the explicit longterm goal of Islamist movements like the Muslim Brotherhood and Hamas.[20]

Still, AMP's invocation of Qur'anic rhetoric and symbols resonates with Islamic conceptions of jihad and the "Holy Land." This complex discursive framing, explicit and implicit, elides non-Muslim territorial claims primarily through an implied reference to Palestine as an Islamic religious endowment (*waqf*). The endowment concept, elaborated within Islamic *fiqh* (jurisprudence), renders the Holy Land an inalienable Islamic trust bequeathed to Muslims in perpetuity. As recipients of this God-given trust, Muslims, especially those for whom Palestine is their national home, incur the responsibility of care and defense of the land, that is, of vigilance and struggle in the face of non-Muslim encroachment. The 2013 conference implied these themes—it did not state them explicitly—by linking the idea of Palestine and the Sham (Levant) as a blessed land to advocacy for Palestine as a "Noble Cause." This phrase, "Noble Cause," resonates with the Qur'anic conception of jihad as a struggle undertaken *fi sabil illah*, "in the cause [literally, path] of God." Such struggle encompasses a wide range of actions: verbal denunciation of oppression; steadfast persistence under conditions of suffering; nonviolent protest and advocacy; armed resistance; internal spiritual effort to overcome the ego so as to achieve unity with divine reality and purpose; and giving of time and money to causes of charity and justice (the spending of one's wealth in the cause of God).[21] AMP's discursive framing situates its advocacy within this spectrum of activities. In AMP's framing, the duty to struggle for the Holy Land through nonviolent public advocacy and protest actions expands to become incumbent upon all Muslims in the United States. American Muslims are to work together to free Palestine as a core concomitant of their submission to God.

Calling the Murabitun

The primary purpose of AMP's annual conference is to educate Muslims about their duties toward Palestine, stir a passionate reaction that can lead to mobilization, and channel action toward participation in AMP's organizational structures. The conference performs this work by instilling a sense of the special role of diaspora Muslims in the struggle for Palestine. It does so in several ways, including by warning against participation in interfaith activities that purposefully deemphasize or suppress the Palestine issue and by instructing attendees about the conflict and about their distinctive responsibilities.

This issue of interfaith forums that de-prioritize Palestine was a particular focus of one of the 2013 conference sessions. Just three months prior, the Shalom Hartman Institute had launched a major initiative to bring Muslim leaders to Israel.[22] The goal of this program was to expose these leaders to Judaism and Jewish life and to Israeli experiences and viewpoints. The AMP session focused on the motives of outreach efforts like this one. The convener pointed to statements by pro-Israel groups concerning the importance of interfaith work as a strategy to entangle US Muslim organizations into cooperative relations and thereby reduce or eliminate their potential to become critics of Israel. He lamented that Muslim leaders had participated in these activities without fully realizing the implications for solidarity with Palestinian Muslims.[23] Any interfaith undertaking, he argued, had to occur strictly on the basis of a prior agreement to oppose Israel's occupation. Palestine had to be prioritized. Collaboration without such shared understanding, especially with Jewish groups, could led to Zionist co-optation. Diaspora Muslims had to be on their guard.

Before the start of this session, two members of Neturei Karta, an anti-Zionist Jewish Orthodox movement, seated themselves in the front row. In the discussion that followed the presentation, these individuals stood up to denounce Israel and proclaim solidarity with Palestinians. Neturei Karta grounds its solidarity in an exclusivist theological agenda. The organization objects to Israel because its existence is the consequence of human initiative and not the result of the Messiah's coming. Jews true to God's commandments are to remain in the diaspora until the Messiah's arrival. Jews who support Israel are in active rebellion against God and therefore sinners. Essentially, Neturei Karta affirms the Jewish claim to territorial sovereignty in Eretz Israel but disputes the Zionist mode of implementing it. This affirmation implicitly contradicts Islamic claims to suzerainty in the Holy Land. The AMP–Neturei Karta convergence thus has less to do with a shared sense of injustice toward Palestinians than with having a shared enemy. Neturei Karta's orientation differs radically, it should be noted, from Jewish Voice for Peace (JVP), whose members also have attended AMP's conference. The anti-Zionist stance of JVP proceeds from an understanding of Judaism rooted in universal values of justice that find expression in support for human rights. JVP is deeply critical of Israel for its perceived failure to enact those principles. Unlike Neturei Karta, it acts in solidarity with Palestinians in response to injustice and the moral necessity to oppose it. On these grounds, JVP comes into alignment with AMP's stated moral and political positions.

The participation of JVP and Neturei Karta, notwithstanding the significant differences between them, produces a common, incidental effect that is useful to AMP: it inoculates the organization against charges of anti-Semitism. Jewish groups that support Israel have leveled such charges in an effort to delegitimize AMP's advocacy. AMP can point to the attendance of Jewish groups that oppose Zionism and Israeli policies as evidence that its activism is not racist toward Jews but rather is a principled stance, shared with Jews, against the repression of Palestinians. The participation of anti-Zionist Jewish groups also provides a model for AMP of proper interfaith solidarity. It poses this model against the cross-religious initiatives of other groups that intentionally deprioritize the Palestine question.

In addition to warning against interfaith alliances that de-emphasize Palestine, the 2013 conference also sought to imbue Palestinian Muslims, especially, with a sense of their Islamic duty to Jerusalem. One of the sessions that emphasized this theme focused on youth. Born in the United States, these youth were at risk of losing touch with the Palestinian cause and of assimilating into US society and culture. They also had to contend with anti-Muslim and anti-Arab racism. Impressing on them their Islamic duties to the homeland could perhaps stem the assimilation danger and reinforce a sense of religious and national self-worth. Young people also represented, if properly educated, potential future activists and supporters of AMP's mission.[24]

The special session for youth featured a young *shaykh* who spoke of the importance of Palestine in Islam. Adept at popular culture references—he compared, for example, Abu Jahl, one of the Prophet Muhammad's great nemeses, to President Snow in the book and film *The Hunger Games*—the *shaykh* emphasized the special status of Palestinian Muslims as the *murabitun*, those believing men, primarily (the term has a collective connotation but is in the masculine plural form) who are "tied" to or "garrisoned" within the land and tasked with remaining steadfast in its defense. He did so while also reminding the gathered youth that Palestine belonged to all Muslims, not just to Palestinians. He conveyed both messages by recounting the centrality of Palestine as the site of the second holiest mosque and as the land of a succession of prophets culminating with Muhammad. Being tied to ("stationed" within) the land (*murabitun*), the *shaykh* said, engendered a deep connection with the Prophet Muhammad. The link was not just to land and lineage and cultural background but the actual Islamic heritage that ties all Muslims, and especially Palestinians as guardians of the Holy Land, to the Prophet. The *shaykh* reinforced this point about the particularity of the Palestinian Islamic binding to the Holy Land by referring to the establishment of Muslim rule of Jerusalem under 'Umar Ibn al-Khattab in 637 CE and the restoration of Islamic control following Salah al-Din Ibn Ayyub's successful retaking of the city from the Franks in 1187.[25]

Beyond its affirmation of the unique Palestinian Muslim status, the *shaykh's* message, wittingly or not, carried a subtle, implicit critique of those Palestinians, especially in the diaspora, who neglected the duty of being garrisoned or tied. *Murabitun* status entailed physical presence—as posted, forward defenders—in the land. Implicitly, however, those who had immigrated to Chicago had relinquished this duty to remain in place. They could ameliorate this condition, presumably, if they dedicated themselves to advocacy, for example, through AMP.

The *shaykh's* remarks conveyed a second underlying message: men, primarily, properly retained the duty of "being tied." This message was the result of an elision. The shaykh did not discuss the *murabitat* (the feminine plural form of the term). In Palestine today, this second term now refers particularly to women who hold vigil through regular prayer and other activities in defense of al-Aqsa Mosque.[26] The *shaykh's* omission indicated a presumption that the status of being tied ("garrisoned") flowed from religious (prophetic) and political (caliphal) leadership—domains that have traditionally belonged to men and were originally integrated within the person and office of the Prophet Muhammad. The *murabitat*, however, demonstrated that women, too, were very much engaged in the political and religious work of "being tied" or "garrisoned." Their invisibility in the *shaykh's* remarks indicated—at least, within this particular space and moment—a persisting patriarchal ordering of political work that privileges men in the public sphere.

As its 2013 gathering illustrates, AMP's annual conferences create a narrative, symbolic, and performative context within which to articulate Palestinian diaspora identity through an Islamic nationalist idiom. The organization replicates and reinforces this articulation in other ways, too. A particularly important mode is public memorialization of key historical events of Palestinian national memory. AMP's commemoration of the Nakba in May 2014 sheds an especially clarifying light on how the organization appropriates the national past as part of its identity work in the Chicago and national diaspora.

AMERICAN MUSLIMS FOR PALESTINE'S NAKBA COMMEMORATION: PALESTINE THROUGH AN ISLAMIC LENS

Commemoration and Contestation

A commemoration is a summons to remember, indicate, and acknowledge through ceremony or observation. A large public commemoration "constitutes the event as an objective fact of the world [. . .] with a social significance and emotional implication of objectively large magnitude" (Frijda 1997, 111, quoted in Damico and Lybarger 2016, 15). The meaning and significance of a commemorative act are open to dispute and resistant to resolution, which are features of any public occurrence (Connerton 1989; Shotter 1997 [1990]; J. Hall 1992; Halbwachs 1992; Confino 1997; Kansteiner 2002; Frost and Laing 2013). The Nakba event that AMP held in May 2014 constituted a commemoration in this sense. As an act of commemoration, it unavoidably intervened within and generated a disputed space of memory. This occurred most obviously in relation to, and against, dominant Zionist and Israeli interpretations of the conflict with the Palestinians, but it also unfolded within Palestinian debates about the symbols and meanings of the national past. AMP melded religious and ostensibly secular political symbols and narratives. It did so in the context of a diaspora community that was and is negotiating its place within US society and culture and in relation to the fraught question of religion and nationalism in Palestine itself.

Nakba in the Suburbs

As I approached the Mosque Foundation and the Aqsa and Universal Schools on that bright May morning in the southwest suburb of Bridgeview, I noticed the parking lots were full. A city police officer pointed at me and then swept his arm to the left. I followed a line of cars south past the mosque. I then turned right, passing again in front of the mosque. I saw a Palestinian flag flapping from the balcony of a large Italianate-style villa. I turned left at the next corner and found parking on the street. A woman with three children had just pulled her large silver Nissan Murano to the curb in front of me. She was dressed in a pink hijab scarf and black 'abaya (formal/literary Arabic, 'aba'a; an ankle-length robe) and was wrangling a stroller out of the back of the vehicle as I angled into the parking spot behind her.

On foot now, I headed toward the mosque. I could see groups of people congregating in the parking areas. As I approached, the atmosphere of a very large, carnival-like family reunion came into focus. A man with a tall brass tea dispenser on his back was pouring out small cups of the sweet black liquid to families strolling about the grounds. The tea man was dressed in a red pantsuit with white gaiters and an embroidered red tarbush-style cap on his head. Wired to the top of his dispenser was a bouquet of red and white roses. Just beneath the roses at the top of the tea dispenser was a black and white *hatta*—a traditional nationalist symbol hearkening to the peasant past—tied around the three brass posts and extending upward from the main vat containing the liquid. The man had wound another *hatta* of the same color and pattern around his waist. Men, women, and children stopped him as he walked amidst the crowd. After accepting a dollar from them, he took a small white plastic cup from the stack sitting in a brass holder attached to his belt, bent at the waist, and poured the beverage.

The tea vendor hearkened to the traditional past, stirring nostalgia in older Palestinians and instilling in younger individuals a tangible sense of connection to the *bilad* ("back home"). Significantly, his outfit and every one of the signs appearing at the different venues and displays in the parking lot featured the same red and white color scheme. Red and white were the hues of the AMP logo, and they appeared in all of AMP's signage and in every one of its publications, print and electronic. The signs were lettered in red and black ink against a white background; the font sizes were uniform; and the AMP logo appeared beneath the signs and placards. This event, focusing on the Nakba and invoking longing for the lost peasant past, was also, in practice, a sophisticated strategy to market the AMP brand and organization as the primary institutional expression and framework for Palestinian identity and politics in the very center of the suburban diaspora community and also beyond it. AMP now claimed the symbols and mantle of the Palestinian national cause that once had been the sole possession of the secular nationalist movements.

Projecting the Nakba: Times Square

During the 2014 Nakba event, AMP's framing of Palestinian identity registered consistently across diverse platforms. The organization, as its name suggests, has sought to project a national presence through its various chapters in different states and through its Washington, DC office. The annual Nakba event provided an opportunity to coordinate cross-chapter initiatives and to project a unified presence. AMP's action in New York during the 2014 commemoration exemplified how this occurred. Real-time and follow-up communications connected the New York action to the commemorations occurring in other cities, including Chicago.

The New York chapter's commemoration on May 16 involved two elements: the projection of an image on a giant screen in Times Square and a silent vigil.[27] The image appeared with the accompanying text "Take a moment of silence for

Palestine." The image persisted for thirty minutes. It also appeared on posters at the simultaneously occurring silent rally in the square. The image, duplicated on screen and street, was then sent with two other photos in a subsequent email message from AMP to its subscribers.

The dominant feature in this multiply replicated image was a young woman's face. She appeared wearing a tight-fitting under-scarf in the traditional checkered black and white pattern of the *kufiya*. Over this scarf was a red hijab—again, the AMP attention to cross-platform branding was evident in the color scheme—which enveloped and framed her head, leaving only her face visible. Across her forehead a string of beads appeared, a gesture perhaps to the gold coins and beads that Bedouin and village women might have worn as signs of family wealth. A gag covered her mouth, a wide adhesive bearing the hastag "#NakbaMSP."[28] This took the viewer to a Twitter feed that on May 19, 2014, was "following" 1,990 accounts, had 503 "followers," and had made 315 tweets. One of the postings in this feed showed photographs of AMP events, including the Chicago event as well as the Times Square televised image. On the posters and on the screen image in Times Square, the AMP logo and the words "Commemorating 66 years of Al Nakba/ Take a Moment of Silence for Palestine/#NakbaMSP" filled the space to the right of the face. In small font beneath this text was an invitation to "post your MSP picture and join the cause." On the other side of the text, in the Times Square televised image, were thin, vertical swooshes of green, black, red, and white, the Palestinian national colors.

The following day, May 17, the AMP website posted an explanation of its Nakba events. The statement declared:

> The New Jersey chapter of the American Muslims for Palestine, supported by AMP-Bronx, took the standard for commemorating the Nakba to the stratosphere in New York City's Times Square with an electronic screen bearing the message: Al Nakba: A Moment of Silence for Palestine.
>
> The message was visible to New Yorkers for 30 minutes during the height of rush hour Friday night. More than 250 people from AMP-New Jersey, AMP-Bronx, Al Awda and other groups turned out to pass out AMP's Palestine 101 brochure and to hold a silent rally to commemorate 66 years of dispossession and occupation of the Palestinian people. The New Jersey chapter also placed a billboard with the same message and launched a successful Thunderclap social media campaign with the hashtag #NakbaMSP.
>
> 'All of our Nakba events are geared toward educating the public about Palestine and its rich cultural and historical heritage,' said AMP Chairman Dr. Hatem Bazian. 'What the New Jersey chapter accomplished was extraordinary. And AMP-Chicago's outdoor event not only educates but it helps our youth take pride in their Palestinian and Islamic heritage in the Holy Land.' AMP held events in New Jersey, New York, Chicago, Milwaukee and Minnesota. Another daylong event, which includes two panel discussions, a film screening and Palestine heritage celebration is slated for

May 24 at the Muslim Community Association in Santa Clara, Calif. The *Middle East Monitor*, a news outlet based in the Great Britain [sic] that covers Palestine globally, a Ramallah-based newspaper, *Al Hayat Al Jadeeda*, and other local news organizations covered AMP's events.

The projection of the AMP image in Times Square was a complex event with diverse audiences. A main audience, as the website posting indicated, was non-Muslim New Yorkers as well as tourists. For this audience, likely possessing little knowledge of the Palestinian situation, the image fused "Palestine," for which one was to pause in silence, with the image of the gagged, hijabbed woman. Palestine was a silenced female Muslim. Other possible conceptions of "Palestine" notably did not register. For example, Palestine has also been home, historically and currently, to Christian and Jewish communities, and secularists envision a multisectarian national society governed through secular democratic institutions. Although, as an organization, AMP acknowledges this diversity and remains non-committal on the form of governance that Palestinians should institute, none of this complexity surfaced in the Times Square image. Also, by presenting the hijab as taken-for-granted, normative practice, the image elided the fact that many Muslim women contested reformist understandings of sartorial orthopraxy.[29] They advanced alternative readings of the Qur'anic hijab passages, arguing that there was no direct requirement to wear a scarf. Moreover, some women rejected the scarf entirely as an expression of their critical stance toward religion. Palestine, Islam, and the hijab were thus not as straightforwardly intertwined, historically or in the present, as the Times Square image seemed to suggest.

A second main audience included AMP's own activists, the US Palestinian community that AMP claimed to represent, and Palestinians globally. To this audience, AMP communicated the success it felt it had achieved. The web posting bragged especially about the exploits of the Bronx chapter. Other chapters, too, received commendation, but the Times Square event was the real achievement because, like a graffiti artist tagging a major public site, AMP's guerrilla-like media action forced Palestine (figured as Muslim) into US public awareness. The organization likely had to pay a fee to project the image, but the fact that it even appeared in a society in which Palestine and Muslims were so deeply marginalized amazed. This was a victory, and AMP celebrated it, passing out congratulations to its partisans and urging donations—a "Donate" button appeared prominently next to the website statement—from supporters.

Displaying the Nakba: Bridgeview, Illinois

In Bridgeview, the AMP Nakba event, which the web posting also noted, took the form of a series of commemorative displays and a formal program. Structured as a series of tents, a symbolic evocation of the Red Cross shelters that Palestinian refugees were forced into in 1948, the displays, aimed entirely at the immigrant community, served a didactic purpose. In the diaspora, where assimilation and the passing of generations born in the United States threatened the continuity of memory, there was a felt need to educate the young, especially. The pedagogical practice that AMP enacted in its event revealed not only this primary emphasis on instilling the core narratives of unjust expulsion, exile, and ongoing suffering but also a specifically religious and nationalist rejection of *tatbiq* ("normalization") and of *taqsim* ("partition," aka the two-state solution).

Public remembrances of the Nakba encode a refusal to relinquish the lands lost in 1948. Indeed, they signify a demand to return. In Islamized contexts, Nakba commemorations connect this demand, typically cast in relation to nationalist claims and international human rights law, with the religious assertion that the usurped patrimony is God's land, which belongs properly under the suzerainty of those who have submitted to God and his messenger, the Prophet Muhammad. Those who have submitted possess a divine right to the land but also incur the duty of struggle to defend it. The appeal at the AMP event, then, was to Palestinians as Palestinians but also to Palestinians as Muslims.

Tent Displays

Except for the main event tent—which featured a large Palestinian flag lying across a blue and white striped top, ironically the colors of the Israeli flag—all of the other tents were white. The attempt to replicate and reference the tents that housed the refugees in large camps in the immediate aftermath of the war of 1948 was unmistakable. The tents also created a distinct contrast with the suburban surroundings, featuring multistory houses, expensive automobiles, and the recently renovated and expanded Mosque Foundation premises. Each white canopy featured small Palestinian flags stuck into the tops of the supporting poles. Inside, thin mattresses and sackcloth were spread on the gravel. Posters with the distinctive red and white AMP colors and logo featured images of Palestinians crowding the narrow alleys in the devastated Yarmouk Camp in Syria.[30] Other images showed the post-invasion destruction of Iraq. Additional posters featured maps of Palestine, pictures of Israeli helicopters and soldiers, and images of destroyed buildings.

Repeatedly, the Islamic framing of the Nakba confronted the onlooker in the tents. One tent featured a poster with an image of al-Aqsa and the appeal to "defend" the iconic mosque by "support[ing] AMP." Behind the tent that displayed this poster was the Aqsa School for Girls, and from another direction the domes and minaret of the Mosque Foundation became visible. The layering of these visual references was striking. The Aqsa School and the Mosque Foundation as built forms purposefully invoke the institutions of the Holy City, the center of the Palestinian cause and global Islamic attachment. To be focused on the Mosque Foundation in one's daily and weekly activities was also to be oriented toward al-Quds (Jerusalem)—as the name of the Aqsa School signaled. Events such as the Nakba commemoration, which took place in the Aqsa and Mosque Foundation parking lots, reinforced the association. The direct funding appeal—"Defend al-Aqsa, Support AMP"—followed seamlessly.

At the same time, however, the schools, mosque, and events such as the commemoration entailed a distinctly American ethos of voluntarism. The AMP's insistent money-raising pitch was evidence of this fact. The annual Ramadan fundraisers at the Mosque Foundation, featuring nightly auction-style pledge drives for the institution and for other charities and organizations the mosque sponsored or approved of, were another example. In the United States market economy, organizations devoted to one cause or another had to compete for the attention and purse strings of potential contributors. In emails, bulk mail, and social media campaigns they conveyed the latest atrocity, positioning the Donate Now button strategically within or beside the text and images conveying the "breaking news" that sought to enrage or elicit sympathy within the target audience. In its Nakba event signage, AMP appealed to the individual moral conscience—al-Aqsa in danger!—and, in the same moment, urged the viewer to join the cause, providing scannable codes on its posters for its Facebook and Twitter sites. In a capitalist society that transformed causes into commodities, al-Aqsa and Palestine had to be marketed. In this context, the degree of one's commitment, one's piety and patriotism, registered in the amounts donated. The success of organizations had also become publicly quantifiable in the number of retweets and site visits—thus the scannable codes—which in turn served as evidence of "influence" for prospective donors. In all of this, AMP differed little from any other US nonprofit organization, cause, or campaign seeking to build a donor base.

A second characteristic of American voluntarism is identification in hyphenated terms with various associations (religious, ethnic-national, political, charitable). At the Nakba event in Bridgeview, this hyphenation was on display through the well-established symbols and paraphernalia of Palestinian nationalism. These symbols carried over from the secularist milieu of the "revolution," which had become an object of memorialization. At a table in one of the tents at the Bridgeview Nakba event, an AMP volunteer sold posters and car pendants featuring Naji al-'Ali's "Handala" figure along with *hatta* (*kufiya*) scarves fringed with the Palestinian national colors and keychains attached to brass cutouts of the map of Mandate Palestine. Prayer beads in the national colors, which, as lettering on their plastic wrapping indicated, were made in China, also were available for purchase. One of the keychains featured the Dome of the Rock. A sign hanging from the table showed the Handala figure with the words, "Palestine, We Will Return," the ubiquitous AMP logo stenciled beside it. The revolution lived on here as postrevolutionary ornaments, some of them now Islamized, which the successful diaspora middle class could exhibit from rearview mirrors and around shoulders as fashion accessories. Through these manifestations, Palestinian suburbanites marked identities within the multicultural milieu of a major US city in which assertions of ethnic pride—such as displays of Mexican flags on Mexican Independence Day—

established one's membership in the spectrum of hyphenated American (associational) belonging. To be American, even a white American now, is to feel the need for an identifiable ethnic location (Gitlin 1996). This is not to denigrate the nationalist feeling that these symbols convey but rather to remark on the other kinds of identity work they do in contemporary US society.

Other expressions of national culture at the event included a tent with Bedouin rugs and pillows. Gesturing to an Americanization and commercialization of tastes, a "Box of Joe" containing brewed "American" coffee sat on the rug next to a short table. In a Bedouin home, the host traditionally roasts, hand-grinds, and boils the coffee on coals to produce a bitter liquid served in small *finjan* cups. In the US suburbs, under the canopy of a recreated Bedouin shelter, the coffee came in a cardboard container from a chain cafe. In this way, as well, Palestine—in the sense of a key Palestinian practice of offering coffee to a guest—had given way to commodification, to a type of consumerist, middle-class Americanization.

Perhaps the most dramatic display was the large replica of the wall that Israel had constructed in the West Bank. Such displays appeared on college campuses elsewhere in the city during Nakba Day events. The DePaul SJP, for example, erected a similar wall in 2014 to commemorate the Nakba. Symbolic of a recurring history of dispossession, expulsion, and exile, the wall conveyed the message of the Nakba's continuing relevance. Each of the panels of the wall served as a medium of communication about the "catastrophe" of 1948. One panel, for example, below the slogan "Free Palestine!," listed the "Impacts of the Wall: limiting Palestinian water supplies; curtails [sic] access to medical facilities; divides [sic] Palestinian farmland and communities." Unsurprisingly, given its attention to branding, AMP's color messaging remained consistent across the display: red and black lettering conveyed the information on the various panels and an enlarged rendering of the abbreviation "AMP" appeared alongside the sizeable, red-colored block lettering running along the top of the wall, calling on the world to "End Israeli Apartheid."

A significant feature of these displays—as well as of the displays in the tents and of the occurrence of the event as a whole within the parking lots of the Mosque Foundation and Aqsa School—was the inward focus. The intended audience was the enclave itself, not the city beyond the enclave. Effectively, the community was mirroring itself to itself through the medium of AMP's brand-conscious displays. The panels explaining the different aspects of Israeli rule in the Occupied Territories—prisoners, land confiscation, settlements, "refugee facts," and the social "impacts of the wall"—indicated this internal pedagogical orientation. In our interview together in October 2013, Kristin Szremski, an AMP staff member, commented on the need to educate Arabs and Muslims who had grown up in the United States. They were as reliant on the "biased US media" as were non-Muslim Americans. AMP therefore saw part of its mission as correcting misunderstandings among US Muslims and Arabs concerning Palestine.

The Formal Program

In addition to the tent displays and the wall, AMP's Nakba event also featured a formal program. At approximately 5:00 p.m., a young man initiated the ceremony with a five-minute-long recitation from the Qur'an. A female moderator then took the stage and called out, "*Takbir!*" ("Magnification [of God's name]!"). The audience responded, "*Allahu Akbar!*" (God is greater!). This ritualized invocation framed the program in Islamic religious and communal terms. In doing so, it cast the nation and its struggles, consciously or not, as an extension of the Islamic *umma* and its duties toward God and toward believers in this one God.

The moderator, a heavyset middle-aged woman in hijab, then came to the stage to speak about the importance of the day and about AMP's work. She also introduced the first speaker, a young man dressed in dark aviator sunglasses and two scarves that combined the *hatta* patterning with the Palestinian national colors. Pacing across the stage, his amplified voice filling the tent, the young activist launched into a review of the key events of Palestinian history, arguing that the Nakba was not a single occurrence in 1948. Rather, it was an ongoing process of dispossession that began with the arrival of Zionist settlers in the 1890s; continued with the British occupation and Mandate; and crested with the wars of 1948 and 1967. It continued today, moreover, in each Israeli attack. Indeed, the persisting Palestinian exile itself was testimony to the Nakba's unending reality. He then remarked on the festive, carnival-like atmosphere of the event in the parking lot, linking it to the somberness of the Nakba memory. Nakba Day marked "our terrible catastrophe" but it also was a celebration of the continuation of the Palestinian people, who remained committed to returning someday, he said. But return would only happen if Palestinians understood their history and got involved to change their situation.

Shaykh Jamal, the head clergyman at the Mosque Foundation, was next on the stage. A powerfully built man with a regal bearing, he came forward in long black robes fringed in gold embroidery. His sartorial display evoked the style of a village headman, a *mukhtar*, and also of an *imam*, or religious functionary, in a Jordanian or West Bank mosque. He wore a white *kufi*-style cap on his head and had a thick, black-streaked grey beard. In a sonorous voice, the *shaykh* spoke of the centrality of the Palestinian question for Muslims. He asserted that Palestine would return to its proper owners one day, but he also stressed—and here he struck a longstanding reformist theme—that the key to this eventual occurrence lay in the return of individual Muslims to Islam. By strengthening their piety, Muslims would hasten the day of their repatriation. The message fit well with the entrepreneurial, small-business, and professional ethos of the suburban middle class. This ethos validated individual empowerment primarily through individual success, wealth accumulation, and moral-ethical rectitude. The *shaykh*'s message reinforced the assumptions underlying this value orientation, adding to it the Islamic imperative to distribute a percentage of one's wealth through charity. Only individual reform, self-discipline, and charitable giving would save the nation ("*umma*"—the Islamic community but also the Palestinian people as part of this community). There was no mention of liberation through social movement, class struggle, and revolution, an idea that had animated Marxist and pan-Arab nationalist activists in previous generations. Still, the notion of individual reform and commitment to the *umma* did contain a sense of the collective beyond the individual. The difference between "the revolution" and the individual turn toward piety, however, lay in the priority that the latter placed on individual morality. It was this morality, the *shaykh* implied, that provided the key to collective success.

After Shaykh Jamal completed his remarks, Shaykh Amin from the Islamic Community Center of Illinois was invited to the stage. Striking a contrast with Shaykh Jamal, Shaykh Amin wore white robes with gold fringe and a white cap on his head. Younger than Shaykh Jamal, Shaykh Amin was from Jordan and had only been in the country for a few years. Like Jamal, he spoke in Arabic and sounded the theme of individual religious return as the necessary prerequisite to political and territorial restitution. He began by emphasizing that Palestine was an Islamic issue. Muslims needed to unify, he said. Only through their individual commitment to Islam would the necessary collective solidarity exist to bring the Nakba to an end.

In the absence of such unity, *nakbas* of all kinds had proliferated among Muslims. Shaykh Amin pointed to the regime-perpetrated atrocities against Syrian civilians. Every hour, he said, five Syrians lost their lives to regime violence. This violence was a "continuing *nakba*." He mentioned as well the ongoing war in Iraq and other parts of the Arab and Islamic world. But Syria was of a different order. The atrocities there constituted a "*nakba* and a half." Shaykh Amin also spoke about the necessity of patience and commitment to the struggle to bring such disasters to an end. And he spoke about the media, saying that it was biased and that through it these *nakbas* were declared to be an irreversible, accomplished fact, simply to be accepted. He noted that the media spoke about how the Syrian regime had conquered different cities and that the opposition was on the run. However nothing could be further from the truth, he contended. "We can't believe the media," he said. If one did so, one would lose hope. The only solution in the face of these ongoing disasters in Palestine, Syria, and Iraq was to bind together as Muslims and to struggle to overcome the situation.

The final speaker, Don Wagner, was a non-Palestinian advocate of the Palestinian cause. At the time, Wagner, an ordained Presbyterian minister, was serving in a national leadership capacity for Friends of Sabeel North America. This organization coordinated a network of largely Protestant churches and individuals who advocated for Palestinian self-determination and who supported Sabeel, a Palestinian liberation theology organization based in Jerusalem. Dressed in dark sunglasses, black pullover, and blue jeans, he reminded the audience of the many non-Muslims working on behalf of Palestine. These others, he said, included Jewish activists, SJP groups on campuses, and many US churches working to divest from Israel and to boycott Israeli products. Wagner ended by invoking the shared point of resistance uniting them across religious and ethnic-national divides: Zionism and the Nakba it produced. It was Zionism above all else, he said, that required their sustained, critical attention. Supporters of the Palestinian cause had to work together to "deconstruct" Zionist claims and support the Boycott, Divestment, and Sanctions campaign.

CONCLUSION

Wagner provided the sole Christian representation at the AMP event, an exception demonstrating the fact that the public expression of Palestinian nationalism in Chicago's suburban diaspora had taken a decidedly Islamic cast in the second decade of the twenty-first century. Wagner's non-Palestinian status heightened this impression: Palestinian Christians were not present in any visible way. This fact did not mean that the Islamic turn had entirely sidelined non-Muslim and secularist voices. Antiochian Orthodox Archbishop Theodosios Attallah Hanna of Jerusalem, for example, addressed AMP's fourth annual conference in 2011. The well-known Palestinian American intellectual Rashid Khalidi, holder of the Edward Said Chair of Modern Arab Studies at Columbia University, had also keynoted the annual meetings. Activists connected to the Arab American Action Network and the national Boycott, Divestment, and Sanctions campaign regularly held workshops at the conference as did leaders and public figures associated with Jewish Voice for Peace, Friends of Sabeel North America, and Neturei Karta.

The presence of these individuals and groups at AMP's conventions, however, occurred within the symbolic and discursive terms that AMP had set. Sectarian and interreligious solidarity, not a desectarianized secular nationalism, now served as the dominant integrating structure for action and identity in relation to the question of Palestine. This was not a mere surface phenomenon, not simply a shuffling of interchangeable symbols on the deck of an essentially secular Palestinian nationalism. Rather, it signaled a substantive change that registered profoundly not only in acts of public commemoration but also in the trajectory of individual lives. These trajectories tracked with the development of the religious institutional presence in Chicago's diaspora community. The next chapter explores the narratives of several individuals who have participated in the institutions constituting the religious milieu in its Muslim and Christian segments. The analysis reveals the mechanisms of the religious turn as well as its dialectical character: the Islamic shift has spurred and reinforced interacting and mirroring Christian sectarian solidarities.

4

The Religious Turn

Generational Subjectivities

Born in 1947, in a farming village near Bethlehem, Muhannad (pseudonym) has been an outspoken advocate of the Palestinian cause and a leader in the Mosque Foundation community in the suburb of Bridgeview. Academically talented, he received a scholarship to an elite private high school in East Jerusalem. In 1975, he immigrated to Chicago, where his uncle lived and was a naturalized US citizen, to pursue an engineering degree. He spent the majority of his career as a civil engineer for the City of Chicago before taking a part-time teaching job in a local community college. He and his wife, a distant relative from his home village, have four children who attended the Islamic schools next to the Mosque Foundation and now work in professional fields.

Muhannad is a contemporary of Musa Samara, Khairy Abudayyeh, and Ali Hussain (chapter 2). Within their generation (1948–67), however, he represents a diverging reformist-Islamic trajectory that ultimately gained ascendancy in Palestine during and after the first Intifada. Muhannad was a forerunner of this trajectory and a founder of its institutions in Chicago. He participated, for example, in the reformist effort to secure a majority on the Mosque Foundation board in 1978 (chapter 1). He was also instrumental, during the 1980s and 1990s, in helping to establish and lead Islamic organizations focused on the Palestinian national cause. These organizations provided a precedent and model for later groups like American Muslims for Palestine (AMP) (chapter 3). Muhannad has also served on the boards of a variety of Arab American civil rights organizations.

These diverse involvements reflect the merging of Arab and Palestinian nationalism with Islamic reformism within Muhannad's outlook. The Islamic framework, however, is primary: it subordinates nationalism and ethnicity in his hierarchy of solidarity. At the same time, the integration of nationalism as the focus of his Islamic orientation leads him to coordinate with secular nationalist leaders and organizations on various campaigns. He has expanded his sense of nationalism to include "Americanism," which he associates with democratic values, especially the value of dissent, which he sees as central to Islam, too.

GENERATIONAL PROCESSES OF THE RELIGIOUS TURN

This chapter describes the generational processes that Muhannad's story highlights. Its purpose is to deepen the analysis of the religious shift that began with the discussion of AMP in chapter 3. The five interviews I have chosen to focus on, including Muhannad's, represent three different generational locations corresponding with three distinct lines of identity articulation.[1] In my data, the first location pertains to the generation of 1948–67, the general features of which are described in chapter 2, and the processes of secular alienation and religious latency that occur within its incipient Islamic trajectory. Alienation and latency here refer to the experience of piety-oriented individuals who came of age politically in the period of secularist ascendancy (the 1950s through the mid-1980s). These individuals reacted against secularism, embracing Islamist political ideology, a latent possibility of their piety orientation. They constituted a distinct religio-political unit that formed synchronically within this generation, which trended predominantly toward secular nationalism (see introduction and Mannheim 1952, 304). Significantly, Muhannad, who represents this unit in my interview data, did not reject secularism entirely; rather, he subordinated it to Islam, which he presented as an all-encompassing framework of unity. His form of religious shift thus was an inversion of pan-Arab secularism, which subordinated religion to an intersectarian, secular national solidarity (exemplified by Khairy Abudayyeh in chapter 2).

The 1987–2001 cohort, which chapter 2 also delineates broadly, is the second main generational location. For this cohort, in my data, the Islamic shift deeply polarized the religious and political field. Among Christians, especially, this polarization sectarianized identity. This sectarianization constituted a reaction against, and a mirroring of, the Islamic shift. The individual I select to illustrate this process moved from a secularist standpoint to a religious-communal one in response to Islamist/Islamic ascendancy in Palestine and in Chicago. In doing so, he participated in the creation of new religious nationalist structures such as the Sabeel Ecumenical Liberation Theology Center.

Finally, I discuss sectarian institutional integration in the post-September 11 generation as it manifests in my data. The religious shift in the two preceding cohorts created and strengthened religious sectarian institutions that then generated a persisting shift after 2001. This continuing, post-2001 dynamic occurred through the integration of the new cohort within these institutions. In some cases, the individuals I profile helped to found new organizations like AMP, but their doing so reflected the prior formation of a religious or religious-nationalist predisposition within already existing sectarian milieus. In my data, two types of identity trajectory emerged in this cohort: sectarianized nationalism and denationalized sectarianism. The first trajectory replicated previous forms of religious shift that produced religious nationalism; the second excluded or ignored nationalism, replacing it with an entirely religious sectarian solidarity.

ALIENATION AND LATENCY IN THE GENERATION OF 1948–1967

The first process I analyze involved a dynamic of alienation and latency within the generation of 1948–67. The individuals who experienced this dynamic grew up in traditional religious milieus but then developed a reformist, religious-nationalist orientation in reaction against ascendant secular nationalism. Their evolution in this direction entailed an embrace of religion that affirmed traditional piety while revising it through a rationalist, text-centered reformism. Reformism answered secular nationalism by deliberately placing Islam at the core of Palestinian identity and of the Palestinian national struggle. The generation of 1948–67 (its religio-political trajectory, or "generation unit" in Mannheim's [1952] terms) concretized this revision by establishing the institutions that grounded the religious turn in Palestine and in the diaspora. Muhannad, who exemplified this process, straddled the West Bank and Chicago, and in doing so provided a bifocal perspective on the phenomenon.[2]

Formational Processes

Three social processes shaped Muhannad's ideological outlook: immersion within a traditional, pietistic village milieu as a child and youth; confrontation with an ascendant secular nationalism and secular pan-Arabism, which simultaneously attracted and repelled him; and immigration to Chicago, where secularism was also ascendant but where an incipient Islamic shift was developing as well. These factors affected the evolution of his orientation in sequential progression. They also interacted simultaneously, in Muhannad's narration, to constitute a distinct Islamic-nationalist space in the Chicago diaspora.[3]

Muhannad began our interview by saying that he was from "a very conservative family" in "a conservative village: we were 100 percent Muslims." Others of the generation of 1948–67, which retained control of leadership at the Mosque Foundation and of other related institutions such as the adjacent Islamic schools, shared a similar background. A contemporary of Muhannad, a teacher at one of the Islamic schools adjacent to the Mosque Foundation, for example, also described coming from a small "conservative" village. In these narratives, "conservative" connoted a patriarchal ethos marked by traditional piety. Muhannad described his father as the "leader of our *hamula*," the extended family or clan. The respect he commanded in the family and in the village, Muhannad explained, came not only from his older age but also from being known for honest dealing. It also derived from his reputation for piety. The father assiduously attended Friday prayers, bringing his sons with him; listened to sermons beaming from mosques in Jerusalem and Cairo on the radio; and asked regularly that Muhannad read to him—he had not learned to do so himself—from the Qur'an and the *sira* (hagiographic stories of the Prophet Muhammad's life).

Muhannad claimed not to have been motivated to perform religious duties in his youth. But, as he observed, he absorbed the culture of his family, developing a pious disposition organically as a result. The family's reputation for piety also served a disciplining end beyond the home: at the village elementary school, for example, Muhannad was asked to lead prayer and be a moral exemplar. "The school didn't ask the boys from the Communist families to do this," he said. Performing this duty not only upheld the family's reputation in public but also further reinforced Muhannad's orientation toward piety.

Muhannad's description of his family's piety and of the village as "100 percent Muslim" conflicted with his mention of "Communists." When I asked him to elaborate on this discrepancy, he described a secular-religious divide in the village, identifying two causal factors: the rise of pan-Arabism and Marxist-nationalist movements after the wars of 1948 and 1967 and the concomitant absence of a viable Islamic political alternative. Friends and neighbors supported the new movements as an expression of their desire to resist the Israeli occupation after 1967. Muhannad also joined in the activities of these movements at his high school in Jerusalem, but he felt ambivalent about doing so.

Rooted within the religious culture of his family, he resisted secularism's implicit demand to subordinate Islam to the priority of national solidarity. He had made an attempt to understand the demand, claiming to have read Marx but finding atheism and "the dialectic" nonsensical. The primary reason for his refusal to join the secular nationalist current, he said, was the religiosity of his parents and a corresponding attachment to Islam "deep in my heart." Secularism alienated him because it challenged this attachment.

The confrontation with secularism, however, did not simply cause alienation. Rather, it provoked a critical appraisal and transformation of the traditional piety that had shaped Muhannad's early value orientation. Muhannad hinted at this effect in his description of the secularist polemics against religion:

> [In our village] the Communists said [religion] was backward and that [religious people] wanted to return to the seventh century [. . .]. We had this idea—even I shared it a little bit—that the Muslim Brotherhood were collaborators with the British and the Israelis [. . .]. Later, I realized the Brotherhood, even though it was weak, was the only credible [Islamic] movement at the time. To this day it is the only credible movement.

The secularist polemic stung. But it also sparked a reassessment. Muhannad, like others who eventually aligned with the Islamic turn, articulated a distinction between religious traditionalism and a deliberate, rational Islam fully compatible with the needs of modern society. Traditionalism had reduced Islam, in this view, to ossified customs perpetuated on the authority of received precedent. There was much to admire in traditionalism, Muhannad remarked, especially loyalty to family and adherence to morality, however unmoored from the foundational texts like the Qur'an and *hadith*. But, there was also "superstition" and a failure to relate faith to the political needs of the moment.

A self-aware, rational Islam, by contrast, Muhannad remarked, rested on a "proper" understanding of the authoritative texts. These texts stressed justice as their essential message. A rational Islam was an activist Islam focused on resisting repression and reestablishing the true order of things as God had ordained it in the Qur'an and *shari'a*. For Muhannad, such an Islam, if it were to mean anything in the Palestinian context, inevitably entailed participation in the project of national liberation because the Palestinian cause was about ending a deep historical injustice. In the 1960s and 1970s, however, Islamic political forces were in disarray. The secular nationalist movements provided the only practical means to address Palestinian suffering. This reality generated fundamental contradictions for those who held to Islam as the only way forward. The tension resolved only with the Islamic shift that Muhannad and others of the generation of 1948–67 led.

The Islamic Revival and Its Generational Trajectory in Chicago

The political-Islamic shift occurred alongside a general revival of Islamic piety among significant segments of Palestinian society during the 1980s. Muhannad observed this phenomenon in his own family: "My family back home has become even more conservative, more religious than it had been when I was a boy; they are more educated, now, religiously." The mechanisms of this process were the new Islamic movements. Through their public advocacy, campus organizing, charitable societies, and preaching in mosques they drew young professionals and students into their ranks, grounding them in reformist piety in the process. Travel to Gulf countries, especially Saudi Arabia, also contributed to this phenomenon. Members of Muhannad's family, along with other Palestinians, had gone to Saudi Arabia for work. When they returned they brought with them the Salafi reformism they had absorbed while in the Kingdom. Salafism—an exceedingly complex phenomenon encompassing a range of intellectual, missionary, and in some cases violent insurgent movements—sought to reform Islam by returning it to its textual sources and to the pious example of the first generations of Muslims.[4] Individuals who had embraced it in the Gulf region often sought to institute it in their families and in doing so helped to create a receptive audience for the later Islamic political shift that powerfully challenged the dominance of Fatah and the PLO.

Muhannad's own entry into these politics, however, occurred within the entirely distinct context of the Chicago diaspora. Secularism was ascendant in this setting too. Incipient reformist networks were nevertheless forming. One such network, comprising businessmen and professionals, organized the initiative to take control of the Mosque Foundation board in 1978. Muhannad participated in this effort and filled prominent roles in the organization in the years following. He also participated in the launching of Islamic organizations that focused specifically on Palestinian advocacy. These institutions formed simultaneously with the Islamic political shift in Palestine.[5] In doing so, they replicated and reflected reformist Islamic orientations that had powerfully challenged secularism in Palestine and were beginning to reorient Palestinian identity in diaspora communities like Chicago. Muhannad was a forerunner and progenitor of some of the key institutions that propelled this process forward in the United States.

At the same time, however, Muhannad explicitly disputed the claim that his activism was merely an extension of the Islamism that had taken root in Palestine. Some secularists in the Chicago community as well as pro-Israel detractors had leveled such charges. He claimed instead that his activism reflected the values of dissent and pluralism that he had come to embrace as part of his self-described "Americanization." US society was certainly, he said, a type of idolatrous *jahiliya* (state of ignorance) inasmuch as some of its values opposed Islamic monotheistic belief.[6] Nevertheless, not everything in the American *jahiliya* was bad. On the contrary, there was much to affirm, including democratic principles and respect for cultural and religious diversity. Muslims, he said, were required to see these goods as the "mislaid belonging" that was their rightful inheritance—in echo of a well-known hadith, *al-hikmatu dallatu al-mu'mini fa-haythu wajadaha fa-huwa ahaqqu biha*, "Wisdom is the lost possession of the believer; so wherever he discovers it, he is entitled to it"[7]—since these things were reflective of God's beneficence. Still, Islam had always to command the ultimate allegiance of the believer. Whenever Islamic principle came into conflict with a belief or practice—whether held by non-Muslims or Muslims—the believer had the duty to dissent. Here, too, however, for Muhannad, this necessity to dissent on principled grounds was also in line with the fundamental requirements of citizenship in the United States.

Muhannad grounded his concept of dissent, as well, in the traditional values of his childhood family and especially in the example of his father. He recalled an incident in which his brother brandished a gun in a dispute with other villagers. These villagers came to Muhannad's father, the head of the *hamula*, demanding that he render judgment. His father weighed the testimony and decided against his son, paying a fee of one hundred dollars on his behalf to the aggrieved party. "My brother was furious; but my father believed in Islam and in justice," Muhannad said, "and he was my role model for putting community first."

In this reference to his childhood, Muhannad presented his father, a traditional village elder, as a principled model of specifically Islamic values. This model emphasized a willingness to go against family and tribe in the defense of justice.[8] It also exemplified openness to others beyond one's particular faction, clan, or sect. Muhannad recalled how the Prophet Muhammad spoke positively of the institutions through which Meccan society before Islam provided charity and assistance to the poor. Muhannad, too, sought to emulate this model. He described working with Communists and secular nationalists in his village to create programs in an effort to redirect youth from going into Israel "to drink and get into trouble and have sex and all these things." Understood in this sense, Islam constituted a compelling moral and political alternative to secular nationalism, which too often devolved, he said, into competitive factionalism.

Muhannad's conception of Islam as a moral-political framework that encompassed the nation blurred religion and ethnicity. As he put it, "what's good for the Arabs is good for the Muslims and what's good for the Muslims is good for the Arabs." Islam and nation amounted to the same thing if understood correctly. He explained:

> There are no contradictions [between Islam and nationalism] as long as we keep our priorities straight. The *'aqida* [technically, the Islamic religious conviction, creed, or doctrine, but in Muhannad's usage, also "cause"] comes before everything else. I would do nothing that is nationalistic if it contradicted the *'aqida*. I'll give you an example: in the 1990s, when the Israelis exiled about four hundred people from Hamas to Lebanon,[9] we went to the *markaz* [the Arab Community Center, described in chapter 2] and we proposed to organize a rally. Some in the Islamic movement said, 'Oh, you cooperate with the secularists, but they are *kuffar* [apostates, nonbelievers].' I told them that I'm not [supporting their ideology] but if we can collaborate then let's do so. I can't be affected by leftist arguments and ideology. I know their ideology better than they do. I grew up around them. Chances are, though, that I can affect them, and I did! A lot of them, actually, became practicing Muslims, *al-hamdulillah* [praise be to God]!

Muhannad was a pragmatist, willing to collaborate with secular nationalists on projects that coincided with his sense of Islam and justice. Understood in a true *'aqida* perspective, the cause of Islam was also the cause of the nation. At other points, however, as his comments on the dangers of apostasy indicated, Muhannad insisted on the priority of Islam. He described one such moment occurring during the effort to organize the protest mentioned above:

> At the meeting to discuss the rally, we agreed we all needed to come together as Palestinians, Islamic or secular; but the devil was in the details. I knew how they would want to bring in pictures of Yasser Arafat. I said, 'The best solution is no pictures whatsoever, no Arafat, no Shaykh Yassin [the late founder and spiritual head of Hamas], none of those people.' One of the *markaz* leaders responded, 'Okay, but there will be no saying Allahu akbar! [God is greater!] either.' That hit me in every nerve I had. I said, 'I'm going to tell you something. Allahu akbar means God is the greatest, greater than you, your family, all of Palestine, the whole world. If someone came to me today and said, we'll give you Palestine today, and all the Jews out of it, but you have to renounce God, I would say to hell with Palestine!' I used stronger words than I am using now. I told that guy, 'If you don't want to come to this rally,

I'll do it on my own. I don't need you anyhow! You know it! All of you here at the *markaz* might bring two hundred or three hundred people, but I'm going to bring five thousand. I dictate the agenda if you want to play that game. I'm giving you more than you deserve. I will go a long way to have unity, but unity has limits.' We could have done it without [the secularists], but I don't believe in exclusion. They can believe whatever they want. I'm not responsible for their beliefs. I'll tell them where they've gone wrong [on matters of belief]. I tell them, 'Someday you will have to pray.' I don't have any doubt in my heart that the *markaz* people love Palestine as much as I do. We just come at things differently. Palestine is a cause; but it's more than just about the nation. It's the most important cause of Islam. Palestine is part of the Qur'an. God took the prophet from Mecca to Jerusalem and he prayed with all the prophets in Jerusalem at Aqsa [al-Aqsa Mosque]. He made Palestine of the same level as Mecca and Medina. It does not matter what your nationality is. If you become a Muslim tomorrow, Palestine becomes your *'aqida*, your duty.

For Muhannad, as for other Palestinian Muslims who expressed their nationalism through an Islamic religious idiom, the Islamic *'aqida*, signified in the Prophet's ascension from the Haram platform to the very throne of God, placed Palestine at the center of Muslim ethical and religious duty. This centering of Palestine as Islam's primary concern effectively constituted an Islamic nationalist alternative to secular nationalist conceptions of solidarity. This alternative accommodated the pluralism that the secularist stance sought to enshrine: secularists and Christians were included within Islam's compass because they were part of the nation. Islam, however, was the core of this nation, and secularists and non-Muslims had to accept this fact or acquiesce in their irrelevance.

Muhannad correctly assessed that by the early 1990s, the mosques and Islamic organizations had become dominant. The secular community centers simply did not possess the same degree of mobilizing capacity. Secularists and Islamists could come together because the center of the Palestinian cause was the search for justice. Justice was the heart of Islam, too. But this justice stood above the nation itself. Palestine was a holy land equivalent to Mecca and Medina. It was the pinnacle of Islam's realization on earth, Islam's axis mundi, the point of heavenly ascension. Its redemption required rededication to God's cause above all else. Some day, Muhannad believed, secularists would appreciate this fact; they, too, would learn to pray.

THE GENERATION OF 1987–2001: POLARIZATION AND SECTARIANIZATION

The generation of 1948–67 established the movement structures and institutions of the Islamic shift in Palestine and in diaspora centers like Chicago. In doing so, it polarized the religious and political fields in Palestinian society. This polarization deepened with the rise of Hamas in the Occupied Territories during the late 1980s and 1990s (see introduction and chapter 2). This process marked the generation of 1987–2001. One of its consequences, as reflected in my data, was the sectarianization of identity as secular nationalism lost its cultural and political hegemony in the Chicago community during this period. Sectarianization registered not only in Islamization but also in a type of Christian nationalism, "Christianization," that reacted to and mirrored the Islamic shift.

For Christians, the Islamized space was an ambivalent arena. By definition, Christians stood excluded on the other side of this space even if occasionally they ventured into overlapping zones such as downtown demonstrations, Nakba commemorations, and ad hoc organizing meetings in periods of crisis. As a shared secular space receded, many Christians retreated into their own, alternate sectarian loci. This phenomenon became visible in my interview with Munir (pseudonym), an activist of the generation of 1987–2001. Munir's narrative showed how Christians growing up within a secular nationalist milieu became integrated into the new Christian nationalist structures during the First Intifada in Palestine (1987–93). His narrative also demonstrated how the Chicago diaspora deepened this process. Munir immigrated to Chicago during the early 1990s. In that same period, the Islamic shift and the concomitant loss of a secular, intersectarian space led Christians I interviewed to retreat into sectarian-communal zones. Munir's story provides an example of this process at the individual level.

Early Secular Identity Formation

Munir was born in Jerusalem in 1977. A former political activist, he described becoming mobilized during the First Intifada. Like his peers, he joined street protests after school and church services. His politicization stemmed also from the involvements of his parents in the Communist Party. Israeli police jailed his father administratively (with no formal charges or trial) for eighteen months during the Intifada for serving in the party's leadership. Munir commented that his parents became Communists because the party prioritized nonviolence. They also joined because it emphasized resistance to the occupation as Palestinians, not as Christians.

The alignment of Munir's family with the Communists was not coincidental. Christians disproportionately participated in secular political movements. This participation reflected an interest in a politics that imagined national inclusion in ethnic-linguistic terms—as Arabs first and foremost—rather than along religious-sectarian lines, as had been the case during Ottoman rule. The roots of this nationalist commitment stretched back to the eighteenth and nineteenth century. As European powers, France and Britain primarily, impinged on Ottoman territories in the eastern Mediterranean, Christian merchants, who were forming a new commercial class, forged contacts with the West. They sent their sons to study in Europe. Those children returned with new ideas about nationalism in which Christians and Muslims shared a common, equal identity as Arabs. This development, along with the Ottoman crackdown on Greek Orthodox Christians during the "Greek Revolt," known also as the Greek War of Independence, which started in 1821, stirred lay Arab Christians to challenge the authority of Greek Orthodox hierarchs, whom the Ottoman state had historically privileged as representatives of the empire's various Christian communities. To this day, among Palestinians, the Christian middle classes have supported secular parties and movements as vehicles for their full enfranchisement, political and religious, within an intersectarian national unity (Haddad 1970; Issawi 1982; Braude 1982; Masters 2001; Sharkey 2017, 122, 125–27, 204–12, 228, 251, 282–83).

The adherence of Munir's family to this Christian tradition of nationalist politics contrasted sharply with the sectarian-religious turn in Palestinian society during and after the First Intifada. Christians regarded resurgent Islamism with anxiety. As Hamas grew in power and prominence, Christians worried about the implications for the type of political arrangement that Palestinians would ultimately form following independence. Ensuing Christian responses ranged from redoubling their commitment to secular nationalism to withdrawing into an apolitical and sectarian quietism (Lybarger 2007b).

Other young Christians, however, individuals like Munir, hearkened to new politicized religious frameworks of activism such as the liberation theology movement. The priest at the church in Jerusalem where Munir's family were members played an especially important role in this shift to a political-religious outlook. He was a founder of the Sabeel Ecumenical Liberation Theology Center, an organization that was instrumental in adapting Latin American liberation theology to the Palestinian situation.[10] This theology essentially advocated for Palestinian national independence and Palestinian democratic governance in terms of the biblical mandate for justice. It empowered adherents to simultaneously contest the Islamist construal of the Palestinian cause as an essentially Islamic matter and critique Zionist uses of the Bible to justify maximalist Jewish claims to the land.

Encounter with this new political Christianity not only reoriented Munir ideologically but also began to determine his educational and career opportunities. As he approached his final year in high school, his priest urged him to apply for a scholarship that would enable him to attend a private Protestant Christian college in Chicago which had recently created a Middle East Studies Center and curriculum. The creator of this center was also a clergyman, a non-Palestinian, who was outspoken on the question of Palestine and also a supporter of the Palestinian liberation theology movement. Munir would be among the first Palestinians to take part in this program. His decision to pursue this path would further strengthen his incipient sectarian turn.

Christian Sectarianization

Munir's sectarianization was not a foregone conclusion. The strong secular nationalist commitments he had grown up with continued to influence his political orientation even as he transitioned into a politicized Christian space. The decisive factor in his sectarian shift was the steady erosion of secular spaces in which Muslims and Christians could come together as Palestinians above all else. Munir explicitly commented on this fact, noting that "there has been this real change—in Palestine, the new Islamic movement—it's defining people, defining how people behave and how they identify themselves, whether you're a Palestinian Muslim or a Palestinian Christian, and we Christians have felt the urgency suddenly to hang on to our identity as a Christian community and that's translated to America, to Chicago." Munir, in fact, perceived the sectarian shift in Chicago to be more polarizing than in Palestine. He described this difference in three respects: in the attitudes prevalent in his Arab Evangelical Protestant community, to which his wife belonged before their marriage; in how other Palestinian activists in the city positioned him specifically as "the Christian"; and in relation to the prevalence of Islamic slogans and symbols in presumably nonsectarian secular nationalist spaces.

Grounding this process was the development of distinct institutional spheres:

> Christians are definitely latching on to their churches. Maybe it's because of the lack of those community centers, the secular community centers. The only ones I know of are the *markaz* and the Ramallah Club [which has predominantly Christian membership]. But they're not as active as they used to be, and that leaves people with no option but to affiliate with their religions [. . .]. Churches and mosques are becoming the community centers. They are not just religious institutes anymore; they are shaping us socially, in separate ways.

Munir's description of these processes reflected well-established assimilation patterns in the United States. Religious institutions resituated and revalued the ethnic-national identities of immigrants within a voluntary religious-communal framework that historically typified processes of cultural integration ("Americanization") (Yang and Ebaugh 2001; Breton 2012; Kivisto 2014, 36–39). In the Palestinian context, however, these developments also reflected dynamics internal to Palestinian society in Palestine and in the diaspora. Munir offered additional insight into this fact, highlighting the Islamization of secular nationalist space and the persisting violence against Christians in the Middle East:

> A few years ago we had a national Palestinian conference here in Chicago [. . .]. The organizers asked if I could recruit Christian authorities to speak because they had invited the Mosque Foundation imam and wanted to balance him. I was glad they were aware of this need to balance but my reaction was, why couldn't this just be secular? I agreed to help invite Christians but few came. We were the absolute minority at the conference. The Christians who did come didn't actively participate. During the *hafla* [social event] in the evening, things took an Islamic turn. There were people chanting for "Muslim Palestine" and things like that. The organizers weren't leading the chanting; it was the attendees, the community. It was a reflection of what the community thinks and feels. It was eye-opening. These days, at every gathering of the community, we have to be sure to cater to the Muslims. At every conference

we have to designate rooms for prayers. Because of this stuff, the churches stay away. They have this idea that this is gonna take some kind of Islamic route. And they're right. When I was growing up in Palestine we were so consumed by the Intifada and the occupation and your father's in jail, you know, you don't have time to worry about your Christian or Muslim identity. But as Hamas became more of a force, people felt like they had to hang on to their identities as Christians. And especially in Chicago people feel this. Muslims feel this, too. They are being arrested and interrogated and attacked in the media purely on the basis of their identities as Muslims. This causes a desire to assert and hang on to their Muslim identities. As a consequence, the mosques have become the main voice. And this has shaped us, causing us to stick with our religious institutions after 9/11. One of my friends—he's secular but from a Muslim family—he and I have gotten into arguments about the church bombings in the Middle East and that pastor in Florida who wanted to burn the Qur'an and the dispute about that mosque in New York, the Park 51.[11] It didn't used to be like that between us.

Munir described an interlocking and interactive sectarianization that transcended Palestine and the United States. His bifocality as someone who came of age politically in Jerusalem during the Intifada but then, in that same moment, joined the Chicago diaspora afforded this perspective. He recalled how Christians in Palestine reacted to Hamas by closing ranks as a religious minority. He connected this response to what he saw occurring in Chicago: Christians closed ranks in response to Islamization, which itself was a response to a powerful xenophobic reaction in the aftermath of the September 11 attacks.

The diaspora context in both cases—Christian and Muslim—sectarianized solidarity further, however, by displacing Palestinian identity within an interethnic religious sectarian loyalty. Palestinians had to share space and leadership with non-Palestinian Muslims in the Mosque Foundation. This reality dislocated Palestinian agendas: Syrians contested Palestinian assumptions that Palestinian liberation should take precedence. Munir experienced a similar phenomenon in his North Side evangelical Protestant church, whose members included Iraqi and Syrian refugees and Egyptian immigrants. In this community, strong anti-Muslim sentiments had formed in reaction to the violence targeting Christians in Iraq, Syria, and Egypt during and after the Iraq War and the Arab Spring uprisings (*BBC News* 2015; *Guardian* 2017; Sherwood 2018). Major US Evangelical leaders also had voiced strong anti-Muslim sentiments (Graham 2001; Prothero 2018). In their discourse, the plight of Arab Christians served as evidence that Islam constituted a malevolent force in the world (Merritt 2015; Graham 2017; *Haaretz* 2017). The anti-Muslim discourse in Munir's church echoed the wider Evangelical narrative about an apocalyptic conflict with Islam.

Such sentiments had affected Munir's perspective. He sympathized with the feelings of his fellow churchgoers and drew connections between violence directed at Palestinian Christians in Hamas-ruled Gaza and the violence directed at Christians elsewhere in the region.[12] With anger in his voice, he asserted that

Qur'an burnings, as terrible as they were, did not kill; the bombings of Christian communities in the Middle East, however, did take lives, and Muslims needed to acknowledge that fact.

At the same time, Munir chafed at the support some of his Arab Protestant coreligionists, non-Palestinians, expressed for Israel. Christian Zionism had taken particularly strong root in US Evangelical churches (Spector 2009; Lewis 2010). Many Palestinian Protestants struggled against this political theology (Younan 2007; Awad 2016). Munir also criticized Christian Zionism but felt conflicted and isolated: Christians had been victimized, but Christian Zionism only contributed to Palestinian Christian suffering. Ultimately, for Munir, echoing the liberation theology themes he had absorbed in Palestine, Christian and Muslim Palestinians needed to stand together when violence and racism reared up against them. They needed to build bridges by creating activities that brought them together not as members of different religions but as Palestinians. Palestinians had a tradition of intersectarian accommodation and a commitment to a nonsectarian secular nationalist framework of solidarity. They could revive those traditions, Munir thought, but opportunities were lacking, the space in which they might have occurred disappearing.

THE POST–SEPTEMBER 11 GENERATION

Sectarianization intensified and took new forms in the post-September 11 generation. This generation emerged in congruence with three main historical events: the anti-Arab and anti-Muslim backlash in the United States following the September 11 attacks and subsequent US invasions of Afghanistan and Iraq; the Arab Spring uprisings and their complicated sectarianizing aftermath, especially in Syria and Egypt; the deepening crises of secular nationalism and the peace process during and after the Second (al-Aqsa) Intifada (2000–05); and the fracturing that occurred after Hamas routed Fatah militarily from the Gaza Strip in 2007. The orientations of this cohort, as my data show, formed through integration into the already established institutions of the sectarian milieus. The profiles below exhibit two trajectories: a continuation of sectarianized nationalism in new forms and denationalized sectarianism, which replaced nationalist with religious solidarity.

Sectarianized Nationalism
Christianized Nationalism in the Second Intifada

Hanna (pseudonym) was in his final semester of studies at one of Chicago's universities when I interviewed him on campus in the student government lounge. He had helped lead an effort to win the support of his fellow students for Boycott, Divestment, and Sanctions (BDS). The campaign sought to convince the university to divest from holdings in certain companies doing business in Israel. Hanna and his fellow activists had just succeeded in steering a resolution supporting divestment through the student council.

Hanna seemed an exceptional figure. Most of the Christians I had interacted with had distanced themselves from nationalist activism or had avoided it altogether. All of these individuals had expressed concern about the turn toward Islam they perceived to have occurred in the wider immigrant community. Hanna was different. He not only had voiced support of the Palestinian cause but also provided highly visible public leadership for it. The community's Islamic turn seemed irrelevant to him.

Yet, as our interview progressed, I began to see Hanna's experience as indicative of a religious turn that encompassed Christians, too. Hanna's politicization occurred not through secular nationalist structures but rather through the new politicized Christianity that had emerged during and after the First Intifada and that had eventually become institutionalized in the liberation theology movement. His mobilization highlighted the relative weakness of secular nationalism as immigrants of the post-September 11 generation came to political awareness. It also reflected the critical importance of continuing links to Palestine. Travel to Palestine—and the encounter there with political Christianity—oriented Hanna toward Palestinian advocacy in Chicago. As with Palestinians born in Palestine who then immigrated to the United States, Hanna's visits to the homeland provided a bifocality that led him to view the diaspora through the lens of a struggle transcending the diaspora and homeland. Crucially, a post-Intifada politicized Christianity filtered this view.

Born in the northwest suburbs of Chicago in the early 1990s, Hanna described how his parents and the Christian community generally deemphasized the Palestinian struggle.

> I was talking to a friend of mine who goes to the Melkite Church [St. John the Baptist Melkite Catholic Church in Northlake] about [how Christians distance themselves from Palestine]. She was, like, it was really messed up that Arab Christians don't really affiliate with being Arab and helping people with the situation [in Palestine]. She told me that she tried to get these Christians [to support BDS] but she did not get the same effect as she did with the Muslims. I was like: Preach on, sister! It's really true that a lot of the Arab Christians don't want anything to do with being Arab or Palestinian. I know a Christian family that pretty much killed the Arab culture. They won't even listen to Arabic music. The only thing they might do is go to an Arab wedding. But they are like the outsiders at the wedding. My parents also tried to distance me from my Palestinian identity, but it backfired.

The denationalization and depoliticization in the Christian community that Hanna described echoed Munir's observations (above) about Christian alienation from Islamized activist spaces. Hanna, however, represented an anomaly; de-Palestinianization produced the opposite consequence in his case. Rather than abandon identification with the nation, he embraced it. This counter-trend development in his case occurred, as Hanna described it, for several reasons: the participation of his family in the Saint George Antiochian Orthodox Church in

Cicero; visits from and to family in the West Bank; and encounters, during those visits to Palestine, with the new Christianized nationalism. The involvement at St. George, he said, "kept us connected to an Arab identity even though my parents didn't want us having anything to do with Palestine." St. George's head priest was a Palestinian and advocate for the national cause, and the church's liturgy integrated Arabic and English. Another individual, Leo (pseudonym), profiled further below, indicated in his interview, however, that many Christians of the post-September 11 generation at St. George had become dissociated from "Arabness" and nationalism. The relationship to St. George, therefore, was a contributing but not sufficiently explanatory factor in the formation of Hanna's outlook.

Visits from relatives in the West Bank also perpetuated attachment within Hanna's family to Arab and Palestinian culture and an awareness of the political situation in Jerusalem and the West Bank. Visits to family in the West Bank had a similar effect. Beginning in the 2000s, Hanna accompanied his family or traveled on his own several times to Palestine. The experience of passing through Israeli border security made a distinct impression. On a trip in 2003, he recalled, "we were stripped down and searched at the airport and made to sit in our underwear, [. . .], not something a thirteen-year-old kid would want to experience [. . .]." This ordeal and others like it at military checkpoints made Hanna conscious of his status as a feared and hated presence that Israel, the state, deemed necessary to interrogate, monitor, and exclude. These experiences stirred his anger and his desire to resist.

The nationalizing and politicizing effects of humiliating border rituals coincided with Hanna's integration into a Christian nationalist milieu during these visits to Palestine. Hanna's introduction to this space began during his first summer trip to reconnect with relatives in Beit Jala in 2010. His uncle took him to the Sabeel Ecumenical Liberation Theology Center in Jerusalem, the same organization that Munir, a generation earlier, had helped to establish. Sabeel's leaders invited him to participate as volunteer staff for the organization's annual conference that year. As part of the conference, participants visited the southern West Bank city of al-Khalil (Hebron), where they talked to survivors of the Baruch Goldstein massacre at the Ibrahimi Mosque during Ramadan 1994.[13] "Hearing those testimonies was shocking," Hanna recalled. The conference attendees also went to Nazareth, first visiting the Basilica of the Annunciation and then listening later to a Sabeel leader discuss how the Israeli authorities refused permits to build or buy homes in predominantly Jewish communities to Palestinians who held Israeli citizenship.

The most significant outcome of Hanna's conference experience was his exposure to Sabeel's politicized biblical hermeneutic:

> Sabeel not only took us to the religious sites but Qissis Naʿim [Fr. Naim Ateek, one of Sabeel's founders] explained that Jesus lived under occupation just like we did. That meant something to me. We had a long conversation about it. They have a book called *The Way of the Cross*, which explains the stages of when Jesus was crucified.[14]

It surveys different ways in which the occupation relates to the different stopping places of the Stations of the Cross. There are like thirteen or fourteen stations, right? I can't remember [laughter]. Anyway, each one represents a different part of the occupation. Like, one stage showed settlements, which represented occupation, which Jesus also experienced, and some of the settlements were next to the apartheid wall. Going through those stages and seeing the parallels really hit me.

In the same way that the American Muslims for Palestine oriented Muslim Palestinians, Sabeel provided Hanna with a religio-political perspective through which to make sense of the Palestinian predicament. The perspective was liturgical, involving the reader in an imaginative re-enactment of Jesus's humiliating march to Golgotha. Significantly, the fusion of Jesus's suffering with Palestinians' tribulations, a logical conclusion derived from Christ's "option for the poor and the oppressed," elided the historical Jesus's Jewishness. Sabeel's Jesus was a Palestinian: his suffering was Palestinian suffering.

Upon returning to Chicago, Hanna joined the Students for Justice in Palestine (SJP) chapter at his university. He was one of only two Christians in the group. He described the chapter as committed to affirming a secular Palestinian identity but also willing to work with religious organizations. During his senior year, the group held a conference on Palestine at the university in collaboration with activists from American Muslims for Palestine, Friends of Sabeel North America, and Jewish Voice for Peace. Hanna provided the conduit to Friends of Sabeel. The goal was to create a citywide coalition in support of BDS and to support campus efforts to pass BDS resolutions. The central role of Palestinian advocacy groups with religious ideological underpinnings in this effort was notable: in the aftermath of the religious turn of the 1990s and 2000s such groups had come to the fore as primary mechanisms of mobilization. Individuals like Hanna, who had become politicized through a type of Christianized nationalism, reflected this phenomenon.

Islamized Nationalism in the Period of Israel's Wars in Gaza

The importance of religious milieu structures and religious-nationalist advocacy organizations registered, as well, in a second example of mobilization in the post-September 11 generation. Born in 1984, Sara (pseudonym) came of age politically during the post-September-11 anti-Muslim reaction in the United States and during Hamas's ascendancy in Gaza and its armed conflicts with Israel. She was among the activists who helped to start American Muslims for Palestine, which took form in response to Israel's attacks on Gaza beginning in 2006.

Sara grew up on Chicago's North Side. This geographic location determined the particular form of the Islamic religious shift Sara experienced. Lacking easy access to the Southwest Side community centers, Sara's parents increasingly became active in the Muslim Community Center (MCC). The MCC catered primarily to South Asian Muslim immigrants; however, a small group of North Side Palestinians had also established themselves there by the time Sara and her siblings started to attend school. Concerned about ensuring cultural and moral continuity in the family, Sara's parents enrolled their children in the MCC's youth programs. Sara and her siblings attended "weekend and night schools for Arabic and Islamic studies and Qur'an," beginning at the pre-K level and continuing to age fourteen. At age twelve she began attending a Qur'an memorization class led by a Pakistani *shaykh*. Her parents then enrolled her in the private K-12 Islamic school in which this *shaykh* also taught. Through this educative process she developed a primary identity as a Muslim oriented toward the core Islamic texts as the basis for piety and cross-ethnic solidarity.

Within this context, too, Sara learned to fuse Islam with advocacy for Palestine. The MCC and the Pakistani school had explicitly embraced the Palestinian cause. This support reflected a sympathetic response to the concerns of the Palestinian minority in the mosque and, as Sara asserted, to a key Islamic mandate. Islam itself, Sara observed, had primed MCC's South Asian majority to support the issue. "It's in the Qur'an," she said—a claim echoing Muhannad's assertions above—"all the prophets went through [the Holy Land]." Palestine was Islam's axis mundi and therefore, in Sara's view, advocating for it was an essential duty, indeed, the very essence of the faith. That MCC made this central to its mission and identity made perfect sense to her. The universalizing of the Palestinian cause in Islamic terms at MCC went beyond verbal exhortations to include participation in direct actions. During Israel's war with Hezbollah in 2006, Sara recalled, Palestinians and South Asians boarded buses at the MCC to join a mass protest in Chicago's downtown.

The interethnic Islamic framework of Palestine solidarity at the MCC modeled for Sara the type of advocacy politics that she and other activists would seek to institute in AMP. Sara described how the idea for the organization arose in 2005. That year, while still a student at a university in the city, Sara attended the annual convention of the Islamic Society of North America at the McCormick Place Convention Center. MCC youth typically attended this annual conference, and Sara had agreed to volunteer at a booth. During one of her shifts, she met individuals discussing the need for a Muslim organization focused exclusively on Palestine activism. They invited Sara to help organize two conferences, one later that year and another one in 2006, to raise awareness and gauge public support. These activities led to further meetings and the creation of AMP in 2006. Barely two years later, Israel launched its "Operation Cast Lead" bombardment of the Gaza Strip. AMP responded quickly, taking the lead in organizing protests downtown. That same year, the organization held its first fundraiser at the Aqsa School, raising enough money to open its national office in Palos Hills, a southwest suburb, and to expand its staff considerably. "It was amazing," Sara said. "After 9/11, the work for Palestine died because people didn't want to speak about Palestine, didn't want anything to do with it for obvious reasons, but Operation Cast Lead opened the floodgate."

The new post-September 11 Palestine activism, originating within an incipient interethnic Islamic context, departed from the secular nationalist forms of advocacy that had prevailed from the late 1960s through the end of the 1980s. It also diverged from the forerunner Islamic organizations that Muhannad and others in the generation of 1948–67 had launched. Those earlier groups "focused specifically on the Palestinian Muslim community," Sara remarked, "but we go beyond that." AMP sought to mobilize all US Muslims; cultivated support among non-Muslims; and lobbied lawmakers in Washington, DC. This broader focus reflected the post-September 11 generation's experience of integration into the Islamic institutions that had formed during and after the 1990s. These institutions instituted a transethnic and Islamic ethos. Sara's schooling within the interethnic MCC context exemplified the process. The resulting ethos shaped the direction of response to Cast Lead in 2009: pan-Islamic solidarity, not ethnic-national identity, became the basis of unity and action. This religious solidarity, as AMP construed it, and as Sara experienced it at the MCC, amalgamated the nation, orienting those drawn into its orbit toward an understanding of the struggle for the Holy Land as the supreme Islamic duty.

Denationalized Sectarianism

The religious turn, however, did not always lead to a sacralized political (religious-nationalist) activism in either the 1987–2001 or post-September 11 generations. Another trajectory—"denationalized sectarianism"—emerged across both cohorts in my data. This orientation almost entirely ignored nationalism, constituting identity exclusively in religious sectarian terms. The primary factors producing this trajectory included a high degree of participation in religious institutions and a corresponding lack of integration within the structures of secular nationalist or religious-nationalist activism.

Denationalized Sectarianism among Muslims

'Aziza (pseudonym) illustrates how denationalized sectarianism manifested within the Islamized suburban enclave. Born in Bridgeview in 1966, 'Aziza was the oldest daughter of immigrants who came to the city just before the war of 1948. Her date of birth placed her in the generation of 1987–2001 but her autobiographical account revealed parallels with the post-September 11 generation. Like this later cohort, 'Aziza's primary formational experiences occurred within the institutions that propelled the religious shift. 'Aziza was, in this sense, a generational forerunner, marking a trajectory that would reappear in the narratives of other interlocutors in the post-September 11 period.

Like Sara, 'Aziza grew up in isolation from the secular nationalist community centers in Chicago's Southwest Side. She described her family as highly assimilated. They had moved to the suburbs before the waves of relocation in the late 1980s and 1990s. They had little contact with Palestinians elsewhere in the city, never travelling to the Southwest Side:

> First time I went [to the Southwest Side] was after I got married and went to visit my husband's sister. I was twenty years old, and I remember driving into the area

and seeing all the Arab stores and women in their *thawbs* [traditional embroidered dresses], and I was like, 'Wow! What is this place!' [laughter] We never ate falafel. We ate corned beef and cabbage and my mom made turkey with stuffing! My grandma picked things up from her [white] neighbors. So, people [other immigrants] were like, 'Who are you people!?!?'

Her suburban isolation excluded 'Aziza from the institutions and mechanisms of cultural transmission within the immigrant community. 'Aziza never learned to read, write, or speak Arabic fluently. Had her family lived on the Southwest Side she might have participated in afterschool language and cultural programs and absorbed the nationalist politics of the community centers, which were dominant during her generation.

A form of cultural transmission did occur nevertheless through the family. This transferal involved the reconstitution of gendered hierarchies derived from the patriarchal ethos of the West Bank village in which 'Aziza's parents and grandparents had grown up prior to immigrating. Her parents restricted 'Aziza's socializing beyond the home. As previously noted, families often justified these restrictions in relation to fears for the safety of children traveling through Chicago's urban expanse. 'Aziza remembered the curtailment of her movements, however, as deriving from "traditional ideas" about female propriety. It was "shameful" (*'ayb*) for girls to move beyond the home unaccompanied. Her brother, 'Aziza told me, did not have to contend with the same limits. Significantly, 'Aziza did not perceive this repatriarchalizing ethos as distinct from "American identity." The gendered constraints were simply how the family did things. "I never really saw my parents as immigrants," she told me, "[we were] as American as you could get."

The isolation and assimilation—the transferal of the rural patriarchal ethos notwithstanding—stemmed, in 'Aziza's view, from a failure to systematically institute religious identity and practice, in particular. Religious transmission, if it occurred, took place in an ad hoc fashion. She offered her grandfather as an example: "My father told me once that after they arrived in the 1940s he asked his father if they were going to do the Ramadan fast and my grandfather said, 'You can do it if you want, but I'm not!'" 'Aziza's grandfather apparently still kept the daily prayers, even "praying twice if he missed a prayer," but "he never encouraged us to pray and this is what I thought about as I got older: why didn't he pass that along?" Her parents, too, especially her mother, attempted sporadically to instill religious knowledge in their children by organizing a Sunday school to learn Qur'an and uttering pious phrases like "*ashhadu an la ilaha illa llah* [the first part of the statement of faith, the *shahada*, 'I bear witness there is no deity save the one God'] every single day when we left to go to school."

In the absence of mosques and formal religious leadership, individuals like 'Aziza's mother improvised. Their efforts were unsophisticated and occurred in a disconnected fashion. There was no systematic integration of practice. The result was an inchoate "God-consciousness"—'Aziza's choice of phrase in English glossed the Qur'anic notion of *taqwa*, or "God awareness." She and her family were adrift in America, she seemed to indicate, no longer retaining a connection with Islam other than, in her telling, a few formulaic phrases and a rudimentary encounter with scriptural revelation.

Standing on the other side of her conversion or "reversion" to "proper Islam," 'Aziza viewed her previous life as mired in ignorance, immersed in a mistaken fusion of culture and faith. Her interpretation of the past reflected a long-established reformist Islamic explanation for the putative decline of Islam in the face of North Atlantic (Western) culture and power. This explanation pinpointed the weakening of Islamic orthodoxy and of a corresponding ignorance of "true Islam" among believers. Assimilation among immigrant Muslims constituted one example of this problem. Subjectively, 'Aziza experienced the "truth" of this diagnosis of Muslim weakness as a personal crisis of identity that only became resolved through her counter-assimilation into reformist ideology and practice ("proper Islam," in her terms).

The key event in this resolution for 'Aziza and her family was the establishment of the Mosque Foundation as the predominant institution of the suburban enclave. Along with their friends and neighbors in their suburban community, 'Aziza's parents and husband began to participate in prayers and other activities at the mosque. As they did so, they adopted the form of piety that the mosque leadership, following the reformist ascendancy in the late 1970s and early 1980s, advocated.

'Aziza, too, gradually joined in this process. With her husband, she began to attend prayers at the Mosque Foundation. She felt initially awkward, however, having "learned prayer incorrectly from my mother." She also did not immediately conform to reformist expectations for women's dress. She began wearing the scarf and a robe, as mandated by the mosque, during prayers but regularly removed these garments when she left the mosque's premises. The sartorial question confronted her from multiple directions. At the mosque's Qur'an study circles for women, the discussion often centered on the Qur'anic passages addressing hijab and women's clothing. Discussion leaders interpreted these texts as mandates to women to remain properly covered in public spaces beyond the mosque's premises (see Q 7:46, Q 19:16–17, Q 33:53, Q 41:5, Q 42:51 on hijab and Q 24:31, Q 33:59 on clothing practices). 'Aziza's husband, too, lobbied her to wear the scarf continuously. "My husband wasn't a good teacher," she reflected, "he just said he didn't want me to end up in hell; we had issues about this for like three years."

She resisted the pressure but finally, in 1993, during Ramadan, she made the decision to wear the hijab continuously: "By the time of the *'id* [the three-day feast that ends Ramadan]," she recalled, "I remember my daughter saying, 'Take off your scarf, we're going out to eat,' and I said, 'No, I'm not taking it off,' and that was that." The decision marked her definitively as a "Muslim" to non-Muslims and to Palestinians, including her grandmother, for whom veiling was "old world," not something one did in America. She described the decision as a "radical mastectomy" that cut off her former self. Years later, in the moment of our interview in 2012, the realignment had taken hold, the scarf and *jilbab* coat now fully integrated into her sense of who she was.

Alongside these processes, and central to them, was the creation of the private Islamic schools, Universal and Aqsa. These new institutions offered an opportunity to 'Aziza to integrate her children into an Islamic religious milieu that simultaneously preserved Arab ethnic attachments and religious values without contradictions. As she discussed what these schools meant to her, she recalled a young man who was helping to organize the effort. During a planning meeting, he spoke of a "lost generation" in Chicago. He described the schools and the mosque as a return to authenticity, a path out of the American wilderness. The young man's words reverberated within 'Aziza. They voiced what had been an inchoate feeling, an unspoken sense of perdition. Recalling what he had said still caused her to weep: tears came to her eyes as she recounted the moment to me.

Toward the end of our conversation, I observed to 'Aziza that I did not notice any display referring to Palestine in her home. Instead, Qur'anic verses framed in gold calligraphy decorated the walls. "That's true," she said. "I know I'm Palestinian, but I'm a Muslim above all else." Recently, however, she had begun to absorb a political perspective, especially through her son-in-law, who was an immigrant from the northern West Bank. A devout Muslim committed to reformist ideals, he sympathized with the Islamist movements in Palestine, claiming they were pure in their intentions, unlike "the corrupt [Fatah-led] Palestinian Authority." 'Aziza agreed with this idea. Echoing a well-established reformist argument, she asserted that the plight of Palestinians was the result of their falling away from Islam. The oppressors—the Israeli and US governments but also corrupt secular Palestinian leadership—were God's sword wielded against the people to bring them back to Islam: "There's a *mathal* [saying] in *'arabi* [Arabic]: *inna al-zalim sayf allah*," she remarked, "which means, 'the oppressor is Allah's sword,' that the oppressor is not an accident; he's there to remind us, bring us back."

'Aziza had felt deeply the communal falling away from faith she described. She recounted the public ridicule and rejection she confronted after she began to wear the scarf. Her detractors, Palestinians opposed to the Islamization occurring in the suburbs, accused her of embracing a backward ideology that would retard Palestinian progress. But 'Aziza had come to see herself first and foremost as a Muslim, and through her scarf and *jilbab* and through her volunteer work for the mosque she presented herself publicly as such. She was profoundly concerned for the injustice that Palestinians suffered. But her politics, to the extent she expressed them, emphasized the necessity of conversion or reversion to Islam. Only in this way would Palestinians discover a path out of their wilderness in Chicago and in the Holy Land, too.

Denationalized Sectarianism among Christians

A second example of denationalized sectarianism comes from the Christian milieu. It bears strong parallels with 'Aziza's case: a specifically religious-sectarian affiliation and a corresponding sense of distance from ethnic-national identity emerge as dominant themes. These orientations, also as in 'Aziza's trajectory, reflected weak or absent integration into secular nationalist institutions and isolation from the main immigrant enclave. They showed, too, the shaping effect of participation within the religious structures that immigrants of the generation of 1948–67 created.

Born in the late 1970s, Leo (a pseudonym) grew up in South Chicago. His father worked in the steel mills there while his mother supplemented the family income as a seamstress. After the mills closed, his father, along with the majority of other men in their neighborhood, suffered extended unemployment punctuated by occasional work in the local service economy. He eventually secured a permanent and relatively well-paying job as a barge operator on the Chicago River. The family subsequently moved to the Northwest Side to be closer to his work.

The move occurred at a critical juncture in Leo's life. The first Gulf War (1990–91) was nearing its end. During the war, neighborhood children had bullied Leo and his siblings. They taunted them for being Arabs and, erroneously, Muslims:

> When the steel mills closed, parents lost jobs. So a lot of men, fathers and brothers, signed up for the military and ended up overseas. Their kids now saw us as the Arabic kids. They started bullying us. A couple of guys beat up my brother. They were like, 'My brother's fighting your dad over there.' I was like, 'No! My dad is working at Little Caesar's trying to get by! He's trying to do the American dream thing!' They just assumed this 'Muslim versus us' thing. They'd ask, 'Is your mom dressed up in a scarf?' And, I'd say, 'No, no we're Christian! You saw me at church last Sunday!' We were going to the Orthodox Church [St. George Antiochian Orthodox Church in Cicero] during the holidays, but we'd go to this local Methodist church during the week 'cause it was close by. It was a nightmare until we moved to the Northwest Side. In our new neighborhood, everybody was accustomed to differences.

The spike in anti-Arab and anti-Muslim racism during the Gulf War stripped Leo's family of their quiet attempt to assimilate. His father's new job and the diverse neighborhood that became their new home offered refuge from the collapsing economy and war-driven bigotry in South Chicago. The family's social center, however, increasingly became the Antiochian Orthodox milieu and its institutions, principally the St. George Antiochian Orthodox Church in Cicero. Integration into this milieu led Leo to see himself as primarily Orthodox Christian, not as Arab or Palestinian. His family's mixed ethnic and sectarian background also influenced him in this direction.

Leo's grandfather immigrated to Palestine following the genocidal violence targeting Armenians in eastern Anatolia during the First World War (1915–17). He settled, like most of the refugees, in an area of Jerusalem's Old City now known as the "Armenian Quarter." The grandfather eventually married a Greek Orthodox woman from the town of Beit Sahour, which lies adjacent to Bethlehem just southeast of Jerusalem. Leo's father, who grew up in South Chicago, also married beyond the Armenian and Palestinian communities. His wife had grown up within the Chaldean Catholic community in Iraq.

Leo's family were among the original members of St. George. From its beginning, the church integrated Arab immigrants of diverse backgrounds from across the Chicago metropolitan area. It did so through an explicitly Orthodox sense of identity that elided nationality and even Arab ethnicity. Leo described how this occurred:

> At St. George Church there are Iraqis, Syrians, Jordanians, Lebanese, and Palestinians. Most of us, the young adults, are mixed. My vice-president [of the young adults group] is half-Jordanian and half-Palestinian. We don't have this sense of national pride. It doesn't get discussed. Some of us identify with the term 'Arab,' some people do; and other people don't identify with the term at all. They think that 'Arab' means 'Muslim.' It's weird. You'll hear somebody say, like, 'how Arabs are,' and somebody else will say, well, 'we're not Arabic.' And, it's like, really? It's weird because at St. George the liturgy is half in Arabic and our parents speak Arabic and understand it [. . .]. The only connection those of us who are younger have [to Arab ethnicity] though is the food. I'm kinda of like that, too, no strong connection to Arab or Palestinian identity. What I care about is whether someone shares the same values I have with respect to Orthodoxy. If I met a girl who was Protestant and she shared the same values I did, I wouldn't have an issue with it. It's a deep-rooted sense in me: this is the Christian faith.

The denationalization that had occurred within St. George—and among the earliest Muslim Palestinian residents in the suburbs, like 'Aziza's family—replicated a classical assimilation trajectory in the United States in which sectarian or denominational identities elided ethnic particularities. But in Leo's case there were other reasons, too, for national disaffiliation, or, in the terms employed here, denationalized sectarianism. Like 'Aziza's, Leo's family never lived within the Palestinian immigrant milieu. Instead, they lived on Chicago's far southern edge and, later, on the city's Northwest Side, commuting on Sundays to St. George in Cicero. As Christians, moreover, they increasingly perceived the main Arab immigrant concentrations, including the Palestinian one, as "Muslim." US wars in the Middle East and the consequent spiking anti-Muslim reaction reinforced the sense of distinction. Many Arab Christians such as Leo and his family sought to distinguish themselves from Islam in response to this reaction.

Leo described this dynamic of alienation further as he discussed his interactions with Muslims during his college years. This period, the 1990s, corresponded with the Islamic shift occurring among immigrant Muslims, including Palestinians. Leo's Muslim classmates, he stated, adopted an "extreme, combative" stance toward him, emphasizing religious differences:

My college had a big Muslim student organization. There were no Arab Christians on campus, I never met one, never had a class with a Christian Arab in it—'Oh, you're a Christian and you're an Arab, that's cool'—never had that experience. It was always Muslim guys and they always made a big deal of their religion with me [. . .]. They could not stop taking potshots at me because I was Christian. They'd come up with these stories I'd never even heard of. I couldn't find them in the Bible. I'd go to my *abuna* ['father,' that is, priest] and he'd go, 'Oh, that was a story in the Qur'an.' They'd claimed it was from the Christian Bible. I'd come back and correct them and then they'd be like, 'Oh, okay, but what about this or that?' So, it became this back and forth to the point of exhaustion. I was like, 'Okay, I have to continuously prove my faith to you? Why every time we hang out you gotta like test my faith?'

Leo's experience with Muslim women was different. "Muslim women were the best, the girls my age, including the *muhajjaba*s [*muhajjabat*, women who wear the scarf], they have always been insanely sweet to me and caring." He recalled a grade-school friend who brought him things to eat from her father's store. The sectarian prejudice he encountered with men did not register with the same intensity in these interactions with women. Leo thought the difference might have had to do with the need of men to perform a type of combative masculinity: "Maybe it's just being a man," he said, "Maybe we're testosterone driven and looking for a fight." When religion did arise as a topic with his female acquaintances, the women would express curiosity about why Leo followed a "Jewish religion" and not the religion that the Prophet Muhammad, "who they said was a Palestinian," had proclaimed. Such comments, as Leo reported them, illustrated the extent to which Islam particularly had come to link tightly with national-ethnic affiliation. Islam was Palestinian; Christianity was other, even possibly, vaguely, Jewish. Christians, too, as Leo reported, absorbed these distinctions, associating "Palestinian" with "Muslim" and consequently placing "Christian" in a separate, de-ethnicized (non-Arab) category.

In contrast with individuals who questioned his religious identity, either by challenging it or by expressing puzzlement over it, Leo described interactions with "agnostic" Muslims who communicated a skeptical view of religious claims generally. These students seemed more interested in simply "hanging out" than with demarcating sectarian distinctions. Leo found acceptance in their attitude. Significantly, he did not describe their outlook as secular but rather as focused on the individual and rooted implicitly in a Christian-like notion of service and love—he used the Greek New Testament's term "caritas," a love of humankind or charity—that looked beyond sect and nation to the individual. The Muslims and Christians he respected were those who said, in Leo's words:

> 'I love you as a human being and I'll help you regardless of what denomination you are.' A Muslim and Christian can be friends in a deep-rooted love for God. The true Christian never says, 'I'm a Palestinian first, a Christian second.' They say, 'I'm a servant of the world regardless of ethnicity.' I'm assuming true Muslim belief says the same thing.

CONCLUSION

The religious turn as it manifests in the narratives of the individuals featured in this chapter unfolds along generational lines. In my data, religious revitalization in Palestine affects the diaspora religious turn primarily through the experiences of immigrants of the generations of 1948–67 and 1987–2001 who are born in the homeland. These individuals establish the core institutions through which the religious shift shapes the subjectivities of individuals in succeeding generations. In some cases, the generational lines in my data overlap: 'Aziza's trajectory, for example, arcs between the 1987–2001 and post-September 11 cohorts.

In the aftermath of the emergence of distinct sectarian milieus, the evolution of religious subjectivities moves, in my data, along the diverging axes of sectarianized nationalism and denationalized sectarianism. The factors determining these trajectories have to do with the degree to which an individual becomes integrated within religious-nationalist structures, Christian or Muslim. Equally significant for this process, however, is the relative absence of a desectarianized secular space that integrates individuals as Palestinians across sectarian lines. This lack reflects the impact of the sectarianization process, particularly through the mechanisms of the religious shift and the consequent decentering of secularism.

The sectarianization trajectories described in this chapter are not, however, the only possible outcomes of these processes. The next two chapters explore religious-secular hybridizations that result from the same sectarianizing dynamic. In doing so, they shift the analysis from a generational to a typological approach. This change allows for a mapping of the range of syncretic orientations that have formed since the 1990s.

5

Dynamic Syntheses

Reversion, Conversion, and Accommodation

"They're basically Marxists in hijab!" The exclamation punctuated an exchange early in my fieldwork with a longtime friend who had been a founder of the Arab Community Center (ACC), the *markaz*, and an activist in the Union of Palestinian Women Associations. I had asked her about the collapse of the political left and of PLO nationalism, generally, and about the parallel rise in the prominence and power of the mosques. I noted, particularly, the presence of younger activists who performed prayers and other ritual activities in the course of their work at the *markaz*'s successor organization, the Arab American Action Network (AAAN). My friend insisted the shift was superficial: a secular commitment to justice and liberation persisted beneath the trappings of piety. The young men and women who appeared to have embraced the Islamic shift were, she said, really leftists in beards and scarves. They were devoted to the same work and to the same liberation goals as the previous generation of secular activists. The AAAN's Executive Director, Hatem Abudayyeh, agreed. "Take Nawal [pseudonym], for example," he told me, "she's committed to the same things as we are [at the AAAN] but layers on this Islam piece."

Born in the old immigrant enclave of Chicago's Southwest Side, Nawal, who was twenty-eight years old when I interviewed her, worked as a coordinator for a domestic violence shelter located in the southwest suburbs. She often collaborated with the AAAN on projects that focused on women's empowerment. She had also volunteered at the AAAN after graduating from college. This volunteer work allowed her to explore career options in community development and women's advocacy within an institution that shared her dedication to the Palestinian cause.

Nawal's commitment to Palestine advocacy, women's empowerment, and community mobilization aligned directly with the value orientations of secularists like Abudayyeh. Islam, however, was far from incidental to Nawal's moral and political commitments. Whatever the "Marxists in hijab" moniker might have meant in her case, her piety had significant implications for her negotiation of identity: Nawal's narrative, in fact, revealed an oscillation of the religious and the secular. The terms did not collapse into one or the other, in her account, but rather co-existed in a shifting, interacting relation.

SYNCRETIC SECULARITY

The religious shift and corresponding attenuation of secularism documented in the previous chapters have spurred a range of complex identity configurations that do not easily align with a simple secular-religious dichotomy. Indications of this complexity have already surfaced in the discussion of the generational processes underlying the formation of distinct secular and religious trajectories. This chapter and the next map this complexity further, demonstrating dynamic syntheses—vital hybridizations[1]—that occur as individuals travel back and forth across secular and religious spaces.

The discussion that follows depicts a typological range of identity. The types are meant to be descriptive. They are not intended as a value scale.[2] The narratives selected for analysis exemplify the array of articulations among my interlocutors. Whether they represent broad or statistically dominant trends beyond my data requires additional research. The profiles do not establish general representativeness, but rather indicate the range of orientations among my interviewees and, in doing so, show and explain how those orientations subjectively mediate and integrate the secular and the religious.

The outlooks I document underscore Eipper's (2011) claims concerning "syncretic secularity," which, he says, emerges from "the influence of religious and secular worldviews upon one another." He explains further:

> [Syncretic secularity is] the union or reconciliation of diverse, even opposed, beliefs, tenets, procedures and practices, the different elements having been brought into some kind of agreement or accord (see Droogers 1989; Stewart and Shaw 1994; Stewart 1999). In these circumstances, religious genres, allegiances, understandings and behaviours blur and blend in ways that require an acceptance of diversity, even a willingness to embrace it and enter into dialogue with it (34).

This conception of syncretism relates to the ambivalent situation that Taylor (2007) refers to as "fragility." Fragility describes the condition of uneasy awareness that one's worldview is not universally accepted, that it in fact co-exists with other competing value orientations. Individuals experiencing such pluralism—almost everyone, globally, today—become aware of the tenuousness of their positions: they might claim universal validity for their stances but nevertheless must confront the fact of limited acceptance. They must contend, as well, with transgressions, desertions, mergers, and conversions as "one's own" cross lines, join other sides, and blur distinctions.

Long before Eipper and Taylor, Weber (1946b, 148) and Simmel (1955 [1922]) spoke respectively of "a polytheism of values" and the "crossing of social circles" as individuals negotiated the distinct and competing value spheres to which modern rationalization processes gave rise. But what Eipper's concept of syncretic secularity gets at that these other ideas do not—or at least not with the same sensitivity to the complexity of lived social reality—is the interactive, mutually conditioning quality of the polytheism of values and of the crossing and overlapping of spaces in one's daily life. The value spheres and milieus that Taylor, Weber, and Simmel so aptly identify are not discrete spaces but rather dynamically interrelated. They flow into one another transversely, churning, blending, and eddying as their currents cut into each other.

Eipper is perhaps too categorical in his emphasis on "agreement or accord," given the dynamism of the syncretic process. The blurring and blending that occur are, as the hydraulic metaphor conveys, dynamic and provisional. Confluences that reconcile the secular-religious tensions do not stand still. Instead, they flow at varying rates, merging and separating at different points. They can reverse direction or branch sharply to form new diverging or opposing currents. In this sense, Eipper's syncretic secularities are active, often momentary secular-religious convergences.[3]

Further, gender, race, and class inflect the negotiations of these convergences.[4] The urban space of Chicago, as seen previously, mediates this inflection. It enables, for example, encounter with other religious and activist traditions (including African American Islam and Puerto Rican nationalism) and with other types of social milieu (for example, youth party scenes; culturally diverse artistic milieus; anti-domestic violence networks) that challenge gender, race, and class hierarchies as well as the moral proprieties of the new suburban, middle class piety. The previous chapters have already shown the effects of these interactions on individual trajectories. This chapter and the next highlight their impact further in the elaboration of the syncretic range.

REVERSION, CONVERSION, AND ACCOMMODATION

The syncretic types I will analyze in this chapter describe movements from a secular to a religious orientation. I refer to these types of shifts as movements of "religious secularity." In arcing from the secular into the religious, individuals undergoing this transition selectively accommodate or resignify the secular; the individual embraces piety, partially or wholly, but in doing so adapts—rather than cancels or suppresses—secularity within the terms and practices of the religious milieu into which she or he now enters. The process is not necessarily unilinear. It can oscillate, shifting in its expression as it does so.

In my data, this particular type of movement manifests in three ways: reversion, conversion, and accommodation. Reversion refers to a shift from piety to secularism back to piety. Conversion indicates a change from an original secularity to a new religiosity. These two orientations, as will become evident below, constitute themselves partially as a critique, implicit and explicit, of the class and gender hierarchies that suburban reformism aligns with through its support for individual wealth accumulation tempered by an ethos of tithing, charity, and gender complementarity.[5]

By contrast, accommodation, the third type of religious secularity, entails adaptation to, and partial identification with, the religious milieu and the suburban middle-class piety that marks it culturally. This partial convergence is social and political: the individual who exemplifies it in my discussion participates, for example, in the suburban Islamic institutions and collaborates, professionally, with the Mosque Foundation leadership. However, she stops short of a full acceptance of reformism, embracing only certain aspects of piety (prayer) while selectively ignoring other practices (wearing the scarf, fasting during Ramadan).

REVERSION

Social Background and Early Identity-Formation Processes

Nawal exemplifies the first type of religious secularity: reversion, which entails fluctuation and a complex negotiation between religious and secular spaces. Her initial encounter with and integration into the religious milieu tracked with the class and demographic shifts that coincided with the rise of reformist Islam in the suburbs. Nawal's parents arrived in Chicago in 1977, ten years after Israel occupied the West Bank. Her father found work on an assembly line—"He has a lot of burns on his hands from that time," Nawal remarked. Incrementally saving his money, he eventually opened a small store, one of many ("it's been store after store for twenty years.") Her mother was a homemaker. In 1991, when Nawal was nine years old, the family moved to the near southwest suburbs. Asked what prompted the shift, Nawal explained that her parents wished to shield her brother from gang violence. Also, many Arab families had already moved to the suburbs, so taking the family to a homogeneously white area created during the "white flight" of the 1950s seemed less intimidating than it might have been.

The move to the suburbs proved crucial to the formation of Nawal's early identity orientations. No longer in close proximity to the community centers on the city's Southwest Side, the family gravitated toward the new Mosque Foundation that anchored the emerging enclave in the suburbs. This change had a transforming effect on the family. Initially, Nawal said, her family was "[not] very practicing." They abstained from alcohol and said "*bismillah al-rahman al-rahim*[6] before [eating] and that was about it." Her mother had always worn a scarf but "towards the back [with the scarf pulled back and tied behind the head rather than pinned under the chin in front] so you could see she was a Muslim, but culturally to the back [that is, in a style that did not comport with the *shari'a* requirements of Islam as Nawal understood them]; so, she didn't wear [the hijab] because she identified as a *muhajjaba* [a woman who is deliberately committed to the scarf as a sign of Muslim identity]; for example, [even though she wore a scarf] she would still wear short sleeves and a skirt above the knees, but a scarf to the back, so she wore it because of culture and not so much because of Islam."[7] Gradually, however, as Nawal's mother began to participate in mosque activities, she conformed to the reformist norms that it instituted. She began to pin the hijab scarf under her chin in the style of a *muhajjaba*, and she started to pray regularly. Apparently desiring to make up for a perceived failure to transmit religious values to the other older children—Nawal recounted that her older siblings never learned to pray or to read the Qur'an—her mother urged her father to enroll the two youngest kids in the new Aqsa School, despite his concerns about the financial cost of doing so.

The move to the new school had a profound impact on Nawal. She described how she "LOVED [the school], I really loved it! I liked the content." She also embraced the disciplines through which the school sought to instill reformist values within the children and staff. As a matter of course in the mosque and in these schools, girls were urged to wear the hijab scarf and the *jilbab* coat—forms of clothing that marked alignment with book-centered reformism.[8] The instruction she received also systematized her religious knowledge. For example, she described, in a manner similar to 'Aziza (discussed in chapter 4), having to "correct" the prayer and recitation practice that she had originally learned from her mother. In contrast to her mother's "cultural Islam," Nawal became grounded in the study of texts and in the "proper" formation of practices. Her decision to embrace these revised practices, especially by wearing the scarf in a reformist style (pinned under the chin, showing only the face), also caused her to stand out against the majority non-Arab and non-Muslim culture beyond the suburban enclave.

Nawal's Islamic (re)formation, however, was not unidirectional. As with a number of other participants in my project who attended the private Islamic schools, financial considerations forced Nawal's family to send her to a public high school. This shift substantially altered the institutional ethos within which she lived out her daily life. One consequence, as she described it, was the weakening of her piety. She described this period, however, not as a turning away from all religious belief and practice per se: "When I was in high school, I was a Muslim, and like, I never experimented with drugs or alcohol or ate pork [. . .] but I [also] didn't pray." Unlike the Islamic school, where "you had to pray," the public school offered other types of extracurricular activity: "My top priority [in high school] was being involved [in clubs] [. . .]. I was not very devout in high school." In addition to not praying regularly, she also stopped wearing the scarf other than when she attended events at the mosque.

The alteration that occurred in Nawal's engagement with Islamic and public institutions illustrated the fluidity in, and negotiation of, practice across different kinds of space. Her family's precarious class situation—working class, attempting to transition to the suburban middle class—produced this fluidity by rendering uneven their integration into the institutions of the piety-minded milieu. As she tacked back and forth between mosque and public school, disenchantment and re-enchantment of daily life acted simultaneously upon her: she removed her scarf and ceased to pray at school; she wore the hijab and returned to prayer at mosque. In doing so, she absorbed a sense of the limits of each distinct space, each zone co-existing with, but not extending into, the other. She adapted to the norms of each space, functioning within each according to its terms.

Nationalist-Islamic Confluences

Nawal's transition to college—an event that stabilized her movement into the middle class—reconfigured and heightened her experience of secular-religious tension. Interaction with Muslim student organizations and the death of her mother propelled a reversion to piety. Gendered expectations and patriarchal authority demands in the home intertwined with this reversion. At the same time, an encounter with Palestine solidarity activism on campus and the development of ties with the Arab American Action Network (AAAN) led her into the secularist political milieu in the old urban immigrant enclave in which she had been born and lived her early childhood. The AAAN context, especially, generated tensions with the reformist piety that she had begun to reinhabit on campus. The tensions led her to revise her bimodal adaptive approach—that is, enacting different practices in different spaces—in an effort to achieve moral consistency across all spaces.

Nawal's entry into Palestine solidarity circles marked a honing of a previously amorphous sense of national identity. She described not being active on Palestine before college. "The most I had ever done was write rap lyrics about *filastin* [Palestine]," she said.

> I was passionate about *filastin* but I didn't know much about it. I wasn't active. I was just passionate. When I was in high school I just knew I was Palestinian; and at that time I called myself "Arabian" like many high schoolers and many young adults still do. That was what I thought I was. I didn't know.

On campus, however, she learned about Students for Justice in Palestine (SJP) from students she was tutoring on campus. Joining the group drew her into citywide activist networks. The key event in this process was a SJP silent sit-in: "We were going to break the silence by performing spoken word and songs [. . .]. I had written some lyrics about Palestine and shared them there and they liked them [. . .] and then the next thing I know they tell me about this new thing called Café Intifada, and they said, 'You've gotta go lay down your verse there!'" The "Café" turned out to be a AAAN-sponsored event in Chicago's Southwest Side, where Nawal had lived before her family moved to the suburbs: "It was so amazing for me. I had never been exposed to these things. Not only that but I was like, 'It's the 'hood, it's where I grew up!'" After her performance, AAAN Executive Director Hatem Abudayyeh asked if she would be willing to offer a series of hip hop classes for youth. She agreed and soon was traveling weekly to the Southwest Side to work with a group of middle and high school students.

At the same time that her integration into the Southwest Side secular activist milieu was occurring, Nawal was also beginning to re-encounter Islam on her university campus. The experience renewed her attraction to the piety that had so powerfully shaped her childhood at the Mosque Foundation. One crucial impetus for this awakening of her dormant religiosity was the university's Muslim Student Association (MSA).[9] Nawal described the MSA activists as providing her with a positive example of piety as an option for young adults. She had thought that she would wear the scarf again, but only when she was older. With her mother's trajectory as a model, she associated adult piety with passage into marriage and full adulthood. The MSA, however, modeled an alternative understanding. She found herself asking, "Why do I have to wait until I'm old to start praying and getting involved?" The MSA also exposed Nawal to the diversity of Islam. Meeting Muslims from different backgrounds forced her to see that what she often took to be "Islam," especially notions of shame (*'ayb*) and consequent restrictions on the activities of girls and women, in reality reflected particular "Palestinian" cultural mores.

This understanding of what she took to be her family's "traditional" or "cultural" piety led, with the help of peer mentors in the MSA, to a critical study of the authoritative textual sources of Islam. A close friend in the group was especially knowledgeable about the *fiqh*—jurisprudence relating to *shari'a*—and "introduced me to authors and sources that were authentic compared to, like, the *shaykh* on the street that gave the *fatwa* [traditionally, the learned opinion of a religious scholar on practice and doctrine] about whatever." She described that "street" Islam as focused on how it was "*haram* [forbidden in Islamic law] to blah, blah, blah," but "you never questioned sources, you never went back down and asked, 'Well, where did that come from? What's your source?'"[10]

Empowered by a new, critical knowledge of the foundational texts, Nawal negotiated an expanded autonomy to attend Palestinian activist meetings that would extend into the late evening, well past the hour when daughters of "respectable," aspiring middle-class families returned home. To do so, she effectively invoked the superseding authority of God (Allah) to counter the limitations imposed by her family's "cultural" patriarchy. Nawal enacted this countervailing authority by wearing a scarf, engaging in prayer, and adhering to various restrictions on cross-gender interactions.

Alongside the engagement with the MSA and her discovery of the counteracting authority of its type of piety, a second key impetus of Nawal's reversion to Islam was the crisis of her mother's terminal illness. Nawal took primary responsibility for caring for her mother in the hospital. She prayed and read Qur'an to her at her bedside daily. These practices reactivated the physical, mental, and emotional dispositions she had absorbed in the Islamic schools as a child. She stated: "During that time, even though I wasn't a *muhajjaba*, wasn't constantly wearing the hijab, still, because I was praying around the clock, I kept the hijab on, I would just walk around with it, and again, it felt very comforting. I just felt protected."[11]

Nawal's references to comfort and protection reveal the complex sources and meanings of her reversion to reformist piety. Death can occasion a search for significance, solace, and stability among the living. Prayer and recitation of the Qur'an met those needs for Nawal by reactivating deeply embedded connections to her mother. Nawal's initial path into Islamic religiosity as a child was through her mother's tutelage and example. The comfort and protection she spoke of were a metaphoric allusion to a kind of divine nurture: maternal care was a quality that Nawal experienced in her relationship to the divine as she faced her mother's death. This sense of the feminine divine heightened the contrast with the majority male family Nawal would continue to be a part of after losing her mother.[12]

A third and related source of Nawal's return to piety lay in the effects of the ritual practice that she began to re-embrace. Nawal indicated the importance of these effects in her comments about wearing hijab in order to meet the conventional requirements for prayer. The sheer frequency of her engagement in the practice caused her to rehabituate to the discipline the prayer imposed. Very soon after her mother died, Nawal had other similar reacclimating experiences. One such instance occurred during her first year as an AAAN volunteer. That summer, the AAAN cosponsored a youth camp on the premises of a nearby mosque.[13] Nawal typically put on her scarf just before entering the mosque and then removed it at the end of the day. This donning and discarding of the scarf caused parents and camp participants to ask: "Are you a *muhajjaba* or not?" The questioning heightened her consciousness of an inconsistency in her actions. At the same time, the sheer frequency of wearing the scarf during the day "allowed me to practice, practice, practice wearing hijab, and so little did I know how comforting it was, just to wear it, and I *took* to it, I felt much more comfortable wearing it."

The comfort that came with rehabituation paralleled a new sense of security. Street catcalling ended, she told me. The hijab had redefined her body, creating a boundary around it. It also imposed new borders in her workspace; but, in this instance, rather than deflecting attention, her clothing decisions drew direct challenge. One person told her "it was just a phase" she would presumably grow out of, while another expressed dismay, saying, "I thought you supported women's rights!" Nawal reacted, saying to herself, "But what about my right to choose to wear this?" Moreover, Nawal had continued to advocate strongly for women's social, political, and economic equality: her reversion to piety had not changed this fact. In retrospect, Nawal came to realize "it was generational and political [. . .]: they saw me going down this religious route, which signaled to them [in their mind] that I was going away from them [politically]."[14]

At home, perhaps because she sensed that especially in this space she might encounter resistance, Nawal was careful to avoid calling attention to her piety. Ultimately, in a moment she humorously referred to as "getting busted," her family found her out. Nawal had been careful initially to perform her prostrations in the seclusion of her bedroom. Her brother stumbled in on her one day, however, initiating an unwanted exposure and recognition of her new identity as an observant Muslim within the family. The discreet manner in which Nawal at first enacted her return to piety served to authenticate the transition in her own eyes—"I wanted to lock myself away and make sure I'm doing it for my own reasons"—but also for those around her: she would show herself and others that she was not seeking public affirmation and status or performing piety in response to pressure from piety-minded friends or family members.

Achieving consistency of practice across all domains of her life was also important to Nawal as she sought to authenticate her reversion. This attempt at consistency, however, generated tension. Conflicting expectations about bodily comportment and their implications for sociability in different milieus produced the greatest stress. As part of her enactment of piety, Nawal began refusing to shake hands with non-*mahram* men.[15] Among her family, this refusal created problems whenever she greeted older male cousins who, according to Islamic *fiqh* (jurisprudence), retained the right to marry her. Growing up, she had been accustomed to referring to these cousins as "uncles" and acknowledging them by shaking their hands and hugging and kissing them (socially, as part of the greeting practice). Declining to hug and kiss created deep awkwardness. Her father at one point became so exasperated that he attempted to compel her physically to shake hands: "I remember once my father introduced me to a cousin of his, and I was standing like this [holding her hands behind her back]. He *pulled* my hand and said, 'Shake his hand!' It was *so* uncomfortable." She encountered a similar tension among her activist friends. Within this social circle, she explained, hugging between and across the sexes signaled comradeship. At the mosque, by contrast, "I don't have to worry about Brother Ahmad coming over to hug me or to shake my hand."

Nawal eventually resolved the tensions her refusal to shake was creating by essentially abandoning her attempt to be consistent in this practice across the social spaces in which she interacted. For example, contradicting the *fiqh* consensus on the matter as she saw it, she decided that she would shake hands with fellow male activists at the AAAN and in other secular organizing spaces. She would do so, as well, with close non-*mahram* relatives in her family. She described the decision as religiously incorrect but socially necessary, given her need to interact across milieus that did not conform to Islamic orthopraxy as she understood and desired to enact it.[16] "It wasn't comfortable for me not to shake someone's hand," she told me, "and it wasn't comfortable for that person who was being rejected." Nawal had brought the religious into the secular, requiring others to adapt to her, but in doing so, she encountered resistance. Ultimately, because she desired to maintain relationships across morally heterogeneous spaces, she chose to modify her practices, accepting the inconsistency that accompanied this decision.

Nawal subsequently left her work at the women's shelter to take a position as a program coordinator with an Islamic social service organization on Chicago's Northwest Side. Nawal's transition to this new institutional setting represented not only an opportunity to advance in her career but also a chance to return to an explicitly Islamic milieu that likely resolved the contradiction between her commitment to piety and the expectations for cross-gender interactions in secular activist spaces. In her new organization, she represented a transethnic Muslim community, not a specifically Arab or Palestinian one, and yet, to the extent she made her political sensibilities known, her presence likely injected Palestinian concerns into the stream of discourse in her new workplace. Whether at the AAAN and the women's shelter or at the new Islamic organization, Nawal's reversionary movements rendered secular and religious into dynamically syncretic forms.

CONVERSION

Whereas reversion, as Nawal illustrates, involves a shifting from piety-minded spaces to secularist milieus and back again to the piety-minded sphere, conversion, the focus of this next section, moves in a single direction from secularism to piety. As with reversion, conversion as a syncretic process is complex: rather than wholesale replacement of one worldview with another, the movement integrates and reinterprets secular orientations—particularly those that emphasize pluralism and intersectarian unity—within a new religious perspective. This reinterpretation, in my example, entails a critique and transcendence of secular nationalism and also, ironically, of the suburban Islamic shift. Secularism is seen as a limiting, provincializing mode of solidarity, which privileges the suffering of one's own ethnos or nation above that of others.[17] The reformist Islamic shift, in this same view, is seen as leading to a similar end by reducing Islam to an alternative, sacralized nationalism. Conversion as a syncretic mode resists the reduction of religion, Islam, in this case, to a singular identity presumed to be equivalent to a particular expression or practice or ideological construal. It speaks rather of "perspectives" and universal "aspirations" present quintessentially within Islam but also extending beyond it. In this sense, conversion generates a type of cosmopolitanism that parallels and resignifies secular pluralism.

Rami Nashashibi, founder of the Inner-City Muslim Action Network (IMAN), illustrates the conversion trajectory in my data with particular vividness. Nashashibi has gained national attention for his work through IMAN, a Muslim-identified social service organization and community center situated in the predominantly African American and Latinx Chicago Lawn/West Englewood area on Chicago's South Side. He and IMAN have been the focus of academic studies and a New York Times profile (Karim 2009; Freedman 2014; Khabeer 2016). In 2016, former US President Barack Obama appointed Nashashibi to his Advisory

Council on Faith-Based and Neighborhood Partnerships. A year later, the MacArthur Foundation awarded him a "genius" grant.

I first met Nashashibi in the mid-1990s. The son of a Palestinian-Jordanian diplomat, he was, at the time, a young and rising activist leader within the Arab Community Center (the *markaz*). His integration into this sphere had a series of unforeseen consequences, leading ultimately to his exit from the *markaz* and its secularist ethos. This departure coincided with his "going the path of a true convert to Islam." As I will show, Nashashibi's "conversion" transformed his "antireligious" secularism into a type of religious secularity. In Nashashibi's narration, the headwaters of this transition lay in the intersecting currents of nationalism and "Americanization" in the lives of his parents and in his childhood.

Social Background and Early Identity-Formation Processes

Nashashibi's parents were from Jerusalem. His mother's family fled the village of Ein Karem on the outskirts of the city during the war of 1948. The family eventually settled in the Palestinian enclave in Chicago's Southwest Side. Nashashibi's father belonged to a wealthy and established political family in Jerusalem that remained in the city through the war. He traveled to the United States for college, completing his studies in California. He met Nashashibi's mother either in Chicago or during a trip home to see family in the Jerusalem area—Nashashibi was uncertain of the exact circumstances. After their wedding, Nashashibi's parents established life together as a couple in Amman and then moved to Jerusalem just prior to the war of 1967. The couple lived through the events of Black September (1970–71), during which the Jordanian regime violently suppressed the Palestinian resistance organizations that had created a quasi state-within-a-state inside the kingdom. Nashashibi's father subsequently served as a Jordanian diplomat in Tunis.

Nashashibi was born in Amman in 1972. He attended a boarding school in Rome during high school. He often visited his father in Tunis. During one such trip, his father arranged for him to meet top PLO leaders, including Yasser Arafat.

Religion seemed entirely absent from Nashashibi's childhood and adolescence. He recalled:

> My father didn't practice at all. I was not being raised in any way, shape, or form as a Muslim, not even as a nominal Muslim. My mom did make sure I would identify as Muslim. But I never once walked into a mosque, I never opened up a Qur'an, we didn't even do the kind of cultural stuff with *'id* [the feasts that mark the end of Ramadan and also the end of the Hajj season] or anything like that.

As Nashashibi described the situation, the family was not "ideologically secular" but rather apathetically areligious. If religion registered at all in his mother's home—Nashashibi's father and mother divorced when he was still a child—it did so in her display of Santa Clauses and other similar trappings of the commercialized public Christmas. The observation of this holiday had more to do, however, in Nashashibi's view, with his mother's assimilation of "Americana" during her childhood in Chicago than with any sort of religious influence per se. Nashashibi mentioned knowing at some point that he was a Muslim "to the extent to which I knew I wasn't Christian, whatever that meant [. . .]. I ran into a couple of other Muslims and learned about the role of Jesus and God, but that really was the extent of it. Other than that there wasn't really any education." Nashashibi's early sense of himself as a Muslim was passive, apophatic: Muslim meant "not Christian."

By contrast, for his mother sustaining one's identity as a Palestinian was of far greater importance than religion. Nashashibi commented:

> My mother was much more intent on Palestinian identification [. . .]. Of course, this was true of my father, but my father didn't spend too much time trying to lecture about it [. . .]. My mother was intent even after the divorce to make sure I stayed connected to the Palestinian thing [. . .]. I definitely as a kid was very much identifying with the [Palestinian] cause.

The methods his mother used to instill nationalist sentiment included intentional exposure of her children to global media news coverage and documentaries about key traumatic moments like the Sabra and Shatila massacres during the Israeli invasion of Lebanon in 1982. A second method was the act of returning "back home." Even after the divorce, Nashashibi's mother took her son on frequent visits to Palestine to maintain a relationship with his father's prominent Jerusalem family. Nashashibi recalled his first experience of crossing into Israel. Still a grade-schooler, he was separated from his mother and strip-searched at the border. "My mom [was] screaming [. . .]," he said, "the whole traumatic thing. It was my first encounter with military occupation and seeing tanks and guns [. . .]."[18]

Nashashibi's sense of nationalism as an identity and as a guiding moral and political commitment deepened during his years as a high school student in Italy. The main catalyst was the First Intifada: "By that time I was a kid who was really politicized," Nashashibi recalled, "and in Europe the people were very sympathetic to the Palestinians, particularly during the Intifada, wearing *kufiyas* [the emblematic checkered scarves]; the Intifada was the first time the Palestinian cause became a global solidarity issue." He became connected during this time with solidarity groups that were "Communist." "I didn't ideologically buy into all of that," he remarked, "but I did align with some of those [solidarity] politics."

Of Re-ve-láy-shun and Li-ber-áy-shun

In 1990, Nashashibi left Rome for Chicago to pursue undergraduate studies. His arrival coincided with the beginnings of the suburbanization of the Palestinian community and the corresponding Islamic shift and secularist attenuation. Yet these developments were not the principal factors in his religious transition, or "conversion." Instead, as Nashashibi narrated the process, the most significant influences were his encounters with racism and his relationships with Black Nationalists and Black Muslim activists on Chicago's South and Southwest Sides.

After he arrived on campus, Nashashibi recalls, officials warned the first-year students not to cross into "certain neighborhoods" bordering the college grounds. The admonition caused him to question the interdiction's rationale. He had never been warned away from any spaces in Rome. Curious about the forbidden zones, he began exploring those off-limits terrains, discovering as he did so a "horrifying" contrast of "two completely separate existences." The first Gulf War, which began just four months after his arrival, unexpectedly forged a sense of connection to this geography of exclusion: white students on campus, he said, hurled racial epithets like "sand n . . . r" at him, effectively linking him to the very neighborhoods he had been told to avoid. The experience of this racist backlash led him to transfer to another university. As in Nawal's experience, Palestinian solidarity groups at this new campus provided Nashashibi with a supportive student community and a structure through which to express his nationalist politics. These groups also had ties with the *markaz*. These connections subsequently facilitated Nashashibi's integration into the secular nationalist activist milieu on the city's Southwest Side.

Assimilation into the *markaz* space marked a crucial transition leading ultimately, and ironically, to Nashashibi's disenchantment with nationalism and to his corresponding conversion process. The origins of the shift lay, according to Nashashibi's account, in his encounter with Third World anti-imperialism and transnational solidarity orientations at the community center. As noted in chapter 2, the *markaz* founders had forged ties with other ethnic-national formations, especially anti-apartheid and pro-African National Congress groups. Activists linked to these groups were often present at the *markaz* to attend meetings or to socialize. One such individual, Thomas [pseudonym], an African American with previous Communist Party and Black Panther links, became an important mentor to Nashashibi. Thomas helped Nashashibi "connect the dots" of his experience as a Palestinian with the experience of other oppressed groups. In his own writings later, Nashahibi would characterize this particular perspective as emerging within "ghetto cosmopolitanism" (Nashashibi 2009, 271–82).

Through this lens, Nashashibi came to understand that, in the United States and globally, the intersecting lines of race and class produced hierarchies of privilege that oppressed all peoples of color, even within progressive circles putatively committed to liberation. He described this insight unfolding gradually through his interactions with Thomas. "[Every weekend] I would literally go with a notebook and sit with [Thomas at the factory in which he worked]," he recalled. Thomas would lecture, and Nashashibi would write notes "all night long." During the day, they would drive through the different South Side neighborhoods. "[Thomas] clued me into the different brothers and the different sets [during these tours]," Nashashibi remembered. "It was my first real exposure to groups like the

Blackstones and the Vice Lords and the connections to older struggles." Through this encounter, he "began to think [for the first time] about the Palestinian experience beyond just the Palestinian context." He realized, he said, how "frivolous" Palestine solidarity work was without these sorts of connections. From that point onward, he began to identify with other justice struggles, for example, in Central America and Puerto Rico. "I started really connecting with black students, Latino students" on campus. He collaborated with these other formations' sit-ins, agitating against the US interventions in Nicaragua, El Salvador, and Panama. "Now, again, I was doing this from an absolutely areligious vantage point," Nashashibi commented. In fact, he said, he was "getting a little more ideologically areligious," viewing religion as an obstacle to the "people of color, solidarity kind of thing" to which he had increasingly committed himself.

Nashashibi's assumptions about religion, however, gradually began to change as his interaction with the milieu of South Side Black Nationalism and Black Islam deepened. Activists in these spaces—who had, as Nashashibi put it, "that black 'street cred' thing," something Nashashibi respected—cast Islam as a liberating, transcendent, and transnational spiritual brotherhood. Nashashibi remembered responding skeptically to their assertions, asking, "How can you really take this seriously?" He began reading the Qur'an so that he could debate them. He would ask "about this verse and how can you really believe this verse, how is this verse in line with progressive principles in terms of liberation and stuff like that." He recalled that in Europe he and his friends had ridiculed the piety-minded Muslims they encountered in the streets: "We would joke about the brothers all being—I mean, I never had that experience—but we would joke that they were all trying to hit on young men and asking for weed when we would go to Amsterdam, you know, we kind of saw all the hypocrisy, you know, so, that's how we kind of filtered [our perspective on religion]."

Gradually, however, through his interactions with his Black Muslim interlocutors, Nashashibi's perspective shifted. "[I was] beginning to take the idea of revelation seriously," he reflected, "that there was actually revealed text from God, and just that idea was so alien [to me]." He described a growing fascination with the thought of an actual verifiable record of the Prophet Muhammad's statements and deeds through which one could test the veracity of his claims.[19] He also discovered the Qur'an to be a theologically rational text that anticipated and "disproved" his skeptical assumptions about revelation. He finally "came to the point where spiritually I started taking [Islam] really seriously but I had not made the adjustments for my lifestyle [because] I never grew up with any prohibitions about anything [. . .]. I had no kind of discipline in those [spiritual] areas."

Nashashibi's gradual opening to Islam through Black Nationalist and Black Muslim circles entailed a parallel process of assimilation into "black" and "person of color" identities. As he talked about this experience, his hand gestures and speech began to mimic an urban hip hop cadence. He pronounced "revelation" as "re-ve-láy-shun," each syllable distinctly and deliberately articulated with stress on the third syllable, as he described his period of intense Qur'anic study. Later in the interview he described finally assenting to the Black Muslim perspective that Islam properly understood was a message of "liberation," again pronounced with a hip hop cadence, as "li-ber-áy-shun." This stylistic transition in Nashashibi's speech, as well as the physical gestures that accompanied it, projected and performed symbolically the assimilative shift—in the sense of an assimilation to South Side Black Muslim and hip hop culture—that Nashashibi had undergone. The *kufi* cap that he wore completed the image of his black-Palestinian synthesis.[20]

Nashashibi's subsequent decisions to establish a family on the South Side—pointedly, not in the suburban Palestinian enclave—and to found his Islamic social service agency in the heart of an economically depressed African American and Latinx neighborhood also symbolically marked his movement away from a strict Palestinian-centered identity toward a countercultural, black (inter)nationalist ("ghetto cosmopolitan") Islamic one (Nashashibi 2009). In both cases, Nashashibi inverted the terms of identity. He subordinated Palestinian solidarity to "blackness" as instituted in the ethos and structures of the neighborhoods in which he had chosen to forge a life. Effectively, he had integrated not into whiteness but into blackness.

This transposition of his solidarity frame—from antireligious, secular Palestinian nationalism and Third World internationalism to an Islam mediated through Black Nationalism and the challenge from, and attraction to, Black Muslims—brought Nashashibi into parallel with the global reformist Islamic revival. Hamas, the predominant Islamic-nationalist movement in the Occupied Territories, had, by this point, established itself as a formidable force in the Palestinian political field. Nashashibi encountered participants in this milieu during a summer-abroad experience at a West Bank university. He saw the potential of a movement united in Islamic commitment. At the same time, however, he rejected the "overconflat[ion]" of Islam with "the Palestinian conflict and this Palestinian struggle." Islam, he sensed, was in danger of becoming subsumed within a narrow Palestinianism, of becoming merely a substitute for secular nationalism rather than a radically transcending force capable of resituating the question of Palestine within the shared struggles of diverse oppressed groups.

Rejecting this type of Islamic political vision, Nashashibi returned to Chicago, seeking to enact his "black" conception of transethnic "people of color" mobilization within an Islamic mode on his campus. He quickly discerned that the Muslim Student Association (MSA) groups, despite their appeal to religious universalism, remained attached to the ethnic identities—mainly Middle Eastern and South Asian—that defined their membership. Nashashibi had committed himself to a different understanding of Islam: "It was very important that the experience of the black and Latino communities and other communities really aligned with the version of Islam I was going to take in." Nashashibi began looking beyond his university for a means to achieve this alignment.

At this critical juncture, he received a call from Najwa (pseudonym), a longtime community activist who had mentored him in the traditions of pan-Arabism and anti-imperialist internationalism at the *markaz*. Najwa offered Nashashibi a job working at the Arab Community Center in a program aimed at Palestinian immigrant youth living on the Southwest Side. Nashashibi accepted the position and very soon succeeded in leading a resurgence of youth participation in the *markaz*'s programs. As part of this effort, Nashashibi encouraged discussions of religion and gradually began implementing organized prayer for youth on the *markaz*'s premises. Almost instantly, older, established staff and leadership objected:

> I would get up, and I'd be denouncing the bankrupt [laughing] secular vantage point. Then the [*markaz* leadership] would call me in [. . .] and they would be like, 'You offended half the people from our community,' and I was like: 'The only reason I got entire families back into the center is because [of this]. You can't talk about the Palestinian thing without talking about how important spiritual religious identity was for [the families], so why are you dismissing this?' [. . .] Remember at that time that 63rd [Street] was really configured along these [community] centers and how many of them were secular, and some of the mosques were just beginning to emerge at the time [. . .]. So the families were just shocked that I was having programming in the center where there would be *salat* [the mandated five daily prayers], you know, that kids were coming back [to their parents] and they would talk about learning about *salat* in the *markaz* and you know that was such a foreign concept for them . . . because the *markaz* was completely not associated with *salat*, and matter of fact some of the families were not sending their children to the *markaz* because [they thought] 'they were Communists.' [So], we started bringing to the *markaz* Muslims from all over the city who were coming to connect with these Muslim kids and so Muslim identity became [central for us]. And then a group of African American Muslims from the East Side started coming through, you know, it was the first time Palestinian Muslim kids started thinking about Islam in a way that connected them to these other Muslims, and started connecting them to the African American Muslims. [This was] the early evolution of IMAN. At a certain point working out of the *markaz* we realized we [needed] to have our own separate nonprofit [that] really highlighted Islam, where it didn't have to constantly contend with the conflicting ideologies [at the *markaz*], where we didn't have to rationalize [the Islamic focus].

The formation of IMAN signaled Nashashibi's definitive break with secularism. He chose premises immediately to the east of the soon-to-close *markaz* on West 63rd Street. Many of the young activists he had recruited and oriented toward Islam followed him to help establish the new initiative. The shift eastward situated IMAN in the heart of the African American and Latinx communities of West Englewood and in doing so announced a corresponding distancing from the *markaz*'s orientation toward Palestinian and Arab empowerment and liberation. The new organization, which began to draw significant donor support, quickly became a magnet for young Muslim volunteers from diverse ethnic communities across the city. Its programs focused predominantly on black and Latinx needs: ex-prisoner reentry, medical needs for the surrounding neighborhoods, arts events and programming, and public forums.[21] Through these activities, IMAN enacted a vision of Islam as a transethnic solidarity frame rooted principally in South Side black cultural forms and Black Muslim traditions and practices.

In addition to breaking with *markaz* secularism, Nashashibi's shift eastward also repudiated what the wealthy middle class mosque institutions in the newly suburbanized Palestinian enclave seemed to represent: upward mobility and abandonment of the South Side communities in which Palestinians had lived for decades. Nashashibi and IMAN refused to follow this trend and in doing so resisted Islamic reformism and its affinity with the professional and business-oriented middle class ethos in the suburbs. Commenting on this fact, Nashashibi stated: "It was very symbolic, 'cause even though we are only a mile, really only a mile and a half at most east of where we are right now [the mosque in which we held the interview], we went the opposite direction of where the migration pattern was happening." Nashashibi was speaking enthusiastically at this point in the interview: this contrast was a good thing to him.

The dual rejection of suburban reformism and *markaz* secularism stemmed ultimately from Nashashibi's deep disenchantment with the privileging of Palestinian or even strictly Muslim suffering and demands for liberation above all other experiences of oppression. He commented: "[What I resented about the] obsession about the Palestinian framework and even the Muslim-national discourse was its just utter lack of creativity, its inability to really draw on the human experience and make those connections real, and the total self-centered way in which people thought about [the Palestinian cause]." He pointed especially to how wealthy Palestinians had built "massive villas alongside refugee camps the same way folks [Israeli settlers] build settlements along refugee camps." A similar phenomenon, by implication, appeared to be manifesting in the shift to the suburbs.

Against this individual self-dealing and accompanying ethnocentrism, Nashashibi invoked the late Edward Said's appeal to a universal humanistic outlook.[22] Originally critical of Said's "eliticism" (sic), Nashashibi had come years later to see the views of this preeminent public intellectual as echoing the Islamic cosmopolitanism he desired to enact. He interpreted Said as offering a global humanistic perspective that brought the diverse experiences of peoples who struggled with the aftermath of colonialism into conversation. He advocated for the Palestinian cause within this universal framework and in doing so was able to draw others into solidarity with Palestinians.

Nashashibi viewed Islam in a similar way: as a universal spiritual canopy under which communities of color, including Palestinians, could come together in a common struggle for justice. But, by the same token, each community's struggle had to coexist alongside others. This required a critical reflexivity that revealed one's own connection to, and possible complicity in, the suffering of others. In Nashashibi's view, Palestinians had failed to see beyond their own trauma, to connect profoundly with the experience of others, and this had led to their isolation. The national liberation movement had not drawn in new allies. It had become repetitive and hollowed out.

Nashashibi cited the behavior of Palestinian activists at the 2001 United Nations conference on racism in Durban, South Africa as an example of this failure of empathy. He remarked: "[The conference was] totally being, on some level for me, somewhat hijacked [in its] ability to move forward unless and until we denounce Zionism as racism." The Palestinians, he recalled, were refusing any forward movement until this explicit denunciation happened. The message Palestinian attendees seemed to be conveying was that only Palestinian suffering mattered. To Nashashibi, this obstinacy was hypocritical in view of the "rampant but unacknowledged racism in the Arab world, the rampant racism that even exists within the Palestinian communities here in Chicago [. . .]." He pointed to the Arabic expression "*sakin 'ind al-'abid*" ("living near the slaves," to refer to living near black communities) as an example of the casual, unexamined bigotry in the community. The failure to address racism in their own midst, argued Nashashibi, "to really immerse ourselves in a deeper humanity," not unlike what Said did, had "led to a lack of moral authority on this position [that is, that Zionism was racism and that Palestinians were victims of racism]."

Nashashibi's sensitivity to the question of race and the hypocrisy implicit in a Palestinian nationalism that, in his view, had demoted the suffering of others led him to clash openly with community leaders. He recalled one incident in which he criticized a delegation of Palestinian lawyers who had come to the *markaz* to meet with local activists. The lawyers seemed to lecture the group, which included African Americans from the surrounding community, for failing to see how their taxes supported Palestinian oppression. Nashashibi criticized the lawyers for failing to understand how taxation actually hurt the local community because of the unequal distribution of public funds. They had failed, as well, he said, to see the racism of local Palestinian shop owners whose stores exploited their African American and Latinx customers, operating "under the same logic as settlers in the West Bank." The lawyers "FLIPPED!" he recalled, retorting angrily, "'How can you compare that to this!'"[23]

The incident underscored Nashashibi's growing alienation from Palestine advocacy and from nationalism generally. Nationalist agitation, secular or Islamic, had become stale and ineffective. He commented: "[In the community], every crisis leads to the same type of emotional demand to take 15–20,000 people downtown in front of the Plaza Center." But these protests had little if any real effect on policy. The same people continued to appear at these demonstrations. The community seemed only to be speaking to itself. What was needed, instead, was "deep community building" that went beyond a "static framework of advocacy for *filastin* [Palestine]." The older secular nationalist leaders at the *markaz* had done "phenomenal work in reaching out and working with Harold

Washington [the first black mayor of Chicago]; there were those pioneers in our community." But the efforts of these secularist forerunners of internationalism had failed to establish the necessary deep connections to sustain the intercommunal solidarity:

> A lot of that solidarity was prompted by the black community's understanding of, like, the symmetry between South Africa and the anti-apartheid alignment with Israel and some of the international socialist frameworks that existed at the time. It wasn't done by deep community building grassroots stuff on the ground. [Deep community building] has the possibility of fundamentally changing the political discourse, but I think we need to do this in a way that is not just politically expedient.

Deep community building, in other words, inherently removed Palestine as the central focus of solidarity and mobilization. This shift inevitably called into question the nationalist framing of the Palestinian cause. Nashashibi explained further:

> [We have] to deconstruct some of our own "isms" [. . .]. [For example] we can't still be locked in a very sentimental kind of construction about Zionism. I'm not defending Zionism [. . .], [but] there's a passage in Qur'an where even Allah is [. . .] telling the Muslims, 'Don't curse the gods of the *mushrikin* [idolaters],' right? [Qur'an 6:108] And if this is coming from [. . .] the Supreme Entity of the Universe telling you not to curse what in Islam is seen as one of the most grave sins, calling on other gods, but not to curse those gods, [then] why [is God saying this]? And the logic is because you may then invite them to turn around and curse Allah. But there is another principle there about cursing what other people find sacred [. . .]. We have to understand how some segments of the Jewish community found solace in a discourse that tried to provide them with a sense of national identity [. . .]. Zionism has translated into different things for different people. The writings of Jabotinsky are very different from the writings of [. . .] Herzl or others. [But, also], nationalism as an early twentieth century discourse had many things that were antithetical to the spirit of human dignity and justice [. . .], including [for] many Arab people and Muslims in other parts of the world [. . .]. You can go to parts of the Khalij [the Arabian Gulf region] today and see Muslim workers living essentially in modern-day concentration camps [. . .]. We just need to think in a new framework. Palestinians have always been the ones to shift the discourse.

For Palestinians, as Nashashibi hints, perhaps the most difficult "ism" to confront was the set of assumptions through which they understood Zionism. Nashashibi's Qur'anic-Saidian universalism did not deny the suffering of Palestinians; rather, it decentered it, placing it alongside the suffering of others, including that of Jews, whose embrace of diverse forms of Zionism had to be grasped empathetically as an attempt to come to terms with devastating persecution. And yet, Nashashibi's criticism of nationalism in all of its forms extended as well to Zionism. The bankruptcy of all types of nationalism lay in how these ideologies sundered intercommunal human solidarity rooted in an empathetic immersion in the struggles of other oppressed groups.

As a Palestinian who had entered into the urban black experience of Chicago's South Side, Nashashibi sought to "shift the discourse." He did so by reframing the question of Palestine within the universal symbols and institutions of an emergent, transethnic Islam that engaged politics at the intersection of race, class, and ethnicity "back home" and "in the 'hood." But, within this cosmopolitan vision, Nashashibi refigured Islam itself as well, rendering it into a syncretic form that even as it affirmed the One God nevertheless refused to curse the gods of others. Islamic brotherhood and sisterhood—and the ties of faith, broadly—replaced the ethnic nation as the horizon of solidarity prima facie. But this solidarity required a reflexive, relativizing stance that decentered both the ethnos and, at its logical extreme, the religious community itself. In a personal communication to me in March 2019, Nashashibi gestured toward this transcendent horizon:

> I typically avoid talking about Islam as 'one thing' and typically will avoid the term 'Islamic' as an adjective to ever describe any facet of our work. I rather try to talk about how I'm drawn to a particular approach to Islam or how living out commitments in the Muslim tradition are things I aspire towards.

This was a subtle point: IMAN, Nashashibi implied, was a framework spanning diverse instantiations of piety and practice as well as of race, class, and ethnicity. Islam was not one thing but rather a range of perspectives to which Nashashibi and possibly also IMAN's staff and program participants were oriented. At this furthest extent, Islam became an empathetic, spiritual union of individuals across race, ethnicity, nation, class, and creed. The *umma* was the new cosmopolitan frame, secular in its Saidian humanism, religious in its spiritual horizon.

ACCOMMODATION

The third typological variation I focus on in this chapter is accommodation. As with reversion and conversion, the movement in this type is from secularism toward piety. Yet, also like the other two types, the shift is syncretic. Accommodation adapts to and partly integrates piety while maintaining practices, orientations, and organizational ties with the secularist milieu. As in the other cases, race, gender, and family ties to Palestine play critical roles in shaping a self-perception as Palestinian, a member of a negatively privileged group in the United States and in the Middle East. Community networks, secular and religious, provide a contrasting, empowering context within which Palestinian and religious identity receives positive valuation. Historical and structural factors—the First Intifada and the September 11 attacks, especially, as well as the suburban demographic and religious transition—also exert a determinative influence.

The individual I have chosen to illustrate the accommodation trajectory was a community organizer in her mid-thirties when I interviewed her. Intisar (pseudonym) began her career as an intern with the AAAN. At the time of our conversation, she had recently completed law school and started work as a civil rights attorney for a small firm downtown. She retained ties with the AAAN nevertheless, and met me at its premises on West 63rd Street for our interview. It was Ramadan when we spoke. I found her taking a cigarette break on the back fire escape. She was wearing a white blouse and blue jeans, no scarf.

Social Background and Early Identity-Formation Processes

Intisar was born in the Occupied West Bank during the 1970s. She arrived in Chicago with her parents when she was only two months old. Like Nawal's family, Intisar's mother and father followed in the path of relatives who had established themselves in the city. Her uncles had settled in a North Side neighborhood with a high concentration of Puerto Rican families. They had come to the United States, arriving first in Puerto Rico, just before the war of 1967. After working in factories and then engaging in peddling, a well-established trajectory for Palestinian immigrants, the uncles pooled their capital to set up small businesses in the area. Intisar's father joined his brothers in their businesses. Her parents soon divorced, however, forcing Intisar's mother to earn money by providing childcare for neighborhood families and selling homemade cheese and yogurt in the local Arab shops.

As other relatives from their West Bank village arrived, a small nucleus of Palestinian families gradually established itself in Intisar's North Side neighborhood. The community was diverse yet divided. Intisar described the solidarity she felt with non-whites, especially. "It was African-American, Latino, and Arab, basically," she said, "we were kind of stuck together." Against this front, "you had the Caucasian community but we didn't mix with them." For Intisar, as with Nashashibi, in the American diaspora, learning to be Arab entailed learning that one was not white, indeed, that one was essentially black and thus negatively privileged within the racial hierarchies structuring Chicago.

Yet the micropolitics of race in her neighborhood were not Intisar's only identity determinant. Equally influential was a family and community life focused intensely on Palestine. Her mother and uncles attended Palestinian events across the city and were loyal participants in the activities of the Arab Community Center. As one AAAN leader put it, Intisar was "a child of the *markaz*," regularly joining in its Arabic lessons and *dabka* instruction.

An important moment in the formation of Intisar's secular nationalist orientation occurred in 1986, when her mother took her and her sister to Palestine, intending to remain there permanently. Her mother had maintained ties "back home," desiring to preserve the continuity of Palestinian traditions, family affiliations, and Arabic language in her daughters. Eighteen months after their arrival in the West Bank, the First Intifada began. Like so many other youth, Intisar was swept up into the daily demonstrations. Through these experiences of protest, she absorbed the Intifada's culture of activism. Ultimately, lacking residency permits—the family had been issued three-month tourist visas at the airport, which they had overstayed—and worried about re-entry to the United States, they returned to Chicago as the uprising continued to surge in 1988.

As she reflected on these events, Intisar melded her memories of that time with other formative historical traumas she had witnessed through televised media. One such event stood out: the massacre in the Sabra and Shatila refugee camps in Lebanon in September 1982. "I heard my uncles and my family yelling and screaming at the TV," she recalled "saying, 'The US government is not going to do anything for us!'" Commenting on this, she said the understanding was "we're just here to work, and eventually we're going to go back home, that's our goal [. . .] 'cause here, even if you become a US citizen it's not going to matter, and we're not any better than the other Palestinians back home.' That's the way we grew up."

The succession of traumatizing events strengthened this presumption across generations. As Intisar related, "Sabra and Shatila have often come back to me." In 2008, as the Israeli "Operation Cast Lead" bombing and invasion of the Gaza Strip was underway, she returned from a meeting to plan protest demonstrations in Chicago's Loop to find her daughters watching footage of the violence on the Al Jazeera satellite feed in their home. Mediated political events "back home" or close to home—as in Sabra and Shatila or in Gaza—continually restaged, in the diaspora, the repression, dispersion, suffering, and resistance that constituted the core symbols and themes of Palestinian memory. Just as she had experienced, Intisar's daughters also absorbed Palestinian identity through this process.

Diaspora institutions reinforced this phenomenon, channeling incipient nationalist feelings into various forms of advocacy and activism. After returning from Palestine, Intisar, for example, underwent a process of training and mobilization through participation in protest actions organized by the *markaz*. She also, like Nawal and Nashashibi, became connected with student activism on university campuses. She joined the General Union of Palestinian Students (GUPS) during her first year of university studies. GUPS provided a broad organizing structure that instilled secular nationalist orientations within university youth. In joining GUPS, Intisar entered directly into this stream of politics and identity.

Significantly, Intisar underwent this mobilization process at the very moment—the first Gulf War of 1990–91, which substantially weakened Fatah and the PLO—in which secular nationalism began to lose its hegemonic position. The subsequent Oslo Peace Process and formation of the Palestinian National Authority furthered this weakening by effectively demobilizing the diaspora as a political force (Frisch 2012). In Palestine, political Islamic groups stepped into the breach, offering a vision of continued armed struggle with sacred intent (*jihad fi sabil illah*). In Chicago, Islamic religious institutionalization, the demographic shift to the suburbs, the disappointing results of the Oslo Process, and, finally, the events of September 11, 2001, caused some secularists to reevaluate their affiliations and orientations.

"The Islam in Me Exploded!"

September 11 provided a powerful, paradoxical impetus for Palestinians to identify as Muslims above all else. A new framing of the global order—posing a "victimized" US society against a malevolent Islam—dominated national discourse. Locally, the aggressive enactment of this framing, as it occurred, for example, in a march by white suburbanites on the Mosque Foundation, caused Palestinian Muslims to respond as Muslims (Goodstein and Niebuhr 2001; Fountain 2001). Intisar, who was working with youth at the AAAN at the time, described how some participants in her program responded by asserting their identities as Muslims: "After 9/11, a lot of our community really turned toward religion, people were looking for something to hold on to [. . .]. My students described it as, 'The Islam in me exploded!,' right?"

"'The Islam in me exploded,'" I said. "That's a powerful image, especially after 9/11."

> "Yeah," she replied.
> I had to defend myself as a Muslim now. I had no choice. When they are attacking Islam, they are attacking me. Maybe we're not wearing hijab [and Intisar did not], we're not praying, we're not fasting or whatever, but the fact is you're attacking me as 'Islam,' as Muslim. The Islam in me just exploded, right? And I'm not gonna stay quiet. A lot of our young women started wearing the hijab at that time. It became like a political statement.

As reflected in Intisar's narrative, the September 11 attacks intensified a transposition of Palestinian identity into an Islamic framework that had already begun during the previous decade. For the young Muslim women that Intisar described, the hijab was a sign, not of piety per se, but of a new political solidarity. This embrace of an Islamic identity in response to the post-September 11 anti-Muslim reaction occurred simultaneously with the continuing expansion of Islamic organizational structures in the suburbs.

This transformation affected Intisar directly, not just her students. In 2003, only two years after the September 11 attacks, Intisar and her family moved to the southwestern suburbs. Initially, Intisar placed her daughters in the public schools. White classmates taunted her eldest daughter, calling her a terrorist. Intisar conferred with other parents and teachers, suggesting that the school institute anti-racism trainings. The school resisted this idea, according to Intisar. The harassment continued. Her daughter then asked to be enrolled in the Aqsa School, the private Islamic institution across from the Mosque Foundation. Concerned that she be protected and affirmed in her Palestinian identity—Aqsa drew its students primarily from Palestinian Muslim families in the suburbs—Intisar agreed to her daughter's request after making sure she understood she would have to conform to the school's Islamic disciplines (prayer and wearing the hijab scarf, for example). This decision, a response to the racist backlash, led Intisar into direct interaction with the piety-minded milieu of the suburbs; it also reshaped the ethos of the family generationally, as her daughters embraced the religious practices that marked membership in the new suburban enclave.

The second impetus for Intisar's integration into the Islamic institutions flowed from cultural and strategic shifts within the secularist milieu itself. These changes directly affected the trajectory of Intisar's career. During the late 1990s, Intisar's immediate supervisor at the newly established AAAN, a person who, like Intisar, had been thoroughly imbued with the secularist ethos, began to respond to the religious shift that Nashashibi had been encouraging. The supervisor began to pray regularly and gave up drinking alcohol. He also astutely observed that secularists had no choice but to work with the mosques. The immigrant community had moved to the suburbs, and the mosques in these areas, the Mosque Foundation especially, had now become its primary institutional anchors. The mosques could mobilize large numbers for demonstrations and other public actions on behalf of Palestinian issues. The centers could either cooperate with them or become isolated and irrelevant. With this understanding, her supervisor urged Intisar to approach the Mosque Foundation leadership to develop collaboration on a range of social programs. Intisar hesitated. Among secularists, the mosque's imam had the reputation of being a humorless ideologue who refused to interact with un-scarved, un-coated women. She contacted him anyway, however, and to her surprise he welcomed her overture.

Intisar's engagement with the Mosque Foundation also coincided with a gradual shift in her career. In 2006, a civil rights organization offered her a position as an organizer. Her AAAN mentors encouraged her to take the job, arguing that it would enable her to establish bridges between Palestinians and other important groups across the city. Soon after beginning her work for the organization, a Latinx colleague challenged her refusal to participate in voting. Intisar had viewed voting as pointless in a country so thoroughly committed to Israel. Through her interactions with her new coworker, however, she began to see the rationale for mobilizing the Palestinian and Arab base: in coalition with other groups, Palestinians could advocate for their interests at different levels of government.

This shift in her views about political participation and mobilization led her to deepen her working relationships with Mosque Foundation leaders in the suburbs. The intensified cooperation she developed with them soon evolved into close coordination on civil rights advocacy. It also eventually led to an unexpected professional opportunity. Because of its centrality to the growing Arab immigrant community in the suburbs, the Mosque Foundation had become a central force in the city's Islamic coalitions. And through this role it began to create working relationships with other coalitions like the civil rights group with which Intisar was associated. Intisar's position within these cross-cutting networks made her an attractive candidate for a position with a new Muslim advocacy organization that the Mosque Foundation leadership had helped to create. This structure brought together the major Islamic formations in the city to act as a single, coordinated force in local and state politics. Intrigued by the possibilities, Intisar accepted the offer to work in the new organization.

Intisar's narrative illustrates the transformations that could occur as individuals traveled through and across secular (nonsectarian) and religious spaces. She remained a "non-hijabi" and smoked during Ramadan, at least whenever she found herself alone on the premises of the Arab American Action Network, "back in the 'hood." But she also claimed during our interview to have started to pray and fast. She spoke of the Mosque Foundation as "my home." She defended the *shaykhs* who led the mosque, describing them as "uncles" who staunchly supported her work, even in the face of attempts within the community to delegitimize participation in the US political system as *haram* (proscribed by Islamic law). She recounted one of the Mosque Foundation imams telling her: "Look, it's very important for us to show our power, so don't give up whenever an issue comes up; you need to keep doing this work."

As she prepared to take up her new job, Intisar blurred the lines dividing secular and Islamic milieus. She selectively integrated elements of reformist piety into her own secularist demeanor, casting her work with the Islamic structures as an extension of the civil rights advocacy she had been engaged in all along. Seemingly there was no tension, no internal division. The community included the mosques; the mosques defended the community. The secular encompassed Islam; Islam incorporated the secular.

In this apparent fusion, Intisar exemplified a trajectory whose impetus lay in the post-Oslo crisis that weakened PLO-led secularism. This trajectory responded pragmatically to the shifting circumstances, forging a syncretic secularity that overcame the crisis of secularism through an accommodation of the religious. This accommodation effectively sacralized the secular, recasting political empowerment and mobilization in terms of Islamic solidarity. The transposition represented more than a mere instrumental or strategic shift: at the time of our interview, Intisar had seemingly integrated some Islamic practices into her daily life and had come to see Islam as continuous with her political and moral commitments. She stopped short of a complete identification with reformist piety, however, and four years after our interview she had left the Islamic organization to embark on a career as an attorney with a firm whose staff included individuals from a wide range of ethnic and religious backgrounds. Nevertheless, she maintained links with the Islamic milieu by participating in the annual conference of American Muslims for Palestine and consulting with the Mosque Foundation on civil rights issues.

CONCLUSION

Reversion, conversion, and accommodation, as I have defined these terms in this chapter, describe movements from secular or secularist milieus into religious institutional spaces. These movements result in various types of syncretic secularity that I have termed "religious secularity." Reversion entails an oscillation from religious to secular back to religious. Conversion involves a single movement from secular to religious. Accommodation is a partial shift from the secular to the religious. In each of these cases, the secular is never fully relinquished but rather repositioned and resignified within a sacralizing framework.

In Nawal's case, there was a modification of reformist orthopraxy to facilitate social interactions within secular space, but, at the same time, Nawal, through the enactment of her piety, sacralized the secular spaces within which she worked. Rami Nashashibi's conversion similarly resulted in a religious modification of the secular: his embrace of Islamic piety produced a religious variation of the transnational Third World solidarity frame of the leftist movements that cohered in the former *markaz* during the 1970s and 1980s. Finally, Intisar, in her partial shift toward the Islamic milieu, elided the secular-religious boundary as she transposed her political activism into religious structures.

In all three of these profiles, gender, race, class, and the historical convergence of secularist attenuation with Islamic ascendancy revealed the causes and direction of the syncretic shift. The weakening of secularism, the demographic shift to the suburbs, and the expansion of Islamic organizations created the conditions for a generational transformation of value orientations and solidarity structures. Nawal, Nashashibi, and Intisar's narratives registered this phenomenon in the transitions each of these individuals underwent in their orientations and affiliations. Gender especially shaped Nawal's trajectory. Her struggles for autonomy within her family led her to adopt a reformist Islamic critique of patriarchy as "culture." Her relationship with her mother, as well, provided a gynocentric matrix for her embrace of piety: prayer, Qur'an recitation, and modest dress, including the scarf, became conduits of emotional connection and continuity as her mother faced death.

Race and class, by contrast, emerged as the most powerful determinants of Nashashibi's movement from secular to religious. In his case, the religious shift occurred as part of his assimilation into Black Nationalist and Black Muslim contexts. The site of this shift, the economically depressed South Side, contrasted sharply with Nashashibi's elite upbringing and with the middle class piety of the new suburban Palestinian communities. Race affected Intisar, too, but her response was to affiliate with the suburban religious milieu. These same factors of race, class, and gender appear in the next chapter, too. The typological focus changes, however, to a focus on syncretic movements whose origins lie in dynamics internal to the sectarian religious space.

6

Dynamic Syntheses

Rebellion, Absolute and Spiritual

It was just as big a deal as coming out gay! It completely blew up in my face. My father threatened to pull me out of school. He wanted me to quit my job. He would talk to my sisters about disowning me. Eventually he cooled down. I learned really quick I had to pretend to give religion a chance. But, there's a point of no return—where once you've separated yourself from it, you're not gonna go back.

Ibrahim [pseudonym] was twenty-four years old when we met. Within the first moments of our conversation, he impressed upon me that he was an atheist. Within the Islamizing ethos of the suburbs, to be a good person was to be a good Muslim as defined within the terms of reformist orthopraxy. But Ibrahim increasingly resisted being molded within this piety. The justifications for it made no sense to him. He especially questioned how an omnipotent, omniscient, yet just God could punish human beings. "I asked my mom if God has predetermined what I'm gonna do then why do I get punished for it?" he said. "She's like, 'Oh no, God gives you choices, you choose,' but I was like, he knows what I'm gonna choose. That was the first time I thought God is unfair." His mother recited Qur'anic passages and stories from the lives of the prophets but "eventually, you're sick of hearing stories and you let it go, and after that, you can't trust this whole thing."

SYNCRETIC REBELLIONS

This chapter continues the discussion of syncretic secularity by focusing on trajectories that, in my data, originated in the religious milieu but then arced into nonsectarian outlooks. I characterize these arcs as "rebellion." The individuals I profile, including Ibrahim, resist and reject the Islamized or Christianized milieu. Their rebellion entails a search for alternative orientations within or beyond those spaces. This search ends in "secular religiosity," a type of syncretic secularity enacted in an abandonment of reformist piety and of sectarian identity. This syncretic form retains religion, the idea of it, and religiosity in certain modified ways, however, as part of an alternative, "polytheistic," or pluralized sense of self.

Rebellion manifests in my data in two subforms: absolute rejection and spiritualization. Absolute rejection leads to atheism. Religion—the idea of it—ironically persists in this stance. It stamps this atheism with its particular character by providing the background and specific points of contrast against which the act of rejection occurs. To the extent the contrasting relation is maintained, the atheism to which absolute rejection leads marks the furthest extreme of the secular religiosities I describe.

The second form of rebellion, spiritualization, embraces religious pluralism and individual "spirituality." Its validation of the polytheism of values (pluralism) in which deinstitutionalized, highly individual, and selective religious sensibilities become possible constitutes its secularity. This stance, too, bears the marks of the Islamized or Christianized milieu. Its secularity gains its coherence through the rejection of the orthodoxies/orthopraxes that define these milieus as well as through its embrace of individualized religiosity and cultural pluralism as the contrasting option.[1]

Class, generation, and gender as well as alternative moral-cultural and leisure spaces within the wider urban zone of Chicago shape these two trajectories (absolute rejection and spiritualization) in various ways. Rebellion against the religious milieu, for example, can have its impetus in a woman's traumatic experience of religion as an enforcement mechanism of gendered inequalities during childhood. The impetus can also lie in generational upheavals, such as the two Intifadas, that open up possibilities for individual self-assertion within and against the religious sectarian milieu. A related conditioning factor is the encounter with social spheres offering different moralities and identity possibilities. These possibilities provide a critical contrast with the Islamized/Christianized milieu. By embracing the alternatives, an individual gives form to the rejection stance not merely as the negation of a particular set of norms but also as an affirmation of a distinct, competing value orientation.

I document and analyze these dynamics in detail in the profiles to follow. Whether the profiles represent general tendencies in the wider immigrant community is beyond the scope of my discussion in this chapter. The goal of the profiles rather is to identify and elaborate the range of identity trajectories—in this case, rebellion leading to atheism or spiritualization—as they emerge typologically in the narratives of my interlocutors. Further research can and should test the validity of the typologies beyond my data. The profiles also serve a second goal: to substantiate my argument that the dynamics of the religious shift in Palestinian Chicago, as they manifest in the narratives of my interlocutors, ironically generate disenchantment leading to new, unanticipated forms of secularity and secularism.

ABSOLUTE REJECTION

My first profile, of Ibrahim, illustrates absolute rejection leading to atheism. The narrative reveals two intertwining acts of rebellion; alongside rejection of the religious milieu, there is a discarding of Palestinian national identity in favor of an "American" one. Atheism and Americanism form a single trajectory in this case. As in the other profiles I present, there is a spatial-social displacement: the journey to a godless America is also an exodus from the immigrant enclave to the city beyond. Still, the enclave remains present in this narrative, albeit at a remove. Family ties are not entirely severed. Further, narratively, religion, which is rejected, provides the negative term that defines and imparts coherence to the resulting atheism.

Atheism in the City Beyond: Ibrahim
Origins of the Heresy

Born and raised in the southwest suburbs, Ibrahim had recently graduated from college with a major in finance when we met for our conversation. His parents had grown up in Palestinian refugee camps in Lebanon. He mentioned that his father had served in "the resistance"—a reference to membership in a PLO faction. After the expulsion of the PLO and its militias from Lebanon in 1982, Palestinians remaining in the camps confronted dire circumstances, including revenge attacks and massacres carried out by Lebanese militias that had opposed the Lebanese National Movement, which the PLO had supported. The deteriorating conditions drove his parents to immigrate.

Despite the direct political heritage of his father, Ibrahim conveyed a strong sense of alienation from Palestinian politics and identity. He, in fact, refused to identify himself as a Palestinian altogether, insisting instead, in reply to my questions, that he was an American above all else. One reason for his alienation seemed to reside in the fact that he had had very little contact with Palestinian life in the Middle East. Ibrahim recounted a single trip with his mother to visit his aunt in Lebanon when he was ten years old. He remembered little of the visit other than his shock at the conditions of the camp in which his aunt continued to live. He never returned to Lebanon and had never been to Palestine itself.

The local diaspora mechanisms for instilling nationalist sentiment had also failed in Ibrahim's case. Ibrahim described going to several protest actions when he was young, but stated categorically that he would have nothing to do with those sorts of events now, or with any other similar nationalist ritual. For Ibrahim, attendance at political events carried the demand for unquestioning loyalty and communal conformity. "My mom and sister would get mad and guilt me when I said I didn't wanna go," he recalled. "They'd tell me: 'you don't really care that people are dying over there.' I told them I do care, but that this protest is not going to change anything."[2] Ibrahim reacted to the pressure to conform politically by rejecting identification as a Palestinian entirely. Desiring to pass as "American," he avoided all discussion of politics in his daily life beyond the family.

Later in his interview, Ibrahim described feeling tension whenever colleagues at work, especially Jewish colleagues, asked about his ethnicity.

> They'd see the name and ask where I'm from and for the first few months I'd say, 'Lebanon,' just 'cause I didn't wanna get into the whole conversation, but then I'd tell them Palestine and Lebanon were where my parents were from and then the Palestine talk would start and I'd try to brush it off [. . .]. It's not something that's pleasant to talk about.

The experience of having to contend with Jewish colleagues and their desire to debate the Palestine question was not unique to Ibrahim. Other Palestinians related similar stories. In Ibrahim's narrative, however, the desire to derail uncomfortable discussion at work connected, as his description of forced attendance at protests indicated, to a deeper estrangement from public identification as a Palestinian generally.

This estrangement extended to religion, too. Ibrahim's atheism developed gradually. Islamic piety had not been a dominant feature of family life when his older sister was growing up. This sister did not wear a hijab scarf or pray, Ibrahim told me. She never learned these disciplines in the home and never became integrated into Islamic communal structures. By the early 1990s, however, when Ibrahim and his younger sisters were toddlers, the Mosque Foundation had become established and its associated schools had launched. The ethos of the suburban enclave began to register the impact of these organizations as community members embraced the practices they instituted. Like their neighbors, Ibrahim's mother began wearing the hijab and his father started attending Friday prayers. She also began to feel during this time that her child-rearing methods had fallen short and that piety was necessary to raising disciplined, moral children—these two qualifiers, disciplined and moral, being intimately linked for Ibrahim in his recounting of this transitional period: "With four kids, it was a way to keep us in line, to instill morals, I guess," he said. "I think she had a picture in her head that Muslims are, like, peaceful, loving, very accepting. She really wanted that with us." Ibrahim resisted the new discipline nonetheless: "The justifications for it just didn't make sense to me, but I was being rebellious, too."

Crossing the Rubicon: Rejecting Faith and Nation

Ibrahim's rejection of reformist piety—expressed as an inability to reconcile moral and logical contradictions—crested when he began attending a college on the North Side. In that space, well beyond the suburban enclave, he finally relinquished his identification with Islam: "Once my separation from God was done, Islam meant nothing to me." But, since he continued living with his parents, he continued outwardly comporting with their expectations of piety to avoid conflict.

He drank water during our interview, held in a downtown café, despite the fact that it was Ramadan. At home, "I still put on this show for my parents and the rest of my family, more out of respect for my parents, but in the city I don't care."

Ibrahim's reference to "the city" was significant. Access to its spaces beyond the enclave facilitated his ability to inhabit other non-Islamic, "secular" personas. However, within the enclave, in which he continued to live, he had to conform to the norms of piety. The price of not doing so became starkly clear when he "tried coming out as an atheist in 2009." Faced with his father's threat to disown him, Ibrahim learned to dissimulate. He cursorily read the books on faith and practice his father gave him, absorbing "just enough to talk to him so he would think, okay, this kid turned over a new leaf." The most difficult time was Ramadan, when everyone was expected to fast and pray. "I think my mom has caught on that I don't fast; I think it hurts their ego." Ibrahim expressed empathy for his parents, stating: "I never expected them to say, okay, he's an atheist, that's cool; a big part of Islam is instilling the belief in your children—that's part of what gets you to heaven—and it's kind of a big deal to them."

Ibrahim did not condemn his parents for their sharply negative reaction to his atheism, but the sense of estrangement from them was palpable in his narrative. Membership in the family required conformity to piety as much as it did to nationality. Ibrahim rejected both, placing his familial membership in question. Financially vulnerable, he tried to mute the dissonance, feigning repentance and piety. But the dissemblance barely disguised his persisting resistance, especially in moments like the Ramadan fast that demanded public adherence to convention.

Elsewhere in the city, however, Ibrahim could shed the pretense. He described having a girlfriend, a Palestinian university student who also had grown up in a newly pious family. Like Ibrahim, she resisted demands that she adopt reformist practice. She refused to fast, pray, or wear the hijab; she also rented her own apartment on the North Side. She and Ibrahim met for dates and long walks there. He had not expected to become romantically attached to an Arab woman. "I always had that picture in my mind of what I saw," he commented, "you know, [Arab women] are really religious and you gotta like stay away 'cause of what it means in the culture [to show a serious interest in a woman]."

Ibrahim was surprised to find someone within "the culture" who, like him, had rebelled against the strictures of piety. "She's essentially in the same boat as me," Ibrahim reflected. The city spaces beyond the enclave allowed them to sustain their shared nonconformity and to stake out independent lives as "Americans." As Ibrahim put it: "We can't go anywhere in the suburbs without worrying about being seen and rumors spreading quick [. . .]. If we were stuck in the suburbs and that was the only way, it wouldn't work."

This was true especially because of the gendered double standard his girlfriend faced in the suburbs. Men, even within the piety-minded milieu, were given unspoken latitude to engage in liaisons with women. Women, on the other hand, faced public shaming, exclusion, and even violence if they ignored the norms governing courtship. This double standard, Ibrahim told me, was yet another reason for his alienation from the enclave and from the patriarchal norms it had instituted. Girls were "like prisoners in the home, especially in Islam," he said, "[. . .] groomed to cater to their husbands—be obedient, don't talk, don't do this or that. I can't support it. That's probably also an American influence on me: women having all their rights, being independent."

The "American influence," which Ibrahim equated with egalitarian gender relations, re-emerged as a theme at the end of our interview. He elaborated on it in response to a question about his hierarchy of identity:

> I'm American. [My family] wants me to say I'm Arabic-American with the Arabic first. But, no, I'm American and my family is Arabic. I was born in America. Arabic culture [. . .] doesn't promote equality as well as the American [one]. If I ever tell my parents, hey, I'm gonna marry a black girl, they're gonna be like, no you have to marry a girl of our culture and no one will ever understand our culture like that. I don't want to raise my kids to think like that. I want them to be raised with an American style—like, hey, whatever is okay.

In Ibrahim's narrative, "American" had ceased to function, in contrast with its usage in the discourse of many Palestinian immigrants I had interacted with, as a negative term against which an authentic "Arab" self was set in relief.[3] Rather, for Ibrahim, Americanness connoted an alternative set of values that one could adopt by virtue of living in Chicago or anywhere else in the United States. Those values and the identity they encoded constituted a point of moral contrast with, and critique of, "the Arabic culture, the Muslim culture" as well as a path out of that culture and its piety and patriarchy, as Ibrahim characterized it. The expectations of moral conformity; the moral contradictions of monotheism as expressed in the injustice of an omniscient and omnipotent deity who predetermined every event; and the gendered double standard—all of this could be transcended in the diaspora. In the exile, other possibilities existed for the trajectory of one's life. Those possibilities lay beyond the enclave, within the majority culture that one could join simply by declaring one's Americanness—so long, at least, as one was able to dodge uncomfortable questions at the office or at home about one's suppressed yet ever present alterity. Ibrahim had secularized this alterity, abandoning its distinctive markings.

Yet, in his narration of his transformation, and in his continuing relations with the immigrant milieu he had rejected, Arabness and Islam persisted as the defining negative image of the American identity he had embraced. At times, too, when back in the suburbs, piety imposed itself on him, and, in his desire to avoid conflict, Ibrahim simulated assent by participating grudgingly in its forms. It was in these ways that his atheism came within the compass, albeit at its extreme edge, of what I am calling secular religiosity. His atheism rejected yet perpetuated, through the very act of negation or in moments of pragmatic capitulation, the piety it purported to have left behind.

SPIRITUALIZATION

In contrast with Ibrahim's absolute rejection of the reformist, piety-minded milieu, the next three profiles map forms of secular religiosity that I characterize as "spiritualization." Spiritualization, like absolute rejection, rebels against the orthopraxy/orthodoxy of the religious milieu. Rather than leading to atheism, however, spiritualization generates a highly idiosyncratic form of religiosity comporting with an embrace of pluralism beyond the immigrant enclave.

Rejecting Sect and Patriarchy, Embracing Pluralistic Alterity

The next profile focuses on the Christian context. Sawsan (pseudonym), an artist, described her confrontation with the mechanisms of patriarchal control within the religious-sectarian milieu in which she grew up. This confrontation produced disenchantment with Christianity and a subsequent search for an alternative moral community and identity. The process began in Palestine, where Islam and nationalism, both of which intertwined during the Second Intifada (2000–05), provided these other possibilities. The embrace of these options led to a series of transformations that ended in the assertion of a highly individualized spirituality and in an affirmation of pluralism on the margins of the Islamized/Christianized milieu in the Chicago diaspora.

Familial and Political Matrices of a Religious Rebel

Sawsan grew up in an Orthodox-Catholic community in the West Bank town of Beit Jala. She immigrated with her family to Chicago in 2002, when she was a university student. Her father, whose bakery business had collapsed during the Second Intifada, desired to take advantage of his brother's invitation to help launch a restaurant in the city. Economic reasons were not the only motives for the move. The family also worried about the political and religious paths that Sawsan had begun to travel during her teenage years.

Sawsan described her upbringing in Beit Jala as "tough." Alongside the violent political circumstances of the military occupation and the uprisings against it, her parents often fought bitterly with one another. "My mom and dad were not a happy couple," she said. "My mom could not stand up to my dad." In response to the pressure, her mother sought emotional shelter and support in her local Catholic parish church and its piety.

> My mom's refuge was church and Jesus. I would always see her pray the rosary—pray and cry, pray and cry. My dad would complain about how religious she was and how she could not miss a mass. She forced us [the children] to go with her to Sunday school.

The refusal of Sawsan's father to attend mass with his wife, indeed, his resentment of his wife's piety, possibly indicated frustration with the intrusion of a superseding patriarchal authority in the home. Like Nawal (chapter 5), who also appealed to religious strictures to contest patriarchal norms, Sawsan's mother not only found consolation in saying the rosary and attending mass but also discovered, through the institutions of the church, the capacity to exercise a countervailing authority.[4] Church piety empowered her. It gave her autonomy. This autonomy entailed the assertion of the right to leave home and participate in public space (the church). It also endowed her with the capacity to assert a moral authority within the home. She took her children to weekly Sunday mass and, against her husband's resistance, enrolled them in Catholic grade schools.

Sawsan quickly began to resent her mother's attempts to impose Catholic discipline and identity. The priest at the church, she said, shamed her "for being chubby [...]. That was one of my earliest memories of being bullied, and it was by a priest, so, I hated going to Sunday school and being around that community." She also recalled the harshness of the nuns toward her if she were late for morning mass.

> If I was late, even by a minute, the church doors would be locked and I would be punished. I would always run and join the Muslim girls. I always felt that their teacher was a lot more loving and peaceful looking than the nuns [...]. That was one of my earliest memories of being drawn to Islam.

Feeling "out of place in my church community, in my own community [...]," Islam appeared to Sawsan as a contrasting, open site of belonging, "which [was] crazy." Pressed on why it "was crazy" that Islam attracted her, Sawsan invoked the strong communal prohibitions against conversion: "Back there [in Palestine] you cannot even consider changing your religion [...]. You could die and it would be easier [to die than to convert] [...]. That's why [it was crazy]."

Sawsan's growing revulsion against the Christian sectarian milieu occurred just as the al-Aqsa Intifada (the Second Intifada) was beginning in the late summer of 2000. During this period of prolonged violence, Hamas increasingly claimed the status of sole remaining champion of uncompromising resistance to the Israeli occupation. The peace process, to which the PLO and Fatah, especially, had linked their fate, lay in ruins. Hamas seized the initiative, carrying out a series of suicide bombings in response to Israel's violence. These actions, which other groups like the al-Aqsa Martyrs' Brigade emulated, resonated with many Palestinians, who saw them as justifiable reactions.[5] Hamas now stood for principled refusal to surrender and in so doing linked Islam to national liberation for a new generation of activists. Sawsan's narrative reflected the impact of this development.

Sawsan described watching Muslim preachers on television during this time. She also began listening to Qur'an recitation on the radio at night—"it would help me sleep and make me feel better"—and started defending Islam to her family whenever the topic arose in discussion. Islam increasingly seemed to her to be the authentic core of Palestinian identity:

I always felt as a Palestinian that there was a relationship between being Palestinian and being Muslim [...]. In Islam, it is a duty to defend your land. I did not see that in Christianity. During the Second Intifada, as a teenager, it just made sense, that explanation [that to defend one's land was a God-given duty].

Sawsan described her political sympathies at the time as leaning toward secular-leftist factions that Christians in the Bethlehem and Beit Jala areas traditionally supported. She claimed, however, never to have formally joined any of these groups. Hamas also did not attract her as a vehicle for her politics. Still, the movement had made jihad a compelling way for her to imagine and justify resistance in the context of Israel's violent suppression of the Second Intifada.

Her budding nationalism and fascination with Islam coincided with and intensified in a romantic attraction that threw her family into crisis. Sawsan had discovered a talent for painting and sculpture and had begun to exhibit her work in galleries in Jerusalem and Ramallah. At one of these exhibits, she met a correspondent for a local TV station in Ramallah. "I fell in love with him [...]; he was my first love," she told me. She was eighteen years old; he was a Muslim. The relationship developed secretly. Sawsan feared the reaction of her father. He had refused to allow her to attend parties, even at church, at which boys were present. The restriction reflected a shared patriarchal ethos in Palestinian society generally. "You could not have a relationship with a young man back home," Sawsan reflected, "like, you know, go out with each other and go have coffee or whatever, unless you were engaged or married."

Endogamy, which reinforced sectarian, class, and familial distinctions, also powerfully constrained Sawsan:

> As a teenager I heard all of these horrifying stories of honor killing, of Christians killing their women or girls, and Muslims killing their women, too. If they found out that I talked to a Muslim man, much less even having a relationship, I would have been finished in the Christian community. Such girls are labeled whores, sluts. I've heard stories of Christian families ringing the church bells to pronounce their daughter dead if she marries a Muslim man. One family put their daughter's picture in the newspaper, saying they disowned her.

Her family discovered her relationship with the journalist. Her brother read their email messages. Her mother found her personal diaries. The family's reaction was sharp. "My mom made me feel so much guilt for betraying Jesus," Sawsan recalled, "[telling me], I'm not good enough, I betrayed my family, I'm gonna bring shame to them, they're Muslims, they're garbage," this last in a suppressed voice. Her father never directly threatened her but said simply, "If you care about him, you should let him go, because he's worth only one bullet." She realized, "It's either I'm gonna get killed or he's gonna get killed."

Sawsan's parents increased their pressure on her. They confiscated her phone and computer and forced her to remain at home. As this was happening, the Second Intifada deepened. Sawsan's father shuttered his business and then decided to take the family to Chicago. Sawsan remembered being made to feel as if she were the sole reason for the family's departure. She recounted her mother saying, "We are leaving because of you, before you bring shame to our family." Sawsan began weeping at this point during the interview. "I had to carry that burden of guilt that we immigrated," she said, "[that] we left the homeland because of me," even though her father's business problems were the primary motive for their departure.

Exilic Transformations of Sawsan's Rebellion

Immigration allowed Sawsan's father to recover financially. However, the buffer they hoped exile would afford against Sawsan's rebelliousness proved illusory. Sawsan described the move to Chicago as deeply traumatizing. In Chicago, she withdrew emotionally, sequestering herself in her room. "It was a very messy, dark time," she commented. And yet, in the midst of this difficult passage, rather than break from her past she immersed herself in it: "my connection to Islam continued [. . .], it intensified [. . .], and I finally converted in 2010," eight years after leaving Palestine.

The trajectory of Sawsan's conversion contrasted significantly with the reformist Islam that had taken root in the southwestern suburbs. The primary impetus for her transition was her encounter with an "American [white] professor" at a local university who had converted. Bosnian friends whom she met while working as a waitress on the city's North Side had invited her to one of the "spiritual talks" that this professor convened every Sunday in his apartment. She began attending the gatherings regularly. "It was amazing!" she commented. "I had never heard anything like it from any Arabic Muslim speaker [. . .], you know, giving us stories about the Prophet or the [Shi'i] Imams; just so much spirituality, and I fell in love with it and felt ready." The professor took the group on a trip to visit a large Shi'i mosque in Dearborn, Michigan. "That's where I declared myself a Muslim," Sawsan remembered.

Sawsan's idiosyncratic trajectory—in the Sunni-majority Palestinian context, Shi'ism was heterodoxy—reflected the depth of her alienation from both the Palestinian Christian and Muslim segments of the immigrant community. Her rejection of the city's Christian milieu stemmed from her refusal to abide the anti-Muslim, anti-nationalist sentiment of the community. The Christians she interacted with wanted, in her view, "to get rid of their Arabness and assimilate to white; their emphasis and focus [was] so much on religion and let's forget about our identity [as Palestinians and Arabs]." As well, at the church her mother had joined, the priest spoke in his homilies about "how our worst enemy was atheism and Islam and that we moved here [to the United States] as religious refugees, we were persecuted by Muslims." The comments enraged her: "I mean, are you kidding me! He never once mention[ed] the Israeli occupation. I just would get sick and would go home crying afterwards."

The Islamized suburban enclave also repulsed her. "I just did not like [the Mosque Foundation], how the *shaykh* was saying, oh, if you pray this way, it's *haram* [forbidden], you should pray that way. I was, like, oh, for God's sake! The crowd is being talked to like cattle." The *shaykh*'s refusal to talk with the women who came to worship also "insult[ed] my intelligence." She recalled sensing from the imam "this feeling of shame that I am a woman, like I should look down and away from men, be ashamed; and men, if they see a woman, they [should] run away." She explained further:

> I'm a feminist. A woman should not feel ashamed, like she's a source of sin, you know, that Muslim male interpretation of women. I felt it in Bridgeview, I felt it in other Arabic mosques. But I didn't feel it in the Shi'i mosque or the Bosnian or Albanian mosques. There wasn't such a harsh division between male and female [in those mosques].

Her conversion in Michigan had failed to sustain itself, however. "Honestly," she said, "I haven't been to a mosque since, well, since that trip to Michigan." She also was reticent to tell other "Arabs that I'm a Muslim [because] they wouldn't believe me." They would likely point out that she didn't pray and that she had tattoos. But, she said, "at the end of the day, it's between me and God." She explained further:

> To me, my interpretation of the faith would just be that connection and spirituality. I don't think I'll go to hell because I have tattoos. I don't think I have to fear God. So, I guess I can't even be a Muslim. But, still, every time I listen to the Qur'an, I feel at home, connected to Palestine.

The tattoos had caught my attention from the moment we met for our interview. I asked her about them at this point in our conversation. Her reaction provided further insight into the spiritualized trajectory that her rebellion had taken. "I have this [tattoo]," she said, as she angled her wrist toward me. "It's the first one I designed when I came here. It says, 'There are three things in my soul: Love, God, and Palestine.'" This triune declaration—a striking nationalist reconfiguration of the Christian conception of the divine—appeared in elaborate Arabic calligraphy. She pointed to another etching on her other wrist, also in Arabic. "This one is *ruh*," she said, "it means 'spirit.'" Again, the reference to the Third Person of the Christian notion of God was unmistakable. The same concept was central for Muslims, too: the *ruh* suffused "the night of power," during which, Muslims believe, Muhammad first recited the divine revelation. It was also the agent of Maryam's (Mary's) miraculous impregnation in the absence of a man.

She mentioned two other tattoos on her back. "I won't say what they are," she said, "but you can see one of them." She lifted the bottom of her shirt to reveal an image of an iconic leftist female resistance figure from the 1970s. "My father was afraid I would get into trouble for that one," she whispered, "but it's just a memory of the old times of the Palestinian revolution." Her father, she said, worried about her outspoken criticism of Israel's occupation: "He tells me it won't get me anywhere but prison and if I go back home it'll get me in trouble."

Sawsan's understanding of her nationalism reflected continuity with the PLO's original demand for a single democratic state in Palestine. "I am one of very few Palestinians who believes in a one-state solution," she said. "I don't agree with two states." She explained this commitment, however, not in ideological terms but rather in relational, cultural, and spiritual ones. She had developed friendships with Jewish activists in Chicago who opposed Israel's policies and advocated for Palestinian freedom. She also listened to the music of Jewish Israeli artists of Arab cultural background (Mizrahi Jews). These connections led her to see possibilities for a shared, binational life as Arabs and Jews and for a single society that affirmed diverse individualities. She commented further:

> I do open my heart. I can see a human being in front of me and not a label or a flag. Part of my soul is just so tired of all this nationalism and blood. Maybe this is one blessing this country [the United States] gave to me. [It] is a blessing that I am not judged [here] for having the sides of my head shaved [which they were at the time of our interview] and that I can look at a human being and judge them by their character and not by what they are wearing, whether they are wearing hijab or covered in tattoos. Not everyone thinks the way I do, but this country, this city, gives me the room to do so, [the room] to be an individual.

Her skin tattooed, her head partially shaved, Sawsan embraced the exilic freedom to transcend religion, gender, and nation, transforming the questions of Palestine, patriarchy, and sectarian loyalty into a vision of pluralized religious-national fusion. This fusion received vivid expression in the trinity of "Love, God, and Palestine" inked into her skin. As a form of secular religiosity, Sawsan's idiosyncratic synthesis constituted a reaction against, and syncretic expansion beyond, the patriarchal ethos of Christian sectarianism and Islamic reformism. She had refused the dominant terms and hierarchal logic of sectarian belonging, instead articulating an alternative spiritualized individuality that fully affirmed the playful possibilities of a pluralized secular religiosity beyond the enclave.

Leaving "Arabville," Finding a "Secular Islam"

My second example of rebellion as spiritualization focuses on Muna (pseudonym), a twenty-five-year-old graduate student at a prominent university in Chicago when I first met her. Her story provides additional insight into the role of patriarchal authority as instituted within reformism in shaping the spiritualization trajectory. Muna's particular path arced from an initial, traumatizing immersion within the reformist milieu to an embrace of, in her terms, "secular Islam." This evolution indexes the disenchanting impact of the religious shift and the role of the pluralized, secular society beyond the immigrant enclave in facilitating the reorientation of values. At the center of this process is Muna's provocative notion of "leaving Arabville."

Social Background

Muna grew up in a mixed family. Her father, a Palestinian, had spent much of his life in the Arabian Gulf region. Soon after immigrating to the United States, he met Muna's mother, a recent immigrant from Mexico, who quickly became pregnant with Muna. The couple married, settling briefly in Atlanta, Georgia, where they had met. They then moved to Nashville, Tennessee before finally transitioning to Chicago to be near the husband's family. Muna was uncomfortable describing what her father did for a living. "He told us, like, used car dealerships, but he did other activities, too," she said. "Some of it might have been traveling back and forth between here and the Middle East, getting goods and bringing them back, and who knows what else."

Muna's parents had a tempestuous relationship. They frequently fought, separated, reunited, and finally divorced. After the ending of the marriage, her mother moved Muna and her sister to Texas to be near the mother's sister and her family. Completing high school there, but also getting involved in the local party scene, Muna returned to Chicago to separate herself from her "bad influences." She enrolled at a suburban community college and then transferred to a public university in the city. During that time, she got married to Isma'il (pseudonym), who had grown up in the southwestern suburbs and served in the US Air Force during the first Gulf War.

After trying to live in the northwest suburbs—"away from 'Arabville'"—the couple returned to live near family in the Palestinian enclave. Traveling across the metropolitan expanse for family events had become too burdensome. Muna was also attempting to complete her graduate studies while holding down a part-time job. The couple did not have the resources to place their daughter in childcare. In the suburbs, at least, grandparents could watch her infant daughter. The move made practical sense, even if it meant having to contend with the pressures of conformity. Muna saw the move as temporary. She was determined to leave "Arabville" as soon as she finished her studies.

The Pious Reformist Milieu and Confluences beyond It

In contrast with Nawal (chapter 5), who embraced the reformist disciplines of the Mosque Foundation, the regimes of piety within the Islamizing milieu disenchanted and alienated Muna. Her parents had modeled an inconsistent adherence to religious strictures. Her mother, for example, had grown up as a Catholic. She converted to Islam to marry Muna's father. She often went to the Mosque Foundation to visit with women friends there. But, as Muna recalled, she would convert and un-convert whenever she reunited or separated from her husband.

Muna described her father as outwardly pious: he regularly attended Friday prayers at the Mosque Foundation and performed *salat*—the five mandated daily prayers—in the home. At the same time, however, "he had an alcohol problem even though he sent us to Islamic school, and we'd learn it's *haram* [forbidden in Islamic law] to drink, but I'd see him at home with a beer." Muna also remembered him as being "very adulterous" when she was growing up. Reflecting on these memories, she stated: "I'm still trying to figure it out, because I mean he still prays and he's more religious now than before [. . .]. My upbringing was one big contradiction."

Beyond the inconsistencies, Muna also experienced the piety instituted in the family and community as an instrument of coercive manipulation and forced female socialization. Muna perceived that her father's religiosity had less to do with honoring divine law than with reinforcing his power in the home. According to Muna, he attempted to restrict his wife's social circle, telling her that, as a Muslim, she could not leave the home without his permission. He was also very concerned that Muna and her sister learn proper female obedience as dictated in patriarchal understandings of Islamic practice. He enrolled them in the Mosque Foundation weekend school to instill this submissive orientation. She commented:

> I remember very much believing everything I heard and trying to be a good Muslim girl, [. . .] doing what I was told, listening to elders, not talking back, observing religious fasting, putting on the scarf when it was appropriate [. . .], speaking Arabic fluently to this day, which I do [. . .]. I can still fool a lot of people today into thinking I'm a quote-unquote 'good girl' because of how good my Arabic is [. . .]. So pretty much the whole patriarchal bullshit [. . .], being told what to do [. . .].

Later, after the family moved—a frequent occurrence—Muna was placed in "Islamic school full time in [a northwestern suburb]." This institution, a Pakistani-run school, required that Muna wear the hijab scarf and long *jilbab* coat throughout the day. She described the curriculum as "a fundamentalist version of Islam." She recalled, "My sister learned that if you use the bathroom and any of your urine dries on you, then those parts of you will burn in hell [. . .]. So, she's seven years old on the toilet and doesn't have any toilet paper and she's screaming, 'I'm gonna burn in hell, give me some toilet paper!'" She also described being told, "it's *haram* to sleep on your stomach 'cause on the Day of Judgment sinners will be dragged on a rope of fire on their stomach to hell or whatever [. . .], so, I remember waking up at night [on my stomach] and being so freaked out and being like, 'Oh my God! Oh my God!'"6 She spoke of how such experiences resulted in the "unraveling of the whole version of Islam that was shoved down my throat [. . .]. I saw this stuff and it just didn't make sense [. . .]." In response to my question about whether she had tried talking to her parents about these feelings, she replied, "it seemed non-negotiable [. . .], so many aspects of it are still non-negotiable [. . .], like, for example, Ramadan is coming up and I haven't fasted since I was fourteen, when I started thinking about this stuff and what it means to me." Because she and her husband lived with her husband's family, she had to "pretend to fast [. . .]. It's ridiculous how I can't tell them I'm not fasting without getting an outburst about how I'm gonna go to hell [. . .]."

Muna's schooling until age fourteen had occurred entirely within the Islamic confessional structures of the Palestinian and Pakistani immigrant contexts. These structures, geared toward reinforcing religio-communal norms and insulating individuals, especially girls and women, against the majority non-Muslim US society, had in Muna's case produced the exact opposite of the intended result.

By age fourteen or fifteen, she had begun to question the strictures the schools required her to embrace and embody. It was at this point that the family moved again. Unable to afford the private tuition for the Islamic school, her parents placed Muna and her sister in the public system. She described continuing to wear her hijab scarf during the first year, but then, freed of the disciplining norms of the Islamized milieu, she made the decision finally to remove it for good. She recalled how "I [talked] with my aunts who wore the scarf about taking it off [. . .]. They were, like, 'No, you can't! You already have put it on, you can't take it off [. . .].' But I decided it wasn't for me [. . .]."

As with Nawal (chapter 5), immersion in a non-Islamic setting weakened the moral influence of the Islamic institutions that had constrained and oriented Muna earlier in her life. By removing the scarf, and also, at this time, deciding no longer to fast during Ramadan, she signaled the embrace of an alternative value structure made possible by her movement beyond the enclave's disciplinary space and by her growing perception of moral contradiction within its piety-mindedness.

When Muna moved with her mother and sister to Texas, her break from the patriarchal-reformist norms that had been so central to her early upbringing deepened. She recalled:

> When I left the community and saw other ways of life, had other influences, the whole ingraining started to leave me [. . .]. I mean, three or four years after leaving 'Arabville,' when I moved to Texas, I took my first sip of alcohol. I thought I was going to be struck by lightning [. . .]. Your whole life, it's like, it's so bad, you're gonna go to hell, even though I saw my dad drinking [. . .]. I just remember that moment, like, ahh, so this is it, sinning.

Far from "Arabville," in Texas, she began "to go wild," she told me, drinking frequently and "smoking a lot of pot." "Sinning" had become the means and the marker of her break with the religious patriarchal regime.

After returning to Chicago to pursue a college degree, consuming intoxicants still figured as a crucial differentiating practice and symbolic barrier with the immigrant community. This move back to Chicago followed an earlier decision, while she was still in Texas, not to enlist in the US Air Force, which had recruited her to serve as an Arabic language interpreter. After determining she didn't want to "go to some shithole," she thought she would "give Chicago a chance." Her father had been encouraging her to return, offering to support her until she could get established. So she returned and lived with her father, attending a community college with a large population of Palestinian students from the suburbs.

Soon after her arrival, she began work at the college café. It was there, across the counter as he ordered an espresso, that she first met Isma'il. She resisted his overtures for weeks but then relented. "I call him all my 'nevers,'" she said:

> [. . .] because I said I would never marry an Arab guy, never a Muslim, I didn't think he'd accept me smoking weed, but he was okay with that, which kind of broke the

whole stereotype I had in my head [. . .]. And he drank, and he was open, and, you know, not conservative, not religious, even though when Ramadan comes, he's like, 'Okay, I'm gonna try to fast this year.' He goes one day and then quits [. . .]. And he was in the Air Force, which was weird, 'cause I almost signed up!

Isma'il was a different kind of Palestinian, a different sort of Arab and Muslim. Through him she could cross into the Palestinian community without having to conform to the norms she had rejected. This led Muna to explore her identity as a Palestinian as an alternative to reformist Islam. Nationalism was never emphasized in her family during her childhood. She had not yet traveled to Palestine, and her father's family had long ago relocated to Jordan, the Gulf, and the United States. Through Isma'il's family, however, she began to connect with Palestine even though Isma'il did not seem to prioritize it in his life. "My husband, both his parents are Palestinian," she said. "They're the ones who experienced it; my mother-in-law grew up in refugee camps [. . .]. I heard their stories and learned [. . .]. I really didn't have any of this [growing up]."

As an expression of her incipient nationalist feelings, Muna began volunteering with a charity founded by a Palestinian businessman in Chicago that supported schools and clinics in the West Bank. She began attending fundraisers and meeting other activists through this network. Additionally, during her college studies, Muna took courses on the Middle East; when I met her, she was completing a master's degree in this field of study.

"A Secular Muslim"

In December 2013, Muna traveled to Palestine for the first time and discovered in urban centers like Haifa and Ramallah a culture far less concerned with piety and conformity than the Chicago suburbs in which she had grown up. The party scenes in those places were as active as any she had encountered in Texas and in Ramallah, surprisingly, she met individuals from Chicago's suburban enclave. Some of these fellow Chicagoans were "married men who put on a big show of being pious back home" but who, she said, indulged themselves in hashish, alcohol, and extramarital liaisons during their sojourns "back home." Her discovery of Palestine thereby heightened her perception of moral contradiction in the piety-minded Chicago enclave, but it also appeared to have opened a path for her beyond the suburban patriarchal ethos. In Haifa and Ramallah, she encountered a nation that, in certain urban locales, at least, seemed to be ignoring the religious revival altogether in its embrace of a hip party culture in which women and men could interact freely. Within these homeland spaces, one could "be Palestinian" without being Muslim, at least in the reformist, orthopraxical sense.

After returning from Palestine to "Arabville," Muna's sense of alienation from the piety-minded milieu persisted. At the same time, however, she indicated in subsequent conversations that she had not given up religion entirely, even if she felt deep ambivalence about it. She acknowledged how alienated from orthopraxy she had become but expressed a continuing sense of spirituality. She stated: "Sometimes, I don't consider myself Muslim at all [. . .]. When I look at the fundamental things, I'm like, 'Well I really don't believe in that.'" She refused to wear the scarf and did not consider it necessary for the prayers (*salat*). Moreover, she argued, the prayer itself actually did not matter; and it certainly did not matter that one pray as a Muslim. There were multiple ways to pray, and not praying at all was fine. Muna even expressed a desire not to have a Muslim burial:

> I don't wanna be buried in a Muslim cemetery because I feel like my whole life I've struggled against that and to be right next to everybody I've tried to distinguish myself from? [. . .] I wanna be cremated; and I want my ashes to be strewn over somewhere beautiful.

At the same time, however, she had not fully rejected Islam. She said she continued to think of herself as a "cultural Muslim" who shared patterns of speech—"you know, the way we'll go into Arabic or say '*hamdulillah*' [Praise be to God!], '*masha'allah*' [God wills it!], or '*subhan allah*' [Glory be to God!] just as part of how we speak." There was also the shared food culture that she considered "Muslim."

Muna viewed Islam as a strategic resource, too. In follow-up conversations, she described how she had started using Islamic legal provisions to resist her retired parents-in-law, who, she said, were pressuring her husband to help defray their monthly expenses. "I went to the *shaykh* at the Mosque Foundation at one point," she told me, "and told him about this, and he said that my husband had to see to our family expenses and needs first and then, if there was anything left over, he could contribute to his parents' needs. Also, he told me that in Islamic law I had the right to control the income I earned from my work." Her parents-in-law were unhappy with the fact that she had sought outside intervention, but, because they accepted the moral parameters of the Islamized milieu, they could not argue with the *shaykh*'s authority. Thus, even if she did not adhere to Islamic strictures in her daily life, she deployed Islamic norms, like Nawal (in chapter 5) did, to defend and expand her autonomy. She also wondered whether Islamic prohibitions on alcohol might actually be good for her and her husband. "I have given up alcohol and am cutting back on pot and I wish my husband would do the same," she told me.

Muna's ambivalence toward Islam and its social forms as enacted in the suburban enclave led her to oscillate between adaptation and refusal. Reflecting on this seeming irresolution, she stated again that she thought of herself as a "secular Muslim." This secularity did not exclude "spirituality." She explained:

> I still consider myself a spiritual person. I would be interested in a mystical form of Islam, I think. Islam has been a victim of politics. There are very many versions practiced and suppressed and even the Qur'an itself might even be a different version because it didn't have dots [diacritical vowel markings] or anything whenever they wrote it. I think maybe if it was just the Qur'an, maybe that would be okay; but

whenever Muslims start throwing in the *hadith* and *sunna* [the Prophet Muhammad's remembered practices] and everything, it's very much to me a human project, not of God. I still sometimes think, 'Oh, the Qur'an is the word of God.' But other days, I'm like, 'Oh, [religious texts] are all just man-made written books or metaphorical ways of dealing with phenomena.'

For Muna, the seeming equivocation of her secular Muslim identity found a consistency in an inner "connection with God." Within this inner realm, she carved out an autonomous spirituality. She was a secular Muslim inasmuch as she did not "really show[. . .] typical Islamic features [like] not wearing the hijab, not praying, not fasting." But she was not an atheist, which she said was "different from secularism." Rather, she expressed a type of secular religiosity that allowed her to retain a relationship to the immigrant community on her own terms. Since returning to Chicago, she had been "meeting other Palestinians and Muslims and Arabs" and through that experience "learning the different ranges of being Muslim [. . .]. It's not like the one formula I was raised with [. . .]." These different ways were similar to "how you meet Jews and they drink and eat pork and everything, so I think it's through the influence of being in America [. . .]. I know so many Arabs and Muslims like me who drink alcohol [. . .], the ones I went clubbing with [before she got married]." Muna also had found alternative spaces—she was part of a feminist reading group at her university, for example—in which women collaborated to challenge the patriarchal norms that imposed female subordination. Crossing between these zones and the immigrant enclave, she found a way to remain connected to "Arabville" as a skeptical, "secular Muslim" who refused to abide the orthopraxical reform.

A Secular Sufi amidst the Suburban Jahl

A similar type of spiritualized autonomy characterizes the secular religiosity of the individual who is the focus of my final profile. As with Muna, the Islamized suburban milieu generated disenchantment and a search for moral alternatives. The process here, however, did not stem from the felt inequities of the patriarchal gender hierarchy of reformism but rather from a reaction against reformist doctrines that deem certain artistic expressions, music, specifically, to be *haram*. Ultimately, a Sufi-inspired spiritual cosmopolitanism that affirms the polytheism of values offered an alternative to this prohibition, but its discovery required leaving the piety-minded suburbs for the multicultural artistic spaces of Chicago's near North Side.

Social Background and Identity Formation

Born in the late 1970s, Jubran [pseudonym] grew up in the rapidly expanding and Islamizing Palestinian suburban enclave. The inner culture (ethos) of Jubran's family was at odds with this turn toward reformist piety. Jubran's father was a musician who had taught his sons to play the instruments used in classical and contemporary Middle Eastern musical styles. He led various ensembles that toured cities in the Midwest, and his sons played in those groups. In high school, Jubran expanded his repertoire, exploring heavy metal as well as classical Andalusian (Middle Eastern) music. He eventually formed his own musical groups devoted to resurrecting Andalusian traditions and fusing them with jazz and other musical styles in Chicago's multicultural music scene.

The musical arts became "an escape" or "shelter" from the surrounding piety-mindedness for Jubran and his brothers and father. They provided alternative possibilities for leisure, identity, and participation in the urban space beyond the enclave. These possibilities enabled and sustained the family's distinct microculture in the midst of the reformist shift.

The family diverged from the piety-minded enclave in another way, too. It was part of the established core of Beitunian families that had provided the original impetus for the Mosque Foundation. These families envisioned the new mosque as a center for communal gathering and worship and not as the instrument of an ideological program that viewed Islam as an all-encompassing identity structure. Jubran, who lived with his grandparents for a period after his mother and father divorced, took part in this communal culture. He characterized the religiosity of this culture as open and accepting. His grandparents exemplified its characteristics:

> My grandparents didn't mind [the fact that his father was a musician] at all. My grandfather [. . .] wasn't very strict about religion. '*Al-din yusr, mish 'usr*' ['religion is ease, not hardship'], is the way he would talk about it, you know, you wanna come to the religion. You do it of your own accord; we're not gonna force you. But, you know, I'd see him pray, I'd take him to the mosque, and I remember when he helped build the mosque, you know, in Bridgeview, with his friends.

Jubran participated in the activities of the Mosque Foundation during its early years. His description of these activities emphasized the mosque's role as a center for a "secular" community life. He studied Arabic at the mosque. His teacher did not wear a hijab scarf and "her husband was a chef at the Berghoff downtown and, in fact, his picture was on the bottle of one their beers." The language lessons, moreover, were not tied to the Qur'an: "It wasn't about religion at all. It was more like, *dar, dur,*" that is, learning to decline nouns and other grammatical tasks. The secularity of the mosque manifested, too, in Jubran's memory, in the fact that the original imam's daughters "were not *muhajjabat* (scarf-wearing) whatsoever, but they were very educated[. . .]; there was this notion that our daughters and our sons needed to be educated before [taking up] religion. There was no indoctrination."

The reformist ascendancy on the Mosque Foundation board, and the implementation of reformist piety that followed during the 1980s, alienated Jubran and his father and brothers. Not only had Jubran grown up with a notion of Islam as *yusr* (ease), not *'usr* (hardship), and thus accepting of diverse lifestyles, he was also the son of a mother who possessed an urbane outlook. Jubran attributed his mother's cosmopolitanism to her childhood in West Jerusalem during the 1930s and 1940s. She had grown up with Jewish neighbors, including "Moshe Dayan's nephew [who was] living in one of their apartments after World War Two and the arrival of all the Jewish refugees!"[7] His grandfather, moreover, had "employed Iranian Jews" at the quarry he owned near the current location of the Israeli Knesset (Parliament) building.

His mother's openness to intersectarian and interethnic coexistence and cooperation continued in Chicago, too. The support of non-Arab, non-Muslim women had been especially important for Jubran's mother after her divorce from Jubran's father. Needing to support herself, his mother found work in a local factory that employed women from a broad range of ethnic backgrounds. "[There were women from] the Polish tradition, Indian, Hispanic, etc., Arab, as well. She became kind of adopted by this one Polish woman, who took her under her wing for the next five years, became like her mother, helped my mom, encouraged her, told her, look these are things that happen in people's lives, save your money."

His father, through music, also modeled an embrace of cultural diversity that spanned the Middle Eastern immigrant community:

> Through the music, I saw the insides of many more churches—Arab churches—than I did mosques. Our singer was Jordanian Christian, there were Iraqi Armenian Christians, Arab Jews who were *'iraqiyin* [Iraqis], you know, who we ended up playing with, you know, Tunisians, North Africans. So the scope of the Arab world really started to broaden for us through music, solely through music, not any other route. That's when I knew that music held a universal truth that I wanted to really latch on to.

Jubran commented that he would never have encountered this diversity had he grown up in Palestine. The US diaspora had thrown all of these individuals together, and through music they had found one another.

Confronting the Suburban Jahl

The openness to, and reliance on, cross-cultural solidarities that Jubran's parents modeled oriented Jubran toward multiculturalism and pluralist secularity. In the suburbs, however, the cultural trajectory was moving increasingly toward orthopraxic uniformity. Jubran referred vividly to this shift as "the emergence of *jahl* [narrow-mindedness]." His choice of terms was striking for its resonance with a core concept in the Salafi-Islamist moral and political lexicon. During the 1960s, Sayyid Qutb, one of the foremost theorists of the Muslim Brotherhood, claimed that modern Arab states and societies comprised a new *jahiliya*, an age of ignorance. The original *jahiliya* traditionally referred to the period in the Arabian Hijaz before the arrival of Islam. Qutb's use of the concept effectively cast contemporary Muslim-majority societies as apostate and thus as legitimate targets of jihad (violence with sacred intent).[8] Jubran's invoking of the term unwittingly inverted Qutb's polemical formulation: the real *jahiliya*, as Jubran saw it, was not secularized modern societies but rather the narrowness that had resulted from the reformist shift.⁹

One characteristic of this narrow piety-mindedness, as Jubran experienced it, was the refusal to affirm the multireligious pluralism of Arab societies. When Jubran mentioned that he had played in Arab churches, the reaction among some of those who had embraced reformism was hostile: "They said things like, don't affiliate with those *kuffar* [heretics]; I heard these things at the *masjid* [mosque] and from people who went to the *masjid*!" Jubran saw this hostility stemming from the fusion of ethnic and religious identity. In the suburbs, the unspoken assumption had become that if one were Palestinian one was also a Muslim in the narrow reformist style. The problem with this merging of sect and ethnicity, Jubran observed, was that it ignored the existence of non-Muslim Arabs and Palestinians. These groups included not only Christians but also Druze, Jews (the "Mizrahim," or Arab Jews, especially), atheists, agnostics, secularists, and so on.

Jubran was careful to say that the turn toward a narrow orthopraxy was not a type of political Islam, or "Islamism," but rather a matter of "taking Islam [simplistically] at face value." To approach Islam in this way was to embrace a type of strict, exclusionary view—he used the term "*al-ta'assub*," "intolerance" or "chauvinism"— and not necessarily to shift toward Islam as political ideology.¹⁰ This intolerance was defensive, he said. It was a reaction to the derogation of Islam in the wider US society. But it was also a deeply limiting attitude that demanded unquestioning conformity. "I have to ask questions," he told me, "I can't simply accept what the *shaykh* says on authority." But in the suburbs today, this non-questioning attitude had become entrenched. "There is no awareness that this style of Islam, this *muta'assibi* [intolerant, chauvinistic] attitude, is just one possible approach to Islam," he commented.

Jubran especially refused to accept the hostility to music and musicians that had accompanied the embrace of "intolerant" orthopraxic reformism.¹¹ Jubran told a humorous story about his brother that illustrated this hostility. For a brief moment, his brother flirted with becoming more pious. The brother approached the Mosque Foundation *shaykh* to tell him of his interest in Islam. The *shaykh* promised his support and then asked him what he did for a living. "I'm a musician," the brother replied, "I play in the nightclubs around here." The *shaykh*, in Jubran's recounting, shook his head gravely and replied: "We must find something else for you to do." Jubran laughed at the memory, saying, "This is precisely what I'm getting at: as a musician, I felt unwelcome in this environment."¹²

The characterizing of music as *haram* by the guardians of the new orthopraxy effectively meant that Jubran had no place to exist as an artist within the suburban enclave as it had come to constitute itself since the late 1980s. The negative attitude was pervasive in the community. He stated:

> I had people coming up to me, telling me that what I believed in, what I espoused to be my religion, secretly, of music, telling me this is *haram*! You're telling me the one

thing that religion wasn't able to do for me, which is expose me to the world and love people for who they are, not for what they are, you're telling me that's *haram*?

No longer able to abide the narrowness, Jubran decided to move to a trendy near North Side neighborhood near Chicago's world music scene. Recently divorced—his first marriage, arranged through his family with a Palestinian woman, had fallen apart relatively soon after the wedding—he began to date individuals from diverse cultural and religious backgrounds.

> My first girlfriend was Italian, after my divorce. Then I dated a woman who was an ordained witch in the Wiccan tradition. Very spiritual, very pagan, she was my yoga instructor. I thought, okay, I wanna start studying new kinds of things and open up to bigger cultures.

Jubran eventually remarried. His new wife was from a Croatian Catholic family. He had met her through music-making circles. She was now managing his performances and recording activities.

Beyond the Jahl: *A Multi-Cultural Sufi Secularity*

Jubran's move to the North Side not only symbolically marked his break from the Islamizing enclave in the southwest suburbs but also initiated a spiritual search leading to a type of secular religiosity. He had, by this point, ceased strict adherence to the norms of Islamic ritual practice—the five mandated daily prayers, fasting during Ramadan, etc.—and had started to read Buddhist sutras and Hindu texts such as the Bhagavad Gita. He also discovered Sufism.

The discovery occurred during a concert tour in Spain—a journey that exposed him to an entirely new Islamic milieu. "[In Spain] I discovered a lot of North African folks who practiced Sunni Islam but a very different version of it," he said, "including Sufism." Unlike the reformists in Chicago, these Sufis embraced music:

> I started doing recordings with them. There was a Sufi group that came from Sudan. They mixed with some Algerian Sufis. We went to a studio and recorded a bunch of Sufi *anashid* [hymns]. I was also really into the Turkish Sufi groups, as well. After returning to Chicago, I sat in with the Jerrahi order, extensively. I didn't start praying with them but became musically involved with them [. . .]. Their form of Islam, though Sunni, was *very* open and Sufi oriented and very spiritual and accepting. I didn't find the same prejudices I saw sprawling up in the Palestinian community and in the Muslim community, generally. The Sufi path really started to appeal to me, I found a lot more poetry in it, a lot more metaphors; it was very metaphorical, it spoke to life and one's connection to spirituality. And I saw it akin to the way I saw music. In fact it's the Sufism and that aspect of Islam that enhanced my understanding and appreciation of the music as a spiritual practice more than anything. So, I'll do *dhikr* ["remembrance" of God through chant, song, and dance]. I will fast, observe, but I'll do it on my own terms. So, this is really the path I think I found myself in; but again I

had to experiment with so many religions, and not to say I converted, I never did, I've always considered myself Muslim; but I consider myself a Muslim who doesn't have an aversion to Hinduism or polytheism or other people in the world who believe the way they do by circumstance.

Jubran's Islam was fully accepting of the polytheism of values that typified contemporary secularity in the wider cultural space of Chicago and globally. Significantly, this acceptance even extended to the *muta'assibi* (intolerant) reformism that had so strongly repulsed him in the suburbs. He declared his readiness to defend those who had chosen it even if he did not fully share its values. "You have the right to believe as you want," he said, commenting on piety-minded orientations. "All I ask is you give me the same."

Jubran's particular appropriation of Islam was highly idiosyncratic: it indicated the extent of his separation from the suburbs. He did not pray five times a day but rather did so "with every breath I take [. . .] and every step I take. I pray with every note I play."[13] He commented further, saying:

> It took the arts to help me see that I could be Muslim in this way. It didn't take somebody indoctrinating me; it didn't take me discovering some document [such as the Qur'an]! It took an approach to life and a critical thought process to question my own existence. We are all sinners but we are all redeemable, as well. We have to help each other in that quest. This particular path was prevalent during the Islamic period in al-Andalus [Spain] from the eighth to the fifteenth century.

Jubran's discovery of an Islamic cosmopolitanism in Sufism coincided with his musical projects. These efforts focused on fusing Andalusian classical music with musical traditions from other parts of the world. He had begun to explore these connections in parallel with his move to the North Side and then deepened them in Spain. This musical and spiritual discovery process paralleled his rejection of orthopraxic-reformist constraints. It also coincided with a new, cosmopolitan perspective on Palestine and the national struggle with Israel:

> You know, it was from being able to discover my own path like this that I began to find out these things also exist in Palestine. There are Sufis in Palestine doing the same work trying to bring people together. There's an amazing documentary I saw on Al Jazeera a couple of weeks ago about a Jewish scholar who moved to the mountains with his wife and discovered Rumi and began translating Rumi into Hebrew and started to do the whole whirling dervish thing to the point [where] he went to Turkey, to Konya, to seek out Rumi's teachings and meet some dervishes and learn how to do the *sama'* [a type of Sufi ritual practice involving musical instruments, chant, and dance] properly. So, they took him in. He was the first Israeli to find his way into the circle out there. He came back and is preaching Rumism, if you will, a version of Islam that's very tolerant as opposed to what people have perceived it to be. It showed him coming back to Israel and sitting in groups in al-Nasira [Nazareth] with the Sufi order that is Palestinian. I remember in Palestine [during a visit

following the trip to Spain] that I sat in [played music] with the Baháʾís for some time who established themselves in ʿAkka after being pushed out of Iran. I thought to myself, okay, this [Palestine and Israel] is a very multicultural and very multireligious area. It's futile to think we are going to make it entirely Jewish or entirely Muslim or entirely Christian.

Jubran had grown up absorbing a basic nationalist outlook. His parents told stories of their lives in Palestine before 1948 and they took their children to events at the community centers in the Southwest Side immigrant enclave. As an adult, he performed at fundraisers for Palestinian and Arab nonprofit organizations. Jubran's evolving musical-spiritual cosmopolitanism, however, had led him to embrace a multicultural perspective that rendered relative the claims of any single ethnic, national, or religious group. Palestine was as diverse as Spain or the United States or any other society. If there was any viable solution to the Palestinian and Israeli predicament, it lay within an interethnic, interreligious solidarity that recognized the futility of attempts to impose exclusivity and dominance at the expense of other groups.

A Jubran Postscript

I interviewed Jubran—we completed two in-depth conversations in a two-year span—at his Near North Side apartment. When I arrived for our first conversation, I saw shoes neatly stacked at the top landing just before the entrance to the apartment. I removed mine and as I straightened, noticed a large skeleton key hanging on the doorframe. Such keys were the quintessential symbol among Palestinian refugees of their lost homes and of their desire to return. Inside the apartment, incense wafted. A Washburn steel-string sat propped in front of a blue-tiled fireplace. An ʿud—ancestor to the European lute and staple of Middle Eastern music—leaned against the southeastern wall. In an adjoining room, electronic sound equipment, a second ʿud, and another guitar filled every corner. "That's my studio," Jubran told me, as he showed me around the apartment. "The landlady downstairs is almost deaf and doesn't care if we crank up the sound."

We returned to the living room and began the interview. Ramadan had begun but Jubran offered me tea and poured himself a cup, too. Halfway through the four-hour conversation, Jubran asked to pause so that he could help his wife finish lunch preparations. Within minutes, he had brought out a chopped salad and a special dressing he had made along with the quiche that Marija (pseudonym), his wife, had baked. "We've been fasting," Marija said. "Actually Jubran fasted all day yesterday." I asked self-consciously if my visit had derailed their abstention from food and drink. "No, not at all," Marija replied, "Jubran isn't real strict about it." I remembered then how right before our interview Jubran had excused himself so that he could finish his hand-rolled cigarette. He walked to the porch, where I noticed him and Marija smoking on their enclosed back porch. Like Intisar (chapter 5), Jubran had retained a taste for tobacco during the daylight hours when Muslims are to fast.[14]

After lunch, I asked about a book on their shelf titled "Jubran and Marija Get Married!" The book contained their wedding pictures. Showing me the pages, Jubran recounted the story of their ceremony in Bali, a Hindu region of Indonesia. They had been spending a year traveling the world. Their Balinese hosts had learned of their plans to formalize their union at the end of their journey. The hosts insisted right there and then on giving them a "Hindi [sic] wedding." In just four hours they drummed up suits and dresses and rounded up musicians. During the preparations, their hosts asked who should preside at the ceremony. Jubran was a Palestinian Muslim, Marija a Croatian Catholic. "It seemed to me we should split the difference and ask a Hindu to officiate!" Jubran laughed. The hosts promptly recruited a Brahmin priest to oversee their vows. They married, Marija said, "under the night sky," a full moon lighting their ceremony, waves gently lapping the Balinese shore.

CONCLUSION

As manifested in my fieldwork data, the "rebellion" form of syncretic secularity led either to spiritualization or to atheism as types of secular religiosity. The primary matrix of both trajectories was the disenchanting effects of the religious shift. In Jubran's case, the disenchantment stemmed from the reformist-orthopraxic devaluing of music, and specifically of its openness to diverse cultural influences and diverse cultural participants. For Ibrahim, the disenchantment process derived from a perception of the fundamental injustice of an all-powerful, all-knowing God condemning humans for their predetermined sinfulness. Muna and Sawsan reacted against the patriarchal control instituted within the religious-sectarian and reformist-orthoprax milieus in which they grew up. They experienced this control as coercive and traumatizing.

In each example, the countervailing response embraced a multisectarian, pluralist ethos. Interaction with diverse intersectarian and nonsectarian spaces beyond the immigrant enclave—North Side neighborhoods, musical circles, youth party cultures, and unconventional religious milieus—presented alternate possibilities for identity. These possibilities became the foundation for the secular religiosities that evolved in each instance of rebellion. These secular religiosities retained a certain adherence to religion within a broad pluralist outlook.

At the furthest extreme, Ibrahim's atheism denied religion's centrality entirely; nevertheless, he pragmatically simulated adherence to piety and held onto the idea of religion as the inverse image of the atheistic values he affirmed. By contrast, the spiritualization that characterized Muna, Sawsan, and Jubran's outlooks replaced orthopraxic uniformity with an expansive universalism that rejected ethnic and religious exclusivity. Muna spoke of a "secular Islam" that she attempted to affirm in the midst of the reformist orthopraxy that confronted her in the suburbs. Sawsan invoked a trinity of "love, God, and Palestine" that denied priority to any particular sectarian claim, Christian or Islamic. And Jubran embraced a Sufi universalism at home with polytheism in Chicago, Palestine, and globally. In each case, the secular and the religious had interacted to create new trajectories of syncretic identity beyond the sectarian milieu.

Conclusion

On April 25, 2017, two years after I had completed my fieldwork, Rasmea Odeh, Associate Director of the Arab American Action Network (AAAN), walked into a federal courtroom in Detroit, Michigan to plead guilty to one count of fraudulently obtaining United States citizenship. Ending a three-and-a-half-year legal and political struggle, she agreed to admit to not having disclosed a previous conviction and imprisonment on her 2004 naturalization application and to accept immediate loss of her citizenship and deportation in return for the waiving of prison time beyond the period she had already served prior to her release on bail. The incident Odeh was accused of not disclosing pertained to her sentencing by an Israeli military court to life imprisonment for membership in the Popular Front for the Liberation of Palestine (PFLP) and participation in two bombings in 1969.[1] Odeh firmly and consistently denied the charges on which she was convicted. Soon after her release as part of a prisoner exchange in 1979, she testified at the United Nations General Assembly in Geneva, Switzerland to having been tortured and sexually assaulted during her initial, forty-five-day detention and interrogation (United Nations General Assembly 1979). A psychiatrist who evaluated Odeh in Chicago determined that she suffered from post-traumatic stress disorder related to the abuse she had suffered and that this condition, which can cause repression of traumatic memories, likely accounted for her not indicating the 1969 arrest in her United States citizenship application form.[2]

In 1997, three years after Odeh's arrival in the United States, the US State Department listed the PFLP as a terrorist organization.[3] On this basis, federal prosecutors threatened to charge Odeh retroactively with membership in a terrorist group if she refused to accept the plea deal they offered her in relation to the immigration charge. Convinced she would never receive a fair trial as spiking anti-Arab and anti-Muslim racism had accompanied the Trump election in 2016 (Lichtblau 2016; Jouvenal and Zauzmer 2017; Southern Poverty Law Center 2018), Odeh's lawyers urged her to accept the offer.[4] Her decision brought to an end forty-two months of political organizing, fundraising, mobilizing, protesting, media work, and legal advocacy on her behalf. Her supporters expressed resignation and sorrow but also claimed victory, declaring, "For three and a half years we put Israel on trial in the United States."[5]

The campaign to support Odeh was an immediate response to her need for backing. But it also stemmed from a deeply rooted practice of protest and mutual aid among Chicago's Palestinians against a US society and government frequently hostile toward Arabs and Muslims (M. Suleiman 1996; Cainkar 2009; Pennock 2017). In Odeh's case, this self-protective reflex unified the various segments of the community—secular and religious—to resist yet another threat against one of their own.[6] The campaign's organizing committee (I attended several of its early meetings) drew from the established leadership in the secular and Islamic activist milieus. Palestinian Christian organizations did not form part of the core leadership, although the head of Friends of Sabeel North America, the Palestine solidarity group primarily supported by non-Arab Protestant denominations (see chapters 1, 3, and 4), did participate. Organizing meetings occurred in restaurants, at the AAAN offices, and in the assembly rooms of the Aqsa Islamic School for Girls situated across from the Mosque Foundation. American Muslims for Palestine (AMP) issued statements and raised money alongside the AAAN.[7] The women associated with Odeh's Arab Women's Committee program, many of them practicing Muslims, and participants in the AAAN's youth programs consistently attended the organizing meetings and travelled to Detroit to demonstrate in front of the federal courthouse where Odeh underwent arraignment and trial. Their signs and slogans decried Odeh's arrest and conviction as unjust and racist.

The campaign also activated longstanding alliances with Puerto Rican nationalist groups, Black Lives Matter chapters, Jewish Voice for Peace, feminist academics, and other progressive and people of color (POC) activists. Prominent African American activist-scholars like Angela Davis adopted Odeh's cause. Reciprocating the solidarity, representatives from the AAAN travelled to Ferguson, Missouri to join the protests against the killing of Michael Brown in August 2014 (Grant 2019). AAAN youth leaders connected this violence against African Americans to the surveillance and racial profiling of their own communities and to US and Israeli law enforcement coordination.[8]

At the center of the campaign was Odeh herself, who emerged from her relatively quiet life as a Southwest Side community organizer to become a national symbol of the resistance against oppression of Palestinians, of other POC groups, and of women. Notably, Odeh did not explicitly invoke religious symbols and tropes despite the involvement of groups like AMP. She did not wear a hijab scarf, for example. In an interview with me, she expressed her belief, derived from her Marxist principles, that religion gave a false understanding of reality and thereby was an impediment to liberation, especially women's liberation. Still, she collaborated with religious activists working on her behalf. With those activists, some of them connected to AMP, she shared a fundamental commitment to justice. A symbol of that commitment during her arrest and hearings, she willingly integrated the diverse segments of Palestinian activism in Chicago within the revived Palestinian solidarity and antiracist coalition that supported her.

RECONSIDERING THE RELIGIOUS SHIFT: CONCLUDING POINTS

The campaign to prevent Odeh's deportation brings into view the main concluding points of this book. First, it highlights the unresolved Palestinian national situation and the role of US policy in favoring Zionism and Israel while opposing the Palestinian demand of return and independent statehood. This lack of resolution continues to generate profound uncertainty and insecurity within Palestinian diaspora communities like that in Chicago. Law enforcement interventions targeting community leaders like Odeh dramatize and reinforce this insecurity. They corroborate for Palestinians the longstanding perception that the exile cannot and should not become the normative state. The condition of exile and occupation is the ongoing Nakba ("Catastrophe"), a distorted reality deeply at odds with universal principles of law, justice, and morality. Only liberation and return (al-'awda) to the stolen homeland can restore the arc of history to its rightful course. Given these presumptions, the exile can only be the site of inauthenticity and alienation, a space and condition to be survived until the moment of restoration.

The recent election of Rashida Tlaib (D-MI, 13th District) and Ilhan Omar (D-MN, 5th District) to the United States House of Representatives has, ironically, further underlined the uncertainty of the exile. Tlaib, whose constituency is predominantly African American, is the first Palestinian-American elected to Congress. She and Omar, the first Somali-American to join Congress, have been outspoken critics of US financial and political support for Israel and concomitant refusal to address Palestinian national demands.[9] In response, they have become targets of a sharp backlash that has included accusations of anti-Semitism (Barbaro 2019; Keating 2019). For Palestinians, these rebukes reinforce the sense of the exile as a hostile space—a site defined by the experience of state surveillance, arbitrary attack, and racist exclusion. The attacks have also underlined the necessity to fight back through mass political mobilization and, increasingly, through the ballot box.

It is this sense of being under siege, and the repressive interventions that provoke and confirm it, which intergenerationally re-enlivens nationalism and its emphasis on the ethnos. This orientation is fundamentally secular to the extent that it imagines an independent national existence within territorially delimited, intersectarian terms. Secular nationalist movements, and the community centers that historically aligned with them in diaspora communities like Chicago, have expressed this secularity explicitly. The orientations carried within these movements have persisted even after the withering of the PLO and the closing of the community centers such as the *markaz*. Successor organizations like the AAAN have provided this continuity even if they no longer are the primary anchors of immigrant community life. As this book has pointed out (especially in chapter 2), secularism has continued through these structures and through families in which secular nationalism has remained a dominant tradition.

A second and related concluding point is that the inherent secularity of the national question has also affected the reformist Islam that has gained ascendency since the late 1980s. It has done so by counterposing the moral imperative of Palestinian unity and liberation against the reformist Islamic devaluing of national solidarities in favor of the transnational Islamic *umma*. Hatem Abudayyeh (chapter 2), Executive Director of the AAAN, explained the reason for this phenomenon in these terms:

> You can't say there's this transnational Islamic experience that we all have. Maybe it helps to organize across nationalities when people look at this concept of *umma islamiya* [the global Islamic community]. But there are very specific issues based on nationality. There are black issues; Mexican issues; Arab issues, beyond Islam. It liquidates the national question when you organize religiously.

As Abudayyeh points out, even if there can be overlap between secular and "faith-based" organizing frameworks, at key junctures the religious focus contradicts the priorities of national liberation. At a certain point one must decide between nation and *umma* as the locus of solidarity. A primary emphasis on *umma* ultimately dilutes the commitment to the nation and its liberation. Conversely, a commitment to the nation entails, at some point, a demotion of the *umma* to secondary importance in the hierarchy of solidarity.

This fact holds true even in instances where the two priorities, *umma* and nation, seem to coincide. AMP, despite appearing to weld nation and *umma* into an undifferentiated whole, has effectively nationalized Islam by rendering Palestine and its liberation Islam's preeminent focus and duty. This transformation has remained unstable, susceptible to challenge from both nationalist and Islamic perspectives. AMP's responses to these challenges reveal the instability of its position.

When AMP prioritizes Islamic solidarity, for example, it risks censure for contradicting the principles of human rights, national liberation, and national unity. This conundrum came into sharp focus during the commemoration of the centenary of the Armenian genocide. On April 19, 2015, the US Council of Muslim Organizations, of which AMP was a founding member, issued a statement that refused to label the Ottoman state's systematic extermination campaign as "genocide."[10] Almost instantly, progressive Muslim American activists and columnists as well as Palestine solidarity social media sites demanded that AMP clarify its position.[11] In an attempt to do so, AMP issued a statement that acknowledged Armenian "suffering and pain" but avoided the term "genocide" as a characterization for what had occurred.[12] Palestine solidarity activists, Palestinian Armenians, and other Christians and Muslims derided this attempted clarification. They pointed out that AMP's refusal to recognize the validity of the term undermined its criticisms of Zionism and Israeli occupation. It was also divisive. As one commenter noted, Palestinian Armenians were among the thousands of Palestinians who fled the fighting or were expelled by force during and after the war of 1948. Armenian Christians were, for this reason, an inseparable part of the Palestinian nation, having shared in its formative traumas.[13] The nation had a reciprocal obligation to stand with its Armenian sisters and brothers in their demand for recognition of genocide. Caught between its opposition to Israeli occupation and its sympathy for Islamic reformism—Turkey, which forcefully opposed the "genocide" label, was led by an Islamic reformist party that had extended support for Muslim Brotherhood opposition groups in Syria and Egypt (Kingsley 2017; Carnegie Middle East Center 2012)—AMP quietly refrained from any further public statements on the matter.

Conversely, when it has emphasized Palestinian nationalist priorities, such as defending al-Aqsa Mosque in Jerusalem, for instance, AMP has sometimes triggered the resentment of other Muslim constituencies (see chapter 3). Syrians, who provide important financial backing and leadership in the Islamic milieu, especially through the Mosque Foundation, have been sensitive to perceived hypocrisy in the stances of Palestinian Muslims whenever their nationalist priorities appear, from their point of view, to sideline the dire plight of Syrian civilians and opposition groups in the ongoing civil war. As its 2013 conference demonstrated (see chapter 3), AMP has attempted to resolve these tensions by placing Palestine at the center of a Holy Land that expands to include the entire Levant and also Iraq and Egypt. In doing so, it has rendered Palestine a metonym of the struggle for justice in the Middle East as a whole. It has also transformed it into a litmus test of religious commitment. This commitment includes advocacy for justice elsewhere—in Syria, for example, or in Ferguson, Missouri—but it is Palestine and its liberation that lies at the center of AMP's raison d'être.

Secularity has persisted and shaped the Islamic turn in a second way: through the emergence of new syncretic secularities—"secular religiosities" (see chapter 6)—that have reacted against the piety-minded milieu. As chapter 6 especially demonstrates, some individuals who grow up in the midst of the Islamized milieu resist its disciplines and norms even as others embrace them. Jubran, for example, a musician, declared the Islamic turn a type of *"jahl"*—a narrow-mindedness that rendered piety into a cheerless iconoclasm. He left the enclave in search of artistic space on Chicago's North Side. He also married a non-Muslim in a ceremony presided over by a Brahmin Hindu priest and pursued syncretic collaborations with jazz, blues, and Indian musicians. As he did so, he formulated a Sufi sensibility open to the diversity of spiritual possibilities within and beyond Islam. His idiosyncratic spirituality comported with the artistic fusion he forged in his professional musical career. His was not the Islam of the reformist movements, the suburban "Islam of the book" and of orthopraxic piety emphasizing the regular performance of prayer, fasting, tithing, and so on. Jubran fasted sporadically, if at all. He prayed occasionally. Not strictly secularist, his Islam was at home with, indeed expressive of, the multicultural, syncretic secularity that he encountered in Chicago's urban expanse. Palestine remained important to him. He performed at fundraisers for Palestinian organizations that advocated for the cause. But neither Islam nor Palestine was necessarily the center of his life beyond the enclave.

In another instance recounted in chapter 6, a young woman, Muna, rejected the religious patriarchy she encountered at the Islamic schools she attended. She rebelled by leaving Chicago's "Arabville" for a distant state, where she participated in the youth party scene. She returned later in an effort to "leave [her] bad habits behind" and retrieve her connections to Palestinian-Arab identity. In "Arabville" in the southwest suburbs, she grappled with Islam as she took university courses in feminist theory. The enclave suffocated her. She resisted it by refusing the hijab, refusing prayer, refusing to fast, and consuming intoxicants. Her search for roots took her to Palestine, where she encountered, in Haifa and Ramallah, a much more relaxed, liberal culture than the one she had grown up in, in Chicago. Individuals who made ostentatious displays of their piety in Chicago also sought out these spaces in Palestine. This fact rendered their piety a patent hypocrisy in Muna's eyes. As a refuge from rigorous moralism, Palestine, it seems, could host more than one sort of rebellion against the diaspora's piety-mindedness. Muna, who returned to live in the suburbs, ultimately settled for a "secular Islam," as she described it. She expressed belief in God's existence but rejected reformist orthopraxy. There were multiple paths. No single religion monopolized truth. In these sentiments, she affirmed a polytheistic secularity that denied authority to any single religion even as it allowed religions their place in society.

There were other similar cases of syncretic secularity. Sawsan, who grew up in a Christian family in Beit Jala, embraced Islam as an expression of her nationalism. In Chicago, however, her path evolved toward a highly idiosyncratic spirituality that resisted the sectarianism, Christian and Islamic, of the suburbs. In her triune expression, "Love, God, and Palestine," she upheld a multisectarian vision that transcended the binaries of Christian and Muslim, Palestinian and Israeli. She acknowledged the diaspora, and Chicago's diversity of trajectories in particular, as affording her the space within which to explore and express her individuality.

Ibrahim, too, embraced the urban exile as the space of individual freedom. He refused the demands of nationalist and religious conformity, declaring himself to be an atheist and an American. He fell in love with a likeminded Palestinian woman who had refused the hijab and, like Ibrahim, did not pray or fast. Their relationship evolved on the North Side beyond the southwest suburban enclave: the morally and culturally diverse space of the city afforded them this chance. As a form of secular religiosity, Ibrahim's represented the furthest end of the syncretic spectrum. Religion persisted within his orientation, faintly, in as much as he pretended to adhere to piety when at home with his parents or invoked it negatively to explain and define his atheism.

As these examples have demonstrated, secularism and secularity have persisted and re-emerged under the conditions of the religious, sectarian shift. They qualified the shift, casting its terms within an affirmation of a multisectarian, polytheistic, or, at the extreme, atheistic ethos. But the dynamic worked in the reverse direction, too. This is the third main concluding point of this book: within the secular-religious interaction, the religious shift, in conjunction with the shrinking of secular space, also profoundly altered the path of secularism and secularity. It did so, as chapters 3 and 4 showed, by institutionalizing the ethos and disciplines of piety and thereby instilling the priority of Islam as the enclave's dominant framework of identity and by reinforcing a mirroring sectarianization among Christian Palestinians.

Chapter 5 further highlighted the diverse ways in which this process of religious qualification of the secular occurred in my data. It specifically profiled individuals rooted in the secular milieu who had moved toward an embrace, fully or partially, of the new piety. Nawal, Intisar, and Rami Nashashibi illustrated this type of development (that is, "religious secularity"). In each of these examples, significantly, the shift was not a matter of a complete and pure exchange of orientations. Nawal embraced the disciplines of piety within the new Islamic structures in the suburbs, but she also continued to immerse herself—at least until she accepted employment with an Islamic social service organization—in secular nationalist spaces that affirmed her Palestinian identity in ways that did not occur within the reformist Islamic milieu. As she crossed in and out of these spaces, she negotiated competing moral demands. In doing so, she arrived at a mutually conditioning compromise: she relinquished elements of "correct" reformist orthopraxy, especially as it pertained to physical contact between marriageable men and women, but otherwise held to the remainder of her orthopraxic comportment—principally, prayer, fasting, and the hijab—within the secular spaces in which she worked. In doing so, she both adapted to and transformed those spaces.

Intisar similarly modified her secularism by enrolling her daughters in the new Islamic schools, primarily as a way to shield them from anti-Arab and anti-Muslim racism. She also did so by redefining her activism as Muslim and Islamic advocacy. "Islam exploded within [her]" after the September 11 attacks as the anti-Muslim and anti-Arab backlash built. Her response was mainly defensive. But, increasingly, as she became integrated into the Islamized suburban milieu, she participated in events at the Mosque Foundation and at the Islamic schools and cooperated with Mosque Foundation leadership to educate residents of the suburban enclave about their civil rights. She had not completely embraced the disciplines—prayer, fasting, hijab—that signaled alignment with reformist Islamic identity, and she remained a committed nationalist. The center of her identity and work, nevertheless, had now come to encompass Islam and the piety-oriented suburban community it represented.

Rami Nashashibi, by contrast, had abandoned the secular nationalist milieu entirely in favor of a cosmopolitan Islam rooted in the Black Muslim space of Chicago's South Side. Significantly, however, he conceived of this Islam as an analog of the Third Worldism that the previous generation of secular activists, who were committed to the Palestinian national struggle, had pioneered. He explicitly invoked Edward Said to express this congruence. Nashashibi's religious turn generated a religious secularity that displaced particular instantiations of Islam in favor of a diversity of expressions and approaches to questions of justice that one could conceive of as Islamic and as equally and universally human in the Saidian sense, as well.

Nashashibi's example points also to the fourth main concluding point of this book: secular-religious interactions and the identity transformations they produce are conditioned by generation, race, class, gender, homeland-diaspora bifocality, and the multiplicity of narrative trajectories, of "stories so far," within the urban and transnational space of Chicago and Palestine. The generation of 1948–67, responding to the ascendancy of pan-Arabism and the Fatah-led Palestine Liberation Organization, created the core institutions, the community centers, which anchored a secular nationalist ethos in Palestinian Chicago. These institutions, embracing Third World solidarity frames and a sense of shared destiny with other liberation struggles, pioneered relationships with other immigrant and minority communities. Khairy Abudayyeh, Ali Hussain, and Musa (see chapter 2) exemplified the orientations and the organizational leadership of this cohort.

The generation of 1948–67 also harbored a competing political Islamic trajectory, in Mannheim's (1952) terms a "generation unit," that rejected secularism. It asserted, instead, that Islam constituted the center—the 'aqida (core principle and meaning)—of Palestinian identity and the Palestinian cause. The converse also held: Palestine lay at the center of Islam. In Muhannad's view (see chapter 4), to declare that one was Muslim was also to declare one's readiness to struggle for Palestine. Marginal within his generational cohort, Muhannad, who participated in the successful reformist bid for majority control of the Mosque Foundation board in 1978 and who helped create and lead Islamic organizations dedicated to Palestine advocacy, was a forerunner of the Islamic shift that would achieve dominance through the activism of the generation of 1987–2001. This later generation, which came to political maturity during the First Intifada and the Oslo Peace Process, forged its orientations within the Islamic institutions that had come into existence through the organizational efforts of Muhannad's generation.

These processes constituted a phenomenon I have referred to as the sectarianization of identity. Sectarianization highlighted the erosion of nonsectarian or intersectarian secular space and the concomitant movement toward religious conceptions of corporate belonging. Increasingly, to see oneself as Palestinian was to see oneself as Muslim. Rami Nashashibi's conversion (his word) and his subsequent efforts to reorient activism at the *markaz* and AAAN in Islamic terms was one indication, in my fieldwork, of this transformation. Some of my Christian interlocutors who retained a sense of nationalism lamented the consequences of such changes. One individual, a Christian committed to Palestine advocacy, expressed this feeling in relation to AMP, saying, "I wish they had just called themselves 'Americans for Palestine' or 'Palestinian Americans for Palestine,' instead." Other Christians like Munir (chapter 4) noted how sectarianization had affected putatively secular spaces. An event he attended at AAAN had started with the Islamic invocation *bismillah al-rahman al-rahim* ("in the name of God the Most Gracious, the Most Merciful"). It also made accommodations for Muslims to hold group prayers. The Muslim participants in the meeting even used the phrase "Muslim Palestine" in chants. These sorts of phenomena had led Christians to view any Palestine-oriented event, even those occurring in supposedly secular spaces, as "Islamic." The result, Munir observed, was a Christian retreat into parallel Christian sectarian spaces.

Homeland-diaspora bifocality also affected secular-religious interaction and its identity outcomes. Bifocality developed and manifested in multiple ways. One powerful matrix lay in the trips that individuals took to visit with family in the West Bank, Gaza, and East Jerusalem. These journeys served as powerful initiations into one's status as a member of a stateless, policed population. Border crossings were especially traumatic, as were reports on satellite television of massacres, bombings, and invasions of Palestinian communities in Lebanon or Gaza. In other ways, too, however, Palestine could serve bifocally as a lens on something to be rejected: for example, Nashashibi's alienating encounter with political Islam and with PLO nationalism or Ibrahim's revulsion at the humiliating conditions of his aunt's refugee camp in Lebanon. Conversely, it could represent a contrasting space of freedom, possibility, and action: Muna's encounter with liberal party scenes in Haifa and Ramallah; Jubran's experience of Baháʼism in Haifa and his hearing of Israeli-Palestinian Sufi interactions in Nazareth; Hanna's discovery of a Christian-Palestinian nationalism through the Sabeel Ecumenical Liberation Theology Center.

The interaction with other Arab Muslims and Arab Christians, whose reference points were the wars in Syria and Iraq and the political upheavals in Egypt during and after the Arab Spring, provided an additional element of bifocality. These other groups provided a contrasting lens through which to view critically the priority that Palestinians placed on Palestine. In doing so, they appealed to sectarian unity to combat injustice in their own home countries. American Muslims for Palestine responded to this critical view and moral pressure by casting the struggle for Palestine as an Islamic duty that encompassed the effort to achieve justice in the Middle East as a whole. The Holy Land as a divinely blessed Islamic *waqf* (endowment) expanded to include Syria and Iraq and even Egypt. The entire region was "the surroundings of which We have blessed," as the Qur'an stated. Palestinian Christians, too, felt the moral force of Christian solidarity in the face of the anti-Christian violence in other Arab countries such as Iraq, Syria, and Egypt. Munir described the consequences for his own views: his interactions with Palestinian Muslim friends had become tense as each side pointed to the bigotry and aggression of the other.

Sectarian bifocality, however, did not lead inevitably to interreligious distancing. Sawsan's experience of religious communalism in Palestine and also in the immigrant enclave caused her to seek an expansive, inclusive space of identity, first through Islam and then through an individual spirituality. The multifocal polytheism of Chicago's urban expanse provided her latitude to forge her idiosyncratic path in contrast with the homeland and the enclave, both of which had imposed demands of communal conformity and suffocated her as a woman.

Bifocality highlighted how space conditioned the identity dynamics described in this book. As symbols and as arenas of lived experience, homeland and diaspora interacted through a mutually defining relation. Nationalist narratives, secular and Islamic, construed the diaspora as a temporary extension of the homeland: the struggle in both spaces was the same, focused simultaneously on liberation. AMP's conception of the land blessed by God elided the diaspora space precisely in this manner, positing that Muslims globally were to see the meaning of their lives and of Islam as fulfilled in a singular focus on the Holy Land as the all-encompassing center of faith (*'aqida*). Secular nationalism also devalued the diaspora in its insistence on "return." At best, the exile was a site of struggle, at worst a sign of Palestinian dispersion and loss.

Other narratives contested such formulations, however, by embracing the diaspora as a space of freedom and transcendence beyond nation and religion. Sawsan, Muna, Ibrahim, Jubran, and Nashashibi exemplified this trajectory in different ways. In each instance, Chicago, and US society generally, offered alternative sites of leisure and sociability (youth party scenes; world music milieus; diverse religious, activist, and intellectual communities) and the chance to interact with other immigrant and minority communities in which contrasting perspectives on solidarity, activism, and religion become available.

Nashashibi's particular form of Islamic cosmopolitanism developed, for example, in the experience of crossing into Black Nationalist and Black Muslim circles on the city's South Side, a process underscoring both class and race as aspects of the spatial factor. Jubran's multiculturalism formed through his participation in the city's world music networks. Sawsan's journey to "Love, God, and Palestine" passed through her encounter with Shi'i spaces. Muna's secular Islam traveled through the party scenes that afforded her the opportunity to "sin" and, in doing so, to break with the moral norms of the patriarchal, Islamizing enclave. A spatial perspective brings into focus the simultaneity of these trajectories, these "stories so far." It also underlines the fluidity of these narrative lines as well as the spaces in which they form and which they constitute. Spaces intersect and overlap, moreover, as individuals cross through them. This fact undermines any clear and easy distinction between the secular and the religious. The distinction remains useful analytically; empirically, however, spatial edges blur. Nawal Islamized the secular, for example, even as she secularized the Islamic. The forms of syncretic secularity documented in chapters 5 and 6 established this point as well.

The spatial perspective also casts light on how gender and class affect secular-religious identity dynamics in the fieldwork I have described. Gender had ambivalent effects. The traumatizing experience of coercion brought to bear on women who challenged their subordination within religious-patriarchal milieus could lead to disenchantment and the search for alternative, equitable identity frameworks beyond those milieus. Sawsan, Muna, and Ibrahim exemplified this possibility. Encounter with nonsectarian zones beyond the immigrant enclaves—university campuses, women's and gender studies programs, and nonreligious leisure spaces—facilitated their rebellions and their formulations of opposing moral orientations. A similar phenomenon of spatial crossing could also empower women to contest traditional patriarchal authority in the home. In these instances, as Nawal illustrated, religion could provide the countervailing moral authority. Nawal's interactions with Muslim Student Association activists at her university empowered her to invoke Qur'anic authority and reformist Islamic hijab practices to expand the latitude of her individual autonomy against demands to conform to the requirements of female "respectability."

The pressure to perform respectability coincided with a significant socioeconomic class transition. Nawal's family had moved from working class—her father had labored in factories—to the small shop-owning middle class. The shift manifested symbolically and physically in their move to the southwest suburbs. The suburban shift in which they participated was a community-wide process. The formation of the Mosque Foundation and its associated schools accompanied and symbolized this process. The forms of piety instituted within the new reformist Islamic spaces aligned with a middle-class emphasis on a rational, text-based morality compatible with professional and entrepreneurial careers, wealth accumulation, and socioeconomic advancement. The wealth and expansion of the Mosque Foundation signified the success of the enclave, a success narrated through the trope of commitment to Islam as a framework for individual moral discipline and community cohesion.

At the same time, not every member of the enclave had the capacity to succeed in this transition. The AAAN and Nashashibi's Inner-City Muslim Action Network (IMAN) sought to address the needs of poor and working class Palestinian immigrants and non-Palestinian minorities on the city's Southwest and South Sides. These community networks constituted contrasting, competing spaces of identity in relation to one another and in relation to the piety-minded suburbs. They instituted activist trajectories, secular and religious, that resisted the middle-class ethos of career-seeking and economic advancement, asserting instead the priority of solidarity with movements committed to social, political, and economic justice. The AAAN and IMAN shared this alternative class solidarity—both, pointedly, had resisted locating in the suburbs—even if they departed in their respective emphases on the ethnos (Palestinian and Arab advocacy) and the *umma* (Islam as the frame of a transethnic, transnational solidarity).

RELIGIOUS AND SECULAR: WHAT TO DO? HOW TO LIVE?

In his famous address "Science as a Vocation," Max Weber (1946b) spoke of the problem of understanding and cohering with others in modern societies marked by the polytheism of values. Modern societies formed through the rationalization and diversification of autonomous institutional spheres. Each sphere structured status, authority, and significance in relation to its own distinct moral hierarchies. Weber contended that social analysis, which this book has attempted to provide, could clarify "what the godhead is for the one order or for the other, or better, what godhead is in the one or in the other order" but "the great and vital problem that is contained therein is, of course, very far from being concluded" (148–49). That "great and vital problem," Weber went on to say, was the question of how to live and what to do in a situation of competing moral and political orientations arrayed across diverging social milieus and social classes.

For Palestinians, the question of how to live and what to do is especially pressing at this moment. Religious-secular divisions deeply, perhaps irreparably, cleave Palestinian politics and society in the Occupied Territories. In the United States, despite moments of unity in the face of racist backlash and law enforcement interventions, similar tensions have manifested, albeit with important differences within the immigrant context. Palestinians, however, do not live in isolation. The tensions those living in the United States must negotiate reflect and bear on similar divisions, contradictions, and contestations among other groups in the United States and globally. A particular question their experience illuminates pertains to the status of immigrant others in the United States, a nation for which immigration features centrally within the founding myth. How are Americans to coexist across lines of religious, racial, and national differences in an era in which the demonization of immigrants and minorities has received ratification from the highest political office? What are we to do? How shall we live?

Weber's (1946b) answer is equivocal: in the absence of genuine visionaries capable of forging a new consensus, a new solidarity, our moral and political divisions appear unbridgeable. The best we can do is attempt to understand one another, holding to our diverging principles while retaining a sense of responsibility toward others in a shared, inexorably polytheistic society (152–53). In this sense, if citizens of the United States can understand what matters most to others, to those they oppose most of all, perhaps then they can arrive at a modus vivendi that allows diverse and divergent forms of human flourishing to coexist and interact in a type of harmonic counterpoint.

The metaphor of counterpoint is Edward Said's. It is his answer to the question of how one is to "coexist with people whose religions are different, whose traditions and languages are different but who form part of the same community or polity in the national sense" (E. Said and Jhally 2005). He asks further:

> How do we accept difference without violence and hostility? I've been interested in a field called Comparative Literature most all of my adult life and the ideal of Comparative Literature is not to show how English literature is really a secondary phenomenon to French literature or Arabic literature is kind of a poor cousin to Persian literature or any of those silly things, but to show them existing, you might say, as contrapuntal lines, in a great composition by which difference is respected and understood without coercion. And it's that attitude I think that we need (14).[14]

One of the most contested sites of belonging today remains the territory that constitutes Palestine and Israel. This conflict plays out globally through geopolitical calculations of regional and international powers, principally the United States, and through the advocacy politics of the Jewish and Palestinian diasporas. These diasporic politics are not unitary. They are complex and contested, certainly between Jews and Palestinians, but also internally within these two multiply divided communities. On many different levels, Palestine and Israel are a shifting, conflicted question that, as this book has shown, deeply implicates the United States, socially and politically. The question transcends national boundaries. The conflict that defines it shapes US politics at multiple scales, including at the very local. Palestinian Chicago offers important insight into these multilevel complexities and thus provides a point of departure for thinking in new ways about questions of exile and diaspora, intergenerational change, and belonging across racial, spatial, ethnic, class, gender, generational, religious, national, and regional lines.

These complexities should force a hard look at the damaging reductions of Palestinians, specifically, and Arabs and Muslims, generally, to the figure of "terrorist." Contrary to US stereotype, Palestinians, other Arabs, and Muslims have most often been the targets, not the perpetrators, of racism and political violence, including terrorism (Miller 2016; Hayden 2017). This violence and exclusion have had contradictory implications for how Arabs and Muslims view US society and their place in it. Among Palestinians, the struggle against oppression has led to the forging of alliances with other "people of color" (POC) groups that equally lay claim to a history of persecution and resistance. And, through this allied struggle,

Palestinians have defended their civil and national rights and their collective presence against state surveillance and racist majoritarian reaction. This struggle has challenged US social, political, and legal institutions to live up to constitutional principles such as equal protection and due process.

Not every individual discussed in this book has embraced a nationalist or religious identity or a politics of resistance against oppression as his or her primary orientation. Some have ventured into the wider US society, and have forged alternative self-understandings. They have moved in those directions for many reasons, including the desire to escape the moral strictures of a suburban community that has embraced modern reformist piety—a phenomenon with complex origins, as this book has shown, turning on the interrelated dynamics of secularism's attenuation, local religious institutionalization, global religious revival, and the external pressures of bigoted reaction and over-reaching law enforcement intervention. What it means to see oneself as Palestinian and as American is very much in flux for these boundary-crossing individuals. But this fact also holds for those who remain within the enclave, where religion, in the aftermath of the weakening of secularism, has redefined the terms of belonging.

The different narratives presented in this book reveal that religion and nation remain powerful determinants of self-understanding under the contested, polytheistic circumstances of political and social life in the United States and Palestine. Their effects, however, are not unidirectional. In Palestinian Chicago, the interplay of religious and secular, conditioned by gender, race, class, generation, and the multiplicity of space, generates diverse, syncretic trajectories. If there is an answer to the pressing question of what to do and how to live, it perhaps lies here, in this dynamic, diasporic interplay from which new, contingent, and contrapuntal forms of relationship and identity are emerging across lines of difference both in Palestine and in America.

NOTES

INTRODUCTION

1. The flag is a modification of the banner of the Great Arab Revolt of 1916 that the Palestine Liberation Organization (PLO) adopted officially in 1964.

2. I have generally followed the style guide of the International Journal of Middle East Studies (IJMES) for Arabic transliteration. In some cases, however, my transliterations depart from the guide. For example, following Hans Wehr (1994), I render the nisba ending as *iya* and not *iyya*. I also have chosen not to include diacritical markings (macrons and dots).

3. The PLO implicitly accepted the two-state formula in the political communiqué accompanying the Palestinian Declaration of Independence (Algiers, 1988). The communiqué called for Israel's withdrawal from the Palestinian lands it occupied during the war of 1967 in accordance with UNSCR 242 and 338 and the establishment of a temporary United Nations receivership in these areas (the West Bank, Gaza Strip, and Arab East Jerusalem). The PLO made its commitment to the two-state formulation explicit through the later Oslo memorandums and agreements. Hamas as well as the Marxist Popular Front for the Liberation of Palestine (PFLP) rejected the two-state concept and the Oslo process. The PFLP would later shift its position on the peace process. Hamas, too, would signal a willingness to accept a long-term "*hudna*" (cessation of hostilities, truce) along the armistice lines of 1948 (an effective acceptance of the two-state formula). For an English translation of the Declaration of Independence, see https://en.wikisource.org/wiki/Palestinian_Declaration_of_Independence. See also an English translation of Hamas's 2017 statement concerning the two-state formula (especially §20) at http://hamas.ps/en/post/678/a-document-of-general-principles-and-policies.

4. Accurate demographic figures do not exist. This estimate balances self-reported community claims of approximately 200,000 with tallies derived from the 2000 US Census figures that place the total number of individuals of Arab ancestry in Cook and DuPage Counties at 40,196. Cainkar, quoted in Amer (2013), asserts that 25 percent of all Palestinian

immigrants in the United States are concentrated in Chicago and its surrounding suburbs. She also estimates that Palestinians constitute as much as 40 percent of the Arab immigrant population of the greater Chicago area (Amer 2013; Cainkar 2004, 2006, and 2009, 11–20; Association of Religion Data Archive 2017).

5. Said's secularism has been much debated. Robbins (1994) has argued, convincingly, that it constituted an independent critical stance opposed to all forms of authority: religious, academic, nationalist. The stance is of "the intellectual who speaks truth to power" in whatever form it presents itself. This is not the sociological ideal-type of secularism that I employ analytically in this book, as later sections of this chapter make clear, but there is an overlap in the notion of opposition to authority, including religious authority.

6. There were two other centers in addition to the *markaz*. These centers were commonly understood to align ideologically either with Fatah, the main PLO faction, or with other leftist opposition groups in the PLO. These centers, like the ACC, closed during the early to mid-1990s. For more background, see chapter 2.

7. I secured Ohio University Institutional Review Board approval (IRB #09F030) for every year of fieldwork, beginning in AY 2010–2011 and ending in AY 2014–2015. The interview protocols required only verbal consent. This consent was digitally recorded at the start of every interview. Prior to beginning the interviews, interviewees were informed of my anonymity procedures and of their right to withdraw consent at any stage of the research process. Only one of my interviewees requested withdrawal from the research following our interview together. I immediately deleted this interview and all accompanying notes from my records. Throughout this book, I have used pseudonyms and changed or obscured employment, residential, and other identifying details in an effort to protect the anonymity of the participants in this project as much as I possibly could. As part of the informed consent process, I explained that I could not guarantee perfect anonymity. In some cases, I have used real names, but only if the participants in question indicated at the beginning of their recorded interviews or in later written correspondence that they had no objection to being identified in the project. Those who have been identified were given copies of their interview transcripts and the opportunity to correct factual inaccuracies. I have used real names, as well, if individuals are known public figures. I have also used the real names of well-known sites and organizations.

8. Palestine has also served as an important symbol of secular (nonsectarian, pan-Arab, and Marxist) anti-colonial and anti-imperialist movements. In the United States, Black Power and the mainstream Civil Rights Movement found inspiration in the Palestinian liberation struggle (Fischbach 2019; Feldman 2015).

9. See Brookes and Sciolino (1995); Levitt (2006); S. Roy (2007); Nasaw (2008); and Westrop (2017) for examples of the focus on Hamas-diaspora connections. A simple online search for books using terms like "Islamism," "Palestinians," and "Hamas" will demonstrate the plethora of writing on these topics. Cainkar (2004) and Schmidt (2004) are important exceptions and receive discussion further below.

10. Not all Islamic organizations, however, rejected Arab and Palestinian nationalist activism. For example, the Federation of Islamic Associations (FIA), an umbrella structure that brought together "a number of American mosques" whose leadership were sympathetic to the dire situation of Palestinian refugees, formed in 1952 (Pennock 2017, 27). Its emergence prefigured the later tension within Islamist movements concerning the priority

of liberating Palestine. In the 1980s, for instance, the relatively small Islamic Jihad movement openly rejected the Muslim Brotherhood's quietist Islam-first strategy by launching armed attacks against the Israeli military in the Gaza Strip. These attacks helped spark the first Palestinian Intifada in December 1987. The Intifada ultimately pushed the Muslim Brotherhood to reorient its priorities toward the national struggle. The primary expression of this shift was the launching of the Islamic Resistance Movement (Hamas) in early 1988 in a bid to wrest control of the Intifada from the PLO-aligned Unified National Leadership (*al-qiyada al-wataniya al-muwahhada*) (Schiff and Ya'ari 1989 [1990], 188–239; Hunter 1991, 58–67; Lybarger 2007a, 25–26 and 81–85).

11. Some Palestinian proponents of the orthopraxic ideological orientation pejoratively characterize the received Islam of earlier immigrants who arrived before the 1980s as "cultural" (supposedly uninformed, backwards, traditional, reduced to social customs) and not "religious" (text-based, rationally elaborated, reflexive, orthopraxical). In the Middle East, modern orthopraxy often views the Islam of rural communities and of Sufi practitioners as perpetuating incorrect practice and introducing un-Islamic ideas either deliberately or inadvertently due to ignorance of core texts and doctrines. On these matters, see Riesebrodt (1993).

12. These remarks on sociohistorical generations draw primarily from the classic discussion in Mannheim (1952). On event-as-epochal-transformation-of-structure, see Sewell (1996). On the further elaboration of generational analysis, see Schuman and Scott (1989); Dunham (1998); and Turner (2002). See also my use of the generation concept in Lybarger (2007a): 14–19.

13. The dating of the First Intifada remains a matter of debate. I am choosing as the starting point the killing of Gazan day laborers by an Israeli truck in December 1987. In response to this event, Palestinians took to the streets in sustained mass demonstrations. The ending point I have chosen is the signing of the Oslo Memorandum of Understanding in 1993. Scholars have argued with justification that several key events preceded the killing of the day laborers and that Palestinian resistance and civil society organizations had prepared the Intifada's mobilizing structures long in advance of December 1987. Some scholars also choose the end of the Gulf War and start of the Madrid Peace Conference in 1991 as the end date. For more on these matters, see Lockman and Beinin (1989); Hiltermann (1991); Peters and Newman (2013).

14. Massey's thought falls on the subjectivist side of the ongoing debate among geographers concerning space-time (Lagopoulos 2011, 129–82).

15. On the milieu concept, see Riesebrodt (1993, 29).

16. I wish to thank Maha Nassar for suggesting this idea during an extended discussion of the generation concept. Bifocality calls into question the distinction between first, second, and third generations conceived in terms of recentness of arrival and degree of assimilation. The continuing interaction with the *iblad* creates a binational, bicultural, and bilingual experience that does not fit easily into assimilation models that presume a progressive shift in cultural and national identity from one age cohort to the next. Bifocality does not necessarily characterize everyone's experience in the diaspora. Some immigrants might turn their backs entirely on Palestine, embracing an "American" identity instead. Others may reject the United States entirely in favor of a permanent return to Palestine. Many, however, live dynamically and intergenerationally across the *shatat* and *iblad* spaces.

202   NOTES

17. This phenomenon is not unique to Palestinian communities. On religious revitalization and repatriarchalization, generally, and in relation to Korean communities, specifically, see Riesebrodt (1993); Riesebrodt and Chong (1999); and Chong (2008).

18. I must emphasize—because the point is often not grasped—that an ideal-type is emphatically not a claim concerning the transhistorical or transcultural "essence" of a particular way of orienting and acting in the world. Rather, it is a deliberately formulated interpretive standpoint, constituted at a particular moment in time, subject always to refinement or even abandonment in relation to empirical findings and to changing historical conditions that shift the priorities of analysis. The formation of ideal-types proceeds from the assumption that interpretation is unavoidable. There is no direct, unmediated grasp of reality apart from the interpretive lenses through which every individual or group, deliberately or not, makes sense of what is otherwise a meaningless and relentless succession of events. As culture-dependent beings, humans can do nothing else but interpret, and through interpretation render their lived circumstances meaningful. Ideal-typical analysis constitutes a formal, second-order reflection on this first-order reality-making process. As a deliberate method of concept formation, it explicitly recognizes and incorporates the fact that knowledge and understanding are inexorably perspectival and historically conditioned (Kalberg 2012, 99–101; Riesebrodt 2010, 18–19; McFalls 2007; Weber 1946b; Weber 1949; Weber 1978 [1968], 19–22).

19. In ideal-typical terms, secularism is a subjectively meaningful pattern of action: it refers to a recurring position and mode of response that individuals can adopt across a range of spatial, cultural, social, political, and historical contexts. Conceptually, its purpose is not to advance any particular normative position that the term "secular" might imply in its other uses. Instead, its function in this discussion is descriptive and analytical.

20. Religion in this ideal-typical sense just described is distinct from religious traditions, which systematize ideas about superhuman entities into normative ideological and ethical principles and practices or classify religious practices according to key symbols that mark them as belonging to one or another self-identified group (Christian, Jewish, Hindu, Buddhist, Muslim, etc.).

21. Mahmood (2010) raises this question of other conceptions of self in relation to her critique of Taylor's (2007) restriction of "the secular age" to a supposedly distinctly Christian West. She makes the point that Christianity's others have profoundly shaped Western secularism and that there are forms of secularism that exceed Taylor's compass. Drawing tidy civilizational boundaries proves difficult to do. Taylor, of course, seeks to limit the scope of his analysis and explicitly acknowledges the need for further work to trace the differential lines of development of secularism in other cultural zones beyond the West. Still, Mahmood's point remains critical to appreciate: the putative West does not exist in a cultural quarantine. This fact renders impossible any attempt to isolate secularism in the West, empirically, from the historical trajectories of others whose experience intersects with the West.

1. PALESTINIAN CHICAGO: SPATIAL LOCATION, HISTORICAL FORMATION

1. Palestinians have continued to live in Southwest Side neighborhoods such as Chicago Lawn and Gage Park, but the community's predominant area of concentration is now in southwest suburbs such as Bridgeview, Oak Lawn, Orland Park, Palos Hills, and Tinley

Park. This shift occurred during the 1990s. In Bridgeview alone, census data indicate that the Arab population, of which Palestinians are a majority, increased from 2 percent in 1990 to 7 percent in 2000 (Abowd 2007; see also Amer 2013). This trend has continued. Since the 1990s, the suburbs and their institutions have become primary points of entry for new Palestinian immigrants.

2. The boundaries of the Black Belt expanded with time, giving rise to discrepancies in the sources regarding its exact limits. The Chicago Public Library (2019), for example, states that the Black Belt during the 1940s stretched between 12th and 79th Streets and Wentworth and Cottage Grove Avenues. By contrast, Best (2005) states that the zone during the 1920s extended along State Street between 22nd and 31st Streets. It then expanded during the rest of the twentieth century, according to this source, from 39th Street to 95th Street and from the Dan Ryan Expressway to Lake Michigan.

3. The Black Belt also gave rise to important African American business enterprises and to a vibrant artistic, political, and intellectual milieu. This milieu pivoted around institutions like the South Side Community Art Center, the George Cleveland Hall branch of the Chicago Public Library, and the salon that acclaimed artist Margaret Burroughs hosted in her home. Richard Wright, whose *Native Son* depicted the intense poverty and desperation of the Black Belt, participated in this South Side cultural hothouse, as did other luminaries such as Gwendolyn Brooks, Lorraine Hansberry, Langston Hughes, and Zora Neale Hurston (Abowd 2015; Rockett 2019).

4. I wish to thank Sherene Seikaly for alerting me to the nuances of this period and especially to recent studies that have shifted the historiography. Recent revisionist work has challenged the assumption that the Tanzimat reforms drove the centralization of landholdings and the shift to industrial cash crop farming. These changes actually preceded the reforms, which were responses to the changes on the ground. The emergence of new social and political movements is also a critical part of this story: Arab and Palestinian nationalism developed alongside the economic shifts that occurred in this period. They predated the appearance of the Zionist movement and had horizons that extended beyond the conflict with the Yishuv. For revisionist accounts spanning the nineteenth and early twentieth centuries, see Doumani (1995); R. Khalidi (1997); Campos (2010); Seikaly (2016). The earlier work of Haddad (1970) and Vatikiotis (1991) also emphasizes the impact of global markets and the rising political and economic power of Europe. For an account adopting the thesis of the Tanzimat's determining role, see Krämer (2008).

5. Middle minorities occupy the ambiguous border area that separates groups in a status hierarchy. They approximate Simmel's figure of the stranger, who "comes today and stays tomorrow." Never fully assimilating into the prevailing status hierarchies, "strangers" travel across social boundaries even as they forge their own subcultural enclaves in the interstices of those boundaries (Simmel 2009, 601 and passim; Cainkar 1988, 101–2, 133). As a "stranger" group unconcerned with the norms of white and black status, Palestinians were willing to situate their stores in the Black Belt and to sell to blacks when whites were not. They lived apart, creating their own subcultural space in the spatial and status gap that separated blacks and whites. Within this zone, the norms of their home villages, including Islamic norms, prevailed.

6. Oschinsky's (1947) interlocutor specifically described, in provocatively racialized terms, confronting intruders with a gun: "I had a lot of trouble with those damned n...rs" (25).

Oschinsky observed that the bigoted attitudes he encountered likely reflected absorption by the immigrants of the pervasive "insolence pattern" of whites toward blacks (25). This assimilation of white racism likely reflected, he said, the desire of his interlocutors to identify with the dominant white majority (26). Oschinsky also described some African Americans expressing views of Palestinian shop owners as dishonest and greedy (25). Al-Tahir (1952) reported similar derogatory views among Palestinian shop owners. His interlocutors told him that blacks believed whatever they were told about the provenance and quality of the goods for sale, that they could be "persuaded to buy almost anything, that they don't know how to spend money [. . .], and don't care whether the goods are clean and neat or not" (122).

7. During the late 1980s, when I worked in the West Bank during the first Intifada, a fellow teacher described the experiences of his brother, a storeowner in Chicago's South Side. The brother had been a target of an armed robbery. "You had to watch out for the n . . . rs," he told me. His use of the n-word shocked me and led us into a long conversation about racism in the United States. Later, as I reflected on that moment in light of the research for this book, I realized that behind my colleague's comment lay a long history of Palestinian insertion into Chicago's embittered, violent, and deeply entrenched geography of race and power.

8. As described in n6 above, al-Tahir (1952, 122) described Palestinian peddlers and shop owners as telling him that their black customers were easy to deceive, unconcerned about quality, and naïve about money. He did not acknowledge, comment on, or attempt to explain the contradiction between this earlier observation and his later claim that there was no racial tension between the communities.

9. Weisenfeld (2016, 217) identifies this space as a Nation of Islam worship site. Al-Tahir (1952), however, does not comment on this fact. He states simply that this community was Muslim.

10. Al-Tahir failed to discuss the discrepancies between Nation of Islam (NOI) ideology, which members of the Arab Club would have encountered at the "Negro Muslim Temple," and traditional Sunni Islam, which Palestinians practiced. These differences likely would have registered as significant for al-Tahir's interlocutors. An individual who participated in my research described his first encounters with NOI adherents on the South Side during the early 1970s. He claimed that NOI ideology was not true Islam and said that he found himself in debates with NOI members about the Qur'an and points of core belief and doctrine. A sense of solidarity rooted in Islam might well have developed for al-Tahir's informants in their interactions with NOI members during the late 1940s and early 1950s; but it is also possible that their interaction generated debate about what counted as Islam. The plan to hold lectures on Arabic and Islamic history in an effort to promote mutual understanding hints at such a possibility.

11. These marriages could have long-term effects not only in the diaspora but also for home communities. In 1989, a colleague invited me to spend the weekend with him in a mixed Christian (Greek Orthodox)-Muslim village near Ramallah. During that visit, I met one of his relatives, an older man who had returned with his grown son from Brazil. My colleague told me this relative had been married to a Brazilian woman but had since divorced her. The man had traveled to South America in search of economic opportunities. After working as a peddler, he opened a series of stores. He had now returned to his home village decades later, his business having faltered. His son, fluent in Portuguese, struggled

with Arabic and with making friends in the village. The friendships he did have seemed to come from his participation in the occasional clashes between the *shabab* (youth, "guys") and Israeli settlers and soldiers. Facing these conditions of the uprising (the First Intifada), his father debated whether to stay permanently or to return to Brazil to try again to make a life there with his son in the *mahjar*.

12. "Imm 'Umar" translates literally as "Mother of 'Umar." In formal Arabic, "Imm" is rendered as "Umm." Individuals typically begin to be referred to in this way after the birth of their first son or daughter. For men, the reference becomes "Abu . . . " (Father of . . .). This style of naming—known in Arabic as a *kunya*—can also serve as a *nom de guerre* or as a nickname. Khalil al-Wazir, a close associate of Yasser Arafat in the Fatah movement, was known by the *kunya* of "Abu Jihad" (Father of Armed Struggle). The choice of the term "jihad" gestured symbolically toward Islam and in doing so signaled the desire of the Fatah leadership to absorb Islam-oriented activists and movements within the PLO.

13. For more information on the current percentage distribution by race and ethnicity in Chicago's different neighborhoods, see the analysis in the Statistical Atlas at https://statisticalatlas.com/place/Illinois/Chicago/Race-and-Ethnicity.

14. Ramallahites, like other town and city dwellers, typically claim an urban identity. They contrast this identity with village-peasant identity. Beitunians and residents of other similar small towns and villages often reverse the polarity, asserting pride as villagers and farmers (*fallahin*). These distinctions are marked linguistically. City dwellers typically transform the "qaf" consonant into a glottal stop. For example, instead of "al-Quds" (Jerusalem), one says, "al-'uds." Those claiming a rural identity will use the "qaf" or even "gaf" and might also change the consonant "kaf" into "chaf."

15. The reason for choosing Oak Park and, later, Cicero remains not entirely clear to me. Fr. Nicholas Dahdal, the priest of St. George Antiochian Orthodox Church in Cicero, explained that these locations presented themselves as a pragmatic compromise: they were centrally situated in relation to the disbursed Christian residential patterns in the city and its northwest and southwest suburbs. These properties, at the time, were also possibly more affordable than other sites, but I have not confirmed this detail.

16. Details of this early history come from interviews with Fr. Dahdal, head priest of St. George Antiochian Orthodox Church during the time of my fieldwork, and from the church's own institutional history, at https://www.stgeorgechi.org/history.

17. As Wofford (2016) points out, this plan provided the template for later measures implemented against Arabs and Muslims after the September 2001 attacks and for the Trump Administration's so-called "Muslim Ban," an administrative order that eventually prevented immigration from five Muslim-majority countries (Iran, Libya, Somalia, Syria, and Yemen) as well as from North Korea and Venezuela.

18. This estimate of the number of displaced Palestinians following the war of 1967 reflects the conservative assessment of Kimmerling and Migdal (2003 [1994]), 241. For alternative estimates, see Bowker (2003, 231) and *Report of the Commissioner-General of the United Nations Relief and Works Agency for Palestine Refugees in the Near East* (1966–67).

19. Israeli settlement policies and their impact have been documented extensively in multiple places. See the documentation, for example, at http://peacenow.org.il/eng and http://www.btselem.org/topic/settlements and United Nations Office for the Coordination of Humanitarian Affairs (2012).

20. Fears for the safety of daughters in the streets beyond the home also motivated their confinement. The phrase *bakhaf 'alayki* (I fear for [what might happen to] you) often accompanied a "no" to a request to visit a friend or attend an event on one's own. Palestinian families shared this worry for the safety of their children with Chicagoans, generally. I am indebted to Maha Nassar for this insight via personal communciation (August 13, 2019).

21. For more on the patriarchal double standard see Naber (2012), Kreager and Staff (2009), and Bogle (2008).

22. The slogan of return—*al-'awda*—resonated not only as a national demand but also with United Nations resolutions such as UNGA 194 that called for the immediate repatriation of Palestinian refugees to their homes and lands and for compensation of those who chose to remain in the countries in which they had sought shelter.

23. See also the collection of Union of Palestinian Women Associations of North America records at the University of Illinois at Chicago, https://findingaids.library.uic.edu/sc/MSUPWA98.xml.

24. See chapter 2 for an extended description and analysis of the secular nationalist milieu and its core organizations.

25. Statistical analyses consistently show a correlation in Chicago between economic disadvantage and high rates of homicide (Stults 2010). Immigration, however, appears to be associated with "reductions in lethal violence in disadvantaged neighborhoods," since recently arrived immigrants revitalize local economic activity, networks, and institutions (Vélez 2009). According to the participants in my study, in the areas in which Palestinians originally settled, lethal violence, especially with the rise of gangs, remained a fact of daily life. A number of my interlocutors identified harassment from gangs when explaining the decisions of their families to move to the suburbs.

26. These figures derive from Abu-Lughod's (1999) data. In 1950, "nonwhites" comprised 492,000 (14 percent) of the City of Chicago's 3.6 million residents (230). Twenty years later, the number of nonwhites (African Americans, Hispanics, others) within the city limits jumped by 35 percent as the total number of non-Hispanic whites declined to 2,200,000 (65 percent) of a total municipal population of 3,366,957 (331–32).

27. Here, I adopt the reported self-perception of my interlocutors as the basis for defining Arab immigrants as non-white. Arab immigrants have long debated their proper racial categorization. The Palestinian immigrants I interacted with generally viewed themselves as non-white and in some cases actively identified as "people of color." This self-perception is at odds with the official census classification of Arabs as white.

28. Palestinians, as I have pointed out, also occupied similar zones.

29. See United States Census Bureau, State and County Quick Facts (2019) at https://www.census.gov/quickfacts/chicagocityillinois. See also the City of Chicago's "Community Area 2000 and 2010 Census Population Comparisons" (2019) at http://www.cityofchicago.org/content/dam/city/depts/zlup/Zoning_Main_Page/Publications/Census_2010_Community_Area_Profiles/Census_2010_and_2000_CA_Populations.pdf. Interestingly, the latest figures actually show an increase of 0.9 percent in Chicago's total population between 2010 (2,695,598) and 2013 (2,831,587).

30. I solicited and received approval from the Mosque Foundation board to carry out research on its premises and with its personnel. Mr. Oussama Jammal, the Chairman of the Board at that time, invited me to attend Mosque Foundation events, activities, and prayers and assisted me in arranging interviews with paid staff and volunteers.

31. The possibility of reclassification from "stranger" or from "white" to non-white other has long characterized Arab American experience within the race hierarchy of the United States (Gualtieri 2009).

32. Palestinian refugees reconstituted within the camps the social structure of the villages from which they fled or were expelled during the war of 1948 (R. Sayigh 1979, 10–53; S. Roy 2001 [1995],16). Camp residents settled into quarters, replicating the spatial arrangements of the home villages. Each quarter appointed a *mukhtar*.

33. The claim here is not that these individuals possessed formal organizational links to the Muslim Brotherhood and other similar movements. No evidence emerged in my research to support such a claim, and I was not searching for such evidence. Rather, the point is that their ideological tendencies, values, and concerns shared an affinity with the orientations of those movements. These orientations stressed the necessity of returning to Islam's foundational texts and of emulating the practices of the first generation of Muslims, who, it was believed, had implemented Islam in its purist form as the Prophet Muhammad intended. For this reason, I speak of "reformism" and "reformist orientations," broadly. Embedded in the call to return to an original Islam was a critique of present practices, which were seen as having become corrupted through the centuries. The corroding impact of colonialism and Western-inspired secularism was a particular focus of this reformism. Reformist tendencies have come to be widely shared among Muslims, globally, since the 1980s (Euben and Zaman 2009; Lauzière 2016). On textualist, reformist Islam as a response to state-driven secularization and and the spread of secular attitudes, see Riesebrodt (1993, 15–19). See Cainkar (2004) and Riedel (2009, 81) for additional discussion of how this type of Islam has manifested in the suburban Palestinian enclave.

34. The details recounted in this paragraph come from interviews with several community members. They also appear, albeit with a sensationalist tone, in Ahmed-Ullah, Roe, and Cohen (2004).

35. Ahmed-Ullah, Roe, and Cohen (2004) recounts these details and describes other conflicts.

36. Two other individuals I interacted with echoed the claim concerning the involvement of Fatah-oriented community leaders but did not provide any additional details. An interviewee who had opposed the leadership transition on the board, however, denied any such intervention by "Fatah people." Regardless of its accuracy, which I was not able to establish, the allegation reflected the spillover into the exile context of incipient tensions between Fatah and the Muslim Brotherhood in the Occupied Territories during that time.

37. Hack and Hantschel (2003) and Ahmed-Ullah, Roe, and Cohen (2004) describe the controversy and the court cases in detail. In doing so, they make unwarranted assertions about hardline radicalization with references to "Wahhabism" and FBI investigations into funding for proscribed groups likes Hamas. Such alarmist characterizations resonated with fears about Islam in the immediate post-September 11 context. They were and are unfounded. Still, key details in these reports pertaining to the transition in board leadership, the new reformist practices instituted at the moque, the court cases, and the confrontations between the groups disputing control of the mosque received corroboration in the interviews I carried out for this project. The mosque has created its own documentary offering its version of the story of the institution. The documentary briefly refers to an earlier effort to establish the mosque but offers no detail. Instead, the history begins in 1981, after the board leadership change; see https://www.youtube.com/watch?v=1wljogRiYnU.

38. See http://www.mosquefoundation.org/programs-services/services-overview for a full description of the mosque's activities and services. See also a video that the mosque prepared for the 2015 annual fundraising dinner that offers a glimpse into the range, size, and centrality of its services within the community (https://www.youtube.com/watch?v=lVzOb_DQNHs). With the permission of the Mosque Foundation Leadership, I spent a Saturday morning observing the activities of the food pantry and the range of clientele it serves.

39. As of August 6, 2019, the mosque's Facebook group had 26,846 "likes" and 27,012 "followers" and its YouTube channel had 1,081 subscribers and 91,492 views.

40. The fact that this book was taught indicated that one concern of the Aqsa School was to impart a "connective" patriarchal orientation and model of domesticity that established the authority but also the solicitous paternal role of husbands in the home and the corresponding complementary role of women as primarily responsible for what Orthodox Jews term, in a different yet parallel context, "*shalom bayit*" (the peace of the house) (Joseph 1993; Heilman 2006). The Aqsa student handbook in 2010 also focused centrally on proper comportment, prescribing the hijab scarf on Fridays for the entire day and during mandatory prayer times but otherwise making it optional. Students had the choice of wearing a "uniform *jilbab*" (an ankle-length coat) or a sweater and skirt with knee-high socks. Individual students, however, might challenge the limits of these restrictions, for example, by wearing the scarf loosely over the head on Fridays (Riedel 2009, 81 and elsewhere). For the text of *The Ideal Muslimah*, see http://www.iupui.edu/~msaiupui/idealmuslimah.html. For the relevant Qur'anic passage concerning *qawwamun*, see Surat al-Nisa', verse 34, which reads: "الرجال قوامون على النساء بما فضل الله بعضهم على بعض" (*al-rijalu qawwamuna 'ala al-nisa'i bi-ma faddala allahu ba'dahum 'ala ba'din*; in my translation, "Men possess authority over women (for their protection) in accordance with what God has preferred for one above the other"). The exegesis of this passage is controversial. Critics point to it as evidence of Islam's patriarchy. Muslim feminists and Muslim modernists place the text in relation to other passages emphasizing mutual respect and complementary responsibilities among men and women. Traditionalists and textualist reform-oriented activists insist on its literal meaning, arguing that God ordains male authority for the proper ordering of the *umma* and the prevention of Westernization. See Wadud (1999) and Barlas (2002) for feminist readings, in particular.

41. Personal communication from Maha Nassar (August 13, 2019). I will address this use of religion to challenge patriarchy within families in a later chapter that profiles a woman who grew up within the Bridgeview community and attended Aqsa School.

42. See also http://www.universalschool.org.

43. Since the 1980s, there has been increasing overlap in the enrollments of the two schools and in the relationship between political, cultural, and religious outlooks. The Mosque Foundation remains central in this nexus through its advocacy of the universal Islamic emphasis embedded within reformism as well as the specific Palestinian concerns, as seen, for example, in its support for American Muslims for Palestine. Personal communications from Maha Nassar (August 13 and August 14, 2019), and see also chapter 3.

44. Personal communication from Maha Nassar (August 13, 2019).

2. SECULARISM IN EXILE

The epigraph is from a poem by Iskandar al-Khouri al-Beit Jali (1890–1973) that Khairy Abudayyeh recited from memory during his interview with me. A Palestinian Christian from Beit Jala in the West Bank, al-Beit Jali dealt frequently with Arab nationalist themes in his work. He was particularly concerned to emphasize Christian and Muslim unity. This emphasis appears in the epigraph and in other poems such as *inna al-nasara ikhwa lil-muslimin* ("Christians are brothers of the Muslims"). I was unable to obtain the published text, either in the original or as a copy, which appeared in one of his collections published in the early 1920s (al-Beit Jali 1923). A segment of the poem is reproduced and analyzed in Musa (2012, 46). For more on Khouri, see Palestinian Academic Society for the Study of International Affairs (2019). Some of Khouri's work is available in digitized form through the Bethlehem University library at https://bethlehem.edu/library-news/2015/iskandar-al-khouri-al-beitjali-books-digitized. Basileus Zeno edited my Arabic rendering and assisted me with the translation of the stanza quoted in the epigraph and in tracking down bibliographic references for the poem.

1. Naji al-'Ali (1938–87) was a Palestinian political cartoonist whose work denounced the corruption and violence of regional and international leaders and powers. Handala, his signature character, often appeared with his back to the viewer of the cartoon. His arms and hands crossed behind him, he bore silent witness to the suffering of his fellow Palestinians filling the rest of the frame of the cartoon. For more on 'Ali, see El Fassed (2004).

2. I distinguish here between secularism as an ideological commitment that rejects or subordinates religious claims and "secular," which encompasses secularist stances as well as religious orientations at home with legal disestablishment of religion and an ethos of pluralistic, multisectarian national solidarity. See the introduction for an extended discussion of my definition of secularism in ideal-typical terms.

3. Approximately half of my interviews for this project (forty) were with individuals whose orientations were secularist or secular in character. The interviews I have chosen to highlight in this chapter were with longtime activists who helped establish and lead some of the main institutions of the secular nationalist milieu in the city, or whose perspectives mark out the broad range of secularist outlooks. Their narratives reflect the key themes of secularism as a distinct orientation.

4. Examples of this focus in scholarship are legion, as any brief Internet search will reveal. A representative example of the journalistic discussion is Inskeep (2017).

5. Many other groups—not just Palestinian Muslim and Christian immigrants—share this same concern to blunt the impact of "secular" influences in American society. Protestant evangelicals, for example, have engaged in a decades-long cultural struggle against secularism (Christian Smith 1998).

6. As chapter 4 will show, Islamic reformist activists who came of age in this period also refer to these wars as formative moments and to secularism as the dominant ideological force. They articulate their religio-political positions in reaction to the challenge of secularism. In this sense, they are also identifiable as part of the cohort of 1948–67.

7. Established in 1920, the British Mandate governed a territory that had formerly comprised part of the Syrian administrative zone of the Ottoman Empire. The British ended this mandate authority in 1948 just prior to the start of the war that coincided with the establishment of the State of Israel. Graduates of the school that Musa attended were sent for advanced studies to universities in London and in Beirut. The school closed after the war of 1948.

8. Musa described praying at Arab-majority churches during important community occasions and crises even though he was a Muslim. He viewed such acts as expressive of a Palestinian and Arab nationalist solidarity that affirmed a shared, intersectarian identity. At his memorial service, following the burial prayer at a multiethnic mosque whose leadership

was known to support the Palestinian cause, Christians in attendance stood, at the invitation of one of Musa's colleagues (a Muslim and a pan-Arabist), to recite the Lord's Prayer (the "Our Father"). "Musa had requested this be done," his wife told me. Musa's Islamic burial ritual, and the unorthodox inclusion of Christians, was yet another reflection of his pan-Arab and multisectarian sensibilities that integrated and subordinated religion within an overarching and essentially secular nationalism.

9. What Hussain described was consistent with the anti-secularist, apolitical position of the Muslim Brotherhood movement in Palestine in this period. Only after Hamas emerged in 1988 did Islamism begin to receive significant backing from Palestinians searching for a viable religious nationalist alternative to the dominant secular nationalist formations (Lybarger 2007a).

10. This secularist orientation continues to define the ACC's successor organzation, the Arab American Action Network (AAAN). In 2010, posters and other artwork on the walls of the AAAN's premises featured the slogans, writings, and visages of secular-left and pan-Arab nationalist icons such as Ghassan Kanafani, Mahmoud Darwish, and Marcel Khalife. The images of younger diaspora artists, such as New York City-based poet Suheir Hammad, who articulated a secular-left and liberationist sensibility, also appeared on the walls.

11. In accordance with IRB protocol, I solicited and received formal permission to carry out research on the premises of the Arab American Action Network. Hatem Abudayyeh, AAAN Executive Director, generously facilitated contacts with AAAN personnel and volunteers and invited me to events.

12. Organizational ties and ideological sympathy had brought Republican forces in Northern Ireland—for example, the Irish Republican Army—into alliance with Palestinian secular nationalist formations, principally Fatah and the Palestine Liberation Organization (Collins 2011; Chamberlin 2012).

13. This center was known in the community to have this ideological sympathy. I have no evidence of formal organizational ties, and I did not seek this evidence.

14. *Nakba* commemorations mark the exodus and expulsion of approximately 750,000 Palestinians from their towns and villages during the war of 1948.

15. The same sort of control constrained women in the immigrant enclave, as well (Cainkar 1988).

16. In the immediate aftermath of the bombing, unsubstantiated and ultimately false reports that Arab and Islamic terrorists were responsible for the attack circulated widely in the national media (Cainkar 2009, 108; Bender 1995, 11–12).

17. Following his election to office in 2011, Mayor Rahm Emanuel restructured the advisory boards, abolishing the specific offices for different communities. This move angered Palestinian activists, who suspected Emanuel of harboring Zionist sympathies. Emanuel's father Benjamin had been a member of the ultranationalist Irgun, which carried out armed attacks against British officials and against Arab Palestinian civilians during the 1930s (Scherer 2008).

18. My relationship with Abudayyeh spans two decades. We met in the context of the effort to start the AAAN during the late 1990s. As the research for this project developed, he and I held several extended conversations, including two recorded interviews that I draw on here. He was in his mid-forties at the time of these discussions.

19. See the AAAN March 6, 2017, press release denouncing the travel ban. The statement lists multiple immigrant rights organizations as well as African American civil rights and justice groups like the Black Lives Matter chapter in Chicago (https://www.facebook

.com/AAAN.Markaz/posts/breaking-we-will-be-live-streaming-the-press-conference-at-1230pm-central-stay-t/10154948212202976).

20. For additional description of AAAN's activities, see https://aaan.org.

21. Abudayyeh's assertion here was possibly not completely accurate. See Moore (2011). On possibly adding Arabic and Mandarin to world language offerings in District 230 schools, which serve the southwest suburbs, see Vorva (2011).

22. Abudayyeh used the phrase "faith-based" to refer to the mosques and their associated organizations as well as to the "Islam-first" orientation they promoted. This phrase ironically had its origins in Evangelical Protestant social activism. President George W. Bush adopted the phrase for his Office of Faith-Based and Community Initiatives (http://georgewbush-whitehouse.archives.gov/government/fbci).

23. See chapter 5 for a discussion of secularist backlash against the new piety within the segment of the generation of 1987–2001 that had embraced the religious shift. The backlash is mentioned, specifically, in the interviews with Rami Nashashibi and Nawal (pseudonym) in that chapter.

24. "Republican" here refers to one of the two main political parties in the United States. Republicans, also known as the Grand Old Party (GOP), are understood to occupy the right-of-center position on the US political spectrum. Both the Republicans and their opposing party, the Democrats, have typically expressed unreserved support for Israel.

3. THE RELIGIOUS TURN: AMERICAN MUSLIMS FOR PALESTINE

1. It is possible that this wall was the same one that appeared at the SJP campus events. AMP and SJP coordinate with one another, and activists in one group can be involved with the other. I did not verify, however, whether or not the wall replica was indeed a portable, shared object.

2. See https://www.ampalestine.org/about-amp/statement-of-principles.

3. The material support charge stemmed from provisions in the Anti-Terrorism and Effective Death Penalty Act, which President Clinton signed into law in 1996. For more on the HLF case see https://archives.fbi.gov/archives/dallas/press-releases/2009/dl052709.htm; Glass (2018); and Nasaw (2008).

4. I interviewed AMP staff at the organization's offices in Palos Hills in October 2013, one month prior to the conference. These individuals mentioned the conference and invited me to come. I paid the registration fee online and attended the conference in November of that same year. At the conference, I confirmed my registration and was given a badge, a program, and other conference materials. I attended for two days, taking notes on presentations during the various sessions. AMP staff also told me about the Nakba Day commemoration in Bridgeview in 2014. The event was open to the public. There was no formal registration that I noticed. In keeping with their advocacy mission, AMP publicly advertised the Nakba event and the national conference through its website, social media platforms, and email. It also published descriptions of the events afterwards on its website and through email.

5. This image is viewable at 0:41 and at 1:22 in the video that the conference organizers produced as part of the publicity package (https://vimeo.com/73333666). The video concludes with an image of the al-Aqsa Mosque, which is situated on the Haram platform.

6. The erasure of Israel in this rendering of the map in AMP's conference poster inversely mirrors Israeli maps that suppress any reference to the Gaza Strip, East Jerusalem,

the West Bank, and the Golan Heights as occupied territories. These maps instead present these areas effectively as part of Israel's territorial expanse, demarcating the occupied areas with the Hebrew Biblical names of Judea and Samaria. For an example, see https://www.factsandlogic.org/ad_151-who-owns-the-west-bank, which appears on a website dedicated to "*hasbara*" (propaganda) on behalf of Israel. A topographical map that appears on Israel's Ministry of Foreign Affairs (MFA) website also uses "Judea" and "Samaria" as the primary geographical references but parenthetically notes that these areas pertain to the West Bank: https://mfa.gov.il/MFA/AboutIsrael/Maps/Pages/Topographical-map-of-Israel.aspx. The same MFA website also provides maps that explicitly delineate the areas occupied in 1967 as well as the proposed territorial arrangements of the now moribund Oslo Peace Process (http://mfa.gov.il/MFA/AboutIsrael/Maps/Pages/Israel%20in%20Maps.aspx).

7. A non-Palestinian activist, in comments made from the floor during one of the plenary sessions, noted this apparent marginalizing of non-Muslim, specifically Christian, landmarks. His comments drew a sharp rebuke from the presenters, who pointed to a small silver dome to the left they said represented the Church of the Holy Sepulcher.

8. For the commentarial context, see the searchable English version of *Tafsir al-Jalalayn* (https://www.altafsir.com/Tafasir.asp?tMadhNo=1&tTafsirNo=74&tSoraNo=17&tAyahNo=1&tDisplay=yes&UserProfile=0&LanguageId=2). For the Arabic version, see https://www.altafsir.com/tafasir.asp?tmadhno=0&ttafsirno=0&tsorano=1&tayahno=1&tdisplay=no&languageid=1. See also Ibn Kathir's commentary at https://islamweb.net/ar/library/index.php?page=bookcontents&ID=991&idfrom=0&idto=0&flag=1&bk_no=49&ayano=0&surano=0&bookhad=0.

9. For background on Jabhat al-Nusra and a list of its attacks, see Adraoui (2017) and https://en.wikipedia.org/wiki/Al-Nusra_Front, which links to news reports, for the group.

10. The US government, in the end, avoided military action after negotiating with the Russian Federation to remove and destroy the Syrian chemical weapons (Chollet 2016).

11. The violent situation in Syria subsequently took a new turn with the rise of the Islamic State movement and with the Russian intervention. Mosque Foundation leaders have explicitly condemned the violence of the Islamic State even as they have also called for pressure on the Syrian regime.

12. The full statement (October 14, 2014) and responses (some from Palestinians who were sharply critical) are available at https://www.facebook.com/m.zaher.sahloulo/posts/10152275648706685. The full text reads:

> Few Israelis have violated the sanctuary of the Aqsa Mosque and provoked the sensitivities of the faithful. Muslims are enraged. Yes, this is unacceptable and we should condemn it. The Syrian regime destroyed hundreds of Mosques including the historic Umayyad Mosque in Aleppo, Omari Mosque in Daraa, Othman Mosque in Deir Alzour, Khaled Ibn Alwaleed Mosque in Homs and many others while killing 200,000 Syrians (including only 17,00 [sic] children and 11,000 tortured to death) and displacing 10 million people inside and outside Syria including thousands of already displaced Palestinians. Syria now is number one in refugees (Yay we surpassed Afghanistan) and number one in boat immigrants (Yippee Yay we surpassed Eritrea) and soon last country in Millennium Development goals (we will surpass Somalia soon inshallah). After 3.5 years, no large Muslim demonstrations against the criminal regime that destroys Mosques and kills children. Muslim reaction anyone?? We condemn Israel! Give me a break for your hypocrisy dear brothers and sisters!

13. The statement and twitter comment thread can be found at https://perma.cc/42ET-274D. The full statement reads:

> It is time for individuals and organizations in the American Muslim, Arab, Jewish and Palestinian communities who promoted and inflated Max Blumenthal and his friends to tell these bozos enough is enough. Max and friends, like Ali Abunimah and Rania Khalek [sic] are the fifth column who have been [sic] promoting war criminals, supporting the genocidal policies of Assad and Putin, promoting idiotic conspiracy arguments, disregarding the scarifies of the Syrian people and probably getting paid by Russian and Assad PR firms. They are the equivalent of the propaganda machine of Hitler. How can they claim that they care about Palestinian children in besieged Gaza while they ignore the suffering of Syrian children in besieged Aleppo? What kind of person devoid of humanity are [sic] these bloggers? It would be shameful if they are invited to speak at conferences or treated with respect. After 6 years of Genocide [sic], anyone with moral ambiguity about what is happening in Syria is a culprit of the crimes against humanity committed every day by Assad and sectarian militias against Syrian children. I invite honorable Palestinian, Arab [sic] and Muslim Americans Linda Sarsour Kifah Mustapha ElMera'abi Hatem Bazian Nihad Awad Ahmed Rehab [sic] and others to uncover the ugly faces of these liars.

The individuals named at the end of the statement were publicly known figures and, at the time, leaders of local and national religious and advocacy organizations such as the Mosque Foundation, AMP, Council on American-Islamic Relations (CAIR), and the Arab American Association of New York.

14. For Blumenthal's views on Israel and Zionism, see Blumenthal (2013). For a critique of this book and Blumenthal's other writings and statements, see Mikics (2015). Salaita (2013/2014) offers a sharply contrasting assessment of Blumenthal (2013).

15. Blumenthal had held strong anti-Assad views while working for the Lebanese paper *al Akhbar*. He left the paper in a controversy with its editors concerning what he viewed as their pro-Assad stance. Later, however, Blumenthal also became critical of groups like the White Helmets and the Syrian American Medical Society. Even as he voiced this criticism, he nevertheless maintained his opposition to the Assad regime. For background, see Dot-Pouillard (2012) and Giovani (2018). For Blumenthal's statement concerning his criticism, see Blumenthal (2012) and also Jay (2012).

16. See Dot-Pouillard (2012) for a discussion of these complicated splits. See Frantzman (2016) for a long polemic that delves into the same issues even as it lambastes the anti-imperialist/anti-interventionist side for its supposed complicity with pro-Assad positions.

17. See the Twitter exchange here: https://twitter.com/maxblumenthal/status/783723876698259456. Abunimah's primary concern has been raising awareness of the Palestinian struggle against Israel. He and the e-zine he founded, *The Electronic Intifada*, have been accused of silence on Syria and of opposing intervention against Assad. For these accusations, see Palmer (2016), which is highly critical of Abunimah, among others. See Abunimah (2016) for reporting on attempts to mediate the dispute in *The Electronic Intifada*. This article quotes Blumenthal at length in defense of the anti-intervention stance.

18. See the discussion of this history and of the semiotics of Palestine in the introduction. See also Collins (2011, 7–8) and Tawil-Souri (2016, 15–28) as well as Feldman (2015) and Fischbach (2019).

19. Hamas, by contrast, refers to this concept. See Article 11 of its charter at http://avalon.law.yale.edu/20th_century/hamas.asp.

20. See AMP's statement of principles at https://www.ampalestine.org/about-amp/statement-of-principles.

21. Since the period of European colonialism, Muslims have engaged in a wide-ranging debate about what jihad encompasses, normatively, and what the conditions are, specifically, under which armed jihad may be undertaken. The debate has become especially intense in the aftermath of the September 11 attacks and the rise of movements like al-Qaeda and the Islamic State. Muslims globally have condemned the violence of these movements as violations of the Qur'anic and *fiqh* stipulations relating to armed jihad. By contrast, supporters of these movements, drawing on the writings of Islamist theorists like Sayyid Qutb, Abu Muhammad al-Maqdisi, Abu Abdullah al-Muhajir, and Abu Bakr Naji, assert that the core of jihad is violence in the service of God against God's enemies. On the range of meanings connected with the jihad concept, including nonviolent meanings, see Firestone (1999) and D. Cook (2005). Articles 12 and 15 of Hamas's 1988 Charter stress a necessary, individual responsibility to resist Israel's threat to the Islamic patrimony in Palestine and elsewhere. See http://avalon.law.yale.edu/20th_century/hamas.asp. On the debate about whether jihad is primarily defensive or offensive and related questions of politics and pluralism, see Safi (2003); Moaddel and Talattof (2000, 71–122 and 223–52); and Maher (2016).

22. For information on the program, see https://hartman.org.il/Programs_View.asp?Program_Id=110&Cat_Id=517&Cat_Type=Programs.

23. Some of the Muslim leaders who were among the early participants in the Shalom Hartman Institute program later issued an apology, stating that they only later came to understand the underlying motives. See, for example, Ziad (2018).

24. Kristin Szremski, an AMP staff member at the time, echoed the point concerning the need for educating the community about the Palestinian issue during our interview together in October 2013.

25. The *shaykh* did not mention that Muslim policy protected Christians and Jews in these historical cases. Although the dating and authorship remain disputed, Islamic tradition nevertheless records that the Pact of 'Umar ibn al-Khattab and al-'Uhda al-'Umariya (the "guarantee of safety" that 'Umar purportedly extended) ensured the right of Christians to remain in Jerusalem after the Muslim conquest of the city in 637 CE. Christians could retain their properties, worship freely, and exercise a degree of legal autonomy in exchange for submission to overall Muslim rule. This submission entailed payment of the prescribed tax and acceptance of various social and symbolic restrictions as subordinate, "protected" people (*ahl al-dhimma*, or "People of the Pact"). Salah al-Din, after conquering Jerusalem in 1187, offered generous terms to the defeated Franks and invited Jews to return to Jerusalem, reversing the ban imposed against them by the Crusaders.

26. For a description of the activities of the *murabitat*, see Staton (2015). I am indebted to Maha Nassar for alerting me to this group.

27. The image is available at https://www.facebook.com/nakbamsp/photos/a.1396050487348514/1401523876801175/?type=1&theater. A variation of the image that zooms in on the young woman's gagged face appears here: https://www.facebook.com/nakbamsp/photos/a.1396050487348514/1396050517348511/?type=1&theater.

28. "MSP" refers to "Management Service Provider," an entity that coordinates information technology services for clients.

29. Orthopraxy and orthodoxy are overlapping terms that nevertheless carry important distinctions in meaning. Orthodoxy refers to established doctrines that define the authoritative ideas and ideals of a community. Orthopraxy refers to the authoritatively instituted practices through which a group enacts its doctrines in the world. Religious studies scholars have typically argued that orthodoxy most appropriately describes Christian emphases on creedal statements and theology while orthopraxy captures the traditional Jewish and Muslim stress on practice. This claim is potentially misleading, since orthodoxy and orthopraxy, in varying degrees, characterize most religious communities. Nevertheless, the distinction does highlight, in general terms, important differences among the monotheisms. Jews and Muslims, for example, have to a far greater degree than Christians engaged in extensive scholarly elaboration of conventions for individual and collective life (*halacha* and *shari'a*, respectively). For this reason, I will, in this book, at times use the term "orthopraxy" in reference, particularly, to Islamic reformism, which has been concerned with establishing *shari'a* norms within the immigrant community.

30. See Najjar (2018) for background on the bombardment of this camp during the Syrian civil war.

4. THE RELIGIOUS TURN: GENERATIONAL SUBJECTIVITIES

1. These interviews are part of a set of forty different recorded conversations with Muslims and Christians who, as a group, center or integrate religious value-orientations, practices, institutions, and interpretive frames within their autobiographical narratives. This centering or integrating of religion occurs in two ways that roughly divide this group of interviews in half: as an embrace of a more-or-less strict or "pure" religious stance that subordinates, ignores, or rejects secularism, sometimes as a reaction, especially among Christians, to the sectarianizing impact of the religious shift; or, as a mediation of the religious-secular tension through articulation of religious-secular hybrid orientations. Mediation/hybridization receives attention in the next two chapters. The focus of this chapter is on the first type, the "pure" religious shift.

2. On the bifocal concept, see the introduction.

3. See the introduction and also Massey 2005, 130 and elsewhere, on how narration, "stories so far," constitutes space.

4. Early Salafists felt that European colonial domination of Muslim lands had resulted from the weakening of Islamic solidarity and Islamic identity. In their view, this weakening had been the result of the accretion of non-Islamic influences such as Greek philosophy, local superstitions, mysticism, and so on. The reformers wanted to purify Islam of these elements and in doing so demonstrate Islam's ability to provide a culturally authentic, rational alternative to European values and political institutions. They also wanted to show that such an Islam was compatible with science and technology and could ground these fields in proper morality. Salafism has taken a variety of organizational forms, ranging from politically quietist missionary groups to social movements, political parties, and violent insurgencies. For more, see Riesebrodt (1993); Euben (1999); O. Roy (2004); Euben and Zaman (2009); and Maher (2016).

5. Whether there were actual material or organizational ties between Islamist movements in Palestine and reformist organizations in Chicago was not of any direct relevance to my project. I do not have evidence of such connections and I did not seek such evidence. What I do note, however, is an ideological sympathy for reformism as mediated

historically through Salafism and the Muslim Brotherhood generally. This ideological tendency followed a distinct developmental path in Chicago.

6. In the premodern period, Muslims used this term to refer to the time before the coming of Islam as the "period of ignorance." The primary characteristic of this period, as the term connoted, was the prevalence of polytheism or of putatively distorted Christian or Jewish ideas that inserted polytheistic ideas ("trinity") into monotheism or rendered monotheism the sole possession of only one ethnic group (Jews as "the chosen people"). Islamists have transformed the *jahiliya* idea into a critique of Muslim-majority societies, which they view as having embraced systems contrary to Islam and thereby to have returned to a state of polytheistic "ignorance." On these matters, see Euben (1999) and Euben and Zaman (2009).

7. My translation. Al-Tirmidhi and other pre-modern commentators apparently viewed this *hadith* saying as unattested because its line of transmission was difficult to verify. See the discussion at https://www.ahlalhdeeth.com/vb/showthread.php?t=144009.

8. Muhannad's story also echoed a set narrative within the Islamic tradition that emphasizes the necessity to oppose unbelief even in one's family. The Qur'an's retelling of the story of Abraham is one example of this type of narrative. Muhammad, however, is the supreme exemplar of this principled stance in his opposition to his tribe, the Quraysh.

9. The actual number was 415 (Haberman 1992; B'tselem 2011).

10. Liberation theology emerged as a response among primarily Catholic theologians and pastors to Marxist-inspired revolutionary movements during the Cold War period in Latin America. These movements demanded fundamental transformations of the conditions of severe poverty and political repression in their countries. Liberation theologians articulate a Christian response that integrates Marxist class analysis into a reinterpretation of the Gospel texts. Their hermeneutical principle is that Jesus evinced a "preferential option for the poor and the oppressed." For the foundational liberation theology text, see Gutiérrez (1988 [1973]). For Palestinian liberation theology, see Ateek (1989).

11. For more on the Park 51 mosque controversy and the Qur'an-burning incident, see the various articles listed at https://www.nytimes.com/topic/organization/muslim-community-center-in-lower-manhattan and *Guardian* (2013).

12. Munir's specific reference was unclear but attacks on churches and tensions surrounding attempts by Christians to build new churches have mounted since Hamas's 2007 takeover in Gaza (al-Ghoul 2013 and 2014).

13. For more on this massacre, see Hedges and Greenberg (1994).

14. The reference is to a publication most recently issued in 2016 (Sabeel Ecumenical Liberation Theology Center 2016).

5. DYNAMIC SYNTHESES: REVERSION, CONVERSION, AND ACCOMMODATION

The data and analyses in this chapter are adapted from Lybarger (2014).

1. See the introduction for a delineation of "hybridization" as I define and deploy the concept in this book.

2. See my discussion of ideal-types in the introduction for further caveats and explanation of the purpose of typological analysis.

3. I have adapted the metaphor of flow and crosscutting currents from Tweed (2006).

4. See the introduction for a detailed elaboration of how this inflection occurs.

5. Reformist piety has affirmed "the sacredness of private property, business, and markets" while also invoking an ethic of paternalistic charity and tithing (*sadaqat* and *zakat*, respectively) (Gamal 2019). In reformist discourse and practice, charity serves ideally to contain the wealth gap while tithing builds the community's institutions. Both function symbolically as signs of the "Islamic solution" to the injustices of a capitalism untethered from *shari'a* morality. The "Islamic solution" seeks to institute a kinder, gentler capitalism in which those who succeed economically redistribute their wealth, seen as deriving from God's beneficence, to the needy through charitable giving and *zakat*. The paternalism of this ethic also dovetails with the reformist emphasis on gender complementarity in work and home. Women can pursue careers but must also fulfill their primary responsibilities as sisters, wives, and mothers. Among its other competing meanings, some of them analyzed further below in this chapter, the hijab scarf serves within the reformist ethos as a symbolic marker of a woman's commitment to her domestic role and to the authority of husbands, brothers, and fathers. Men, too, bear their divinely ordained responsibilities, principally the financial and moral support of their families and of the *umma*'s institutions through public prayer in the mosque, regular payment of *zakat*, etc. As Weber (1946a) observed in relation to Protestant communities in the United States, regular performance of public religious duties of this sort establishes a man's status as a trustworthy partner in business and professional interactions. It also integrates him into the community's professional and commercial networks. I should point out, too, that the redistributive ethic, instituted through the *shari'a* mandate to tithe, is present across diverse Muslim communities, not just those oriented toward reformism. On the competing meanings of the hijab and women's roles within reformist understandings, see Ahmed (2011, 1992); Tarlo (2010); Lazreg (2009); Lybarger (2007a, 169–73); Mahmood (2005); Joseph (1993); Riesebrodt (1993).

6. "In the name of God, the Most Gracious, the Most Merciful"—the traditional invocation uttered before recitation of Qur'anic passages, the beginning of meals, and the start of any new venture.

7. By "culture," as becomes clear later in this section, Nawal also meant the traditional expectation that as one grew older, one needed to dress in a manner appropriate to one's age. The scarf thus signaled a life-course transition for her mother, and not an ideological change or internal metanoia. The distinction between "culture" and "Islam"—understood in this context as the difference between an unthinking traditionalism and a rational, self-aware, and book-centered orientation toward praxis—that features so prominently in Nawal's discussion of her mother's scarf-wearing has been a standard trope in reformist discourse from its inception (Ahmed 1992; Riesebrodt 1993; Moaddel and Talattof 2000; Euben and Zaman 2009; Lazreg 2009; Tarlo 2010; Ahmed 2011).

8. In implementing this orientation, the long-serving imam of this mosque carried forward reformist tendencies that he had likely absorbed while undergoing training in the Middle East. For more on reformism as it manifests in Salafism in its multiple forms, see Euben and Zaman (2009); Scott (2010); Wickham (2013); Mouline (2014); Lauzière (2016); and Maher (2016).

9. Historically the MSA, as a national organization, aligned ideologically with the Muslim Brotherhood. In Palestine, the Muslim Brotherhood, until the rise of Hamas in the late 1980s, opposed Palestinian nationalism, emphasizing instead the necessity of

reorienting Palestinian society as a whole toward reformist-type Islam prior to launching concerted mass resistance against Israel. In the Middle East, generally, the Muslim Brotherhood has actively recruited membership on university campuses by providing tutoring, financial help, and a community in which to receive social support, friendship, and professional and political connections after graduation. For more on the MSA-Muslim Brotherhood ideological alignment in the United States, see Pennock (2017, 27 and elsewhere). For a history of the Muslim Brotherhood in the Middle East, see Wickham (2013).

10. Arguably, by questioning sources, Nawal not only acquired the capacity to deconstruct the patriarchal dictates of the "street" preachers but also of Islamic reformism. Reformism, as noted already, had generally emphasized the re-institution of patriarchal gender norms within the family and community. Debates about the hijab scarf among Muslims revolved, in particular, around this question of gender norms, specifically, the proper role of women in society. For background on reformism as repatriarchalization, see Riesebrodt (1993).

11. Prayer requires women and men to adhere to conventions of modest dress (*sitr al-'awra*—"covering one's nakedness," that is, genitals and other sexually significant parts of the body). According to the Shafi'i *madhhab*, the tradition of *shari'a* jurisprudence predominant among Palestinian Muslims, men at a minimum must cover the area from the navel to the knees. Women, however, must cover all areas except for the face and hands during prayer and while engaging in activities outside of the home. See the sections on prayer and *sitr al-'awra* in al-Misri (1994 [1991]).

12. Her mother, before dying, expressed concern that her husband and Nawal's brothers would force Nawal to withdraw from college because of the cost. Nawal commented that her mother's fear was misplaced because her father was proud of her and her accomplishments as a student.

13. The AAAN recognized the pragmatic necessity of collaborating with religious organizations to amplify its reach. Consistent with this pragmatism, it had forged cooperative relations with different mosques. The particular mosque that Nawal interacted with was known to possess strong Palestinian nationalist orientations. Also, at about the time that Nawal began work, arson had destroyed the AAAN's premises, requiring the organization to find alternative venues for its programs.

14. Islamic reformists, too, conceivably might have interpreted her adherence to these practices as aligning with the concern to "repatriarchalize" the family that has been a focus of contemporary Islamist movements and other forms of religious fundamentalism. On these matters, see Riesebrodt (1993), 176–208. It bears emphasizing that other religions, including Judaism and Christianity, have supported patriarchal norms, and especially so within the fundamentalist movements that have opposed "liberalism" within these religions. Like Islam, they have also witnessed diverging appropriations that have challenged those same norms.

15. Islamic *fiqh* (jurisprudence) deems non-*mahram* men to be potential marriage partners because they are beyond the boundaries of immediate blood relations (consanguinity). Thus, a brother or a father is *mahram*—forbidden as a marriage partner—but a first cousin is not. Refusing contact with a marriagiable individual serves to maintain a person's ritual purity (*tahara*). Ritual purity is required for the performance of duties such as prayer. Loss of *tahara* normally imposes the necessity of ablutions with water prior to undertaking

prayer, etc. Refusal of contact assists someone to avoid having to do ablutions prior to the arrival of the next prayer time. Beyond its practical motivations, refusal of physical contact with non-*mahrams* also signals adherence to sexual propriety as interpreted in contemporary reformist orthopraxy. Engaging in the practice is of a piece with the decision to embrace other dimensions of reformist piety, such as the hijab, prayer, and so on. Refusal of contact is thus a performance of this type of piety. It signals alignment with this piety and the orthopraxy that supports it.

16. On the definition of orthopraxy in contrast with orthodoxy, see chapter 3, n28.

17. Intersectional perspectives that relate the suffering of one's own ethnos to the suffering of other oppressed groups would challenge this assertion. From an intersectional standpoint, emphasis on national particularity does not necessarily have to lead to ethnocentrism. Rather, it can become the foundation for empathy and solidarity with others sharing a common experience of exclusion and repression. The conversion trajectory described in this chapter aligns with this intersectional understanding at the point at which the ethnos is relativized and transcended within a new, overarching transnational solidarity. By definition, at this point, the ethnos no longer constitutes the primary basis of identity but rather gives way to intersubjectivity (interethnicity) that conversion expresses in terms of a transcendent spiritual community.

18. Nashashibi's story echoed similar accounts of border crossing among my interlocutors. These acts of pilgrimage "back home," and the crossing of the fortified borders that they required, resulted in a direct confrontation with what it meant to identify and be categorized as "Palestinian." A ritual process in Turner's sense, the act thrust these individuals into a traumatizing and transforming liminality (V. Turner 1969). The mechanisms of this process were the procedures of humiliation that unfolded in several stages: separation from loved ones at passport control; isolation within interrogation rooms; and, finally, if fortunate, reintegration with family on the other side as a member of a policed population in an occupied territory.

19. Nashashibi stated: "What really intrigued me was [. . .] that there was an ability to really engage with primary sources about the life of the Prophet Muhammad, to look at [. . .] what he says [and to ask whether] is he a liar, and the fact the Qur'an was engaging these things, and engaging these arguments, thinking about these things, and the Qur'an invited you [to think about this]." His thoughts here reflect the traditional doctrinal standpoints of Islam concerning the veracity of the sources about Muhammad. Nondoctrinal historical-critical and text-critical analyses have raised numerous unresolved questions about the origins of Islam and about the extent to which the *hadith* texts and the Qur'an reflect those beginnings in any direct, empirically verifiable way. These views remain controversial. See inter alia Wansbrough (1978, 2004 [1977]); Crone (1987); Cook (1983, 2000); F. Peters (1994); Noth and Conrad (1994); and Donner (1998, 2010).

20. The *kufi* cap is a style of head covering that many African American Muslim men have adopted. For more on the cultural impact of hip-hop and Black Islam on American Muslims generally, see Khabeer 2016.

21. The IMAN website details the current programming. The site reflects deep ties with African American communities and African American Muslims. Arab and Palestinian connections are gestured to, but these relationships are embedded within IMAN's public identity as a South Side Muslim organization focused on social justice. IMAN's website

conveys these terms, explicitly, through the description of the organization's mission, policy initiatives, and programs. Its photographs also convey these terms. Equally revealing is what IMAN's site does not convey: a specific immersion within, or explicit commitment to, a particular immigrant expression of Islam. There is no programmatic reference, for example, to the Palestinian struggle—a clear contrast with American Muslims for Palestine. Arabs and Palestinians appear in three ways on the IMAN website: as members of IMAN's staff; as a target of "the Corner Store Campaign" to convince Arab owners of small grocery stores to carry affordable, healthy produce for their local customers; and, occasionally, as artists listed in the artists' registry.

22. Edward Said (1935–2003) was a literary theorist, defender of secularism, and outspoken critic and advocate of the Palestinian national cause in the diaspora. His oeuvre includes *Orientalism* (1978), *The Question of Palestine* (1979), and *Culture and Imperialism* (1993) among many other books and articles. He came to Chicago often to speak at community events such as the AAAN fundraiser I describe in the introduction.

23. It is not uncommon for shop-owning classes to possess ethnic identities that differ from those of their patrons. The "communistic" ethos of ethnic and neighborly ties can make commercial enterprise difficult to sustain. In this ethos, one is not to exploit one's brothers and sisters in the ethnos or one's neighbors. Rather, one is to give as one can to those who are in need with no expectation of repayment, and certainly not with interest. Ethnic distance and difference, however, cancel such obligations, thus making capitalist commercial transactions sustainable. Nashashibi's critique mobilizes religious communism—the idea that one is not to exploit one's sisters and brothers in the faith—against this cross-ethnic commercial relation between Palestinians and African Americans, a relation he characterizes as exploitative. His appeal is to a shared brotherhood and sisterhood in Islam that transcends this ethnic division and resituates relations within the ethos of "from each according to his abilities, to each according to his needs." The reaction of the lawyers to Nashashibi's criticism bears out the logic of these dynamics, too: the reaction registered a feeling of betrayal triggered by the perception that Nashashibi was failing to abide by the communal requirements of ethnic and national solidarity. On the tension between communistic and commercial ethics, see Graeber (2014 [2011], 89–126).

6. DYNAMIC SYNTHESES: REBELLION, ABSOLUTE AND SPIRITUAL

1. See chapter 3, n28, on the distinction between orthopraxy and orthodoxy.
2. Recall that Nashashibi also argued that protesting, at least in the way Palestinians typically did it, was pointless. Palestinians were simply talking to themselves whenever they demonstrated downtown. They needed, he said, to immerse themselves in other people's struggles so as to expand the sphere of solidarity. Ibrahim, by contrast, viewed these sorts of politics in their entirety as futile.
3. For many Palestinians in Chicago, the term "American" in conversation often was a reference to the majority-white society. "American" was distinct both from "Palestinian" in this ethnic-racial sense and from the political status of US citizen. One could see oneself as Palestinian and a US citizen but not as "American."
4. For an explanation of why some women might embrace conservative religious traditions, see Riesebrodt and Chong (1999).

5. The al-Aqsa Martyrs' Brigade drew its membership from Fatah. It took its name from the al-Aqsa Mosque on the Haram al-Sharif in Jerusalem. In 2000, soon-to-be Israeli Prime Minister Ariel Sharon toured the Haram with a heavily armed escort in a bid to reinforce Israeli claims to Jerusalem in its entirety. Palestinians demonstrated against this highly provocative act. The militarized Israeli response sparked an escalating spiral of devastating reprisals that led to the Second Intifada. For background, see Usher (2000, 2003); Shikaki (2001); and Carey (2001).

6. On such matters, see the canonical collection of *hadith* in *Sahih Bukhari* Volume 1, Book 4, Number 247, which specifies that one sleep on one's right side as if one were a corpse in a coffin. Should one die at night, one will then be in the proper position to meet God. For this reference, see the searchable online version featuring the Arabic original and English translation in parallel columns at https://sunnah.com/bukhari/4. A website operated by the Saudi Salafi Shaykh Muhammad Al-Munajjid provides textual references explicitly linking sleeping on one's stomach, and not on one's right side, to the practice of those who have been cast into hell. These references include *hadith* reports conveyed in several collections, including Al-Tirmidhi: https://islamqa.info/en/answers/827/the-reason-why-it-is-forbidden-to-sleep-on-ones-belly.

7. Moshe Dayan (1915–1981) was a militia commander during the war of 1948, Israel's Chief of Staff during the Suez Crisis of 1956, and Defense Minister during the war of 1967.

8. By labeling modern Muslim-majority societies in this way, Qutb was able to respond to the traditional proscription against *fitna*—conflict that fractures the *umma*—in Islamic *fiqh*. Societies characterized by *jahiliya* ceased to be Muslim and in doing so became legitimate targets of jihad to the extent they posed a threat to Islam. Qutb and his ideas have received extensive scholarly attention in multiple languages. For background, see Euben and Zaman (2009). For additional nuanced discussion, see Euben (1999).

9. I remarked on this resonance to Jubran during our conversation. He had not known of Qutb's use of the term.

10. O. Roy (2004) parses Jubran's distinction in terms of "neo-fundamentalism," which is a totalizing form of life that transcends national borders. "Political Islam," by contrast, seeks to impose Islamic institutions within specific nation-states through the mechanisms of state power. Neo-fundamentalism ignores the state. It focuses instead on the transformation of social norms and social practices at the individual level, primarily through missionary (*da'wa*) activity. The goal is the creation of a subcultural milieu defined in terms of the sort of exclusionary ethos that Jubran's describes.

11. There has been a long-running debate among Muslims concerning music. Scholars of Islamic law have tended to view Qur'anic recitation and sacred hymn singing as licit. These forms of soundmaking are not classified as "music" but rather in relation to other terms such as *tajwid* (elaborated recitation of the Qur'an) that refer to a religious liturgical practice. "Music" is reserved for profane forms of soundmaking ranging from classical musical performances, which, in legal debates, have a morally ambiguous status (because possibly a frivolous use of time), to performances associated with morally proscribed "red light district" activities (singing and dancing in taverns, for example). Sufi mystics, by contrast, have adopted an expansive interpretation of sacred soundmaking. Sufis have incorporated musical instruments, chant, singing (for example, Indo-Pak Qawwali), and dance. They see these forms of soundmaking as devoted to sacred purposes—achieving *fana'* (annihilation

of the ego in God), for example—and thus licit. Salafi-inspired movements, endeavoring to impose strict orthopraxy, have, by contrast, adopted a strict interpretation of the traditional legal dichotomies distinguishing licit sacred soundmaking from illicit "music." Otterbeck (2004) notes that modern hardline Islamist movements view music as a serious challenge to orthopraxy because it offers alternative avenues for leisure, creativity, feeling, and spiritual experience. It also opens avenues to a pluralist global culture and especially to Western cultural influences. For more, see Shiloah (1997) and al-Faruqi (1985).

12. The proscription of music in the suburbs was not entirely complete, however. Couples still wanted music at their weddings. But, now, typically, these celebrations occurred in gender-segregated spaces. "We had to get extra long cables and speakers to reach the women's area," Jubran recounted, "and the women had to use couriers to convey their requests and often the men intervened to say they did not want to listen to what the women wanted to listen to: it was a mess!" Recently, however, Jubran noted, there were signs of a relaxing of the practice of separation in these gatherings. "Maybe things are loosening up," he said.

13. Jubran here gave expression to a quintessential Sufi conception of prayer (Chittick 1983, 153–55). His particular gloss on this practice invoked the song "Every Breath You Take" by the Police.

14. Ramadan fasting restrictions include abstention from smoking and sexual intercourse as well as food and beverage of any sort during the daylight hours.

CONCLUSION

1. The Israeli military court system is notorious for convicting almost every indicted Palestinian brought before it. The conviction rate in these tribunals in 2010, for example, stood at 99.74 percent (Levinson 2011; Naber 2014).

2. The United Nations General Assembly document (1979) includes background information about the charges brought against Odeh and about the abusive conditions of interrogation and detention that she and several other Palestinian political prisoners confronted at the time. Israel's use of torture in its interrogations of Palestinian detainees is well documented; see the various reports at https://www.btselem.org/topic/torture. For documentation of one of the most recent cases—the torture of Samir Arbeed—see Amnesty International (2019). For additional background on Odeh's 1969 detention and on her immigration case, see Khoury (2004); American Friends Service Committee (2013); Naber (2014); Warikoo (2016, 2017); Dabaie (2017); Mustufa (2018).

3. For the full list of the groups that the federal government designates as terrorist organizations, see https://www.state.gov/j/ct/rls/other/des/123085.htm. The designation of terrorist organizations resulted from the passing of the Antiterrorism and Effective Death Penalty Act in 1996 (Broxmeyer 2004). Prior to the passage of the antiterrorism act, membership in groups like the PFLP or actions that supported such groups—contributing donations to affiliated entities, distributing supportive literature, etc.—were not explicitly illegal. Federal prosecutors nevertheless made attempts prior to the legislation to deport Palestinians it deemed to be a threat (Goodman 2007; Abowd 2007).

4. Beginning in 2015, the Federal Bureau of Investigation collected hate crime data pertaining to violent discriminatory acts committed against Arab Americans (1.1 percent). The majority of hate crimes involving religion in 2015 targeted Jewish Americans (52.1 percent)

and Muslim Americans (21.9 percent). See https://ucr.fbi.gov/hate-crime/2015/topic-pages/victims_final.

5. See http://justice4rasmea.org/news/2017/04/25/supporters-join-rasmea-at-plea-hearing and https://www.facebook.com/678264732186412/videos/1508754542470756.

6. Odeh's indictment and conviction occurred in the midst of renewed, intensified, and ongoing law enforcement interventions against Arab and Muslim communities after the September 11, 2001 attacks. These interventions had resulted in crippling legal action against organizations like the Holy Land Foundation and the Islamic Association for Palestine. Individuals also became targets of antiterrorism probes. Prior to Odeh, the Muhammad Salah case had been the most recent and prominent (Sander 2007). Odeh's arrest occurred seemingly in connection with a grand jury investigation into the activities of antiwar activists in Wisconsin and Illinois. In 2010, Hatem Abudayyeh, the Executive Director of the Arab American Action Network (see chapter 2) and Odeh's supervisor, became a target of this probe (*ABC7* 2010; Grimm and Dizikes 2010). Federal agents searched his home and the homes of the other targeted activists and confiscated computers, books, and files. The investigation remained open but had failed to result in formal charges against Abudayyeh. Odeh's supporters believed that her arrest stemmed from this open-ended investigation of Abudayyeh (Silver 2016). Politically, they asserted that the law enforcement raids and the Odeh arrest formed part of a longstanding effort to undermine the viability of activism on behalf of the Palestinian struggle and of Arab and Muslim civil rights in the United States. Revealingly, the description of Abudayyeh as a "Muslim community leader" in *ABC7*'s (2010) reporting of his arrest was incorrect. Abudayyeh identified explicitly as a secular leftist and Palestinian and Arab activist, not as a Muslim per se. *ABC7*'s description indicated how "Muslim" had come to serve as the primary media frame for Muslim-majority immigrant communities. This designation reflected the post-September 11 discourse about Islamic radicalism. The construal of Arab immigrants as "Muslims," regardless of their internal cultural, religious, and political differentiation derived from this discourse. On these matters, see the discussion in the introduction of this book.

7. See, for example, https://www.ampalestine.org/newsroom/amp-stands-solidarity-rasmea-odeh.

8. See https://www.arabamericannews.com/2014/09/12/Activists-call-for-political-solidarity-between-Arab-and-African-Americans/ and Daghash (2015).

9. Media and Muslim organizations have primarily referred to Tlaib and Omar as "Muslims." Omar wears a hijab scarf; Tlaib does not. Both women affirm their identities as Muslims. But, in an extended interview with "The Daily" podcast (Barbaro 2019), Tlaib defined herself in other terms, too, saying, "I grew up more Palestinian than Muslim." She also stated that "I have never felt so Palestinian than I [have] in Congress." But in Palestine, she is "the *amrikaniya*" and in Detroit, "I'm just a Detroiter, I'm Rashida from the Southwest [of the city], or 'You're the girl from the Southwest.'" Later in the interview, she described how the anti-Muslim backlash following the September 11 attacks imposed "Muslim" as a defining negative category. This assertion of complexity in her identity reflects and reinforces the core arguments of this book. Omar's explicit embrace of the Palestinian cause also shows how Palestine has become symbolically central to solidarity networks spanning secular-left, African American, and immigrant and Muslim activist circles. The mobilization to support Odeh drew on these networks and on Palestine as symbolic frame. See Naber (2012) for background on these sorts of convergences.

10. See United States Council of Muslim Organizations (2015).

11. See, for example, S. Suleiman (2015) and Moghul (2015).

12. The AMP statement is embedded in S. Suleiman's (2015) polemic against the organization's stance on the issue.

13. Palestinian Armenians have long claimed to be, and received acceptance as, members of the Palestinian nation. In the view of AMP's critics, consistency of principle required affirmation and support of the history of Armenian oppression, especially since it paralleled so closely the Palestinian experience of violent dispossession. See Hintilian (1998) for how Armenians are presented as Palestinian nationalists.

14. Perhaps Said's most significant and direct expression of this utopian vision was his collaboration with Israeli pianist and maestro Daniel Barenboim. Said, also an accomplished pianist, and Barenboim created the West-Eastern Divan Orchestra that brought together Jewish Israeli and Palestinian and other Arab musicians. For more on the idea and the project, see: http://www.west-eastern-divan.org; https://www.barenboim-said.ps; and https://barenboimsaid.de/about/history. For Palestinian criticism of the West-Eastern Divan, see Palestinian Campaign for the Academic and Cultural Boycott of Israel (2009, 2010); M. Said (2010). The Boycott, Divestment, and Sanctions campaign has continued to intervene against attempts by the West-Eastern Divan to perform in Arab capitals, most recently in Qatar in 2012 (Palestinian Campaign for the Academic and Cultural Boycott of Israel 2012).

REFERENCES

ABC7. 2010. "Muslim Community Leader: 'No Rhyme or Reason' for Raids." December 17. https://abc7chicago.com/archive/7850679.

Abowd, Mary. 1995. "In Memoriam: Samir Odeh, 1951–1995." *Washington Report on Middle East Affairs*. January/February: 35, 88. https://www.wrmea.org/1995-january-february/in-memoriam-samir-odeh-1951-1994.html.

———. 2007. "Arab Community has Deep Roots in Chicago." *The Chicago Reporter*. September 24. http://chicagoreporter.com/arab-community-has-deep-roots-chicago.

———. 2015. "Students in the College explore Richard Wright's Chicago." *UChicago News*. June 18. https://news.uchicago.edu/story/students-college-explore-richard-wrights-chicago.

Abu El-Haj, Thea Renda. 2015. *Unsettled Belonging: Educating Palestinian American Youth after 9/11*. Chicago: University of Chicago Press.

Abu-Lughod, Janet L. 1999. *New York, Chicago, Los Angeles: America's Global Cities*. Minneapolis: University of Minnesota Press.

Abunimah, Ali. 2006. *One Country: A Bold Proposal to End the Israeli-Palestinian Impasse*. New York: Metropolitan Books, Henry Holt and Company.

———. 2016. "Debating Escalation of the War in Syria." *The Electronic Intifada*. November 4. https://electronicintifada.net/blogs/ali-abunimah/debating-escalation-war-syria.

Adraoui, Mohamed-Ali. 2017. "Jabhat Al-Nusra in the Syrian Conflict." *Oxford Research Group*. December 20. https://www.oxfordresearchgroup.org.uk/blog/jabhat-al-nusra-in-the-syrian-conflict.

Ahmed, Leila. 1992. *Women and Gender in Islam: Historical Roots of a Modern Debate*. New Haven, CT: Yale University Press.

———. 2011. *A Quiet Revolution: The Veil's Resurgence, from the Middle East to America*. New Haven, CT: Yale University Press.

Ahmed-Ullah, Noreen S., et al. 2004. "Hard-liners Won Battle for Bridgeview Mosque." *Chicago Tribune*. February 8. https://www.chicagotribune.com/news/chi-0402080265feb08-story.html.

Ahmed-Ullah, Noreen S., Sam Roe, and Laurie Cohen. 2004. "A Rare Look at Secretive Brotherhood in America." *Chicago Tribune*. September 19. http://www.chicagotribune.com/news/watchdog/chi-0409190261sep19-story.html.

Alba, Richard, and Victor Nee. 1997. "Rethinking Assimilation Theory for a New Era of Immigration." *International Migration Review* 31, no. 4 (Winter): 826–74.

Alonso, Andoni, and Pedro J. Oiarzabal. 2010. "The Immigrant Worlds' Digital Harbors: An Introduction." In *Diasporas in the New Media Age: Identity, Politics, and Community*, edited by Andoni Alonso and Pedro J. Oiarzabal, 1–15. Reno: University of Nevada Press.

Amer, Robin. 2013. "Forget Poles: Palestinians Find a Home in Suburban Chicago." *WBEZ91.5CHICAGO*. February 7. https://www.wbez.org/stories/_/b14f6828-24ad-4cca-973b-6a584502e862.

American Friends Service Committee. 2013. "AFSC Chicago Calls for Justice for Palestinian Activist." October 30. https://www.afsc.org/story/afsc-chicago-calls-justice-palestinian-activist.

Amghar, Samir, Amel Boubekeur, and Michael Emerson. 2007. *European Islam: Challenges for Society and Public Policy*. Brussels: CEPS.

Amireh, Amal. 2003. "Between Complicity and Subversion: Body Politics in Palestinian National Narrative." *South Atlantic Quarterly* 102, no. 4 (Fall): 747–72.

Amnesty International. 2019. "Israel/ OPT: Legally-Sanctioned Torture of Palestinian Detainee Left Him in Critical Condition." September 30. https://www.amnesty.org/en/latest/news/2019/09/israel-opt-legally-sanctioned-torture-of-palestinian-detainee-left-him-in-critical-condition.

Appadurai, Arjun. 1991. "Global Ethnoscapes: Notes and Queries for a Transnational Anthropology." In *Recapturing Anthropology: Working in the Present*, edited by Richard G. Fox, 191–210. Santa Fe, NM: School of American Research Press.

———. 1996. *Modernity At Large: Cultural Dimensions of Globalization*. Minneapolis: University of Minnesota Press.

Asad, Talal. 1993. *Genealogies of Religion: Discipline and Reasons of Power in Christianity and Islam*. Baltimore, MD: Johns Hopkins University Press.

———. 2003. *Formations of the Secular: Christianity, Islam, Modernity*. Stanford, CA: Stanford University Press.

Association of Religion Data Archives. 2017. "County Membership Report: Cook County, Religious Traditions, 2010." http://www.thearda.com/rcms2010/rcms2010.asp?U=17031&T=county&Y=2010&S=Name.

Ateek, Naim Stifan. 1989. *Justice, and Only Justice: A Palestinian Theology of Liberation*. Foreword by Rosemary Radford Ruether. Maryknoll, NY: Orbis.

———, Marc H. Ellis, and Rosemary Radford Ruether. 1992. *Faith and the Intifada: Palestinian Christian Voices*. Maryknoll, NY: Orbis.

Awad, Sami. 2016. "Christian Zionism and the Conflict." *Christ at the Checkpoint*. March 7–10. https://www.youtube.com/watch?v=JdAyhQ4iwvY.

El-Awaisi, Abd al-Fattah Muhammad. 1998. *The Muslim Brothers and the Palestine Question, 1928–1947*. London: Tauris Academic Studies.

Barbaro, Michael. 2019. "The Freshmen: Rashida Tlaib, Part 2." *The Daily* (podcast). May 14. https://www.nytimes.com/2019/05/14/podcasts/the-daily/rashida-tlaib-israel-palestinians.html.

Barlas, Asma. 2002. *"Believing Women" in Islam: Unreading Patriarchal Interpretations of the Qurʾān*. Austin: University of Texas Press.
Bates, Karen Grigsby. 2019. "Red Summer in Chicago: 100 Years after the Race Riots." *NPR Code Switch: Race. In Your Face*. July 27. https://www.npr.org/sections/codeswitch/2019/07/27/744130358/red-summer-in-chicago-100-years-after-the-race-riots.
BBC News. 2007. "British Muslims Poll: Key Points." January 29. http://news.bbc.co.uk/2/hi/6309983.stm.
———. 2015. "Syria's Beleaguered Christians." February 25. https://www.bbc.com/news/world-middle-east-22270455.
Al-Beit Jali, Iskandar al-Khouri. 1923. *Daqqat al-qalb* [Heartbeats]. Jerusalem: Bayt al-Maqdis.
Bender, Penny. 1995. "Jumping to Conclusions in Oklahoma City?" *American Journalism Review* 17, no. 5 (June): 11–12.
Bernal, Victoria. 2014. *Nation as Network: Diaspora, Cyberspace, and Citizenship*. Chicago: University of Chicago Press.
Best, Wallace. 2005. "Black Belt." *Electronic Encyclopedia of Chicago*. http://www.encyclopedia.chicagohistory.org/pages/140.html.
Bhabha, Homi K. 1994. *The Location of Culture*. London: Routledge.
Blackistone, Kevin B. 1981. "Arab Entrepreneurs Take Over Inner City Grocery Stores: Over 350 Stores in Chicago." *The Chicago Reporter* 10, no. 5 (May).
———, and Paula Corrigan. 1986. "Chicago's Arab-Americans Fight Ethnic Stereotypes." *The Chicago Reporter* 15, no. 4 (April).
Blumenthal, Max. 2012. "The Right to Resist Is Universal: A Farewell to Al Akhbar and Assad's Apologists." *Rise Up Times: Media for Justice and Peace*. July 31. https://riseuptimes.org/2012/07/31/part-i-blumenthal-the-right-to-resist-is-universal-a-farewell-to-al-akhbar-and-assads-apologists.
———. 2013. *Goliath: Life and Loathing in Greater Israel*. New York: Nation Books.
———. 2016. "Inside the Shadowy PR Firm that's Lobbying for Regime Change in Syria." *Off Guardian*. October 7. https://off-guardian.org/2016/10/07/world-inside-the-shadowy-pr-firm-thats-lobbying-for-regime-change-in-syria.
———. 2018. "How the Syrian American Medical Society Is Selling Regime Change and Driving the U.S. to War." *Truthdig*. April 12. https://www.truthdig.com/articles/how-the-syrian-american-medical-society-is-selling-regime-change-and-driving-the-u-s-to-war.
Bodnar, John. 1985. *The Transplanted: A History of Immigrants in Urban America*. Bloomington: Indiana University Press.
Bogle, Kathleen A. 2008. *Hooking Up: Sex, Dating, and Relationships on Campus*. New York: New York University Press.
Bowker, Robert. 2003. *Palestinian Refugees: Mythology, Identity, and the Search for Peace*. Boulder, CO: Lynne-Rienner.
Bowman, Glenn. 1993. "Nationalizing the Sacred: Shrines and Shifting Identities in the Israeli-Occupied Territories." *MAN* 28, no. 3: 431–60.
———. 2001. "Two Deaths of Basem Rishmawi: Identity Constructions and Reconstructions in a Muslim–Christian Palestinian Community." *Identities: Global Studies in Culture and Power* 8, no. 1: 47–81.
Broxmeyer, Eric. 2004. "The Problems of Security and Freedom: Procedural Due Process and the Designation of Foreign Terrorist Organizations under the Anti-Terrorism and Effective Death Penalty Act." *Berkeley Journal of International Law* 22, no. 3: 439–88.

Brachear, Manya A. 2010. "Muslim Liquor Store Owners Get Help with Moral Dilemma." *Chicago Tribune*. June 20. https://www.chicagotribune.com/news/ct-xpm-2010-06-20-ct-met-muslim-liquor-store-20100619-story.html.

Braude, Benjamin. 1982. "Foundation Myths of the Millet System." In *Christians and Jews in the Ottoman Empire: The Functioning of a Plural Society*, edited by Benjamin Braude and Bernard Lewis, 69–88. New York: Holmes and Meier.

Breton, Raymond. 2012. *Different Gods: Integrating Non-Christian Minorities into a Primarily Christian Society*. Montreal and Kingston: McGill-Queen's University Press.

Brinkerhoff, Jennifer M. 2009. *Digital Diasporas: Identity and Transnational Engagement*. Cambridge: Cambridge University Press.

Brooke, James, and Elaine Sciolino. 1995. "Bread or Bullets: Money for Hamas—A Special Report; US Muslims Say Their Aid Pays for Charity, Not Terror." *The New York Times*. August 16. http://www.nytimes.com/1995/08/16/us/bread-bullets-money-for-hamas-special-report-us-muslims-say-their-aid-pays-for.html.

Brubaker, Rogers. 2005. "The 'Diaspora' Diaspora." *Ethnic and Racial Studies* 28, no. 1: 1–19.

Brynjar, Lia. 1998. *The Society of the Muslim Brothers in Egypt: The Rise of an Islamic Mass Movement, 1928–1942*. Foreword by Jamal al-Banna. Reading, UK: Garnet.

B'tselem. 2011. "Mass Deportation of 1992." January 1. http://www.btselem.org/deportation/1992_mass_deportation.

Buder, Stanley. 1967. *Pullman: An Experiment in Industrial Order and Community Planning, 1880–1930*. New York: Oxford University Press.

Al-Bukhari, Muhammad Ibn Isma'il. c. 1971. *Sahih al-Bukhari. The Translation of the Meanings of Sahih al-Bukhari*. Arabic Text and English Translation in Parallel Columns, translated by Muhammad Muhsin Khan. Gujranwala: Taleem-ul-Quran Trust. Available at https://sunnah.com/bukhari.

Cainkar, Louise A. 1988. "Palestinian Women in the United States: Coping with Tradition, Change, and Alienation." PhD diss., Northwestern University.

———. 1998. "The Arab American Action Network: Meeting Community Needs, Building on Community Strengths." https://aaan.org/wp-content/uploads/2018/07/AAANneedsassessment.pdf.

———. 2004. "Islamic Revival among Second-Generation Arab-American Muslims: The American Experience and Globalization Intersect." *Bulletin of the Royal Institute for Inter-Faith Studies* 6, no. 2 (Autumn/Winter): 99–120.

———. 2006. "The Social Construction of Difference and the Arab American Experience." *Journal of American Ethnic History* 25, no. 2–3 (Winter/Spring): 243–78.

———. 2009. *Homeland Insecurity: The Arab American and Muslim American Experience after 9/11*. New York: Russell Sage, 2009.

Calder, Mark D. 2017. *Bethlehem's Syriac Christians: Self, Nation and Church in Dialogue and Practice*. Piscataway, NJ: Gorgias Press.

Campos, Michelle U. 2010. *Ottoman Brothers: Muslim, Christians, and Jews in Early 20th Century Palestine*. Stanford, CA: Stanford University Press.

Carey, Roane, ed. 2001. *The New Intifada: Resisting Israel's Apartheid*. London: Verso.

Carnegie Middle East Center. 2012. "The Muslim Brotherhood in Syria." February 1. https://carnegie-mec.org/diwan/48370.

Casanova, José. 2011. "The Secular, Secularizations, Secularisms." In *Rethinking Secularism*, edited by Craig Calhoun, Mark Juergensmeyer, and Jonathan VanAntwerpen, 54–74. New York: Oxford University Press.

Chamberlin, Paul Thomas. 2012. *The Global Offensive: The United States, the Palestine Liberation Organization, and the Making of the Post Cold War Order*. New York: Oxford University Press.
Chicago Commission on Race Relations. 1922. *The Negro in Chicago: A Study of Race Relations and a Race Riot*. Chicago: University of Chicago Press.
Chicago Public Library. n.d. "Housing and Race in Chicago." https://www.chipublib.org/housing.
Chittick, William C. 1983. *The Sufi Path of Love: The Spiritual Teachings of Rumi*. Albany: State University of New York Press.
Chollet, Derek. 2016. "Obama's Red Line, Revisited." *Politico*. July 19. https://www.politico.com/magazine/story/2016/07/obama-syria-foreign-policy-red-line-revisited-214059.
Chomsky, Noam. 1999 (1983). *The Fateful Triangle: The United States, Israel, and the Palestinians*. Updated Edition. Foreword by Edward W. Said. Chicago: Haymarket Books.
Chong, Kelly H. 2008. *Deliverance and Submission: Evangelical Women and the Negotiation of Patriarchy in South Korea*. Cambridge, MA: Harvard University Press.
Clifford, James. 1994. "Diasporas." *Cultural Anthropology* 9, no. 3 (August): 302–38.
Collins, John. 2011. *Global Palestine*. New York: Columbia University Press.
Confino, Alon. 1997. "Collective Memory and Cultural History: Problems of Method." *The American Historical Review* 102, no. 5 (December): 1386–1403.
Connerton, Paul. 1989. *How Societies Remember*. Cambridge, UK: Cambridge University Press.
Cook, David. 2005. *Understanding Jihad*. Berkeley: University of California Press.
Cook, Michael. 1996 (1983). *Muhammad*. Oxford: Oxford University Press.
———. 2000. *The Koran: A Very Short Introduction*. Oxford: Oxford University Press.
Crone, Patricia. 1987. *Meccan Trade and the Rise of Islam*. Princeton, NJ: Princeton University Press.
Dabaie, Marguerite. 2017. "Rasmea Odeh: Woman without a Country." *The Nib*. September 28. https://thenib.com/rasmea-odeh.
Daghash, Manar. 2015. "Arab American Action Network Youth Launch Anti-Profiling Campaign." *Chicago Monitor*. August 20. https://chicagomonitor.com/2015/08/arab-american-action-network-youth-launch-anti-profiling-campaign.
Damico, James S., and Loren D. Lybarger. 2016. "Commemoration, Testimony, and Protest in Argentina: An Exploration of Response and Responsibilities." *Ubiquity: The Journal of Literature, Literacy, and the Arts* 3, no. 1 (Spring): 7–44. http://ed-ubiquity.gsu.edu/wordpress/damico-and-lybarger-3-1/.
Dearden, Lizzie. 2014. "Israel-Gaza Conflict: 50-day War by Numbers." *The Independent*. August 27. http://www.independent.co.uk/news/world/middle-east/israel-gaza-conflict-50-day-war-by-numbers-9693310.html.
Deaux, Kay. 2006. *To Be an Immigrant*. New York: Russell Sage Foundation.
Donner, Fred M. 1998. *Narratives of Islamic Origins: The Beginnings of Islamic Historical Writing*. Princeton, NJ: The Darwin Press.
———. 2010. *Muhammad and the Believers at the Origins of Islam*. Cambridge, MA: Harvard University Belknap Press.
Dot-Pouillard, Nicolas. 2012. "Syria Divides the Arab Left." *Le Monde diplomatique*. August 4. https://mondediplo.com/2012/08/04syrialeft.
Doumani, Beshara. 1995. *Rediscovering Palestine: Merchants and Peasants in Jabal Nablus, 1700–1900*. Berkeley: University of California Press.

Drake, St. Clair, and Horace R. Cayton. 1993 (1945). *Black Metropolis: A Study of Negro Life in a Northern City*. Introduction by Richard Wright. Foreword by William Julius Wilson. Chicago: University of Chicago Press.

Droogers, André. 1989. "Syncretism: The Problem of Definition, The Definition of the Problem." In *Dialogue and Syncretism: An Inter-Disciplinary Approach*, edited by Jerald D. Gort, et al, 7–25. Grand Rapids: W.B. Eerdmans.

Dunham, Charlotte. 1998. "Generation Units and the Life Course: A Sociological Perspective on Youth and the Anti-War Movement." *Journal of Political and Military Sociology* 26, no. 2 (Winter): 137–55.

Eipper, Chris. 2011. "The Spectre of Godlessness: Making Sense of Secularity." *The Australian Journal of Anthropology* 22, no. 1 (April): 14–39.

Erakat, Noura. 2018. "Contemporary Renewals of Black-Palestinian Solidarity." November 27. Global Solidarities Lecture Series, Ohio University, Athens, OH.

Euben, Roxanne L. 1999. *Enemy in the Mirror: Islamic Fundamentalism and the Limits of Modern Rationalism: A Work of Comparative Political Theory*. Princeton, NJ: Princeton University Press.

———, and Muhammad Qasim Zaman, eds. 2009. *Princeton Readings in Islamist Thought: Texts and Contexts from al-Banna to Bin Laden*. Princeton, NJ: Princeton University Press.

Al-Faruqi, Lois Ibsen. 1985. "Music, Musicians, and Muslim Law." *Asian Music: Journal of the Society for Asian Music* 17, no. 1 (Fall/Winter): 3–36.

El Fassed, Arjan. 2004. "Naji al-Ali: The Timeless Conscience of Palestine." *The Electronic Intifada*. July 22. http://electronicintifada.net/content/naji-al-ali-timeless-conscience-palestine/5166.

Feldman, Keith P. 2015. *A Shadow over Palestine: The Imperial Life of Race in America*. Minneapolis: University of Minnesota Press.

Firestone, Reuven. 1999. *Jihad: The Origin of Holy War in Islam*. Oxford: Oxford University Press.

Fischbach, Michael R. 2019. *Black Power and Palestine: Transnational Countries of Color*. Stanford, CA: Stanford University Press.

Fountain, John W. 2001. "A Nation Challenged: African-American Muslims; Sadness and Fear as a Group Feels Doubly at Risk." *The New York Times*. October 5. http://www.nytimes.com/2001/10/05/us/nation-challenged-african-american-muslims-sadness-fear-group-feels-doubly-risk.html.

Frantzman, Seth J. 2016. "Moral Barometer: How the Syria Conflict Divided the Left, Pro-Palestinian Voices and Exposed a Murderous Support for Assad." August 30. https://sethfrantzman.com/2016/08/30/moral-barometer-how-the-syria-conflict-divided-the-left-pro-palestinian-voices-and-exposed-a-murderous-support-for-assad.

Freedman, Samuel G. 2014. "Building Bridges Where Needed on Chicago's South Side." *The New York Times*. November 15. https://www.nytimes.com/2014/11/15/us/building-bridges-where-needed-on-chicagos-south-side.html.

Frijda, Nico H. 1997. "Commemorating." In *Collective Memory of Political Events: Social Psychological Perspectives*, edited by James W. Pennebaker, Dario Paez, and Bernard Rimé, 103–27. Mahwah, NJ: Lawrence Erlbaum.

Frisch, Hillel. 2012. "The Demise of the PLO: Neither Diaspora nor Statehood." *Political Science Quarterly* 127, no. 2 (Summer): 241–61.

Frost, Warwick, and Jennifer Laing. 2013. *Commemorative Events: Memory, Identities, Conflicts*. London: Routledge.

Gamal, Wael. 2019. "Lost Capital: The Egyptian Muslim Brotherhood's Neoliberal Transformation." Carnegie Middle East Center. February 1. https://carnegie-mec.org/2019/02/01/lost-capital-egyptian-muslim-brotherhood-s-neoliberal-transformation-pub-78271.

Gans, Herbert J. 1992. "Second-Generation Decline: Scenarios for the Economic and Ethnic Futures of the Post-1965 American Immigrants." *Ethnic and Racial Studies* 15, no. 2: 173–92.

Gerges, Fawaz A. 2009 (2005). *The Far Enemy: Why Jihad Went Global*. Cambridge, UK: Cambridge University Press. di Giovani, Janine. 2018. "Why Assad and Russia Target the White Helmets." *New York Review of Books*. October 16. https://www.nybooks.com/daily/2018/10/16/why-assad-and-russia-target-the-white-helmets.

Al-Ghoul, Asmaa. 2013. "Do Gaza's Christians Feel Safe?" *Al-Monitor*. April 18. http://www.al-monitor.com/pulse/originals/2013/04/gaza-christians-safety.html.

———. 2014. "Vandals attack Catholic Church in Gaza." *Al-Monitor*. March 11. http://www.al-monitor.com/pulse/originals/2014/03/gaza-catholic-orthodox-church-attack-palestine.html.

Gitlin, Todd. 1996. *The Twilight of Common Dreams: Why America Is Wracked by Culture Wars*. New York: Holt.

Glass, Charles. 2018. "The Unjust Prosecution of the Holy Land Foundation Five." *The Intercept*. August 5. https://theintercept.com/2018/08/05/holy-land-foundation-trial-palestine-israel.

Goodman, Amy. 2007. "The Case of the L.A. 8: U.S. Drops 20-Year Effort to Deport Arab Americans for Supporting Palestinian National Rights." *Democracy Now!* November 2. https://www.democracynow.org/2007/11/2/the_case_of_the_la8_u.

Goodstein, Laurie, and Gustav Niebuhr. 2001. "After the Attacks: Retaliation; Attacks and Harassment of Arab-Americans Increase." *The New York Times*. September 14. http://www.nytimes.com/2001/09/14/us/after-the-attacks-retaliation-attacks-and-harassment-of-arab-americans-increase.html.

Gordon, Milton Myron. 1964. *Assimilation in American Life: The Role of Race, Religion, and National Origins*. New York: Oxford University Press.

Graeber, David. 2014 (2011). *Debt: The First 5,000 Years*. Brooklyn, NY: Mellville House.

Graham, Franklin. 2001. "Franklin Graham Calls Islam a 'Wicked and Evil' Religion." *Bowers Media Group*. https://www.youtube.com/watch?v=I5VF_0MhE54.

———. 2017. "Persecution of Christians Isn't Rare." *USA Today*. May 7. https://www.usatoday.com/story/opinion/2017/05/07/christian-persecution-world-egypt-iraq-mexico-column/101279550.

Grant, Teddy. 2019. "A Look Back on the Death of Mike Brown in Ferguson." *Ebony*. August 9. https://www.ebony.com/news/a-look-back-on-the-death-of-mike-brown-in-ferguson.

Grewal, Zareena. 2014. *Islam Is a Foreign Country: American Muslims and the Global Crisis of Authority*. New York: New York University Press.

Griffith, Sidney H. 2013. *The Bible in Arabic: The Scriptures of the 'People of the Book' in the Language of Islam*. Princeton, NJ: Princeton University Press.

Grimm, Andy, and Cynthia Dizikes. 2010. "FBI Raids Antiwar Activists' Homes." *Chicago Tribune*. September 24. https://www.chicagotribune.com/nation-world/ct-xpm-2010-09-24-ct-met-fbi-terrorism-investigation-20100924-story.html.

Gualtieri, Sarah M.A. 2009. *Between Arab and White: Race and Ethnicity in the Early Syrian American Diaspora*. Berkeley: University of California Press.

The Guardian. 2013. "Florida Pastor Terry Jones Arrested on Way to Burn Qur'ans." September 12. https://www.theguardian.com/world/2013/sep/12/florida-pastor-terry-jones-qurans.

———. 2015. "Islamic State Threatens to Topple Hamas in Gaza Strip in Video Statement." June 30. https://www.theguardian.com/world/2015/jun/30/islamic-state-threatens-hamas-gaza-strip.

———. 2017. "For Iraq's Christians, a Bittersweet First Christmas Home after ISIS Takeover." December 25. https://www.theguardian.com/world/2017/dec/25/for-iraqs-christians-a-bittersweet-first-christmas-home-after-isis-takeover.

Gunning, Jeroen. 2008. *Hamas in Politics: Democracy, Religion, Violence*. New York: Columbia University Press.

Gutiérrez, Gustavo. 1988 (1973). *A Theology of Liberation: History, Politics, and Salvation*, translated and edited by Sister Caridad Inda and John Eagleson. Maryknoll, NY: Orbis. Published originally as Gutiérrez, Gustavo. 1971. *Teología de la liberación: Perspectivas*. Lima: C.E.P.

Haaretz. 2017. "Trump Introduced at Liberty University as the 'Man Who Bombs the Middle East.'" May 14. https://www.haaretz.com/us-news/trump-addresses-liberty-univeristy-1.5471879.

Haberman, Clyde. 1992. "Israel Expels 400 from Occupied Lands; Lebanese Deploy to Bar Entry of Palestinians." *The New York Times*. December 18. http://www.nytimes.com/1992/12/18/world/israel-expels-400-occupied-lands-lebanese-deploy-bar-entry-palestinians.html.

Haddad, Robert M. 1970. *Syrian Christians in a Muslim Society: An Interpretation*. Princeton, NJ: Princeton University Press.

Halbwachs, Maurice. 1992. *On Collective Memory*, edited and translated with an introduction by Lewis A. Coser. Chicago: University of Chicago Press.

Hall, John R. 1992. "The Capital(s) of Cultures: A Nonholistic Approach to Status Situations, Class, Gender, and Ethnicity." In *Cultivating Differences: Symbolic Boundaries and the Making of Inequality*, edited by Michèle Lamont and Marcel Fournier, 257–88. Chicago: University of Chicago Press.

Hall, Stuart. 1990. "Cultural Identity and Diaspora." In *Identity: Community, Culture, Difference*, edited by Jonathan Rutherford, 222–37. London: Lawrence and Wishart.

Hack, Chris, and Allison Hantschel. 2003. "US Investigating Mosque Foundation." *Daily Southtown*. September 23. http://www.religionnewsblog.com/4563/us-investigating-mosque-foundation.

Hanania, Ray. 2015. "Street Named in Honor of Tearing Icon of Virgin Mary." *The Arab Daily News*. March 30. http://thearabdailynews.com/2015/03/30/street-named-in-honor-of-tearing-icon-of-virgin-mary.

Hashimi, Muhammad Ali. 1998. *The Ideal Muslimah*, translated by Nasiruddin al-Khattab. Riyadh, Saudi Arabia: International Islamic Publishing House.

Hayden, Michael Edison. 2017. "Muslims 'Absolutely' the Group Most Victimized by Global Terrorism, Researchers Say." *ABC News*. June 20. https://abcnews.go.com/Politics/muslims-absolutely-group-victimized-global-terrorism-researchers/story?id=48131273.

Hedges, Chris, and Joel Greenberg. 1994. "West Bank Massacre: Before Killing, Final Prayer and Final Taunt." *The New York Times*. February 28. https://www.nytimes.com/1994/02/28/world/west-bank-massacre-before-killing-final-prayer-and-final-taunt.html.

Heilman, Samuel C. 2006. *Sliding to the Right: The Contest for the Future of American Jewish Orthodoxy*. Berkeley: University of California Press.

Hiltermann, Joost R. 1991. *Behind the Intifada: Labor and Women's Movements in the Occupied Territories*. Princeton, NJ: Princeton University Press.

Hintilian, George. 1998. "Armenians of Jerusalem." *Journal of Palestine Studies* 2: 40–44. http://www.palestine-studies.org/jq/fulltext/78237.

Hirsch, Arnold R. 1983. *Making the Second Ghetto: Race and Housing in Chicago, 1940–1960*. Cambridge, UK: Cambridge University Press.

Hroub, Khaled 2000. *Hamas: Political Thought and Practice*. Washington, DC: Institute for Palestine Studies.

Human Rights Watch. 2014. "All According to Plan: The Rab'a Massacre and Mass Killings of Protestors in Egypt." August 12. https://www.hrw.org/report/2014/08/12/all-according-plan/raba-massacre-and-mass-killings-protesters-egypt.

Hunter, F. Robert. 1991. *The Palestinian Uprising: A War by Other Means*. Berkeley: University of California Press.

Inskeep, Steve. 2017. "History of Our Time: Is Islam Compatible with Democracy." *National Public Radio*. June 20. https://www.npr.org/2017/06/20/533617455/history-of-our-time-how-americans-view-islam.

Issawi, Charles. 1982. "The Transformation of the Economic Position of the *Millets* in the Nineteenth Century." In *Christians and Jews in the Ottoman Empire: The Function of a Plural Society*, edited by Benjamin Braude and Bernard Lewis, 261–85. New York: Holmes and Meier.

Jamal, Amaney, and Nadine Naber, eds. 2008. *Race and Arab Americans Before and After 9/11: From Invisible Citizens to Visible Subjects*. Syracuse, NY: Syracuse University Press.

Jay, Paul. 2012. "Max Blumenthal Resigns Al Akhbar over Syria Coverage." *The Real News Network*. June 22. https://therealnews.com/stories/mblumenthal0621.

Joppke, Christian. 2017. "Blaming Secularism." Review of Saba Mahmood, *Religious Difference in a Secular Age: A Minority Report* (Princeton, Princeton University Press, 2016). *European Journal of Sociology* 58, no. 3: 577–89.

Joseph, Suad. 1993. "Connectivity and Patriarchy among Urban Working-Class Arab Families in Lebanon." *Ethos: Journal of the Society for Psychological Anthropology* 21, no. 4 (December): 452–84.

Jouvenal, Justin, and Julie Zauzmer. 2017. "Killing of Muslim Teen near Va. Mosque Stemmed from Road Rage, Police Say." *The Washington Post*. June 19. https://www.washingtonpost.com/local/public-safety/killing-of-muslim-teenager-not-being-investigated-as-a-hate-crime-police-say/2017/06/19/e7670f0a-54f0-11e7-ba90-f5875b7d1876_story.html.

Kalberg, Stephen. 2012. *Max Weber's Comparative-Historical Sociology Today: Major Themes, Mode of Causal Analysis, and Applications*. Burlington, VT: Ashgate.

Kanazi, Remi. 2011. *Poetic Injustice: Writings on Resistance and Palestine*. New York: RoR Publishing.

Kansteiner, Wulf. 2002. "Finding Meaning in Memory: A Methodological Critique of Collective Memory Studies." *History and Theory* 41, no. 2 (May): 179–97.

Karim, Jamillah. 2009. *American Muslim Women: Negotiating Race, Class, and Gender within the Ummah*. New York: New York University Press.

Kårtveit, Bård Helge. 2014. *Dilemmas of Attachment: Identity and Belonging among Palestinian Christians*. Leiden: Brill.

Kastoryano, Riva. 2002. *Negotiating Identities: States and Immigrants in France and Germany*, translated by Barbara Harshav. Princeton, NJ: Princeton University Press.

Keating, Joshua. 2019. "The Uproar over Ilhan Omar's Israel Tweets Is a Sign of Things to Come." *Slate*. February 11. https://slate.com/news-and-politics/2019/02/ilhan-omar-israel-twitter-controversy-democrats-bds.html.

Khabeer, Su'ad Abdul. 2016. *Muslim Cool: Race, Religion, and Hip Hop in the United States*. New York: New York University Press.

Khalidi, Omar. 2009. "Indian Muslims and Palestinian Awqaf." *Jerusalem Quarterly* 40: 52–58.

Khalidi, Rashid. 1997. *Palestinian Identity: The Construction of Modern National Consciousness*. New York: Columbia University Press.

Khoury, Buthina Canaan. 2004. "Women in Struggle." Documentary film. https://www.youtube.com/watch?v=v0Va7-cNxf8.

Kimmerling, Baruch, and Joel S. Migdal. 2003 (1994). *The Palestinian People: A History*. Cambridge, MA: Harvard University Press.

Kingsley, Patrick. 2017. "Decimated Muslim Brotherhood Still Inspires Fear. Its Members Wonder Why." *The New York Times*. July 15. https://www.nytimes.com/2017/07/15/world/europe/muslim-brotherhood-qatar-egypt-turkey-saudi-arabia.html.

Kivisto, Peter. 2014. *Religion and Immigration*. Cambridge, UK: Polity Press.

Krämer, Gudrun. 2008. *A History of Palestine: From the Ottoman Conquest to the Founding of the State of Israel*, translated by Graham Harman and Gudrun Krämer. Princeton, NJ: Princeton University Press.

Kreager, Derek A., and Jeremy Staff. 2009. "The Sexual Double Standard and Adolescent Peer Acceptance." *Social Psychology Quarterly* 72, no. 2 (June): 143–64.

Kruse, Kevin M. 2005. *White Flight: Atlanta and the Making of Modern Conservatism*. Princeton, NJ: Princeton University Press.

Kupferschmidt, Uri M. 1987. *The Supreme Muslim Council: Islam under the British Mandate for Palestine*. Leiden: Brill.

Lagopoulos, Alexandros PH. 2011. "Subjectivism, Postmodernism, and Social Space." *Semiotica* 183, no. 1: 129–82.

Lauzière, Henri. 2016. *The Making of Salafism: Islamic Reform in the Twentieth Century*. New York: Columbia University Press.

Lazreg, Marnia. 2009. *Questioning the Veil: Open Letters to Muslim Women*. Princeton, NJ: Princeton University Press.

Levinson, Chaim. 2011. "Nearly 100% of All Military Court Cases in West Bank End in Conviction, Haaretz Learns." *Haaretz*. November 29. https://www.haaretz.com/1.5214377.

Levitt, Matthew. 2006. *Hamas: Politics, Charity, and Terrorism in the Service of Jihad*. New Haven, CT, and London, UK: Yale University Press and the Washington Institute for Near East Policy, 2006.

Lewis, Donald M. 2010. *The Origins of Christian Zionism: Lord Shaftesbury and Evangelical Support for a Jewish Homeland*. Cambridge, UK: Cambridge University Press.

Lichtblau, Eric. 2016. "U.S. Hate Crimes Surge 6%, Fueled by Attacks on Muslims." *The New York Times*. November 14. https://www.nytimes.com/2016/11/15/us/politics/fbi-hate-crimes-muslims.html.

Livezey, Lowell W. 2000. "The New Context of Urban Religion." In *Public Religion and Urban Transformation: Faith in the City*, edited by Lowell W. Livezey, 3–28. Epilogue by R. Stephen Warner. New York: New York University Press.

Lockman, Zachary, and Joel Beinin, eds. 1989. *Intifada: The Palestinian Uprising against Israeli Occupation*. Boston, MA: South End Press and MERIP.

Logan, John R., and Charles Zhang. 2010. "Global Neighborhoods: New Pathways to Diversity and Separation." *American Journal of Sociology* 115, no. 4 (January): 1069–1109.

Lubin, David C. 2008. "From Bohemian to Brown: Global Migration and the Changing Complexion of a Chicago Suburb." Paper presented at the American Sociological Association, Boston, MA, August.

Lutfiyya, Abdulla. 1966. *Baytīn, a Jordanian Village: A Study of Social Institutions and Social Change in Folk Community*. The Hague: Mouton and Company.

Lybarger, Loren D. 2005. "Palestinian Political Identities during the Post-Oslo Period: A Case Study of Generation Effects in a West Bank Refugee Camp." *Social Compass* 52, no. 2: 143–56.

———. 2007a. *Identity and Religion in Palestine: The Struggle between Islamism and Secularism in the Occupied Territories*. Princeton, NJ: Princeton University Press.

———. 2007b. "For Church or Nation? Islamism, Secular Nationalism, and the Transformation of Christian Identities in Palestine." *Journal of the American Academy of Religion* 75, no. 4 (December): 777–813.

———. 2013. "Other Worlds to Live In: Palestinian Retrievals of Religion and Tradition under Conditions of Chronic National Collapse." In *Palestine and the Palestinians in the 21st Century*, edited by Rochelle Davis and Mimi Kirk, 158–87. Bloomington: Indiana University Press and the Center for Contemporary Arab Studies, Georgetown University.

———. 2014. "Nationalism and the Contingency of the Religious Return among Second-Generation Palestinian Immigrants in the United States: A Chicago Case Study." *The Muslim World* 104, no. 3 (July): 250–80.

Maher, Shiraz. 2016. *Salafi-Jihadism: The History of an Idea*. Oxford: Oxford University Press.

Mahmood, Saba. 2005. *Politics of Piety: The Islamic Revival and the Feminist Subject*. Princeton, NJ: Princeton University Press.

———. 2006. "Secularism, Hermeneutics, and Empire: The Politics of Islamic Reformation." *Public Culture* 18, no. 2: 323–47.

———. 2010. "Can Secularism Be Other-wise?" In *Varieties of Secularism in a Secular Age*, edited by Michael Warner, Jonathan VanAntwerpen, and Craig Calhoun, 282–99. Cambridge, MA: Harvard University Press.

———. 2016. *Religious Difference in a Secular Age: A Minority Report*. Princeton, NJ: Princeton University Press.

Malik, Kenan. 2009. *From Fatwa to Jihad: The Rushdie Affair and its Legacy*. London: Atlantic Books.

Mandaville, Peter. 2001. *Transnational Muslim Politics: Reimagining the Umma*. London: Routledge.

Mannheim, Karl. 1952. "The Problem of Generations." In *Essays on the Sociology of Knowledge*, edited by Paul Kecskemeti, 276–322. London: Routledge & Kegan Paul.

Martin, David. 2014. *Religion and Power: No Logos without Mythos*. Burlington, VT: Ashgate.

Massey, Doreen. 2005. *For Space*. London: Sage.

Masters, Bruce. 2001. *Christians and Jews in the Ottoman Arab World: The Roots of Sectarianism*. Cambridge, UK: Cambridge University Press.

Mattar, Phillip. 1988. *The Mufti of Jerusalem: Al-Hajj Amin Al-Husayni and the Palestinian National Movement*. New York: Columbia University Press.

Mayer, Harold M., and Richard C. Wade. 1969. *Chicago: Growth of a Metropolis*. Chicago: University of Chicago Press.

McFalls, Laurence, ed. 2007. *Max Weber's 'Objectivity' Reconsidered*. Toronto: University of Toronto Press.

Merritt, Jonathan. 2015. "Franklin Graham's Turn Toward Intolerance." *The Atlantic*. July 19. https://www.theatlantic.com/politics/archive/2015/07/franklin-grahams-turn-toward-intolerance/398924.

Mikics, David. 2015. "Wild Thing: Max Blumenthal's Creepy Anti-Zionist Odyssey." *Tablet*. March 10. https://www.tabletmag.com/jewish-arts-and-culture/189172/max-blumenthal-and-anti-zionists.

Millar, Stuart. 2001. "Violent Attacks on Arab Americans, Special Report: Terrorism in the US." *The Guardian*. September 14. http://www.theguardian.com/world/2001/sep/14/september11.usa14.

Miller, Erin. 2016. "Patterns of Islamic State-Related Terrorism, 2002–2015." START Background Report. College Park, MD. https://www.start.umd.edu/pubs/START_IslamicStateTerrorismPatterns_BackgroundReport_Aug2016.pdf.

Milton-Edwards, Beverley. 1996. *Islamic Politics in Palestine*. London: I.B. Tauris.

———, and Stephen Farrell. 2010. *Hamas: The Islamic Resistance Movement*. Cambridge, UK: Polity.

Mishal, Shaul, and Avraham Sela. 2000. *The Palestinian Hamas: Vision, Violence, and Coexistence*. New York: Columbia University Press.

Al-Misri, Ahmad Ibn Naqib. 1994 (1991). *Reliance of the Traveller: A Classic Manual of Islamic Sacred Law*, edited and translated by Nuh Ha Mim Keller. Beltsville, MD: Amana Publications.

Moaddel, Mansoor, and Kamran Talattof, eds. 2000. *Modernist and Fundamentalist Debates in Islam: A Reader*. New York: Palgrave.

Moghul, Haroon. 2015. "An American Muslim Responds to Muslim Orgs Questioning of Armenian Genocide." *Religion Dispatches*. April 24. http://religiondispatches.org/an-american-muslim-responds-to-muslim-orgs-questioning-armenian-genocide.

Moore, Natalie. 2011. "Chicago School to Expand Arabic Offerings to District, Community." *WBEZ 91.5 CHICAGO*. August 30. https://www.wbez.org/shows/wbez-news/chicago-school-to-expand-arabic-offerings-to-district-community/6e316709-c48a-497b-8a4a-6af8655c9376.

———. 2012. "Race Out Loud: Arab Store Owner on Working in Englewood." *WBEZ 91.5 CHICAGO*. August 27. https://www.wbez.org/shows/race-out-loud/race-out-loud-arab-store-owner-on-working-in-englewood/7004fceb-dddd-478b-830f-ce060421d593.

Moser, Whet. 2013. "How Poverty Moved to Chicago's Suburbs." *Chicago Magazine*. June 24. https://www.chicagomag.com/Chicago-Magazine/The-312/June-2013/The-Suburbanization-of-Poverty-in-Chicagoland-1980-2010/.

Mouline, Nabil. 2014. *The Clerics of Islam: Religious Authority and Political Power in Saudi Arabia*, translated by Ethan S. Rundell. New Haven, CT: Yale University Press.

Mullen, William, and Vikki Ortiz-Healy. 2011. "Chicago's Population Drops 200,000." *Chicago Tribune*. February 11. https://www.chicagotribune.com/news/ct-xpm-2011-02-15-ct-met-2010-census-20110215-story.html.

Musa, Ibrahim Namir. 2012. *Iskandar al-Khouri al-Beit Jali: hayatuhu wa shiʻruhu al-watani (dirasa mawduʻiya fanniya)* [Iskandar al-Khouri al-Beit Jali: His Life and Nationalist Poetry (an objective technical study)]. Palestine: Beir Zeit University.

Mustufa, Asraa. 2018. "Rasmea Odeh, Deported but not Defeated." *The Chicago Reporter*. October 1. https://www.chicagoreporter.com/rasmea-odeh-deported-but-not-defeated.

Naber, Nadine. 2012. *Arab America: Gender, Cultural Politics, and Activism*. New York: New York University Press.

———. 2014. "Justice for Rasmea Odeh." *MERIP*. June 19. https://merip.org/2014/06/justice-for-rasmea-odeh.

Nagel, Caroline R., and Lynn A. Staeheli. 2011. "Muslim Political Activism or Political Activism by Muslims?: Secular and Religious Identities amongst Muslim Arab Activists in the United States and United Kingdom." *Identities: Global Studies in Culture and Power* 18, no. 5 (June): 437–58.

Najjar, Farah. 2018. "Syria's Yarmouk Camp: From a 'War on Stomachs' to 'Annihilation.'" *Al Jazeera*. April 24. https://www.aljazeera.com/news/2018/04/syria-yarmouk-camp-war-stomachs-annihilation-180423212111918.html.

Nasaw, Daniel. 2008. "Leaders of Muslim Charity in US Found Guilty of Providing Funds to Hamas." *The Guardian*. November 24. https://www.theguardian.com/world/2008/nov/24/holy-land-foundation-gaza-hamas.

Nashashibi, Rami. 2009. "The Blackstone Legacy: Islam and the Rise of Ghetto Cosmopolitanism." In *Black Routes to Islam*, edited by Manning Marable and Hishaam D. Aidi, 271–82. New York: Palgrave.

Neuhaus, David Mark. 1991. "Between Quiescence and Arousal: The Political Functions of Religion: A Case Study of the Arab Minority in Israel: 1948–1990." PhD diss, Hebrew University.

Noth, Albrecht, and Lawrence I. Conrad. 1994. *The Early Arabic Historical Tradition: A Source-Critical Study*. Studies in Late Antiquity and Early Islam 3, translated by Michael Bonner. Princeton, NJ: The Darwin Press.

Numrich, Paul D. 2012. "Emergence of the Rhetoric of a Unified *Ummah* among American Muslims: The Case of Metropolitan Chicago." *Journal of Muslim Minority Affairs* 32, no. 4: 450–66.

———, and Elfriede Wedam. 2015. *Religion and Community in the New Urban America*. New York: Oxford University Press.

Nüsse, Andrea. 1998. *Muslim Palestine: The Ideology of Hamas*. Amsterdam: Harwood Academic Publishers.

Oschinsky, Lawrence. 1947. "Islam in Chicago: Being a Study of the Acculturation of a Muslim Palestinian Community in that City." MA Thesis, University of Chicago.

Otterbeck, Jonas. 2004. "Music as Useless Activity: Conservative Interpretation of Music in Islam." In *Shoot the Singer! Music Censorship Today*, edited by Marie Korpe, 11–16. London: Zed.

Palestinian Academic Society for the Study of International Affairs (PASSIA). 2019. "Al-Beit Jali, Iskandar al-Khouri (1890–1973)." http://www.passia.org/personalities/505.

Palestinian Campaign for the Academic and Cultural Boycott of Israel. 2009. "*Bayan lil-raʼy al-ʻam hawla al-musharaka al-israʼiliya fi faʻaliya musiqiya fi ramallah* [Public Statement Regarding Israeli Participation in a Musical Activity in Ramallah.]" July 14. http://www.pacbi.org/atemplate.php?id=145.

———. 2010. "PACBI: West-Eastern Divan Orchestra Violates Boycott." *The Electronic Intifada*. March 24. https://electronicintifada.net/content/pacbi-west-eastern-divan-orchestra-violates-boycott/1040.

———. 2012. "A Letter Regarding UN Sponsorship of Joint Palestinian-Israeli Orchestra." July 24. https://bdsmovement.net/news/letter-regarding-un-sponsorship-joint-palestinian-israeli-orchestra.

Palmer, Jamie. 2016. "The Pro-Palestinian Left Is Tearing Itself Apart over Syria." *The Tower* 44 (November). http://www.thetower.org/article/the-pro-palestinian-left-is-tearing-itself-apart-over-syria.

Pennock, Pamela E. 2017. *The Rise of the Arab American Left: Activists, Allies, and Their Fight against Imperialism and Racism, 1960s–1980s*. Chapel Hill: The University of North Carolina Press.

Peters, F.E. 1994. *Muhammad and the Origins of Islam*. Albany: State University of New York Press.

Peters, Joel, and David Newman, eds. 2013. *The Routledge Handbook on the Israeli-Palestinian Conflict*. New York: Routledge.

Pew Research Center. 2007. "Muslim Americans: Middle Class and Mostly Mainstream." May 22. http://www.pewresearch.org/2007/05/22/muslim-americans-middle-class-and-mostly-mainstream.

———. 2011. "Muslim Americans: No Signs of Growth in Alienation or Support for Extremism." August 30. http://www.peoplepress.org/2011/08/30/muslim-americans-no-signs-of-growth-in-alienation-or-support-for-extremism.

Philpott, Thomas Lee. 1991. *The Slum and the Ghetto: Immigrants, Blacks, and Reformers in Chicago, 1880–1930*. Belmont, CA: Wadsworth.

Portes, Alejandro, and Min Zhou. 1993. "The New Second Generation: Assimilation and Its Variants." *The Annals of the American Academy of Political and Social Science* 530 (November): 74–96.

Prothero, Stephen. 2018. "Billy Graham Built a Movement. Now His Son is Dismantling It." *Politico*. February 24. https://www.politico.com/magazine/story/2018/02/24/billy-graham-evangelical-decline-franklin-graham-217077.

Ramadan, Tariq. 2004. *Western Muslims and the Future of Islam*. Oxford: Oxford University Press.

Report of the Commissioner-General of the United Nations Relief and Works Agency for Palestine Refugees in the Near East. 1966–1967. General Assembly Official Records: Twenty-Second Session Supplement, no. 13 (A/6713). July 1,–June 30. https://unispal.un.org/DPA/DPR/unispal.nsf/eed216406b50bf6485256ce10072f637/2a43e4d980f2c20685256a48004d0424.

Riedel, Barnaby B. 2009. "The Character Conjuncture: Islamic Education and its Social Reproduction in the United States." PhD diss, University of Chicago.

Riesebrodt, Martin. 1993. *Pious Passion: The Emergence of Modern Fundamentalism in the United States and Iran*, translated by Don Reneau. Berkeley: University of California Press.

———. 2010. *The Promise of Salvation: A Theory of Religion*, translated by Steven Rendall. Chicago: University of Chicago Press.

———. 2014. "Secularisms: Ideals, Ideologies, and Institutional Practices: An International Conference Organised under the Auspices of the Yves Oltramare Chair on Religion and Politics in the Contemporary World. Opening Remarks." The Graduate Institute,

Geneva, Switzerland: September 25–27. https://www.scribd.com/document/241464183/Secularisms-Ideals-Ideologies-and-Institutional-Practices-International-Conference-25-27-September-2014.

———, and Kelly H. Chong. 1999. "Fundamentalism and Patriarchal Gender Politics." *Journal of Women's History* 10, no. 4 (Winter): 55–77.

Riessman, Catherine Kohler. 2008. *Narrative Methods for the Human Sciences*. London: Sage.

Robbins, Bruce. 1994. "Secularism, Elitism, Progress, and Other Transgressions: On Edward Said's 'Voyage in.'" *Social Text*, no. 40 (Autumn): 25–37.

Robles, Jennifer Jaurez. 1989. "Captive Grocery Market Pits Blacks against Arabs." *The Chicago Reporter* 18, no. 10 (November).

Rockett, Darcel. 2019. "100 Years of History: Timuel Black Takes Readers through Chicago Streets in 'Sacred Ground.'" *Chicago Tribune*. January 28. https://www.chicagotribune.com/entertainment/books/ct-books-timuel-black-0127-story.html.

Roediger, David R. 2005. *Working Toward Whiteness: How America's Immigrants Became White: The Strange Journey from Ellis Island to the Suburbs*. New York: Basic Books.

Rothstein, Richard. 2017. *The Color of Law: A Forgotten History of How Our Government Segregated America*. New York: W. W. Norton.

Roy, Olivier. 2004. *Globalized Islam: The Search for a New Ummah*. New York: Columbia University Press.

Roy, Sara. 2001 (1995). *The Gaza Strip: The Political Economy of De-Development*. Washington, DC: The Institute for Palestine Studies.

———. 2007. Review of *Hamas: Politics, Charity, and Terrorism in the Service of Jihad* by Matthew Levitt. *Middle East Policy* 14, no. 2 (Summer): 162–66. https://mepc.org/hamas-politics-charity-and-terrorism-service-jihad.

———. 2011. *Hamas and Civil Society: Engaging the Islamist Social Sector*. Princeton, NJ: Princeton University Press.

Saad, Hwaida, and Ben Hubbard. 2013. "Bombings Strike Lebanon, as Mosques Are Targeted in Growing Violence." *The New York Times*. August 23. https://www.nytimes.com/2013/08/24/world/middleeast/lebanon-bomb-attacks.html.

Sabeel Ecumenical Liberation Theology Center. 2016. *Contemporary Way of the Cross: A Liturgical Journey along the Palestinian Via Dolorosa*. http://sabeel.org/2016/06/08/contemporary-way-of-the-cross-3.

Safi, Omid, ed. 2003. *Progressive Muslims: On Justice, Gender, and Pluralism*. London: One World.

Said, Edward W. 1978. *Orientalism*. New York: Vintage Books.

———. 1979. *The Question of Palestine*. New York: Vintage Books.

———. 1993. *Culture and Imperialism*. New York: Vintage Books.

———, and Sut Jhally. 2005. "Edward Said on 'Orientalism.'" Transcript. Documentary film. Northhampton, MA: Media Education Foundation. https://www.mediaed.org/transcripts/Edward-Said-On-Orientalism-Transcript.pdf.

Said, Mariam. 2010. "Barenboim-Said Foundation Does not Promote Normalization." *The Electronic Intifada*. March 17. https://electronicintifada.net/content/barenboim-said-foundation-does-not-promote-normalization/8728.

Saint-Blancat, Chantal. 2002. "Islam in Diaspora: Between Reterritorialization and Extraterritoriality." *International Journal of Urban and Regional Research* 26, no. 1 (March): 138–51.

———. 2004. "La transmission de l'islam auprès des nouvelles générations de la diaspora." *Social Compass* 51, no. 2: 235–47.

Salaita, Steven. 2013/2014. Review of *Goliath: Life and Loathing in Greater Israel* by Max Blumenthal. *Journal of Palestine Studies* 43, no. 3: 76.

Sander, Libby. 2007. "Two Men Cleared of Charges of Aiding Hamas Violence." *The New York Times*. February 2. http://www.nytimes.com/2007/02/02/us/02chicago.html.

Satter, Beryl. 2009. *Family Properties: Race, Real Estate, and the Exploitation of Black Urban America*. New York: Henry Holt.

Sayigh, Rosemary. 1979. *Palestinians: From Peasants to Revolutionaries*. London: Zed.

Sayigh, Yezid. 1997. *Armed Struggle and the Search for State: The Palestinian National Movement, 1949–1993*. Oxford: Oxford University Press.

Scherer, Michael. 2008. "Rahm Emanuel's Father Problem." *Time*. November 13. http://swampland.time.com/2008/11/13/rahm-emanuels-father-problem.

Schiff, Ze'ev, and Ehud Ya'ari. 1990 (1989). *Intifada: The Palestinian Uprising—Israel's Third Front*, translated by Ina Friedman. New York: Simon and Schuster.

Schleifer, Abdallah. 1993. "Izz al-Din al-Qassam: Preacher and *Mujahid*." In *Struggle and Survival in the Modern Middle East*, edited by Edmund Burke III and David Yaghoubian, 164–98. London: I.B. Tauris.

Schmidt, Garbi. 2004. *Islam in Urban America: Sunni Muslims in Chicago*. Philadelphia: Temple University Press.

Schuman, Howard, and Jacqueline Scott. 1989. "Generations and Collective Memories." *American Sociological Review* 54, no. 3 (June): 359–81.

Scott, Rachel M. 2010. *The Challenge of Political Islam: Non-Muslims and the Egyptian State*. Stanford, CA: Stanford University Press.

Seikaly, Sherene. 2016. *Men of Capital: Scarcity and Economy in Mandate Palestine*. Stanford, CA: Stanford University Press.

Self, Robert O. 2003. *American Babylon: Race and the Struggle for Postwar Oakland*. Princeton, NJ: Princeton University Press.

Serhan, Randa Bassem. 2009. "Suspended Community: An Ethnographic Study of Palestinian-Americans in New York and New Jersey." PhD diss, Columbia University.

Sewell, William H., Jr. 1996. "Historical Events as Transformations of Structures: Inventing Revolution at the Bastille." *Theory and Society* 25, no. 6 (December): 841–81.

Sharkey, Heather J. 2017. *A History of Muslims, Christians, and Jews in the Middle East*. Cambridge, UK: Cambridge University Press.

Sherwood, Harriet. 2018. "Christians in Egypt Face Unprecedented Persecution, Report Says." *The Guardian*. January 10. https://www.theguardian.com/world/2018/jan/10/christians-egypt-unprecedented-persecution-report.

Shikaki, Khalil. 2001. "Old Guard, Young Guard: The Palestinian Authority and the Peace Process at Crossroads." Ramallah, Palestine: Palestinian Centre for Policy and Survey Research. November 1. http://www.pcpsr.org/en/node/488.

Shiloah, Amnon. 1997. "Music and Religion in Islam." *Acta Musicologica* 69, fasc. 2 (July–December): 143–55.

Shotter, John. 1997 (1990). "The Social Construction of Remembering and Forgetting." In *Collective Remembering*, edited by David Middleton and Derek Edwards, 120–38. London: Sage.

Silver, Charlotte. 2016. "Judge Orders New Trial for Rasmea Odeh." *The Electronic Intifada*. December 7. https://electronicintifada.net/blogs/charlotte-silver/judge-orders-new-trial-rasmea-odeh.

Simmel, Georg. 1955 (1922). "The Web of Group Affiliations." In *Conflict and the Web of Group Affiliations*, translated by Kurt H. Wolff and Reinhard Bendix, 125–95. New York: Free Press.

———. 2009. *Sociology: Inquiries into the Construction of Social Forms*, translated and edited by Anthony J. Blasi, Anton K. Jacobs, and Mathew Kanjirathinkal. Leiden: Brill.

Smith, Carl. 1995. *Urban Disorder and the Shape of Belief: The Great Chicago Fire, The Haymarket Bomb, and the Model Town of Pullman*. Chicago: University of Chicago Press.

Smith, Christian. 1998. *American Evangelicalism: Embattled and Thriving*. Chicago: University of Chicago Press.

Sniderman, Paul M., and Louk Hagendoorn. 2007. *When Ways of Life Collide: Multiculturalism and Its Discontents in the Netherlands*. Princeton, NJ: Princeton University Press.

Southern Poverty Law Center. 2018. "Report: Rise in Hate Violence Tied to 2016 Presidential Election." March 1. https://www.splcenter.org/hatewatch/2018/03/01/report-rise-hate-violence-tied-2016-presidential-election.

Spector, Stephen. 2009. *Evangelicals and Israel: The Story of American Christian Zionism*. New York: Oxford University Press.

Squires, Gregory D., et al. 1987. *Chicago: Race, Class, and the Response to Urban Decline*. Philadelphia: Temple University Press.

Staton, Bethan. 2015. "The Women of Al-Aqsa: The Compound's Self-Appointed Guardians: Meet The Murabitats Who Say They Protect Al-Aqsa But Have Been Accused of Pushing and Grabbing Jewish Visitors." *Middle East Eye*. February 13. https://www.middleeasteye.net/news/women-al-aqsa-compounds-self-appointed-guardians.

Stewart, Charles. 1999. "Syncretism and Its Synonyms: Reflections on Cultural Mixture." *Diacritics* 29, no. 3: 40–62.

———, and Rosalind Shaw, eds. 1994. *Syncretism / Anti-Syncretism: The Politics of Religious Synthesis*. London: Routledge.

Stults, Brian J. 2010. "Determinants of Chicago Neighborhood Homicide Trajectories: 1965–1995." *Homicide Studies* 14, no. 3: 244–67.

Suleiman, Michael W. 1996. "The Arab-American Left." In *The Immigrant Left in the United States*, edited by Paul Buhle and Dan Georgakas, 233–55. Albany: State University of New York Press.

Suleiman, Sami. 2015. "The Moral Hypocrisy of American Muslims for Palestine on the Armenian Genocide." *Mondoweiss*. April 21. http://mondoweiss.net/2015/04/hypocrisy-american-palestine.

Sullivan, Winnifred Fallers, et al, eds. 2015. *Politics of Religious Freedom*. Chicago: University of Chicago Press.

Swedenburg, Ted. 2003. *Memories of Revolt: The 1936–1939 Rebellion and the Palestinian National Past*. Fayetteville: University of Arkansas Press.

Al-Tahir, Abdul Jalil Ali. 1952. "The Arab Community in the Chicago Area: A Comparative Study of the Christian-Syrians and the Muslim-Palestinians." PhD diss, University of Chicago.

Tarlo, Emma. 2010. *Visibly Muslim: Fashion, Politics, Faith*. Oxford and New York: Berg.

Tawil-Souri, Helga. 2016. "Gaza as Larger than Life." In *Gaza as Metaphor*, edited by Helga Tawil-Souri and Dina Matar, 15–28. London: C. Hurst & Co.

Taylor, Charles. 2007. *A Secular Age.* Cambridge, MA: Belknap Press of Harvard University Press.

Terry, Don, and Noreen S. Ahmed-Ullah. 2001. "Protesters Turn Anger on Muslim Americans." *Chicago Tribune.* September 14. https://www.chicagotribune.com/chi-0109140352sep14-story.html.

Tsimhoni, Daphne. 1993. *Christian Communities in Jerusalem and the West Bank Since 1948: An Historical, Social, and Political Study.* Westport, CT: Praeger.

Tweed, Thomas A. 2006. *Crossing and Dwelling: A Theory of Religion.* Cambridge, MA: Harvard University Press.

Turner, Bryan S. 2002. "Strategic Generations: Historical Change, Literary Expression, and Generational Politics." In *Generational Consciousness, Narrative, and Politics*, edited by June Edmunds and Bryan S. Turner, 13–29. Lanham, MD: Rowman & Littlefield.

Turner, Victor. 1969. *The Ritual Process: Structure and Anti-Structure.* Foreword by Roger D. Abrahams. New York: Aldine de Gruyter.

United Nations General Assembly. 1979. Thirty-Fourth Session, Agenda Item 51: "Report of the Special Committee to Investigate Israeli Practices Affecting the Human Rights of the Population of the Occupied Territories." Geneva: November 13. https://undocs.org/en/A/RES/34/90.

United Nations Office for the Coordination of Humanitarian Affairs. 2012. "The Humanitarian Impact of Israeli Settlement Policies." December. https://unispal.un.org/pdfs/OCHA_HumImpact-Settlements.pdf.

United States Council of Muslim Organizations. 2015. "USCMO Statement on 1915 Turkish-Armenian Events." April 19. https://uscmo.org/index.php/2015/04/20/uscmo-statement-on-1915-turkish-armenian-events/; also archived at http://www.icna.org/uscmo-statement-on-1915-turkish-armenian-events.

Usher, Graham. 2001. "Palestine: The Intifada This Time." *Race & Class* 42, no. 4: 73–80.

———. 2003. "Dead End for the Palestinian Resistance." *Le Monde diplomatique.* September. https://mondediplo.com/2003/09/02usher.

Vatikiotis, Panayiotis J. 1991. *The History of Modern Egypt: From Muhammad Ali to Mubarak.* Fourth Edition. Baltimore, MD: Johns Hopkins University Press.

Vélez, Maria B. 2009. "Contextualizing the Immigration and Crime Effect: An Analysis of Homicide in Chicago Neighborhoods." *Homicide Studies* 13, no. 3: 325–35.

Vorva, Jeff. 2011. "D-230 Schools Weighs [sic] Adding Arabic, Chinese Language Courses." *Triblocal Orland Park.* August 3. http://www.triblocal.com/orland-park/2011/08/03/d-230-schools-weighs-adding-arabic-chinese-language-courses/index.html.

Wadud, Amina. 1999. *Qur'an and Woman: Rereading the Sacred Text from a Woman's Perspective.* New York: Oxford University Press.

Waldroup, Regina. 2014. "Thousands of Palestinian Supporters Protest in Chicago." July 26. http://www.nbcchicago.com/news/local/Hundreds-of-Palestinian-Supporters-Protest-in-Chicago-268742291.html.

Wansbrough, John. 1978. *The Sectarian Milieu: Content and Composition of Islamic Salvation History.* Oxford: Oxford University Press.

———. 2004 (1977). *Quranic Studies: Sources and Methods of Scriptural Interpretation*. Foreword, Translation, and Expanded Notes by Andrew Rippen. Amherst, NY: Prometheus Books.
Warikoo, Niraj. 2016. "New Trial in Detroit for Activist Rasmieh Odeh." *Detroit Free Press*. December 6. https://www.freep.com/story/news/local/michigan/detroit/2016/12/06/detroit-palestinian-activist-rasmieh-odeh/95061048/.
———. 2017. "Guilty Plea, Deportation End Terror Case Against Former Michigan Woman." *Detroit Free Press*. April 25. http://www.freep.com/story/news/local/michigan/2017/04/25/rasmieh-odeh-bombing-israel/100884788.
Weber, Max. 1946a. "The Protestant Sects and the Spirit of Capitalism." In *From Max Weber: Essays in Sociology*, edited by Hans H. Gerth and C. Wright Mills, 302–22. New York: Oxford University Press.
———. 1946b. "Science as a Vocation." In *From Max Weber: Essays in Sociology*, translated and edited by Hans H. Gerth and C. Wright Mills, 129–56. New York: Oxford University Press.
———. 1949. "'Objectivity' in Social Science and Social Policy." In *The Methodology of the Social Sciences*, translated and edited by Edward A. Shils and Henry A. Finch, 49–112. New York: The Free Press.
———. 1978 (1968). *Economy and Society: An Outline of Interpretive Sociology, Two Volumes*, edited by Guenther Roth and Claus Wittich. Berkeley: University of California Press.
———. 2004. *The Essential Max Weber*, edited by Sam Whimster. London: Routledge.
Wehr, Hans. 1994. *Hans Wehr: A Dictionary of Modern Written Arabic (Arabic-English)*. Fourth Edition, edited by J. Milton Cowan. Wiesbaden, Germany and Ithaca, NY: Otto Harrassowitz and Spoken Language Services, Inc.
Weisenfeld, Judith. 2016. *New World A-Coming: Black Religion and Racial Identity During the Great Migration*. New York: New York University Press.
Westrop, Sam. 2017. "How American Charities Fund Terrorism." *National Review*. January 12. https://www.nationalreview.com/2017/01/terrorist-groups-american-charities-fund-ufa-hamas-dawah-social-services/.
Wickham, Carrie Rosefsky. 2013. *The Muslim Brotherhood: Evolution of an Islamist Movement*. Princeton, NJ: Princeton University Press.
Wofford, Ben. 2016. "The Forgotten Government Plan to Round Up Muslims." *Politico*. August 19. https://www.politico.com/magazine/story/2016/08/secret-plans-detention-internment-camps-1980s-deportation-arab-muslim-immigrants-214177.
Yang, Fenggang, and Helen Rose Ebaugh. 2001. "Transformations in New Immigrant Religions and Their Global Implications." *American Sociological Review* 66, no. 2: 269–88.
Younan, Munib. 2007. "An Ethical Critique of Christian Zionism." *Journal of Lutheran Ethics* 7, no. 5 (May). https://www.elca.org/JLE/Articles/509.
Zaghel, Ali Shteiwi. 1976. "Changing Patterns of Identification among Arab Americans: The Palestinian Ramallites and the Christian Syrian-Lebanese." PhD diss, Northwestern University.
Ziad, Homayra. 2018. "Why I Left the Muslim Leadership Initiative." *Muslim Matters*. June 6. https://muslimmatters.org/2018/06/06/why-i-left-the-muslim-leadership-initiative.

INDEX

AAAN (Arab American Action Network): *See also* Abudayyeh, Hatem; ACC; and the ACC, 65–67, 210n10; and AMP, 74, 82–83; and black-Palestinian solidarity, 20; Café Intifada, 138–39; and continuity of secular nationalism, 59, 188; and Intisar's secular-religious identity synthesis, 152, 153, 156, 157; and the Islamic shift, 6–7, 133, 140, 156, 218n13; and Nawal's nationalist-Islamic synthesis, 138–42; and Odeh's immigration fraud trial, 186; and persistence of secularism, 59, 83–84; programming, 79, 138–39; social class basis of, 81–82, 195–96; strategic alliances, 79–80; and UPWA, 66, 81

Abudayyeh, Hatem (son) (1987–2001 generation): and the AAAN, 79–83, 210n18; activists as "Marxists in hijab", 133; education and work, 63; impact of the Gulf War on, 80–81, 84; on inability of Mosques to provide political advocacy and community support, 79, 82; and intergenerational reproduction of secularism, 80, 83–84; on moving AAAN to the suburbs, 81–82; on Palestinian secularism as a necessity, 79, 81, 82–83, 188, 211n22; and the piety of young activists, 82–83, 211n23; on services and programming needed in the suburbs, 81–82, 211n21

Abudayyeh, Khairy (father): and 1967 war, 64; as ideal-type for Palestinian secularism, 61–62; on loss of secular milieus, 69, 74, 81; on Oslo Peace Process (1993–Present), 68–69;

pan-Arab nationalist secularism of, 109, 192; on religious sectarianism vs. Arab unity, 58–59, 61–62; social background of, 62–63

Abu Jahl, 97

Abu Jihad, 205n12

Abunimah, Ali (*The Electronic Intifada* founder), 92, 93, 213nn13,17

ACC (Arab Community Center) (*markaz*): failure to move to suburbs, 68, 86; fire and closure (1991–1992), 67; founding and closure of, 65–67; and GUPS, 71; and Intisar, 153, 154; and Nashashibi, 143, 145, 148, 156; outreach and Youth Delinquency Program, 66, 148; as pan-Arab Palestinian secular-nationalist milieu, 6, 14, 26, 65–67, 80, 145; secular-Islamic reformist collaboration of (Muhannad), 114–17, 216n9; and UPWA, 72; volunteer orientation of, 69, 74

accommodation: characteristics of, 152–53, 157–58; early identity-formation processes, 153–54; "Islam in me exploded" post-9/11, 155–57; vs. other forms of religious secularity, 135–36; as subform of syncretic secularity, 134–35

Advisory Committee on Arab American Affairs, 67

Advisory Council on Faith-Based and Neighborhood Partnerships, 142–43

African Americans: and the "Black Belt," 203n2, 203nn3,5; in the "Black Belt," 30, 45–46, 57, 142, 203n2; Black Islam, 21, 144–49, 219nn20–21;

245

246   INDEX

Black Lives Matter, 20, 186, 210n19; Black Panthers, 145; and Southwest Side corridor Palestinians, 29, 66–67; Third Worldist and black liberation, 20, 33, 44, 145, 192
Al Bawadi Grill, 55
alienation: and Christian Palestinians in Islamized spaces, 118–19, 121–23; and latency of piety-oriented individuals in the 1948 and 1967 generation, 109, 110–12; and law enforcement intrusions and media stereotyping, 16, 40; and Palestinian Christian sectarian-denationalization, 129–31; and turn to religion, 111
Alien Terrorists and Undesirables: A Contingency Plan (1986), 40
al-ʿAli, Naji (political cartoonist), 58, 103, 209n1
Al Jazeera TV station, 55
al-Qaeda, 90
American-Arab Anti-Discrimination Committee (ADC), 64, 77, 79, 84
American Arabian Ladies Society (AALS), 48–49, 51–52, 207n36
Americanization: "American" identified vs. bifocality, 201n16; and cultural assimilation through religious institutions in, 118; to escape Arab/Muslim identity (Ibrahim), 163–64; and Islamic reformism, 113; of the Nakba, 99–104; in Nashashibi's black-Palestinian synthesis, 143, 145–47; vs. Palestinian identity, 164, 220n3
Amin (Shaykh), 106
AMP (American Muslims for Palestine): See also AMP Conference (2013) Americanness of, 87, 103–4, 211n3; "Aqsa in danger," 91–92, 97, 102–3; and the Armenian genocide, 188–89, 224n13; collaboration with SJP, 85, 123, 211n1; erasures of, 90, 211–12nn6–7; founding and sectarianism of, 67–68, 72, 88, 123, 124; logo, 99, 102, 103; Muslim-American solidarity frame of, 3, 87–88; and Nakba commemorations, 68–69, 85, 98–101; and the post-9/11 generation, 123–25; and Odeh, 186; and Palestine nation-umma elision, 68–69, 188–89; predecessor organizations of, 108; as religion prevailing over secularism, 59, 73–75, 82–83; as sectarian-religious transethnic solidarity, 88, 123–25, 193; secular critique of, 85–86; Syria, 91–93, 188–89, 193–94, 212–13nn12–13; and youth, 96–97, 100
AMP Conference (2013): and community political divisions, 90–93; discursive framing in title "A Blessed Land, A Noble Cause," 93–95; and interfaith forums vs. Palestinian cause, 95–96; and Israel issues, 94; on the *murabitun* in the diaspora, 97–98, 214n25; "Noble Cause" as non-violent jihad, 93, 95, 214n21; promotional materials as discourse, 89–90; representation of the "Holy Land" tropes in, 93–95, 189, 194; research methodology, 88, 211n4
anti-colonialism: and Arab revolts, 11, 35, 61, 94, 199n1; Jerusalem/Holy Land proxies for, 94, 123–25; of Third Worldist and black liberation, 20, 33, 44, 145, 192
anti-Muslim/anti-Arab backlash: and the 1967 war, 39–40; and children's bullying, 129, 155–56; and denationalized Christian sectarianism, 130; and the Gulf War, 129–30; law enforcement intrusions/media stereotyping, 16, 39–40, 185–86, 187, 205n17; and 9/11, 11, 59, 86, 119, 123, 223n6; and post-9/11 "US as victim of Islam," 155; and Odeh's immigration fraud case, 185–86; and the Oklahoma City bombing, 40, 77, 86, 210n16; and the religious shift, 8, 59, 86, 87, 119; and sense of exile in hostile place, 187–88
Antiochian Orthodox Christians. See Palestinian Christians
ʿaqida (core doctrine), 114–15, 192, 194
al-Aqsa Intifada. See Second Intifada
al-Aqsa Martyrs' Brigade, 166, 221n5
al-Aqsa Mosque: and AMP, 89, 94, 189; "in danger," 91–92, 97, 102–3; in diaspora Nakba commemorations, 102–3, 211n5; Islamic religious-nationalism, 12, 115
Aqsa School: as an Islamic religious/Arab ethnic milieu, 128; compared with Universal School, 54, 208n43; Islamic reformism of, 53, 137, 155–56, 208n40; Nakba Day commemoration at, 85, 102–3; and Odeh's trial, 186; and patriarchy, 53, 208n40
Arab American Association of New York, 212–13nn12–13
Arab American University Graduates (AAUG), 14
Arab Bible, 56
Arab Christians: See also Hanna; Leo; Palestinian Christians; and bifocality, 193–94; and denationalized sectarianism (Leo), 129–31, 193; vs. Greek orthodox Christianity, 117; interactions with Muslims, 55; and St. George Antiochian Orthodox Church, 121–22; sectarianization of (Munir), 117–20; and sectarianized-nationalism (Hanna), 120–23

INDEX 247

Arab community centers/clubs, 8, 11, 14, 37–38
Arab nationalism. *See* Abudayyeh, Khairy; ACC; Fatah; generation of 1948–1967; pan-Arabism; PLO
Arab revolt (1936–1939), 11, 35, 61, 94
Arab Spring: and bifocality, 193; impacts in Chicago, 91–93; and the post-9/11 generation, 120; uprisings, 59, 90
Arab Students Association (ASA), 45, 64–65
"Arabville," 171, 173, 174, 176, 190
Arab Women's Committee, 186
Arafat, Yasser, 11, 76, 114, 143
Armenian Palestinians, 129–30, 188–89, 224n13; genocide, 188–89
ʿAroubi, Shaykh (Dearborn Michigan), 49
al-Assad, Bashir (regime), 91–92. *See also* Syria
assimilation: and AMP Nakba commemorations, 101–2; and AMP youth messaging, 96–97; "becoming white," 21; and bifocality vs. "American" identified, 201n16; vs. bimodal migration and homeland family and religious bonds, 32, 34–35; and Gulf War backlash, 129–30; of Nashashibi (Black culture), 146–47; patterns and religious institutions in, 118; and reformist Islam leadership, 49–50, 207n32; and religious transmission, 126–27; and Santa Claus at Christmas, 143–44; and "stranger" groups, 26, 32, 36, 39–40, 203n5; and suburban "browning," 48–52, 125–26
atheism, 159, 160–65, 191
autobiographical axis, 17, 18–19. *See also* narrations
"autonomous immigrants," 41
al-Azhar University, 49
ʿAziza: and denationalized Islamic sectarianism, 125–28; and the hijab, 127–28; identity formed in isolation, 125–26; and *taqwa* "God awareness," 127

Baʿathism, 80
Baghdad Pact, 59
al-Banna, Hasan (Muslim Brotherhood founder), 11, 94
baraka (divine blessing), 90
Bazian, Hatem (Dr.), 100
BDS (Boycott, Divestment and Sanctions): and anti-"Protective Edge" protests, 2–3; beyond the secular-religious binary, 27; and Christianized nationalism (Hanna), 120, 121; as deinstitutionalized secularism, 59; and Fatah, 27–28; and inter-racial/inter-ethnic countercultural resistance, 20;

at Nakba Day commemorations, 85; and non-Muslim solidarity, 107; and secular deinstitutionalization, 59
Bedouin culture, 55, 100, 104
al-Beit Jali, Iskandar al-Khouri, 58, 208–9
bifocality: and the diaspora as a space of freedom, 163–64, 191, 194–95, 195; of homeland-diaspora, 19–20, 201n16; intergenerational, 22; and intersectionality in immigrant space, 57, 194; and Muhannad's religious nationalism, 110; Munir's, 119; as narrated contexts, 19–20; Nashashibi's, 192; and religious identities, 121, 193–94
bimodal migration patterns, 30, 35, 39
"Black Belt": boundaries, 203n2; as cultural and business milieu, 203nn3,5; and early Palestinian bimodal immigrants, 32, 203n2; and Nashashibi, 146–49; and racial violence/border wars, 30, 45–46
Black Islam, 21, 144–49, 219nn20–21; and countercultural identity and space, 20–21, 144–47; and hip hop re-ve-láy-shun and li-ber-áy-shun, 146–47; and IMAN's social justice orientation, 147–49, 219n21; and the *kufi* cap, 147, 219n20; and revelation, 147
Black Lives Matter, 20, 186, 210n19
Black Panthers, 145
BLM (Black Lives Matter), 20, 186, 210n19
Blumenthal, Max, 92, 93, 213nn14,17
"border wars," 30, 45–46
Boycott, Divestment and Sanctions (BDS). *See* BDS
Bridgeview Mosque, 77, 169
Bridgeview suburb, 48–52, 55, 77, 125–26. *See also* Islamic reformism; Mosque Foundation
British colonialism, and pan-Islamic colonial resistance, 11
British Mandate, 9, 10*map*, 62, 103, 209n7
"browning," 48–52
Brown, Michael, 20, 186

Cainkar, Louise, xiv, 14, 16, 39, 42, 43
"chain" immigration, 35, 40, 153
chemical weapons, 92
Chicago, industry and demographics (1860–1890), 30
Chicago Coalition for Justice in Palestine, 1
Chicago diaspora: and Christian response to new Islamic movement, 118; and hijab and *jilbab* coat wearing, 127–28; and identity displacements, 119–20; Islamic-nationalist spaces in Muhannad's story, 110; and rise of sectarianism in the 1987–2001 generation, 116

Chicago Lawn (Southwest Side): boundaries and racial demographic, 35, 36*map*, 142; a secular enclave, 7, 35, 65–66, 67–68, 81, 202n1
Chicago Mercantile Exchange ("the Merc"), 47
Christianity, disenchantment with, 165
Christian Palestinians. *See* Palestinian Christians
Christian Zionism, 120
Cicero township, 38, 46, 55, 56, 121, 129, 130, 205n15
class. *See* social class
clubs (village based), 37–38
commemoration: *See also* Nakba; defined, 98
communism: and Communist Parties, 44, 145; and liberation through revolution, 44; religious (Nashashibi), 144, 220n23
community centers (secular), 6–7, 200n6. *See also* AAAN; ACC
community leadership: traditional, 49; transformation of in the diaspora, 50, 59, 68–69
concentration camps for Palestinians, 40
conversion: characteristics, 142–43; as critical of Islamic reformism and secular nationalism, 142; dynamic processes of, 142–43; early identity-formation processes in, 143–44; Nashashibi's from anti-religious secularism to religious secularity, 142–52; Re-ve-láy-shun and Li-ber-áy-shun, 144–52; vs. reversion and accommodation, 133–58, 135–36, 157–58
Council of Islamic Organizations in Chicago, 54, 59, 91
Council of Islamic Schools in North America, 54
Council on American-Islamic Relations, 59, 93, 213
Council on American-Islamic Relations (CAIR), 93, 212–13nn12–13
crossing of social circles, 24, 135
cross-pressures, 24–25, 135. *See also* fragility/fragilizing; syncretic secularity

dabka (village line dances): and secular nationalism, 43, 43*fig*, 65, 153; and women's political activism, 43, 43*fig*, 65, 71, 72
Dahdal, Nicholas (Father), 56
Daley, Richard M. (Mayor), 77
Davis, Angela, 186
Democratic Party, 77
denationalized sectarianism: of Arab (Palestinian) Christians, 121–22; characteristics of, 125, 129; Christian (Leo), 129–31; of Christians in St. George, 129–31; Islamic ('Aziza), 125–28
diaspora. *See* Palestinian Chicago entries

diaspora identity: *See also* anti-Muslim backlash; assimilation and AMP's positioning on assimilation, 89; and commodification of the Nakba, 103; and contingency in forming subjectivity, 15–17; and diaspora-homeland space, 13, 22, 57; and gender, 22, 41–42, 206n20; and ongoing Nakba (Catastrophe), 187; and patriarchy, 22–23, 41, 42, 206n20; religious revival in reaction to racism, 13, 179; re-traditionalization and guilt related to "back home," 42; and sense of exile and uncertainty, 187–88
diversity: in Chicago and the US, 20, 113, 178, 190; in Islam, 139, 190, 192; in Palestine, 101; and syncretic secularity, 134–35
Dome of the Rock (*Qubbat al-Sakhra*): in AMP conference materials, 89, 94, 211n5; as Arab-Muslim unifier, 55, 89–90; barbed wire-Israel symbolism, 94; as identity symbol (signifier), 1, 3*fig*, 103; and Palestinian national-territorial claims, 54; and re-Palestinianization, 42
Dow v. United States (1915), 33
dynamic syntheses: *See also* absolute rejection; accommodation; conversion; reversion; spiritualization syncretic rebellions, 159–60

East Jerusalem, 35
Egypt, 90, 91, 120. *See also* Arab Spring
Eipper, Chris, 25, 27, 134, 135
The Electronic Intifada (Ali Abunimah founder), 92
epochal events: the First Intifada (1987–1993), 18, 201n13; the Gulf War (1990–1991) and the 1987–2001 generation, 70, 80–81, 84; Israeli invasion of Lebanon (1982), 18, 65–66, 114, 144, 154, 161–62, 193; 9/11 as, 19; the wars of 1948 and 1967, 18
epochal-historical axis, defined, 17, 201n12
ethnicity: *See also* pan-Arabism; race and hybrid identities, 24; and identity projection, 88; and Palestinian Christians, 56, 130; rejection of, 162; sectarian elisions and hierarchies of, 108–9, 114, 130–31; transcending, 152, 179, 219n17
ethnos, 9, 142, 152, 187, 196, 219–20
evangelism, 118, 119–20, 209n5, 211n22
exilic difference, 13

"false consciousness," 9, 86
Fatah (Palestinian National Liberation Movement): and Abu Jihad, 205n12; and

the al-Aqsa Martyrs' Brigade, 166, 221n5; and diaspora secular nationalism, 63, 65, 67, 76, 192, 210n13; vs. Hamas, 5, 12, 27; and the Irish Republican Army, 210n12; vs. Islamic reformism, 112, 128; vs. MAN (Movement of Arab Nationalists), 63–64; and secular nationalism in Palestine, 7–12, 27–28, 59, 154

FBI (LA Eight case), 39–40

Federal Housing authority, 45–46

first Gulf War. *See* Gulf War (1990–91)

the First Intifada (1987–1993): and ACC community organizing, 66; as an epochal event, 18, 201n13; as defining trauma of secular identity, 9; events of and dating, 201n13; and Fatah/PLO, 11, 116; and the generational axis, 27; and Islamic reformist-revolutionary nationalist splits, 50–51, 116–17, 119, 200n10; as key event of the 1987–2001 generation, 70, 72, 144, 153–54; and the Muslim Brotherhood/Hamas, 200n10; and new Christian nationalism, 116, 120–23; and West Bank, 5

fitna (Muslims killing Muslims sin), 91

fragility/fragilizing, 9, 24, 134, 135, 202n21

Friends of Sabeel North America, 106–7, 123, 186

Gage Park neighborhood enclave, 35, 36*map*, 65, 202

Gaza Strip: AAAN protests against Israeli actions in, 79–80; and BDS (Boycott, Divestment and Sanctions), 27–28; Hamas domination in, 7–8, 12, 59, 120, 123; and Islamic Collective (Hamas's precursor), 60; Israeli occupation of as key event of the 1987–2001 generation, 70; and Israeli "Summer Rains" bombardment, 72, 87; and Israel's "Operation Cast Lead," 124, 125, 154; Muslim Brotherhood in, 12; violence against Christians, 119–20

gender: and AMP representations of Palestine, 101; and Aqsa School curriculum, 53, 208n40; and cultural transmission of patriarchy through the family, 126; and disenchantment with religious-patriarchal milieus, 195; education and recruitment of women for the "revolution," 44; and family caregiving, 139–40; and the *murabitun* (tied to the land), 97–98; in Nawal's reversion process, 138–39, 140, 158; and piety as social coercion, 139, 168–69, 172; and political empowerment of women through UPWA, 72; and rebellion, 160, 168–69; and religious secularity vs. suburban reformism, 136; and re-Palestinianization, 41–42, 206n20; re-segregation of after religious turn, 69; in secular nationalist narrative and iconography, 43; and sexual double standard, 163–64; and *shariʿa* in reformist Islam, 136, 217n5; and syncretic-secular confluences, 135

General Union of Palestinian Students (GUPS), 14, 45, 71, 76, 79, 84, 154

generational phenomena: *See also* specific generations; axes defined, 18, 26–27; and intergenerational reproduction of secularism, 60–61, 73–74, 80, 83–84, 187–88; locations, 18, 22, 109, 215n1; processes, 109–10; and rebellion, 160; and socio-historical generations, 17–18, 201n12; vs. typologies, 132; units, 18–19, 110, 192, 201n12

generation (post-9/11): *See also* 9/11; and denationalized sectarianism, 125–28; and denationalized sectarianism (Christian), 129–31; and Islamized nationalism, 123–25; and the Second Intifada (2000–2005), 109, 120–23

generation of 1948–1967: *See also* Abudayyeh, Khairy; Hussain; Muhannad; Musa; secularism; alienation and latency in, 110; and creating core institutions of secularism, 65–67, 192; and deinstitutionalization and attenuation, 67–70; formational processes in, 110–12; generational processes in formation of, 40, 63–65; and Palestinian identity and national solidarity, 69–70; and pan-Arabism secular nationalism, 111, 192; religion as in the private-domain, 69–70; social backgrounds of, 36, 62–63; two identity types (secularist and latent piety), 109, 192, 215n1

generation of 1987–2001: *See also* Hatem Abudayyeh; Mahmoud; Manal; accommodation of new religiosity, 70; and Christian sectarianization, 109, 117–20; defined by the secularism-religion split, 70, 115–16; early secular identity formations, 116–17; Hatem Abudayyeh, 79–83; and Mahmoud's multi-sectarian solidarity trajectory, 75–79; Manal's accommodation-persistence trajectory, 70–75, 83–84; and responses to religious turn, 74–75

genocide (Armenian), 188–89, 224n13

"ghetto cosmopolitanism," 145

Great Arab Revolt (1916–1918), 61, 199n1

Greater Syria, 31

Greek Revolt, 116–17

Greek War of Independence, 116–17
Grewal, Zareena, 14
guerrilla fighters (*fida'iyun/fedayeen*), 43
Gulf War (1990–1991): as the 1987–2001 generation's epochal event, 70, 80–81, 84; and anti-Arab backlash impact (Leo), 129–30; and crippling of PLO secularism, 5, 11, 67–68; and the First Intifada (1987–1993) periodization, 201n13; and Intisar, 154; and Nashashibi, 145
GUPS (General Union of Palestinian Students), 14, 45, 71, 76, 79, 84, 154

Habash, George, 64
Hamas (Islamic Resistance Movement), 1; abduction of Gilad Shalit, 72; and BDS (Boycott, Divestment and Sanctions), 27–28; as designated terrorist organization, 87, 211n3; and diaspora scholarly literature, 13, 200n9; expulsion of Fatah from Gaza Strip (2007), 120; vs. Fatah and Israeli "Protective Edge" invasion, 12; Holy Land/Jihad tropes, 94, 214n21; Islamic State critique of, 12–13; and Jerusalem/Holy Land liberation, 94; members exiled to Lebanon, 114, 216n9; and the Muslim Brotherhood, 217n9; and Palestine within global Islamic solidarity resurgence since 1980's, 12; and Palestinian Christian sectarianizing, 12–13; as Palestinian offshoot of the Muslim Brotherhood, 86; vs. PLO (Palestine Liberation Organization) secularism, 7–8; and religious-political polarization, 12–13, 115–16, 119–20, 216n12; and religious theodicies, 24; and the Second Intifada, 166; and *shari'a*-based state, 94; supplanted PLO in Gaza, 59, 123; the two-state solution and *hudna* truce, 199n3
hamula (extended family/clan), 110
Handala (political cartoon figure), 58, 103, 209n1
Hanna: and BDS (Boycott, Divestment and Sanctions), 120, 121; bifocality and liberation theology, 193; humiliating border security rituals, 122, 193; as post-9/11 generation anomaly (reasons), 121–23; and West Bank visits as politicizing, 122
Hanna, Theodosios Attallah (Antiochian Orthodox Archbishop), 107
Haram al-Sharif: and Islamic-reformist discourse and the Palestinian nation, 85, 89; Jewish settler entry into compound of, 91–92; and religious nationalism, 54, 115
haram (forbidden in Islamic law): and Muna's anxiety about sleeping position, 172, 221n6; to participate in US political system, 157; and "street" Islam, 139
hate crimes, 222n4
hattas (*kufiyas*), and hyphenated identity, 103–4, 105
Al Hayat Al Jadeeda, 101
Hezbollah (Lebanon Shi'i), 90–91, 124
hijab: and AMP representation of Palestine, 101; and AMP's branding, 99, 100; and 'Aziza, 127–28; competing meanings of, 217n5; and hijabi vs. non-hijabi women, 156, 157; and Islamic school, 172; and *muhajjabas*, 131, 137, 139, 140, 177; and Muna's spiritual rebellion, 173; and Nawal's religious secularism, 133–34, 136–37, 139–40; as political solidarity signifier (post-9/11), 155; and Qur'anic interpretation, 101, 127; and religious-secular nationalist identity markers, 2, 3, 98; and religious turn, 6, 59, 77; and ritual practice/prayer, 140; *shari'a* requirements of, 136, 217n5
Holy Land Foundation for Relief, 87, 211n3
Holy Land tropes, 93–95, 123–25
al-Husayni, Amin (al-Hajj) (Mufti of Jerusalem), 11–12, 94
Hussain, Ali: arrest and legal defense, 66, 67, 210n12; on Oslo Peace Process (1993–Present), 68–69, 74; pioneer of secular nationalist institutionalization (ACC), 65–67, 192; politicization and generational processes of, 63–65, 210n9
Hussein, Saddam, 80
hybrid identities: *See also* absolute rejection; accommodation; conversion; reversion; spiritualization; syncretic secularity; vs. crossing of social circles, 24, 135; and narrations "stories so far," 8, 17; and secularism-religion dynamic, 24–25; in "syncretic secularity," 25–26
hyphenated identity, 103–4

iblad/shatat (homeland-diaspora). *See* bifocality
Ibrahim: Americanism of, 161–62, 164; atheism of, 159, 162–63, 190–91; bifocality and Aunt's refugee camp conditions, 193; bifocality and the diaspora as a space of freedom, 194, 195; disenchantment and injustice of God (leading to atheism), 183; enclave vs. city behavior (urban exile as space of freedom), 163, 190; family's reaction to atheism, 163; girlfriend, 163; grudging participation in forms of piety, 163, 164–65; North Side

INDEX   251

(beyond the enclave) as space of freedom, 191; on patriarchy, 164; rejection of parents' Palestinian nationalist identity, 161–62, 220n2; rejection of reformist Islamic piety, 162–63, 190–91
iconography, of secular nationalism, 43
'id, 127
The Ideal Muslimah, 53, 208n40
ideal-types: defined, 23–24, 61, 200n5, 202nn18–20, 215n1; (Khairy Abudayyeh) secular, 23, 61, 109
ideal-types (Muhannad), religion, 215n1
identity: AMP's American Muslim/Palestinian fusion of, 88; commemoration as organizational appropriation of, 99; complexity of, 60; defined, 17, 25; hyphenated, 103–4; Islamic reformist-secular-nationalist fractures in, 6; multi-dimensional determinants of, 8, 21, 24, 27, 57, 152, 158, 192, 198; and the need for ethnic location, 104; sectarianization of in the 1987–2001 generation, 116; space, narrative and generational constitution of, 19
identity formation: See also milieus; specific generations; axes of, 17–19; and contingency, 15–17, 16–17, 210n11; and space, 19–20, 57
identity transformations, 17, 23, 192. See also accommodation; conversion; religion-secularism dynamic; reversion; spiritualization; syncretic rebellions; syncretic secularity;
Illinois Voters for Middle East Peace, 67
imam certification, 49
IMAN (Inner-City Muslim Action Network), 142, 148–49, 152, 195–96, 219–20n21; working and poor class base of, 195–96
Imm George, 38
immigrant space, between *amrika* and the *iblad* (back home), 57, 99
Immigration and Nationality Act (1965), 39
Immigration and Naturalization Services, 40
Imm 'Umar: the 1948 and 1967 generation's, impact on the diaspora, 35; on AALS and religious institutionalization, 48–50; on Mosque Foundation power-struggle, 51
Indian Khalifat movement, 12
intercommunal relations, 37–38, 205n14
inter-ethnic coalitions, 7, 44–45, 66–67, 156
intersectionality: and bifocality, 22, 57; and gender, 22–23; and Islam, 33, 152; and Nashashibi's universal humanism, 149–50, 220n23; and race, class, gender and generation, 57, 152; in the secularism-religion dynamic, xiv, 7, 17; and space, 19–20, 57; of space/milieu and race/ethnicity, 20–21; and syncretic formations, 25–27; as transcending ethnocentrism, 219n17
Intifadas, as generational upheavals, 160
Intisar: at the AAAN, 152, 153, 156, 157; background and early identity formation, 153–55; civil rights organization job, 156–57; daughters in Aqsa School, 155–56; the "Islam in me exploded" after 9/11, 155–57; modified secularism of, 191–92; Mosque Foundation influence on, 156–57; and non-white identity, 153; political mobilization of, 153–54, 156, 157; and race issues, 158; and trauma exposure through US media, 154, 193
Iran, 90–91
Iraq War, 80, 92–93
Irish Republican Army, 66, 210n12
Islamic Collective (Hamas precursor), 60
Islamic Community Center of Illinois (ICCI), 52, 106
Islamic diaspora concept, 15
Islamic Jihad: AMP conference discursive framing of, 94–95; and "Noble Cause" (*fi sabil illah*), 95
Islamic milieus: See also AMP; Aqsa School; Mosque Foundation; American Arabian Ladies Society (AALS), 48–49, 51–52
Islamic piety markers: 'abaya ('aba'a) (ankle length robe), 98; beards, hijab scarves, brimless knitted kufi caps, 6
Islamic reformism: See also AMP; 'Aziza; *haram*; hijab; Islamic texts; Jerusalem; Mosque Foundation; Muhannad; Qur'an; *umma*; and Americanization, 113; at Aqsa School, 53, 137, 155–56, 208n40; and assimilation, 49–50, 207n32; and charity, 52, 95, 105–6, 136, 217n5; class and demographics of, 50–51, 136, 207n33, 217n5; vs. "corrupt" US secularism, 54, 60, 209n5; vs. cultural piety, 111–12, 136–37, 217n7–8; definition of, 207n33; disenchantment with, 57, 60, 84, 160, 176, 183; distinct developmental path of in Chicago, 195, 215n5; and duty of principled dissent, 113; and *fiqh* (Islamic jurisprudence)141, 95, 139, 214n21, 218n15, 221n8; generational trajectory of, 112–15; global, 147; ideological tendencies/roots of, 207n33, 217n5; vs. intersectionality in conversion, 142, 219n17; as *jahl* (narrow-mindedness), 178–81, 221n10; and justice, 113–14; and music as *haram*, 176, 179–80,

221n11, 222n12; and the national question, 188–89; in Palestine vs. in Chicago diaspora, 112–15, 215n5; and the primacy of God/ʿaqida, 114–15, 192, 194; and repatriarchalization, 136, 140, 202n17, 217n5, 218n14; and the right of return, 68–69, 101, 105–6; and shariʿa, 112, 136, 139, 215n29, 217n5, 218n11; and Syria, 188–89; and tithing, 52, 136, 190, 217n5; and traditional village leaders, 113; and the transnational Islamic *umma* concept, 188; and wisdom as a "mislaid belonging" *hadith*, 113, 216n7

Islamic shift: *See also* AMP; activists as "Marxists in hijab," 133; and AMP, 26; and failure of secular nationalism with Oslo, 68–69; impacts of syncretic secularity on, 189–92; and Mosque Foundation, 48–52; and private schools, 53–55, 69, 128, 208n40; values, 37

Islamic Society of North American, 124

Islamic State movement, 12–13

Islamic texts: *See also* Muhannad; Qurʾan; *hadith* and Muna, 51, 172, 175–76, 221n6; and Islamic reformism, 137, 139, 217nn7–8; and reformist orthopraxy (*Qurʾan* and *hadith*), 51; and revelation, 146, 219n19; and Sara's cross-ethnic solidarity, 124; and the *sira*, 111; *tafsir* literature, 90; and wisdom as a "mislaid belonging" *hadith*, 113, 216n7

Islamism: *See also* Jerusalem; *umma*; origin and characteristics of (orienting horizon of), 11–12; in Palestine vs. in Chicago diaspora, 11, 94, 113, 117–18, 179, 200n8, 210n9; and the student movement, 14

Israel: in AMP's annual conference, 85, 87–88, 89–90, 91, 92, 93, 94, 95, 96; in AMP's Nakba commemorations, 98, 102, 104, 105, 106–7; border security and Arab Christian politicization, 122, 193; and the Dome of the Rock barbed wire, 90, 94; expropriations for settlements, 40; and Hamas suicide bombings, 166, 221n5; home permit refusals, 122; invasion of Lebanon (1982), 9, 11, 18, 66, 144, 154; vs. Islamic patrimony (*waqf*), 94; and Jewish anti-Zionists, 92; legitimacy question of and AMP, 94; military court sentence of Odeh, 185, 222n1; and Nakba as a disputed space of memory, 98; and the Neturei Karta (Jewish Orthodox movement), 96; "Operation Cast Lead," 124, 125, 154; PLO capitulation to in Oslo, 68–69; representation of in AMP conference materials, 89–90; repression during the First Intifada (1987–1993), 116; rise of pan-Arabism and Marxist nationalist movements, 111; Sahloul's condemnation of, 91–92, 212–13nn12–13; "Summer Rains" bombardment of Gaza Strip, 72, 87; treatment of political prisoners, 221nn1–2; US political and financial support for, 187, 211n24; war with Hezbollah (2006), 124; West Bank wall replica in Nakba commemorations, 85, 104, 211n1

Israeli occupation: and forced exodus of Palestinians, 40, 205n18; Islamic reformists on Armenian genocide, 188–89, 224n13; occupied territories, 11; and Sawsan on whiteness, 168; and the Second Intifada, 166

isrāʾ wa al-miʿraj (Prophet's journey), 11, 85, 89, 115

Jabhat al-Nusra, 90
Jackson, Jesse (Reverend), 67
jahiliya (age of ignorance), 113, 127, 178–79, 216n6, 221nn8–9
jahl (narrow-mindedness), 178–79
Jamal (Shaykh), 105–6
Jerusalem: *See also* al-Aqsa; as al-Quds (Holy Land), 1, 89, 102; in British Mandate Palestine, 10*map*; and gendered re-Palestinianization, 42; and Hanna's bifocality, 122–23; and Haram al-Sharif, 54, 85, 89, 91–92, 115, 221n5; immigration to US, 31; in Islamist and cross-ethnic Islamic and Islamic reformist discourses, 11–12, 20, 89–92, 94, 96–97, 120; and the isrāʾ wa al-miʿraj (Prophet Muhammad's journey), 11, 85, 89, 115; and Jubran's mother's intersectarianism, 178; Manal's return to, 70–71; and Muhannad's bifocality, 108–9, 111; and Munir's bifocality, 116–17, 119, 122; and Nashashibi's bifocality (strip searched), 143–44; and Palestinian Christians, 106, 107, 116–17, 119; retaken from the Franks, 97, 214n25; and Sawsan's bifocality, 167–68; as symbolic proxy for anti-colonialism, 11, 20, 55, 94; wall replica in Nakba commemorations, 85, 104, 211n1

Jerusalem, East (occupied territory), xiv, 5, 11, 35
Jesus as Palestinian, 122–23
Jewish-Arab personal encounters: and Christianity as a "Jewish" religion (Leo), 131; and debates on Palestine, 162; distinguishing Jewish ethnicity from Zionism, 78; and Friends of Sabeel, 122–23; hate crimes, 222n4; and Jewish-American assimilation,

87–88; and Jubran's intersectionality, 178, 181–82, 221n7; non-Zionist and Mizrahi Jews, 170; and Palestine, 101, 197; and Saidian universalism, 151, 224n14

Jewish identity projection, 88

Jewish United Fund of Chicago, 93

Jewish Voice for Peace, 4, 96, 107, 123, 186

jihad: as non-violent "Noble Cause" (AMP), 93, 95, 214n21; Qur'an interpretations, 12, 94–95, 214n21; secular vs. religious framing of, 1, 12

jilbab coats, 42, 127–28, 137, 172, 208

Jordan, Black September (1970-1971), 40, 143, 205n18

Jubran: Bahá'ísm and Sufi influences on, 180–82, 193; bifocality of, 193–94; family's intersectarian and interethnic Islam, 177–78; his idiosyncratic appropriation of Islam, 181–82; and the Mosque Foundation, 177–78; and music, 176–77, 179–80, 221n11, 222n12; pluralism of, 178, 182–83, 189–90; on reformist Islam as intolerant, 179–80, 181, 221n10; social background and identity formation, 176–78; on suburban reformist milieu as characterized by *jahl* (narrow-mindedness), 178–80, 189, 221nn8–9

Kanazi, Remi, 83, 211n24

Karim, Jamillah, 14

Khabeer, Su'ad Abdul, 15

Khalidi, Rashid, 107

Kishawi, Deena, 3

Kraemer, Shelley v., 45–46

kufi cap, and Nashashibi's black-Palestinian synthesis, 147, 219n20

kufiyas (*kaffiyeh* or *hatta*) pattern: as AMP branding, 99, 100; appropriation of and hyphenated identity, 103–4, 105; and the First Intifada (1987–1993) politicization, 144; as identity marker, 2, 3, 4*fig*, 99

kunya naming, 205n12

LA Eight case, 39–40

Latinx, 48

Lebanon: and Arab Spring and occupied holy lands in AMP conference materials, 90; Hamas members exiled to, 114, 216n9; and Hezbollah in Syria's fight with Jabhat al-Nusra, 90–91; Israeli invasion of, 9, 11, 144; Palestinian refugee camps (Ibrahim's parents), 161

Leo: and alienation from Palestinian-Muslim milieu, 130–31; on Christian-Arab identity, 122; denationalized Christian sectarianism, 129–31; early life and move to Northwest Side, 129; interactions with Palestinian-Muslim women, 131; role of church in denationalization, 129, 130; school and family life, 129–30; and weak integration with secular nationalism, 129, 130

liberation theology, (new political Christianity), 86–87, 109, 117, 121, 216n10

Logan, John R., 48

Lubin, David C., 48

MacArthur Foundation "genius" grant, 143

mahjar (the diaspora), 32, 56–57

Mahmood, Saba, 25, 202n21

Mahmoud (1987–2001 generation): ADC involvement, 77, 79; and American-Arab Anti-Discrimination Committee (ADC) at UIC, 77, 84; Arabic classes and fundraisers, 75–76; vs. conservatism, 77–78; disconnectedness with Southwest Side community organizations, 75–76; father's tolerance, 78; and GUPS-Fatah factionalism, 76, 79; impact of religious shift on, 77, 78; multi-sectarian cross-national trajectory (post religious turn), 75; and Oklahoma City bombing (April 1995), 77; personal history of, 75–76; political roles, 77

non-*mahram* men, 141, 218n15

Manal: accommodation-persistence trajectory of, 70–75, 83–84; bifocality of (*Amrikan-Palestinian*), 71; education and social class status, 70–71; and the First Intifada, 72; and gendered comportment expectations, 71, 210n15; and GUPS secular nationalism, 71, 84; importance of the 1948 and 1967 generation to, 71; involvement with ACC, 71–72, 84; involvement with UPWA, 72, 84; and the Mosque Foundation, 73–74; on secularist deinstitutionalization, 72–74

Mandate Palestine, 9, 10*map*, 103

MAN (Movement of Arab Nationalists), 9–11, 63–64

Mannheim, Karl, 18, 110, 192, 201n12

marriage/weddings: and the loss of secular community space, 72–74; at the Mosque Foundation, 49; and sexuality of early migrants, 34, 204n11

Marxism, 43–44, 111, 186–87, 199n3

"Marxists in hijab," 133, 134

memory and forgetting, 17–18

Middle East Monitor, 101

middle minority. *See* "stranger groups"
migrations, 30, 35, 40–41, 153
milieus: *See also* religious milieus; secular-nationalist milieus; space; specific Islamic milieus; and absolute rejection, 161; in accommodation (religious secularity), 152–57; alternative feminist, 176, 195; Arab American professional organizations, 77–78; Christian nationalist, 109, 116–17, 122–23; in conversion (religious secularity), 142–43; and hyphenated identity, 103–4; Islamic, 16, 48–53, 53–55, 60; and the mahjar (Arab diaspora), 20–23, 56–57; and the Mosque Foundation (Islamic-suburban milieu), 48–53; and nationalist-Islamic identity, 138–42; Palestinian immigrant, 130, 164; politicized Christian (sectarian), 117–18; and processes of identity formation, 19, 24–25, 27; and rebellion, 160, 161; in reversion (religious secularity), 136–42; role of in Intisar's accommodation shift to religious secularity, 157; and the secularism-religion dialectic, 25, 84, 107, 134, 191–92, 195; in spiritualization, 165, 170, 176, 182, 194–95; in syncretic identity formations, 135–36, 157–58, 159–60, 183–84; theories of, 135
Morsi, Mohamed, 91
Mosque Foundation: *See also* Aqsa School; AALS legal action against, 48–49, 51–52, 207nn36–37; and AMP's Nakba commemorations, 102–3; Arab Spring Syria vs. anti-Syria divisions, 91–93; and assimilation, 49–50, 103; attendance patterns, 14; and ʿAziza's reformist Islam, 127; and "corrupt" secular practices, 54, 60, 208n5; and Ibrahim's family, 162; Intisar's religious-secularity, 136, 156–57; and Islamization of suburban enclave, 21–22, 39, 48, 59, 195; and Muhannad, 108, 112–13, 192; post-9/11 march of white suburbanites against, 155; non-doctrinaire original vision of, 177–78; and non-Muslim Palestinians, 73; pre-1967 Beitunia immigrants and new post-1967 reformists and fundraising, 50–51; professionalization of vs. volunteerism of ACC, 69; public mobilization capability, 156; and reformist influence on Nawal, 136–37, 139; and religious institutionalization, 48–50; and right of return, 49; Shaykh Jamal, 105–6; struggle for control of, 50, 108, 112–13, 192; and US intervention in Syria, 90–93, 212nn10–11; and the war of 1967, 48–49

Movement of Arab Nationalists (harakat al-qawmiyin al-ʿarab), 59
MSA (Muslim Student Association): and the Muslim Brotherhood, 14, 217n9; and Nashashibi, 147; and Nawal's latent religiosity, 139, 195; and Palestinian national identity in the diaspora, 14; and re-reading of Islamic texts, 22–23; too ethnically identified for Nashashibi, 147
Mubarak, Hosni (President), 91
Muhannad: in a distinct religio-political generational unit, 109; alienated secularism and latent piety in 1948–1967 generation, 110–11; and ʿaqida, 114–15, 192; and Islamic reformism in the 1948–1967 generation, 108, 111–13; and Islam-nation convergence in, 112, 114, 192; pietistic and patriarchal formation of, 110–11, 113–14, 216n8; religious-nationalism of, 110, 114–16; as representative of a generational unit, 109, 192
Muna: and alcohol and party scene, 171, 172, 174–75, 176; alienation from the Mosque Foundation, 171–72; and alternative feminist milieus, 176, 195; as a secular Muslim, 174–76; and bifocality (party scenes), 193, 194–95; burning in hell and *haram*, 171–73; and the hijab and fasting, 172–73; leaving-returning "Arabville" pattern, 171, 173, 174, 176, 190; oscillating adaptation-refusal of Islam, 175–76, 190; rebellion from religious patriarchy, 172, 174–75, 183, 190; recovery of nationalist Palestinian identity, 174; schooling of, 172; social and family background, 170–71; and spiritualization identity form, 174–76
Munir: alienation from Islamized spaces, 118–19, 193; as Christian nationalist, 116; Christian sectarianization of, 117–20, 194; early secular identity formation of, 116–17; on the need to cater to Muslims, 118–19; on religious vs. political identity, 119; and sectarian bifocality, 194
murabitun, 97–98
Musa: intersectarian identity and community role of, 64, 209n8; involvement in the 1967 war, 63–64; on the middle-class immigrants of 1948–1967 generation, 62; on the Oslo Peace Process (1993–Present), 68–69; as pioneer of secular nationalist institutions, 192; on secularism vs. the religious turn, 69–70
Muslim Ban, 5, 205n17
Muslim Brotherhood: *See also* Hamas; vs.

INDEX 255

Fatah funding in Mosque Foundation dispute, 51–52; and Hamas, 217n9; impacts on Palestinian nationalism/liberation, 7–8, 11–12, 217n9; and middle class reformist immigrants, 50, 207n33; and Muslim Student Association (MSA), 14; political alignments of, 91; and religious salvation as response to Palestinian condition, 86; Salafi-Islamist concept of *jahiliya* (age of ignorance), 178–79; vs. secular nationalism, 14, 200n10, 210n9; and *shariʿa*-based state, 94; vs. the 1948 and 1967 generation, 65, 111, 210n9

Muslim Community Association (Santa Clara), 101

Muslim Community Center (MCC), 123–24, 125

Muslim identity projection, 88

Muslim Legal Fund of America, 59

Muslim Student Association. See MSA

"Muslim Travel Ban" (2017), 79, 210n19

Naber, Nadine, 15

Naji al-ʿAli (Handala cartoonist), 103

Nakba commemorations (AMP): audiences, 84, 101, 104; as branding and commodification of Nakba, 99–103; Christian representation, 106–7; Islamic framing of, 102–3, 105–7; and Islamization and Americanization of Palestinian national symbols, 103–4; and Israel's West Bank/Jerusalem wall replica, 85, 104, 211n1; and the reperiodization and proliferation of the Nakba, 105, 106; research methodology, 88, 211n4; and the right of return, 101, 105–6; and suburban religious-nationalism, 98–99, 101–2; tent displays, 101, 102–4; Times Square image projection, 99–101

#NakbaMSP, 100

narrations ("stories so far"): See also specific individuals; and axes of identity formation, 17; Christian nationalist (Munir), 117–20; denationalized-sectarianism (Christian-Leo), 129–31; denationalized-sectarianism (Islamic-ʿAziza), 125–28; ideal vs. hybrid types, 23–24; religious-nationalist/reformist Islam (Muhannad), 108, 110–15, 114–17; research protocols for, 7, 200n7; sectarianized nationalism (Christian-Hanna), 120–23; sectarianized nationalism (Sara), 123–25; secularism (ideal type-Khairy Abudayyeh), 61–62; secular nationalism (second generation-Hatem Abudayyeh), 79–83; secular nationalism with political-religious fusion (Musa), 63–64, 68–70; secular-nationalist-religious pragmatism (Manal), 70–75; secular-nationalist with religious-shift accommodation (Mahmoud), 75–79; secular-religious sub-type, 27; as space constituting, 19, 56–57, 110, 143, 164, 192, 195

narratives: of catastrophic loss/revolution (*thawra*), 9, 11, 64, 103–4, 194; and epochal experiences, 18; and hybrid identity formations, 17; oversimplified, 8; of "return" (*al-ʿawda*) in Islamic reformism, 68–69, 102, 105–6; of "return" (*al-ʿawda*) in secular nationalism, 13, 43, 102, 187, 206n22; of secular nationalism, 43; spatial structuring of, 18–19, 56–57

Nashashibi, Rami: as an apophatic Muslim, 143–44; bifocality, 193–94; and Black Islam, 144–47, 148, 192, 194; break with *markaz* secularism and suburban reformist Islam, 149, 211n23; class and race oppression on the South Side, 145–46, 158, 194; critique of secular nationalism, 147, 148–51; early life and family, 143–44; as example of conversion subform of religious secularity, 142–52; and "ghetto cosmopolitanism," 145; and global reformist Islamic revival, 147; and IMAN, 142, 148–49, 152, 195–96, 219–20n21; and *markaz* secularism (ACC), 143, 145, 148; move to South Side neighborhood, 147; Saidian perspective of, 149, 151–52, 192, 220n22; and sectarianization of identity in conversion, 193; on shop-owner racism/exploitation, 150, 220n23; transethnic cosmopolitanism of, 151–52

al-Nasser, Jamal ʿAbd and Nasserism, 64, 80

nationalism: See also Palestinian nationalism; as an inherently a secular issue, 188–89; as basis of identity during the transition wave (1948–67), 39; blended religious/secular unity displays of, 1–4, 1–4*figs*, 99, 100, 120; disenchantment with, 145; vs. Islamic solidarity movements, 14, 200n10; of Nashashibi's mother, 144; pan-Arabism as ideological framework for, 61; in reformist Islamic religious-nationalist position, 114–15; *tatbiq* (normalization) vs. *taqsim* (partition), 102

nationalism, Christian: ethnic-linguistic-historical orientation of, 116–17; and the Sabeel Ecumenical Liberation Theology Center (Jerusalem), 109, 117, 122–23

National Lawyers Guild, 66

National Network for Palestinian Community Empowerment, 66
Nation of Islam temple, 33, 204nn9–10
Nawal: *See also* reversion; syncretic secularity; adaptive bimodalism of, 138; and boundaries (greetings), 141, 191; counter-patriarchy use of Islamic texts, 53, 139, 195, 218n10; and "divine nurture" prayers for mother, 140; on *fatwa* "street" Islam, 139, 218n10; and gender, 138–39, 158; Islamic private school vs. public high school, 136–37; Islamization of the secular, 118, 195; a "Marxist in hijab," 133–34; milieus and oscillating religious-secularism, 134, 191; modified secularism of, 191, 211n23; mother and family, 136–37, 140–41, 218n15; and nationalist-Islamic influences, 138–42; and reformist Islamization, 136–38; as reversion type of religious secularity, 136–42, 139–40, 218n12; work, 133, 142
Near North neighborhood, 44, 47, 176, 180, 182
Negro Muslim Temple, 33, 204nn9–10
Neturei Karta (Jewish Orthodox movement), 96, 107
"new peasants": vs. chain immigrants, 41; vs. middle class reformist immigrants, 50–51; and PLO Arab nationalism, 43–45; and re-traditionalization, 41–43
9/11: as an epochal event within diaspora space, 19; coinciding with Islamic institutionalization in Chicago, 155–57; as key event of 1987–2001 generation, 70; and racist backlash of exclusion and surveillance, 11, 59, 86, 119, 155, 223n6; "The Islam in me exploded!" response to, 155–57; as trigger for intensifying Islamic identity, 155–57
post-9/11: Arab Advisory Board and Mahmoud, 77, 210n17; Palestine-Jerusalem in cross-ethnic solidarity against US-Israeli state alliance, 20; and sectarian institutional integration, 109–10
Non-Aligned Movement, 64
North American Islamic Trust (NAIT), 51
North Side: and Bosnian "spiritual talks" (Sawsan), 168; as determining form of religious shift (Sara), 123–24; Palestinian community centers, 29
Numrich, Paul, 14, 15

Oak Park neighborhood, 38, 205n15
Obama, Barack, 142
Occupied Territories: *See also* Gaza Strip; Israel; Jerusalem; West Bank; and BDS (Boycott, Divestment and Sanctions) movement, 85; during the first Gulf War, 5; and Egypt/Arab Spring in AMP conference materials, 90; Israeli map erasures, 89–90, 211n6; and Jerusalem as Islam's third holiest site, 89; and protests/criticism against Israel, 3, 92, 104; and rise of Hamas, 67, 115–16; and secular nationalism, 65; and war of 1967, 40, 205n18
Odeh, Rasmea, 185–87, 222nn2–4, 223nn6,9
Odeh, Samir (1951–1994), 65, 66, 67
Oklahoma City bombing, 40, 77, 86, 210n16
"Operation Protective Edge," 1, 12
Organization of Arab Students (OAS), 14
orthodoxy, 56, 127, 165, 215n29
orthopraxy: vs. "cultural Islam" as incorrect practice, 201n11; in Islamic reformism, 51, 159, 165, 174–75; as *jahl* (narrow-mindedness), 178–80, 183, 190; Muna's rejection of, 190; vs. orthodoxy defined, 165, 215n29; and physical contact in and out of religious spheres (Nawal), 141, 151; sartorial (of hijab and *jilbab* coat), 101
Oschinsky, Lawrence, 32, 38–39, 203n6
Oslo Peace Process (1993–Present): and Fatah/PLO, 11; and the generational axis, 27; impact on secular nationalist organizations, 68–69, 166; as key event of 1987–2001 generation, 70, 74, 154; and the post-9/11 generation, 120; and the two-state solution, 199n3
Ottoman Empire: breakup of *musha'* system, 31; crackdown on Greek Orthodox Christians (Greek Revolt), 117; and early Zionist movement, 31; Land Code (1858) socio-economic impacts of, 31; and political-national demands, 31, 203n4

Palestine: and Arab Spring and occupied holy lands in AMP conference materials, 90; British Mandate, 9, 10*map*, 103; *filastin*, 1, 138, 150; as gagged, hijabbed woman, 101; as Islam's axis mundi (as Holy Land), 124; and multilevel political complexities, 197–98; in nationalist iconography and narrative, 43; as place to be Palestinian without being a piety-minded Muslim, 174–75; in the religious-nationalist identity spectrum *'aqida*, 115, 192
Palestinian Chicago: the Christian milieu, 55–56; *mahjar* spaces and narratives, 56–57; racial positioning of, 29
Palestinian Chicago (1890s-1940s early migration), 30–35; ambiguous homeland-diaspora positioning, 34–35; bimodal

INDEX 257

residency patterns of, 32, 33–34; class and religious demographics of migrants, 31–32; Greater Syria background of, 3, 31; marriage and sexuality, 34, 204n11; non-Muslim (mostly Christian) Arab immigrants, 33; Palestinians as a "stranger" group, 32, 36; South Side demographic context of, 30; worklife and leisure of, 33–34

Palestinian Chicago (1948–1967 transition wave), 35–39; Christian-Muslim relations, 36–37; clubs, 37–38; "migration chain" importance, 35; from peddling to store ownership, 36, 153; and religious practice, 38–39; shift in residential locations, 35, 36*fig*

Palestinian Chicago (1967–1980s re-Palestinianizing wave), 39–43; anti-Arab racism and government targeting, 39–40, 205n17; LA Eight case, 39–40; new immigrant characteristics and motives, 40–41; and the new Immigration and Nationality Act (1965), 39; new peasant vs. chain immigrants and impact on community identity, 41–42; re-Palestinianization with new peasant immigrants, 41–42; and re-traditionalization, 42–43

Palestinian Chicago (1967–1990): assimilation processes with Mosque Foundation, 48–50; and "browning" concept, 48; and gang violence, 45, 206n25; impact of rise of Islamism as challenge to secular nationalism in the Middle East after 1967 war, 50; and Islamic private schools, 53–55, 73, 128; and middle-class immigration, 50–51; and movement of Palestinians with "white flight," 47–48; secular nationalism, 43–45; suburbanization and Islamic reformism, 51–52; suburban transitions, 45–48; and "white flight," 45–47, 206n26

Palestinian Christians: and the American-Arab Anti-Discrimination Committee, 64, 209n9; AMP's marginalizing of, 90, 211–12nn6–7; and the anti-Muslim backlash, 119, 216n12; churches, 55, 56; and evangelical narratives, 118, 119–20, 122–23; Greek Orthodox vs. Arab, 117; and Hamas violence, 119–20; and Hanna, 120–23; history of, 31, 116–17; in Islamized spaces, 55, 118–19, 121–23; and nationalism/Palestine liberation, 61–62, 86–87, 116–17, 121–22, 189; responses to Islamic shift, 117; St. George Antiochian Orthodox Church, 38, 55–56, 121–22, 129–30, 205nn15–16; and shift from secularism to sectarianism, 109, 116, 118–19, 121–23; and Theodosios Attallah Hanna, 107

Palestinian Community Center, 67, 210n13

Palestinian condition: core narratives and AMP, 102; defined, xiii–xiv, 85–86; and dispossession, xiii, 9, 85–86, 100, 104–5, 182, 244n13; and liberation theology, 117; Nakba in the diaspora, 83, 187; as ongoing Nakba (catastrophe), 187, 210n14; parallels with African American struggle for Nashashibi, 146; and return (*al-ʿawda*), 13, 43, 68–69, 102, 182, 187, 206n22; a secular and national issue, 85–86, 101, 188–89; and *thawra* (loss/trauma/revolution), 9, 11, 64, 103–4, 194

Palestinian Declaration of Independence, 199n3

Palestinian displacement, xiii, 11, 83

Palestinian Human Rights Information Center (PHRC), 5

Palestinian identity: and Americanness, 87; AMP's appropriation of in logo, 99, 102, 103; and border crossings on trips to the homeland, 122, 144, 193, 219n18; displacement of into sectarianized solidarities, 119–20; race, gender and family roles in shaping of, 152; and trauma exposure through US media, 154

Palestinian nationalism: of the 1948–1967 generation, 63–64; vs. deep community building internationalism, 150–51; and Nakba commemorations, 102; pre-Zionism emergence of, 203n4

Palestinians, as "stranger" group, 26, 32, 36, 39–40, 203n5

Palestinian society: impact of Islamization on secularism and Christians, 118–19; sectarian-religious turn after the First Intifada (1987–1993), 116–17

Palestinian solidarity activism, 92, 188–89, 224n13

Palestinian Students Association, 64–65

pan-Arabism (*qawmiya*): *See also* Abudayyeh, Khairy; ACC; Fatah; PLO; the 1948 and 1967 generation; and the Islamic shift, 109–10; and Khairy Abudayyeh's secular nationalism, 58–59, 61–62; and Nasser variant of, 11, 59, 64; and Palestinian Christians, 61, 116–17; in village milieus, 37, 111

Park 51 Mosque incident, 119

patriarchy, 95, 139; and alternative feminist spaces, 176; and Aqsa School, 53, 208n40; cultural transmission through family, 126–27; and cultural transmission through the family, 126; and diaspora identity, 22–23, 41, 42; feminist use of Islamic texts against, 53, 139, 195, 218n10; and greetings, 141; and Islamic reformism, 202n17, 218n10, 218n14; and the *murabitun*, 97–98; in Nawal's reversion process, 138–39; in pietistic village milieu, 110–11, 113–14; and piety as an instrument of social coercion over women, 172; and preaching shame (*'ayb*), 139, 169; reformist re-reading of Islamic texts, 22–23, 139; and the religious turn, 82; and Sawsan's secular religiosity "beyond the enclave," 170; in secular nationalist narrative and iconography, 43; and sexual double standard, 163–64; use of religious instruction to challenge, 53, 137

people of color (POC), 146–47, 186, 197–98, 206n27

PLO (Palestine Liberation Organization), 5; closure of UN Observer Mission in NY, 40; and diaspora secular nationalism, 9–10, 26, 44–45, 65–66, 156, 192; factions, 9–11, 11, 64, 154; and Great Arab Revolt banner, 199n1; Ibrahim's father as member of, 161; and the Irish Republican Army, 66, 210n12; and Islamic revival in Palestine, 7, 112; one-state solution, 170; and the Oslo Peace Process, 68–69, 166; overtaken by Hamas in Gaza, 59; repatriation ("return") narrative, 43, 206n22

PNA (Palestinian National Authority), 11, 12, 128, 154, 166

Pollack, Lynn, 3–4

polytheism of values (pluralism), 135, 160, 176, 181, 196–97; in spiritualization rebellion, 160

Popular Front for the Liberation of Palestine (PFLP), 39–40, 185, 199n3, 222n3; listed as terrorist organization, 185, 222n3; reconstituted MAN (Movement of Arab Nationalists), 64; rejection of two-state solution, 199n3

prayers/invocations: *adhan* (call to prayer), 6, 82; "al-salamu 'alaykum" "(Peace be upon you"), 69; *bismillah al-rahman al-rahim*, 136, 217n6; 'Id al-Fitr, 55; *maghrib*, 6, 82; modest dress *sitr al-'awra*, 218n11; referencing God, 175; and ritual practice/religious discipline, 140, 180; and ritual purity (refusal of contact), 141, 191, 218n15

Prophet Muhammad: and Abu Jahl, 97, 214n25; *isra' wa al-mi'raj*, 85, 89; and the *mi'raj* and sovereignty claims, 11; stories and Sawsan conversion to Islam, 168

protests: of AAAN against Israeli actions, 79–80; against Gulf War at UCLA, 80–81; and alienation from nationalism (futile), 150, 161, 220n2

al-Qaeda, and Palestinian freedom cause, 12

al-Qassam, 'Izz al-Din, and the Great Revolt (1936–1939) anti-colonial (British and Zionist) resistance, 11, 94

qawwamun (men's authority over women), 53, 208n40

Qur'an: burning of, 119; interpretations of jihad in, 12, 94–95, 214n21; and Islamic reformism (Nawal), 137; and language lessons, 177; and Muna's self-description as secular-Muslim, 175–76; Palestine as part of, 115; reading and Islamic reformism, 137, 217n7

Qutb, Sayyid (Muslim Brotherhood theorist), 178–79, 221n8

race: *See also* African Americans; anti-Muslim backlash; assimilation; segregation; white flight; whiteness; and Arab and Muslim self-perceptions as POC, 206n27; and black solidarity/"blackness," 147; and Nashashibi's "blackness," 147; and negative privilege, 152, 153; people of color (POC), 146–47, 186, 197–98, 206n27; riots and "border wars," 30; and *Shelley v. Kraemer*, 45–46, 206n26; and syncretic-secular confluences, 135

race relations: intercommunal African American-Palestinian tensions, 32; and shopowner-clientele interactions, 32–33, 36, 203n6, 204n8

racism: and African-Arab-Muslim American shared experiences, 16, 186; and external signs of Muslimness, 16; and "insolence pattern," 203n6; in Palestinian communities and movements, 150; of Palestinians towards African Americans, 32, 203–4n6-8; with patriarchy and traditionalism (authentic Palestinianness as rejection of wider society), 42; and "terrorist" label, 16

Rainbow Coalition, 67

Ramadan ritual/restrictions: and the AAAN, 82; adherence patterns in syncretic secularity, 143, 153, 157, 163; defined, 222n14; and identity transformations to Islamic reformism, 78, 126–27; in pre-1948 Chicago Palestinian diaspora, 34, 38; in the suburbs (fundraisers), 52, 74, 91, 103; and syncretic rebellions, 163, 172–74, 180, 182

INDEX 259

Ramallah, *Al Hayat Al Jadeeda*, 31, 36–37, 101
Ramallah club, 72
Red Cross shelter displays, 101
Rehab, Ahmed, 93, 213n17
religion: as an ideal type, 23, 24, 202n20; and the generation of 1948–67, 38–39
religion-secularism dynamics. *See* secularism-religion dynamics
religio-political units, 109. *See also* Muhannad
religious institutionalization: *See also* Mosque Foundation; religious milieus; and the 1948 and 1967 generation, 38–39; and assimilation, 50; and closure of secular nationalist community centers, 8, 14; private Islamic schools, 14, 69, 73, 128; wealth accumulation and suburban enclaves, 8
religious milieus: *See also* AMP, Mosque Foundation; Aqsa School; SJP; and the 1948–1967 generation, 110–12; AMP as religious-nationalist, 123; and Christian denationalized Sectarianism, 129–31; Muslim Community Centre (MCC), 123–24, 125; reformist piety-minded, 156, 165, 170, 171–75, 189, 196; and St. George Antiochian Orthodox Church, 38, 55–56, 122, 129–30, 205nn15–16; sectarian, 132, 160, 165–66, 168, 183, 193; self-construction of through tension with secularism, 84
religious-nationalism, 12, 109–10
religious secularity: *See also* accommodation; conversion; reversion; syncretic rebellions; syncretic secularism; accommodation type (Intisar), 152–57; and atheism, 191; conversion type (Nashashibi), 135, 136, 142–52; reversion type (Nawal), 136–42; three subforms of defined, 27, 135–36
religious shift: *See also* AMP; Christian Palestinians; Islamic milieus; Islamic reformism; Islamism; Mosque Foundation; syncretic secularity; and anti-Muslim backlash, 8, 59, 86, 87, 119; and identity formation, 60, 82, 86, 211nn22–23; impact on secularism, 6–7, 17, 27, 59–60, 72–73, 74–75, 79, 118; and religious-secular dynamics, 60, 86, 196–97; secularist critique of, 85–86; and transethnic Islamic *umma*, 14–17, 86–87, 94, 101
re-Palestinianization: and *'adat wa taqalid* (customs and traditions), 41–42; and chain vs. new peasant immigrants, 40–42; and nationalism, 43–45; and rising nationalism, 43–45
re-traditionalization. *See* re-Palestinianization
reversion: *See also* Nawal; religious secularity; syncretic secularity; vs. conversion and accommodation, 133–58, 135–36, 157–58; dynamic processes of fluctuation in, 136, 142; and gender issues (Nawal), 138–39; and nationalist-Islamic confluences, 138–42; Nawal's background and early identity formation processes, 136–38
"the revolution" (*al-thawra*), 9, 11, 64, 103–4, 194; alternative to re-Palestinianization, 43–44

Sabeel Ecumenical Liberation Theology Center, 109, 117, 122–23
Sahloul, Zaher (Dr.), 91–92, 93, 212–13nn12–13
Said, Edward, 6, 107, 149–50, 151–52, 197, 220n22, 224n14
St. George Antiochian Orthodox Church (Cicero): denationalized sectarianism in, 129–31; and Palestinian Christians, 38, 55–56, 122, 129–30, 205nn15–16; role in new Palestinian Christian nationalism, 121–22
St. Mary Antiochian Orthodox Church, 56
Salafism, 112, 215nn4–5, 217n8, 222n11
Salah al-Din Ibn Ayyub, 97, 214n25
salat, 148, 171, 175
SAMS (Syrian American Medical Society), 91–92, 93, 213n15
Sara: and cross-ethnic Islamic reformism, 124; and Islamized nationalism, 123–25; as picking up where Muhannad left off, 124, 125; role of MCC in religious-nationalist identity formation, 123–24, 125
Saudi Arabia, 69, 89, 112, 215n4. *See also* Salafism
Sawsan: bifocality and the diaspora as a space of freedom, 194, 195; Bosnian influences, 168; conversion to Islam, 167, 168–69; Israel in her rebellion, 168, 169; and Jewish activists/Mizrahi Jews, 170; "Love, God and Palestine" tattoo significance/other tattoos, 169, 170, 190, 194; markers of exilic freedom, 170; post-migration conversion to Islam, 168–70; mother's Orthodox Christian piety, 165–66; multisectarianism of, 190; and patriarchy, 165–66, 167, 170, 195; a religious rebel, 165–69, 183; and the Second Intifada, 166–67; trauma of family migration, 165, 168, 193
Schmidt, Garbi, 14
the Second Intifada, 6, 9, 120–25, 165–68. *See also* generation of 1987–2001; Oslo Peace Process; sectarianization of identity, 117–19, 132, 192, 193
secular: as an ideal type defined (vs. secularism), 24; defined vs. secularism, 209n2; range of orientations within, 209n3

secular deinstitutionalization: and attenuation of, 57–59, 67–70; and BDS (Boycott, Divestment and Sanctions), 59; and hybrid identity formations, 23–24; impact on Mahmoud, 75–79; impact on Manal, 70–75; impact on the 1948 and 1967 generation, 69–70; impact on the 1987–2001 generation, 9, 59–60, 72–74; loss of secular community space, 72–74, 118, 132, 218n13; and rise of Islamic religiosity and leadership, 59, 68–69; and the Syrian civil war, 90–93, 212nn10–11

secularism: in the 1948–1967 generation, 62–65; in the 1987–2001 generation, 70; as an ideal type, 23–24, 61, 202n19; and Arab unity, 58–59, 61–62; core organizational structures of, 9–10; defined vs. secular, 209n2; disenchantment with, 68, 145, 149; of Hatem Abudayyeh, 79–83; importance of, 60–61; institutionalizing of, 65–67; intergenerational reproduction of, 60–61, 73–74, 80, 83–84, 187–88; in Islamizing spaces, 78–79; in Kanazi's poetry, 83; new forms of against the new piety, 17, 23, 28; Palestinian, 61–62, 66–67; persistence of, 59, 83–84; syncretic secular identity formations, 189–91; vs. the Islamic shift, 84, 187–89, 191

secularism-religion dynamics: *See also* syncretic rebellions; in absolute rejection, 161–65; in atheism, 160; as dialectical and transformational, 25, 84, 107, 110; and hybridity, 24–26; living and doing within, 196–98; in reversion, 142; in syncretic rebellions, 160

secular nationalism: and ACC programming, 65; and AMP's appropriation of nationalist symbols, 99; ancestral territory claims (British Mandate), 9; in crisis after the Second Intifada (2000–2005), 120; identity markers and practices of, 43, 65, 99; and intercommunal coalitions, 44–45, 66–67, 156; vs. intersectionality in conversion, 142, 219n17; Nashashibi's critique of, 147, 148–51; and the post-9/11 generation, 124–25; orienting horizon of, 9–10; and Palestinian Christians, 116–17; and the PLO (Palestine Liberation Organization), 43, 68–69; religious identity in, 9–10; and "return" (*al-ʿawda*), 43, 49, 206n22; and the secular ideal type, 23; and *thawra* narrative, 9, 64, 187–88, 194; as unified diaspora identity, 44–45, 69–70, 86; and village line dances (*dabka*), 43, 43*fig*, 65, 71, 72; weakness of in post-9/11 generation, 121

secular-nationalist milieus: *See also* AAAN; ACC; Arab-American, 75–79; Arab Students Association (ASA), 45, 64–65; continuing relevance of, 83–84; deinstitutionalization of, 67–70, 73–74, 81, 83–84; and GUPS, 14, 45, 71, 76, 79, 84, 154; institutionalization of, 65–67; Intisar's integration into, 153, 154; Nashashibi's integration in, 143, 145, 148; Union of Palestinian Women Associations, 71; UPWA (Union of Palestinian Women Associations), 44, 66, 72, 81

secular religiosity: atheism as a form of, 159, 160–65, 191; complexity of, 192; and Muna on the Islamic texts, 175–76; and returns to Islam, 191; of Sawsan's pluralized religious-national fusion, 170; spiritualization as a form of, 160, 165; and sub-type rebellions, 27

segregation: and the African American "Black Belt" zone, 30; and Arab vs. Ramallahite (Christian) immigrants, 36–37; and "border wars" (Black Belt), 30, 45–46; and suburban Palestinians, 29

anti-Semitism accusations, 92, 96, 187, 223n9

shahada, 34

Shalit, Gilad (Israel Defense Force Corporal), 72

Shalom Hartman Institute, 95, 214n23

sharaf (woman's sexual honor), 42

shariʿa: and AMP's Holy Land tropes, 94; and capitalism, 217n5; and gender, 136, 217n5; and modest dress *sitr al-ʿawra*, 218n11; and orthopraxy, 215n29; and rational (book centered) Islam, 112, 139; and the tithe, 217n5

shatat/iblad. *See* bifocality

Shelley v. Kraemer, 45–46

Shiʿism, 168, 194–95

Simmel, Georg, 24, 26

al-Sisi, ʿAbd al-Fattah (Field Marshall), 91

sites of exile, 44–45

social class: base of IMAN, 195–96; basis of AAAN, 81–82, 195–96; and early migration, 31–32; and intersectionality, 57, 152; "Islamic solution" to capitalism, 217n5; middle-class immigrants of 1948–1967 generation, 62; and Nashashibi's rejection of suburban reformist Islam, 149; and "new peasants," 41, 41–45, 50–51; and race oppression in the South Side, 145–46, 158, 194; and rebellion, 160; and religious secularity vs. suburban reformism, 50–51, 136, 207n33, 217n5; and space, 20–21, 26, 33; and syncretic-secular confluences, 135

social spheres, 16–17, 160

sociohistorical generations, 17–18

INDEX

sociopolitical spaces, 18–19
solidarity frames: *See also* secular nationalism; and "Americanism," 109; anti-colonial, Third Worldist and black liberation, 20–22, 33, 44, 145, 192; cross-ethnic Islamic, 15, 20, 44–45, 54, 119, 123–25, 178, 182, 219n17; enclave Muslim, 21–22; hierarchies of, 108–9, 188–89; internationalism, 150–51; Islamic vs. national, 188–89; multiple transpositions of (Nashashibi), 147; nationalist, 39–40, 111; Palestinian-Jewish, 3–4, 88, 92; people of color, 146–47, 186, 197–98, 206n27; transethnic sectarian religious Muslim, 11–12, 14, 88
space: *See also* milieus; in and out of "Arabville" (Muna), 171, 173, 174, 176, 190; and bifocality, 57, 194, 194–96; and the city-suburb divide, 47; and the construction of race, 20–21; and contested memories, 98–99; and cross-pressures/worldviews, 24–25, 134–35, 142; defined as an emergent phenomenon, 19, 201n14; as forming identity and being formed by people, 195; forming identity within narrations, 56–57, 110, 143, 164, 192, 195; and identity displacements, 119–20, 161; institutional and sociomoral, 24; as narrated contexts, 18–20; and secularism-religion dynamics, 25, 84, 107, 191–92, 195; and social spheres, 16–17, 160
space, Palestinian Chicago as: Churches as boundary markers, 21; (diaspora community) size and surveillance of, 5, 199n4; and diaspora-homeland (*shatat-iblad*), 22, 99; identity constituting, 19, 57; immigration patterns, 13–14; as interspatial-intergenerational phenomenon, 19–20; race/class and ambivalence of Palestinian position, 26, 33; secularism and the religious turn in, 13–15; and socioeconomic class relations, 20–21; and the suburban shift, 21
spaces. *See* milieus
spatial axis, 17, 19, 21–22
spiritualization: *See also* Jubran; Muna; Sawsan; and fundamentalist religious schooling, 172–73; leaving Arabville for secular Islam, 170–71; and pluralism, 168–70, 182–83; as rebellion (Sawsan, Muna), 165–68, 170, 176; and religiosity free from social practice (Muna), 174–76; and religious inconsistency in formation, 170–71, 172; role of outside influences on, 166–68, 171–74, 176; and the suburban enclave as *jahl*, 176, 178–82

the state: defined, 25; Islamic State, 12, 212n11, 214n21; Palestinian one-state solution, 94, 170; Palestinian the two-state solution, 3, 94, 102, 199n3
statelessness, xiii, 35, 42
steadfastness (*sumud*), 43
"stranger" groups, 26, 32, 36, 39–40, 48, 203n5, 207n31
student groups: Arab Students Association (ASA), 45, 64–65; General Union of Palestinian Students (GUPS), 14, 45, 70, 71, 76, 84, 154; and Islamic reformist revival, 14; Muslim Student Association (MSA), 14; Organization of Arab Students (OAS), 14; and Palestinian national identity in the diaspora, 14; Palestinian Students Association, 64–65; Students for Justice in Palestine (SJP), 59, 83, 85, 107, 123, 211n1; and the Washington coalition, 44–45
suburban shift, 20–22, 46, 136–37, 202n1
Sufism, and music, 180–81
Sukkot (Festival of Tabernacles), 91
sunna (and Muna), 175–76
Supreme Muslim Council in Palestine, 11–12
syncretic rebellions: absolute rejection subform (Ibrahim), 161–65; characteristics and subforms of, 159–61; and disenchantment with the religious shift, 183–84; multisectarian and pluralist ethics in, 183; and retention of religiosity if not orthopraxy, 183–84; and the retention of the rejected in, 160, 161; spiritualization subform, (Sawsan), 165–70; spiritualization subform (Jubran), 178–83; spiritualization subform (Muna), 170–76
syncretic secularity: accommodation type (Intisar), 152–57; as a religious qualification of secularity in Nawal, Intisar and Nashashibi, 191; as a typological range of identity, 84, 134–35; and the complexity of lived social reality and cross cutting currents, 135; conversion type (Nashashibi), 142–52; vs. crossing of social circles, 24, 135; defined, 24–25, 27, 134–35; and fragility of worldview, 134–35; and home-diaspora identity influences, 27–28; impacts on the Islamic turn, 189–92; race, class and gender inflections of, 135; and religious secularity trajectory, 27; reversion, conversion and accommodation, 133–58, 135–36; reversion type (Nawal), 136–42; three types of, 135–36; and worldviews, 134, 142

syncretism. *See* syncretic secularity
Syria: AMP-Mosque Foundation opposition to (Arab Spring), 91–93, 106; and Arab Spring and occupied holy lands in AMP conference materials, 90; and post Arab Spring sectarianization, 120; and Hezbollah as client of, 90–91; and Jabhat al-Nusra (al-Qaeda linked), 90; and Jewish-Palestinian solidarity positions, 92; and the Mosque Foundation vs. American Muslims for Palestine (AMP), 189; and US intervention, 92–93; and US intervention impacts on Chicago community, 90–93, 212nn10–11; Yarmouk Camp, 102
Syrians, term for Arabs, 33
Szremski, Kristin, 3

al-Tahir, Abdul Jalil Ali, 22, 32, 33, 39, 40, 203–4nn6,8-10
Tanzimat reforms (Ottoman Empire), 203n4
Taylor, Charles, 9, 24, 134–35, 202n21
terrorist designation labeling: and AMP's emphasis on its Americanness, 87; and law-enforcement, 5, 40, 185, 205n17, 222n3, 223n6; and racism, 16, 185–86, 222n4
thawra (loss/trauma/revolution), 9, 11, 64, 194
theodicies, 24
Times Square, Nakba commemoration at, 99–101
torture, 92, 185, 221n2
Trump Administration, 79
Turkey, 188–89
two-state solution (*taqsim*), 3, 94, 102, 199n3
typological ranges of identity. *See* ideal-types

'Umar Ibn al-Khattab, 97, 215n25
umma: as a new cosmopolitan frame (Nashashibi), 152; and Holy Land tropes, 54, 94; and Muslim Brotherhood theory, 221nn8–9; and the national question, 105–6, 188–89; and reformist patriarchalization, 208n40, 217n5; simplified narratives of, 8; and transethnic Islamic solidarity, 11–12, 14–15, 196
United Nations: (General Assembly), 185, 206n22, 222n2; PLO's Observer Mission, 40; Security Council Resolutions, 199n3
United States: citizenship and immigration laws, 39, 40, 185–87; intervention in Syria and Iraq, 92–93; invasions of Afghanistan and Iraq, 120; Palestinian-Americans in House of Representatives, 187, 223n9; society as *jahiliya* (ignorance), 113, 216n6; support for Zionism, 187
United States, Dow v., 33
Universal School, 54, 128, 208n43
University of California-Los Angeles (UCLA), 80–81
University of Illinois at Chicago (UIC), 76
UPWA (Union of Palestinian Women Associations): and AAAN, 44, 66, 72, 81; and food and medicine drives/activism for the First Intifada, 72; nationalism and women against patriarchal norms, 44
Urban Redevelopment Act (1949), 46
US Council of Muslim Organizations, 59

village milieu: communists in, 111, 114; conservative Islamic values in, 110–11, 113–14
Virgin Mary icon (Theotokos), weeping, 56

Wagner, Don, 106–7
waqf (Islamic patrimony/Holy Land), 94, 95, 194, 214nn19,21
war of 1967: and Fatah takeover of PLO, 11; and forced exodus in newly occupied territories, 40, 205n18; impact of defeats on Palestinian nationalist movements, 63–64; and law enforcement and media backlash, 39–40; and nationalist surge in Chicago, 64
war of 1973, 39–40, 185–86, 187, 205n17
wars of 1948 and 1967: diaspora secularism, 11–14, 61, 111; as epochal events, 18; and the generational axis, 27; statelessness and migration to Chicago, 35
Washington coalition, 44–45, 66–67
Washington, Harold, 44, 77
Weber, Max, 24, 135, 196–97, 217n5
Wedam, Elfriede, 15
West Bank: and the 1967 war, 40, 205n18; Baruch Goldstein massacre at the Ibrahimi Mosque (al-Khalil/Hebron 1994), 122; and BDS (Boycott, Divestment and Sanctions), 27–28; Christian/Muslim residence patterns replicated in Chicago, 36–37; Fatah in, 7–8, 12, 59; and the First Intifada, 5; and Israeli occupation of, 70, 79–80, 85, 104; Jordan's annexation of, 35
West Englewood (African American/Latinx neighborhood), 35, 142, 148
West Lawn (mainly white neighborhood), 35, 36*map*, 142, 148
West Side neighborhood, 32, 38, 46
white flight: and "becoming white" assimilation, 21; and black/white income disparity

increases, 47; of Nawal's family, 136; and Palestinian shift to suburbs, 47–48; and *Shelley v. Kraemer*, 45–46, 206n26

White Helmets, 93, 213n15

whiteness: vs. Arab self-perception as POC, 46, 153, 168, 206n27; and assimilation, 21; vs. brownness, 30; and city-suburb divide, 47; and classification of Arabs, 33, 206n27; and Sawsan's critique of Christians getting rid of their Arabness, 168

women: *See also* gender; hijab; patriarchy; and Aqsa School, 53; as the invisible *murabitat*, 97–98; men's authority over (*qawwamun*), 53, 208n40; political activism of and *dabka*, 43, 43*fig*, 65, 71, 72; and reformist-Islamic sartorial expectations, 127–28; representing Palestine in AMP promotional materials, 101; and the "revolution," 44; secularism and rights of, 80

World Islamic Congress, 12, 94

worldviews, 83, 134–35, 142

Yarmouk Camp (Syria), 102
Yassin, Ahmed Ismail Hassan (Shaykh), 114
youth, 11, 64, 66, 96–97
Youth Delinquency Program (ACC), 66

Zaghel, Ali Shteiwi, 39
Zhang, Charles, 48
anti-Zionism, 4, 83, 92–93, 96
Zionism: *See also* Israel; Christian, 120; and the closure of the Arab Advisory Board, 210n17; and early Yishuv (Jewish settlement), 31; and Islamic reformist position on Armenian genocide, 188–89; and Nakba as a disputed space of memory, 98; Nashashibi on, 150–52; and pan-Islamic colonial resistance, 11; as racism, 150; strategies of cooptation, 95–96, 214n23; and US policy, 187
Zoghby, James, 77

Founded in 1893,
UNIVERSITY OF CALIFORNIA PRESS
publishes bold, progressive books and journals
on topics in the arts, humanities, social sciences,
and natural sciences—with a focus on social
justice issues—that inspire thought and action
among readers worldwide.

The UC PRESS FOUNDATION
raises funds to uphold the press's vital role
as an independent, nonprofit publisher, and
receives philanthropic support from a wide
range of individuals and institutions—and from
committed readers like you. To learn more, visit
ucpress.edu/supportus.